THE ANNUAL
OF
PSYCHOANALYSIS

Editorial Committee

John Gedo, M.D.
Robert Kohrman, M.D.
Glenn E. Miller, M.A.
Kate R. Ollendorff
Morris A. Sklansky, M.D.
Harry Trosman, M.D.
Ernest Wolf, M.D.
George H. Pollock, M.D., PH.D., *Chairman*

Manuscript Editor

Janice Feldstein

Editorial Assistant

Jacqueline Miller

THE ANNUAL
OF
PSYCHOANALYSIS

A Publication of the
Chicago Institute for
Psychoanalysis

VOLUME I

Quadrangle / The New York Times Book Co.

Copyright © 1973 by the Institute for Psychoanalysis of Chicago. All rights reserved, including the right to reproduce this book or portions thereof in any form. For information, address: Quadrangle/The New York Times Book Co., 10 East 53rd Street, New York, N.Y. 10022. Manufactured in the United States of America. Published simultaneously in Canada by Fitzhenry & Whiteside, Ltd., Toronto.

Library of Congress Catalog Card Number: 72-91376

International Standard Book Number: 0-8129-0319-6

PREFACE

We have reached the centenary of Sigmund Freud's decision to abandon his ambitions for a career in law and public affairs in order to devote himself to natural science, to "gain insight into thousand year old acts of Nature, perhaps even eavesdrop on its eternal processes." Toward the end of his life, Freud was able to survey the intellectual movement he had founded and to conclude that the psychoanalytic enterprise had a promising capacity for survival. Developments within the core of psychoanalytic psychology and collaboration with a variety of other disciplines in the study of man contributed to Freud's belief that "the whole impression is a satisfactory one—serious scientific work carried on at a high level."

This appraisal serves as an appropriate introduction to our statement of purpose for the new *Annual of Psychoanalysis:* to seek and publish good writings which focus on the theoretical and clinical aspects of psychoanalysis and, beyond that, over the full range of Freud's scientific humanism.

We realize that so high an ambition cannot be attained in any single issue of a publication. So, for example, many areas are missing from this first volume, which concentrates on the history of psychoanalysis, its place in contemporary culture, and its interplay with philosophy and experimental psychology.

We present Volume I with a good deal of satisfaction and with the hope that our readers will contribute their ideas and their best work to make the *Annual* a journal of high quality and significance.

The Committee wishes to express its gratitude to several colleagues who offered their services as readers for this volume: Drs. Michael Franz Basch, Helmut Baum, Haskell Bernstein, Arnold Goldberg, Bernard Kamm, Jerome Kavka, Charles Kligerman, Heinz Kohut, Paul Kramer, William Offenkrantz, Marian Tolpin, Samuel Weiss, and Edward A. Wolpert.

Finally, we wish to dedicate our new book to a collaborator from the earliest days of this venture, a psychoanalyst with vision and concerns far beyond his own field, and a cherished friend, Gerhart Piers.

The Editorial Committee
180 N. Michigan Ave.
Chicago, Illinois 60601

CONTENTS

I

PSYCHOANALYSIS AND CONTEMPORARY SOCIETY

Psychoanalysis in a Troubled World   3
HEINZ KOHUT

Sigmund Freud Centennial Lecture   26
ROBERT WAELDER

II

PSYCHOANALYTIC THEORY AND
DEVELOPMENTAL PSYCHOLOGY

Psychoanalysis and Theory Formation   39
MICHAEL FRANZ BASCH

The Instinct Theory in the Light of Microbiology   53
THERESE BENEDEK

Psychoanalysis and Science: The Concept of Structure   73
SAMUEL A. GUTTMAN

Notes on "Psychoanalysis and Science: The Concept of Structure"   82
HEINZ HARTMANN

Two Prevalent Misconceptions about Freud's "Project" (1895)   88
MARK KANZER

Comments on Some Instinctual Manifestations of Superego Formation   104
HANS W. LOEWALD

Affects and Psychoanalytic Knowledge   117
ARNOLD H. MODELL

Symbolism and Mental Representation   125
PINCHAS NOY

Action: Its Place in Psychoanalytic Interpretation and Theory   159
ROY SCHAFER

III

INTERDISCIPLINARY STUDIES

PSYCHOLOGY

Psychoanalytic Research in Attention and Learning: Some Findings and the Question of Clinical Relevance 199
FRED SCHWARTZ

PHILOSOPHY

Commentary on Freud and Philosophy 216
FAY HORTON SAWYIER

IV

CLINICAL STUDIES

The Role of Illusion in the Analytic Space and Process 231
M. MASUD R. KHAN
Concerning Therapeutic Symbiosis 247
HAROLD F. SEARLES

V

PSYCHOANALYTIC EDUCATION

The Clinical Conference in Teaching and Learning the Psychoanalytic Process 265
PAUL A. DEWALD
The Training Analyst as an Educator 280
JOAN FLEMING

VI

HISTORY OF PSYCHOANALYSIS

Freud's Novelas Ejemplares 299
JOHN E. GEDO AND
ERNEST S. WOLF

CONTENTS

Freud's Cultural Background   318
HARRY TROSMAN

Minister to a Mind Diseased: Freud at the Allgemeine Krankenhaus   336
ERNEST S. WOLF

VII

APPLIED PSYCHOANALYSIS

On Oscar Wilde   345
ALEXANDER GRINSTEIN

*Psychoanalytic Object-Relations Theory, Group Processes,
and Administration: Toward an Integrative Theory
of Hospital Treatment*   363
OTTO F. KERNBERG

I

PSYCHOANALYSIS AND CONTEMPORARY SOCIETY

Psychoanalysis in
a Troubled World

HEINZ KOHUT, M.D. (*Chicago*)

Psychoanalysis is under attack from various sides. As hedonistic—as puritanical. As mystical and unscientific—as hyperrational. As revolutionary—as old-fashioned and tradition-bound. As right-reactionary—as left-communistic. Such accusations may often seem justified, since psychoanalysis observes man from various sides and on different levels; uncovers many layers of human passion; explains—and, while explaining, removes—diverse inhibitions of human activity. Thus one can always accuse psychoanalysis of having disregarded a dialectically opposite psychological finding or explanation with regard to each of the specific empirical discoveries which it claims to have made, and with regard to each of the specific theoretical explanations which it holds to be true. If analysis is put to the test from such a vantage point, the task of the would-be attacker is facilitated while the task of the defender remains difficult indeed. The indictment is simple and concrete; the defense has to rest on the laborious study and slow integration of all the many psychological insights which psychoanalysis has provided—including the acknowledged incompleteness of this science and its capacity to grow. Still, the analyst is on the whole not greatly upset by the aforementioned attacks, which strike him frequently as biased and pedantic; and he will tend to be philosophical about the fact that he cannot convince all the various

Based on an address given, under the title "Is the Investigation of the Inner Life of Man Still Relevant Today?," to a broad audience of students, professionals, and nonprofessionals on October 7, 1970, at the Free University in Berlin, Germany, on the occasion of the celebration of the Fiftieth Anniversary of the Berlin Psychoanalytic Institute (Karl-Abraham Institut).

This address was published by *Psyche* 25 (1971): 298–322; and in *Psychoanalyse in Berlin* (Meisenheim: Anton Hain, 1971).

Although I must take responsibility for this English version of my originally German-language address, I am glad to express my indebtedness to Dr. Ernest S. Wolf, who quickly and skillfully prepared a draft of an English translation which I then took as the basis for my own efforts.

insufficiently informed detractors of psychoanalysis of the value, the significance, the importance of this science.

. Nevertheless, much as the analyst may be able to discount a great number of these generally ill-intentioned, and often flimsy, criticisms, the problem of the worthwhileness of analysis in today's world, which is pondered by many a serious-minded and responsible observer, both inside and outside the field of analysis, must not be lightly brushed aside. It is in fact fully understandable that the question should be raised whether the detailed and intensive investigation of the inner life of man can still be considered as having sufficient relevance to our deeply troubled times—and there exist indeed a number of weighty arguments which could be marshaled in support of a negative verdict.

We are living in a time of great changes. Whole populations must regroup themselves rapidly in accordance with new guidelines of communal organization. Everywhere is the individual suddenly faced with the task of aiming toward newly defined goals and meanings, of grasping new values and of making them his own, of quickly adapting to a new societal order. Such tasks arise not only in territories where a social revolution has prevailed, where a new state has been founded, or where the basic form of government has been altered, but also within those nations—the United States, for example—whose structure appears on the whole to have remained unchanged. One need call to mind only the rapid emancipation of the American Negro and his impetuous tendency to use militant means; or the rapid Americanization of new ethnic groups who, contrary to the traditions of the nation, wave the flag of amoral patriotism, who impatiently push aside all questions concerning the justice of the actions of the state, and who—contrary to historically established ideals—level their self-righteous intolerance against the man who will not disregard his moral scruples. Everywhere new thoughts have to be thought and new plans for action devised if effective participation in the new world is to be accomplished. And everywhere are the Zhivagos dying who are incapable of adapting to the new conditions without the loss of the core of their life-sustaining traditions and ideals.

And how does depth psychology pass muster when it is evaluated against the background of the contemporary situation? Pretty badly—at least if one is satisfied with only scanning its broad outlines rather than undertaking a careful scrutiny of the actual and the potential significance of its functions.

The investigations of depth psychology must in the main be undertaken in the setting of the therapeutic situation. The patient comes to his analyst four, five, or even six times during the week, and for nearly an hour he is encouraged to talk freely about everything that goes through his head, apparently at random. The analyst, employing the skills acquired in many years of arduous professional training, listens with empathic attention to these seemingly disjointed communications; and, whenever it is appropriate, he communicates to his patient the insight which he may have acquired.

This process may go on for years, and if everything goes well, which luckily occurs with increasing frequency, then all this great effort will indeed lead to the deepgoing improvement of a single human fate; to the new, undreamed-of psychic integration of a person who has made peace with his past, has won respect for himself, and who looks to the future with independent strength and initiative. "Well and good," it may be said, "but is all this effort worth it? All these hundreds and hundreds of hours of work, for a single individual? Is not such effort wastefulness, immoral luxury, in a time when uncounted numbers of people are struggling and suffering, and when millions perish?"

I do not wish to involve myself here in a circumstantial and petty defense of therapeutic analysis. I could stress that the assistance which analysis provides is often to the benefit of very valuable individuals. Statistically it has been demonstrated—a fact of which every analyst has been aware without the aid of polls—that we do not treat the idle rich, as is often asserted, but that, in general, we help the educated and potentially creative to liberate their energies from sterile internal entanglement and thus make them available for tasks of social importance. I could also argue that each resolution of a deeply grounded psychic disturbance of an individual father or mother may benefit a whole series of generations—an analogy to (and a reversal of) the biblical punishment leveled against the children and children's children of the sinner. Of the truth of these assertions I have no doubt. But I do not believe that they, by themselves, constitute a satisfactory justification for all the time-consuming and cumbersome effort which the therapeutic endeavors of depth psychology require.

If we wish to affirm that this effort is indeed worthwhile, then we must demonstrate that its therapeutic and scientific goals carry a significance which transcends the fate of the single person and the knowledge obtained about the psychology of the individual. We must show, in other words, that psychoanalysis makes a contribution to the activation of wholesome social, cultural, and historical effects which may influence the future of not only a handful of individuals but of large groups, whole layers of society, and—yes!—even of mankind as a whole.

W. H. Auden, the great modern English poet, may have had something similar in mind when he wrote, in 1940, one year after Freud's death, the following beautiful lines in his poem "In Memory of Sigmund Freud":

> To us he is no more a person
> Now, but a whole climate of opinion
> Under whom we conduct our differing lives.[1]

For us, as Auden tells us here, the name of Freud no longer merely evokes the memory of the great man he was: it has become the symbol of that

---

[1] *The Collected Poetry of W. H. Auden* (New York: Random House, 1945), p. 166. Reprinted with permission of the publisher, Random House, Inc.

whole profound revolution of style and manner that has characterized twentieth-century existence as a result of his work.

Few will doubt that Freud's work has exerted a significant influence on the conduct of life, on the *Weltanschauung* of modern man. Still, there are a number of possible objections to the assertion which Auden presents to us so impressively. It could be said that it was man's outlook on the world that changed first, and that psychoanalysis and Freud's discoveries were the result, not a cause, of the new cultural attitude. (One could, of course, make the same claim with regard to Copernicus or Darwin. How is one to decide about such an issue?) Or one could take the stand that the influence of great men and of their discoveries and actions should not be overestimated. (One is reminded, in this context, of Tolstoi's opinion that even as important a figure as Napoleon was not the initiator of the events which are generally considered to have resulted from his actions, but that, on the contrary, he was just passively carried along by the currents of history.) True enough, terms such as "libido," "the unconscious," and "Oedipus complex" are widely used today; and people are usually ready to admit that a person's unknown thoughts and feelings may be "projected" onto others, and that our parapraxes—the slips of memory, tongue, and hand—reveal our hidden intentions. And the artists, poets, dramatists—they know all this only too well. The modern psychological drama and film are frequently saturated with Freudian discoveries and insights and use them not rarely in all too obvious, inartistically intentional manner. Is that the "whole climate of opinion" of which Auden speaks? "Easy come, easy go!" one thinks. And one calls to mind the ebb and flow of fashions: one day they seem to dominate the world, but on the next day they are gone as if they had never been around.

To be sure, the influence of psychoanalytic thought has maintained itself for some time now in the Western world; it appears to be more a persisting cultural style than a quickly passing fashion. But one is inclined to remember the old saying that "plus ça change, plus c'est la même chose." Every Tom, Dick, and Harry is using a few words of the psychoanalytic vocabulary, and they may have become superficially acquainted with a few new concepts. Some people have even learned to play analytic parlor games; that is, they permit themselves the ill-mannered license of subjecting the actions and the personality of their acquaintances to those—generally malicious—explanations which they consider to be psychoanalytic interpretations. In essence, however, they have remained untouched.

The foregoing comments, however, are only of peripheral importance, since it is by no means my intention to claim that analysis and its insights have already exerted a deep and genuine influence on the present generation. What I do wish to express is the hope that the influence of analysis will indeed be brought to bear broadly on future generations and—what is of at least equal importance—that analysis as an important civilizing force will become actively engaged in man's battle for his biological and spiritual survival. The goal of my presentation is therefore, generally speaking, a moral one.

But first a practical and technical question: is psychoanalysis indeed able to influence society? In other words—leaving aside for the moment the much more important uncertainty whether the broader application of the insights of analysis would have beneficial results—do we have the means for an effective penetration of analytic insights into society; and is there any likelihood that analysis could ever influence the actions of large groups?

It may appear at this point that my inquiry leads into unrealistic directions. Is it necessary to demand such large effects from the professional activity of a small group of psychotherapists? Is it not enough for analysts to concentrate on their therapeutic work and to be satisfied with the appropriately circumscribed results of these therapeutic activities? Is it not a sign of insecurity when a small professional group becomes restless, begins to put on airs, and agonizes ostentatiously about the question whether it could and should influence the future of mankind?

Yes and no. I have complete sympathy for those of my colleagues who, in quiet restraint, want to focus their whole attention on the concrete problems of their therapeutic activity, without spending sleepless nights over the course that the development of mankind is taking. But I think that it also is justifiable to adopt a more comprehensive point of view. I know, of course, how tempting it is to exaggerate the importance of the small events of our workaday life and to see them in a broad historical perspective. But what I wish to affirm appears to me to be a concrete and by no means exaggerated claim, namely, that psychoanalysis—as a form of psychotherapy and as a branch of investigative science—is potentially a cultural factor of considerable importance.

Here I want first to point out, however, that some of the most decisive events in history—events which ultimately came to exert a profound influence on the actions and thoughts of mankind—appeared to be small-scale and insignificant when evaluated within the framework of their original historical setting.

The inconspicuous events, for example, which may have formed the historical basis of the story of the Gospels had reverberations (in the development of culture, in the shaping of morality, in the whole history of Western man) which would seem to be of incomprehensible magnitude if measured against the scale of their tiny beginnings. Clearly, it was the power of a set of ideas which prevailed here so decisively—not the weight of the bigger battalions, not, at least not in the beginning, the trumpet call of a mighty propaganda apparatus. The apparently simple and circumscribed recognition that earth is not the center of the universe has not only revolutionized the thinking of all generations of scientists since Copernicus but has also exerted a considerable influence on historical and cultural development in areas which lie outside of the province of science (in the area of art and literature, for example; and perhaps even in the area of political activity). Darwin's theory of the origin of species had consequences which far transcended its original field of application. Out of Darwin's revolutionary approach to a sector of biology grew not only a new fundamental ordering principle valid within the total biological realm but also a broad new outlook on the world. Darwin's theory of the developmental transience of biological phenomena not only introduced a scientific relativism in the field of biology which stands in sharp contrast to the preceding absolutism of man's grasp of these phenomena (exemplified by the biblical story of creation), but also altered man's whole outlook, from the realm of physics to that of psychology.

But why the emphasis on the banal truth that small causes may lead to large effects? Because the preceding examples can teach us the important lesson that these so-called small beginnings were small only in appearance. Their greatness remains unrecognized as long as we insist on measuring them with yardsticks and weighing them on scales which are not designed to gauge the scope of their intrinsic energy and to respond to their potential impact. One cannot determine the power of a hydrogen bomb by weighing it as if it were a stone.

There are some fields, of course, in which we are willing to treat even inconspicuous activities with respect. We do not expect a researcher who attempts to identify a new virus to be concerned only with large epidemics; we gladly allow him to spend his working days in the laboratory with his test tubes, culture media, and filters. He receives not only our moral but also our financial support. The work of the scientist and teacher in the field of depth psychology, however, finds little public appreciation, and he will hardly be able to obtain adequate public assistance for the research which he pursues in the small arena of his consulting room. The day will come, I think, when people will shake their heads in disbelief about this short-sightedness of our society.

The analyst's attention is focused on small-scale activities, and his psychological inquiry concerns apparent trifles which seem to be far away from the events which are shaping our world. The assertion, however, that these facts speak against the importance of psychoanalytic investigation would be just as unwarranted as the conclusion that the small size of the virus or the atom negates the importance of virological or atomic research.

A short time ago a young patient reported to me that on the preceding day he had become involved in an ugly argument with a neighbor, an elderly man, who had refused him the temporary use of his driveway. Through careful psychological scrutiny of the incident we ascertained that the apparent unfriendliness of the response of the usually friendly neighbor had not been, as the patient had thought, a reaction to his request in itself but had been elicited by the provocative way in which he had made it. I remembered, and I reminded the patient, that a similar event had taken place once before. At that time the patient had started a serious quarrel because he had felt crowded by a man who sat next to him in a busy restaurant. I was able to demonstrate to my patient that at that time, just as now, his actions had been unnecessarily provocative and that he had left the other man no choice but to react with aggression to his own aggressivity.

I don't want to burden this presentation with a description of the details of an analysis. But I must mention briefly that both events occurred shortly before my leaving for a journey; that the patient, who had become fond of me, felt himself excluded when I told him that I would go away; that he became enraged about the inconsiderateness with which he felt treated by me; and that all these events repeated a devastating trauma of his childhood, when the beloved and admired father suddenly left the family and thus abandoned the patient.

I did not report this clinical episode in order to make propaganda for the correctness of the theories of psychoanalysis or for the usefulness of its methods; nor in order to demonstrate that in an analysis the key conflicts of a person's life are reactivated and thus become available for a new attempt to solve them. I adduced the clinical vignette in order to suggest that certain insights which are obtained in the analytic situation may help us understand human behavior in the broad social arena. My patient's request to use the neighbor's driveway and his wish that the other restaurant guest should move away from him were not unreasonable, and a small shift in the way in which he made his demands would have led in both instances to friendly compliance and would not have brought about the ugly confrontation which in fact ensued. Are such considerations without significance with regard to the understanding of the events which determine whether there will be war or peace among nations? Are we really unable to learn anything that illuminates the behavior of large groups from the careful study of the inner life of the individual? Or might we not by this road obtain insights which would allow us to cope in new ways—without having to resort to force and terror and killing—with those reality situations (social injustice, for example; or national insecurity) which up to now have been considered to be the all-important causes of the conflicts of world history?

Psychoanalysis assumes that the existence of a tendency to kill is deeply rooted in man's biological makeup and stems from his animal past. The omnipresent aggressive drive must be taken into account if we are not to yield to the lures of a shallow and misleading optimism which claims that man's pugnacity could be easily abolished if only his needs were satisfied. But analysts are also fully aware of the fact that certain external circumstances—e.g., those which bring about emotional and material deprivations—will arouse man's anger and may lead him to engage in aggressive actions. The influence of the environment on the propensity toward hostile behavior is, therefore, crucial; and the relevant external factors must be investigated thoroughly, whether we are trying to understand the aggressive reactions of the individual patient (in response to the fault-finding and belittling behavior of the marital partner, for example), or those of social groups (in response to discrimination or maltreatment), or, in the arena of world politics, those of nations and large populations (for instance in response to territorial and mercantile injustices).

I am well aware of the danger of one-sidedness and of the loss of a balanced scientific perspective. This danger becomes especially great in areas where multiple factors are involved in the production of the phenomena which we are striving to explain. Under such circumstances it is tempting to lift one set of factors from the whole intricate pattern of causes, to declare that it is primary and fundamental, and to assign a mere secondary and subsidiary role to other influences.

The depth psychologist, for example, who day in and day out observes the manifestations of the enormous power of unconscious motivations, will naturally be inclined to look upon unconscious psychic factors as the decisive, essential, i.e., as the only valid, forces in the life of individuals and of groups. The psychoanalyst must resist this temptation to espouse a naïve attitude of biased one-sidedness; he must not overrate the explanatory power of the insights of depth psychology. The analyst's insights about the role played by the unconscious forces in the depth of the personality do not in fact constitute a complete explanation of the behavior of either the individual or the group.

Still, there are, of course, many instances when psychoanalysis can make a person aware of previously unconscious motivations, thus increasing the control which he is then able to exert over his behavior. Minute as the increment of understanding often appears to be, suddenly—and surprisingly!—a hitherto unbreakable deadlock may become loosened: the patient's attitude becomes more tolerant; his previously provocative behavior becomes transformed into relaxed strength and moral firmness; his aggressions begin to serve constructive aims. Can there be any doubt about the appropriateness of a judicious application of insights such as these to the understanding of the events of history? And might we not expect that an increased grasp of the causal role played by depth-psychological factors will lead us also to greater control over our historical destiny?

"Could be!" it may well be said, "but are these not just empty speculations?" The bacteriologist, the virologist with whose small-scale research in the laboratory I compared the analytical work with individual patients—they have demonstrated, after all, that their efforts lead to far-reaching benefits for mankind. Where are the analogous results of analysis? It may be true that the individual patient benefits from the research which has steadily increased the body of psychoanalytic knowledge and the technical skill of the practicing analyst. And we can perhaps also say that, as a result of our persevering investigations, we are now able to undertake the successful treatment of psychological illnesses which had formerly been therapeutically as unapproachable as was diabetes before the introduction of insulin. Still, analytic research has up to now given us no therapeutic techniques which correspond to the powerful therapeutic agents discovered through biological research; and, above all, it has not provided anything yet that could be made available to the population at large—nothing, for example, that comes near to equaling the brilliant successes which bacteriological or virological research achieved in its fight against the great epidemic scourges of mankind.

I will again resist the temptation of losing myself in narrow argumentation. It could, of course, be stated that the psychological knowledge which is slowly accumulated as the result of work performed in the laboratory of psychoanalytic treatment is also becoming increasingly useful in the broader arena of general psychotherapy. I am thinking here, in particular, of those forms of psychotherapy which set themselves circumscribed and limited goals. The expenditure of time for patient and therapist is here significantly less than in analysis—yet, as in psychoanalysis, the therapeutic work is focused on the individual. With the possible exception of the crudest application of suggestion or of that type of psychological coercion ("conditioning") by which the patient is drilled to behave normally, there hardly exists any form of psychotherapy which does not owe a significant debt to the expanding scientific insights of psychoanalysis—whether this debt is acknowledged or repudiated.

Although claims such as these no doubt sound impressive, I must admit that the adoption and utilization of the findings of psychoanalysis by other forms of psychotherapy do not always lead to favorable results. The particular therapeutic procedure which analysis employs is correlated to a specific conceptual framework and forms an integral part of the analytic situation itself. It is, therefore, not easy to achieve a viable transplant when the technique of psychoanalysis is employed in other therapeutic settings.

Certain forms of psychotherapeutic counseling, for example, which enjoy at present a not inconsiderable popularity, restrict their technique in the main to letting the patient say everything that occurs to him. The counselor's passive attitude seems to be similar to the analyst's attitude of expectant silence: he listens, and either says nothing or merely repeats what the patient has just said himself. But while the analyst employs his method for a specific purpose—he listens in order to understand and then explain, thus enabling the patient to enlarge his knowledge of himself—for the counselor the method of free association appears to have become an end in itself. But when this use of free association is extolled as being superior to psychoanalysis, then the analyst cannot refrain from shaking his head in amazement. He understands, of course, how, in certain instances, temporary improvements are quickly brought about in this way. If we consider a patient, for example, who as a child had not been able to feel certain of the attention of the important adults in his environment, and who never acquired a secure sense of his own worthwhileness and acceptability because he had been criticized too much and lectured at too frequently, it is evident that for such a patient simply the devoted attentiveness on the part of a therapist can be a beautiful and wholesome experience. But among the countless variations in psychological disturbances and human needs, such a constellation represents only one specific kind of problem. It is not a rarity; but it is hardly the form of psychopathology that a therapist is most frequently asked to treat.

Therapeutic benefits such as these remind me of an amusing incident that occurred during the early years of the war. I had an old alarm clock which one day refused to work and just stopped running. As a result of the conversion of industry to the production of armaments no new clocks were obtainable. Yet nobody was willing to accept my old, cheap, nonelectric one for repair. One day I happened to pass by a small hardware store which had a sign in the window advertising the repair of alarm clocks. The owner accepted my clock without hesitation and told me to pick it up the next day. The price, he said, would be two dollars—not exorbitant, I thought, in view of the circumstances. The following day I did indeed receive my clock, which was now ticking again normally, and I happily paid my two dollars. But I was curious, of course; and I asked the shopkeeper to explain how he alone had been able to see his way clear to take on this repair and to carry it out successfully. With disarming frankness he replied that he knew next to nothing about watch repairs, let alone about the repair of alarm clocks, but that it had occurred to him one day that many of these old clocks had simply collected dust and grime in their wheels for too long and needed nothing more than some cleaning and a little oil. He decided to accept some clocks for repair, and put their movements, therefore, into an oil bath overnight. When that simple process did the trick he asked for the agreed payment. When it did not, he explained to his customer that unfortunately even he was not able to repair the clock; he then returned the clock to the owner, and of course demanded no payment. There is no need to spell out the analogy between the so-called watchmaker and the practitioners of certain kinds of psychotherapy—except, I think, that my so-called watchmaker had a higher percentage of successes and knew more about what he was doing than most of the psychotherapists who borrow one or the other insight or technical rule from psychoanalysis and apply it without understanding.

But I don't want to exaggerate. Although the application of the methods and theories of psychoanalysis to many types of abbreviated psychotherapy is indeed unsatisfactory, there do also exist scientifically well-founded and effective forms of short-term psychotherapy which are practiced and taught by skillful and experienced professionals. And analysts are rightfully proud of the fact that the utilization of analytic insights in brief and financially less burdensome forms of psychotherapy opens a path toward emotional health for many who might have remained bogged down in neurotic inhibitions without this assistance.

It would be tempting for the psychoanalyst who is confronted by the accusation that analysis belongs only to a sociocultural elite to reply that the principles of analysis are indeed successfully employed in the service of briefer and less deep-going forms of psychotherapy which can be made available to larger numbers of those who suffer from emotional disturbances. Still, in the context of our present considerations, I do not believe that this argument carries sufficient weight, since even the more broadly available forms of psychotherapy, which are derived from psychoanalysis, continue to deal either with the single disturbed individual or, at most—I am thinking here of forms of group and family therapy which are conducted along analytic lines—with only a comparatively small number of patients. Even if it should be possible in the future, therefore, to extend the availability of psychoanalytic therapy far beyond the present limits, no essential change would be achieved. For is not the problem of the relevance of psychoanalysis, as we are examining it here, to be viewed against the background of the silent assumption that mankind in its totality is in jeopardy—that it is endangered by an affliction which is more ominous and profound than that which is evoked by calling to mind the sum total of the misery of individual neuroses?

Yes, man is in danger. He may be on the verge of destroying himself. He cannot control his cruelty toward his fellow man. He appears to be forced to respond to differences of opinion or conflicts of interest in one mode only: through the mobilization of his readiness to fight and to destroy. The mere otherness of others frightens and disgusts him. And so powerfully impelling is the influence of these feelings on him that he would rather risk total destruction than bear the burden which an attitude of tolerance toward the demands of his fellow men and the temporary renunciation of his own demands and of his own pride would impose on him. An often heard statement, which by now strikes us as an unimpressive truism, is that man's technological power to destroy has risen enormously, while his capacity to control his aggression has at best increased only slightly. Yet, trite as this psychosocial diagnosis appears to be, it points to the heart of the discrepancy in the development of man as an active causative force in history—a discrepancy which calls for a cure. Is it conceivable that the important insights of modern depth psychology since Freud should be irrelevant here? Clearly, we should expect them to help us as we try to control our historical fate. But do they? Does psychoanalysis, for example, make a contribution to the efforts that are being made to bring about greater harmony between ethnic and national groups? Certainly not in any clear-cut and direct way—even though we may console ourselves with the thought that some of the maxims that have been derived from the findings of analysis have filtered through to the masses and to their leaders and are thus exerting their influence in an inconspicuous and indirect fashion.

What reason can we adduce for the fact that psychoanalytic insights have not been brought to bear effectively on the great problems of our times? We will start with the simplest explanation: psychoanalysis is young. Such an assertion may well seem strange when we consider the fact that the first psychoanalytic book—Breuer's and Freud's *Studies on Hysteria*—

was published in 1895 and that the treatment of Breuer's famous case (Miss Anna O.) had begun fifteen years earlier. We can thus say that psychoanalysis has been in existence for about eighty or ninety years—long enough, one might think, to demand from this science clear-cut achievements in the various areas of its potential application. This is indeed an opinion which is held by many—including numerous analysts. But it is an opinion which I do not share. Analysis may, of course, lay claim to having provided an important new instrument which opens the path to the deeper layers of the mind; and it has clearly supplied a powerful therapeutic technique by which one can bring about the relief of certain psychic disturbances. Still, despite the accuracy of these claims, the territory which is staked out by them is too small. For those who thus restrict themselves to defining analysis as a circumscribed profession which employs a specific technology must concede that it is no longer young, that it can hardly expect to make further decisive advances but has reached the final stage in its development as a limited branch of science whose near-exclusive goal has become the painstaking verification and the systematic classification of the discoveries which were made in the days of the pioneers.

No, the preceding evaluation is too narrow. Strange as it may sound to many ears, I believe that the advent of psychoanalysis constitutes an important step in the history of science and, potentially, even a significant turning point in the development of culture. With psychoanalysis man has succeeded in transforming introspection and empathy into the tools of an empirical science. Operations which had previously been harnessed to impressionistic, mystical, and speculative approaches have now become instruments for the systematic exploration of the inner life of man. Through the use of these methods, furthermore, a new field has been opened to science. While scientific methodology in the field of psychology formerly could be applied only to comparatively simple data concerning the behavioral surface, psychoanalysis undertakes the scientific exploration of the complex and significant dimensions of human life in depth. It has found the bridge between the two opposing approaches—understanding and explaining—to the inner life of man. It has achieved the first valid integration of, on the one hand, the observer's ability to understand the endless variety of psychological experiences through introspection and empathy with, on the other hand, the theorist's ability to conceptualize these data at higher levels of abstraction and to formulate their interrelatedness within a system of experience-distant explanations. Mystical introspection may understand, but it does not explain; and pre-analytic scientific psychology explains, but it does not understand. Psychoanalysis, by contrast, explains what is has understood. This combination of empathic-introspective data-gathering with abstract formulation and theoretical explanation in the field of complex mental states, however, constitutes a revolutionary step in the history of science. And I believe, therefore, that analysis, this new and pioneering foray into the hitherto unexplored, is still in its infancy, and that our present analytic investigations do not yet penetrate very far beneath the surface.

He who has fully grasped how great the step was that science took with the establishment of psychoanalysis will have no difficulty understanding why analytic research has up to now remained focused almost exclusively on the psychic life of the individual, why so far only one fundamental insight concerning the psychology of groups has been obtained within the framework of psychoanalytic theory: Freud's realization that the cohesion of certain groups is explained by the fact that the members of these groups hold the same ego ideal in common. It is the relative youthfulness of analysis which justifies our hesitation to transfer the knowledge obtained in the solid central sphere of our observation to the psychology of the group, i.e., to an area in which neither the new methods of observation nor the conceptual framework which is correlated to them can be directly applied.

Another reason why, so far, we have concentrated our attention on the individual is the realization that our ability to find access to the inner life of others is dependent on their willingness to reveal themselves. In general we can, therefore, undertake psychological investigations only when illness and suffering provide sufficient motivation. Without an individual's wish to seek relief or to be cured it is usually difficult to obtain sufficient psychological data.

Still, I am not pessimistic. It is indeed possible to learn a great deal about the inner life of man outside the therapeutic setting. Man's wish to express himself is strong. True, the documents of self-revelation may often have the simultaneously activated tendency to hide and to disguise—perhaps just at the point where they manifestly appear to divulge some decisive secret; yet, the careful scrutiny of the available material may lead us to many insights. Freud thought, for example, that psychotic patients could not be treated by psychoanalysis because they could not come emotionally close to the analyst and lend him their trust. Still, it was Freud's study of an available document, Schreber's *Memoirs of My Nervous Illness,* that allowed him to dispense with the investigation of the mental life of a noncooperative psychotic patient during the treatment process and yet to explain the psychopathology of paranoia (in particular its persecutory and megalomaniac delusions) more comprehensively and cogently than had ever been done before.

Are there analogous methods by which we could investigate the reactions of large groups? Are there ways by which the deep insights which psychoanalysis has gained about the individual can be brought to bear on group psychology in a sensitive and creative fashion, so that we may hope to arrive at a solid understanding of the behavior of large groups, and thus, in turn, may hope to make a decisive contribution to the strengthening of the self-control of these groups and of their leaders?

To be more specific, let us consider the psychic constellation called narcissism—the love for one's self—which, as we are realizing with deepening understanding, plays a decisive motivational role in group psychology. The importance of such vicissitudes in the realm of narcissism as wounded self-esteem and deflated fantasies of omnipotence cannot be overestimated—they lead to the most dangerous form of group tension: the group's readiness toward aggressive action. Our broadened and deepened knowledge in these psychic areas is already assisting us to achieve respectable therapeutic successes with individual patients whose prognosis had formerly been rather poor; and the substantial insights in this area concerning the psychopathology of individual patients raise the legitimate hope that we will eventually be able also to obtain analogous insights in the area of group psychology which will increase the group's ability to be the master of its own destiny.

It would not be difficult to present at this point some concrete illustrations of the important role which narcissism plays in the psychic life of individuals and groups: how, for example, endless hate and lust for revenge—without regard even for one's own survival—can result from wounded self-esteem; and why these reactions come about. But I must not allow myself to be long-winded concerning a favorite topic. And instead of supplying clinical or historical illustrations let me merely mention two literary masterpieces which deal with this theme—not as rigorous, scientific explorations, of course, but with the freedom which an artistic medium provides. I am thinking of a masterful German story about hurt pride and its consequences, Kleist's *Michael Kohlhaas,* and of its English-language counterpart, Melville's great novel *Moby Dick.*

The acquisition of psychological insights, however—be they ever so clearly formulated and validly substantiated—is only a first step. If our insights are to influence others to modify their attitudes and actions, we also must be able to count on the good will and the open-mindedness of those to whom these insights are communicated. You can lead the horse to water but you can't make him drink. We will have to discover methods by which we can make the wholesome potentialities of the discoveries of modern depth psychology not only available but even attractive to the large groups. At the moment there are several opportunities which offer themselves to us as we strive to reach this goal. I will discuss two of these approaches.

The first is the mapping out of a psychological technology designed to influence the masses. I admit freely that I am not at home with such methods—indeed, I feel very uneasy about them. The skilled use of techniques to manipulate the masses smacks of demagoguery, suggests the rabble-rousing of the seducer who is able to intoxicate the listening crowds. And there is, of course, no dearth of historical examples that show how a people was led to ruin by its leader—as were the children by the Pied Piper of Hamlin. I think that we understand such events. The great seducers of mankind have retained from their childhood an unshakable conviction of being all-powerful and all-knowing. It is this pervasive sense of infallibility which shapes their attitudes and forges their actions. Such personalities are prone to formulate certain simple and clearly depicted goals—whether in the realm of religion or of politics; whether as the prophets of a salvation through physical exercise or through the eating of herbs. Although these goals may be rational in appearance, they are, nevertheless, the manifestations of an archaic self which, in accordance with the solipsistic conceptions of early life, is still experienced as possessing absolute power and unlimited knowledge. It is this connection with the archaic self which lends dogmatic certainty to the opinions held by such individuals, and it explains the ruthlessness with which they are able to pursue their goals. These personalities, furthermore, exert a quasi-hypnotic effect on many people. Deeply rooted in our earliest childhood there remains in us a longing to merge with an all-powerful and all-knowing ideal figure. This yearning finds an apparently irresistible fulfillment for many in their total submission to a Messianic leader and to his dogmatic beliefs.

It surely does not have to be explained why we feel instinctively repelled at the thought of advocating methods that resemble those employed by the Messianic leaders and dictators of recent history. But are we not here perhaps the victims of a prejudice? Must we not admit that there are also well-intentioned and constructive leaders who are able to employ irrational forces and to evoke irrational responses—but all this in the service of rational and culture-building goals? What would we not have given—I am speaking here of those of my own generation who lived in Germany and Austria during the thirties—what indeed would we not have given for an inspiring charismatic leader who could have pitted his profoundly held humanitarian ideals effectively against that most pernicious mass seducer of our time who almost succeeded in destroying Western civilization? Under certain circumstances—we have to admit it—pure rationality, however valid its goals, must find support from the irrational depths of the archaic psyche. If not, it will remain impotent vis-à-vis the irrational forces of destruction. It was not by accident that the image of the devil was created by man's symbol-forming mind.

We must ask ourselves, in addition, whether it would indeed be possible for us to use irrational methods with conviction should we ever decide to take such a step in earnest. People who have once fully committed themselves to rationality, whether in individual psychotherapy or in the realm of social action, are in general simply not able to mobilize and exploit the charisma of archaic omnipotence. And furthermore, should we nevertheless succeed in conjuring up those irrational powers that are effective in the social arena, in order to guide and to inspire, then we must not forget that playing the sorcerer's apprentice is not without danger. One begins by using irrational means in the service of rational ends. Yet, before one knows it, the irrational has taken over and has become our master. At first we are pretending omnipotence but soon we may begin to believe in it ourselves. The kind and rational leader is now a tyrant, and the friendly mentor becomes transformed into the Messiah who brooks no contradiction. It is not hard to find examples of such inauspicious developments either in the history of nations or—I will here refrain from pointing at specific instances—in the history of psychotherapy.

The second approach to the masses and their leaders—analogous to the conditions that allow access to the psyche of the individual—is opened by the group's anxiety and need for help. We must not discount the possibility that some extreme, not yet fully foreseeable danger will in the future constitute a turning point with regard to the traditional irrationality of group behavior. Mankind may indeed be facing grave and unusual dangers, since for the first time in history the means for self-annihilation are now at its disposal. Let us assume a dawning awareness in the masses that certain convictions—such as the belief in the perfection, omnipotence, and indestructibility which each individual harbors about himself and about the group to which he belongs—prevent us from acting realistically because they make us blind to the ultimate peril. Could it not then come to pass, in a period of critical danger, that there may emerge the ability to pause, to listen, to ponder—to be insightful before the irreversible deed is done? Might it not happen, under such circumstances, that the seemingly unattainable would become a reality and that the large groups, or at least their leaders, would begin to understand themselves, not only superficially but in depth? That they would grasp the significance of psychic areas which under ordinary circumstances can hardly be penetrated and mastered by the mental efforts of even the most rational and courageous individual? What I am speaking of here is the dawning recognition by the masses or their leaders of how easily the ideas of grandeur and omnipotence which are so deeply interwoven with a sense of national identity can become an unrealistic intoxicant and can thus constitute a great danger. What I have in mind here, furthermore, is the recognition that neither God nor nature has bestowed on us the right to feel ourselves bigger and better than our neighbor and, what is even more important, that we do not *need* this right. That each can have pride in himself and be pleased with himself without degrading the other, without having to do away with those whose only fault is the fact that they are different from us, and who thus remind us that we are not the only-begotten: unique and universal.

I realize that there are objections to these thoughts. It may well be said that in moments of despair and extreme danger men tend to be less rather than more rational; that in such moments they will not turn to a rational leader but that they will be swept toward the charisma of a Messiah. Yet, who can really predict how man will behave when he is face to face with ultimate disaster? At any rate: so long as there is uncertainty, it is the duty of depth psychology to be prepared for the moment when, in a situation of utmost gravity, there might arise a last chance for the ascendancy of reason. We must, therefore, attempt to gather insights which would allow us, if the historical moment is propitious, to exert that influence on behalf of rationality in the arena of public and historical events which depth psychology has up to now exerted in psychotherapy. Beyond that we cannot see today. Yet the mere possibility of such an intervention should be a sufficient incentive for us to devote all our resources to the broadening and deepening of our work.

But I must take a breath. From what I have said so far one might conclude that it is my intention to deflect analysts from treating their patients and to direct them instead to the investigation of groups—that I am asking them to focus their attention on social psychology instead of wasting their time with psychotherapy and with the investigation of the psychology of the individual and his treatment. Nothing, however, is further from my mind. On the contrary, not only am I convinced that the abandonment of the traditional therapeutic goals and investigational tasks of the analyst and their substitution by research in the field of social psychology would lead to very meager results, but I am also certain that such a shift would bring about the drying up of the actual source from which must spring the analyst's insights concerning group psychology.

Cobbler, stick to your last! Analyst, stay in your consulting room! Don't be persuaded to relax your efforts in pursuing the work in which you have become proficient: to understand your patient, to communicate your understanding to him, and to help him through his increasing self-knowledge to become the master of his fate.

These appeals are, however, meant to militate neither against the social psychologist, nor, of course, against those analysts whose predilection and talent have led them to the study of group psychology. The application of analytic insights to the investigation of this field and to related disciplines has already brought us many fine results. Nowhere, however, is the access to the soul of man, to the peak of his love and the abyss of his hate, more open than in that singular, long-term relationship between two people which is called the psychoanalytic situation. And since the fundamental discoveries of the analyst will surely continue to be made only in the central sphere of his work, he must not relinquish his therapeutic activity, for he would otherwise deprive himself of the richest source of new insights.

My conviction that the analyst must not turn away from therapeutic activity is, however, still more broadly based. True, every successfully terminated analysis gives us the satisfaction of knowing that a human life has now been freed from the shackles of neurotic inhibitions. And we may also surely allow ourselves to feel pride when—often as the result of having been privileged to collaborate with an insightful and gifted patient—it is our good fortune to contribute a piece of new psychological insight to the enduring fund of general scientific knowledge. But each favorable therapeutic outcome, each scientific advance signifies still more. Each treatment that reaches a valid termination—yes, even each partial success that brings about the reliable modification of a hitherto deadlocked neurotic state—is an important and auspicious event with regard to the survival of what should be considered as the essence of man. It is a victory of man's planning and thinking individuality over the impersonal anonymity of his fate-bound matrix. With every analytic success a human being has made a step toward autonomy, toward freedom.

What I have in mind here is not the traditional conception of the victory of rationality over the irrational, the ascendancy of reason over passion. Humanness comprises not only reason and equanimity but also irrationality and passion. Still—although man as a thinking machine is no more human than man as a frenzied fanatic—a person's inner freedom and independence, the essence of his human individuality, become enhanced when he begins to discern the determinants of his goals and attitudes; when he knows why he thinks, feels, and acts as he does; and when now, because of his knowledge, it is easier for him to be in control of his feelings and his behavior, and to be the master of his choices and decisions. He now understands why he always had to be cold, logical, and rational; and in consequence of this understanding, he becomes capable of passionate feelings and actions. Or he knows now why all his life he had to move from one frenzied crisis to the other and, in consequence of this knowledge, he is now able to reflect first and not plunge into action. In the terms of Freud's well-known simile: he is no longer the Sunday horseman who claims that he wants to go where in fact his horse is taking him—he is now in truth the master of his horse.

As I get closer to the end of these reflections I realize more and more how difficult it is to state the case of analysis without presenting the empirical evidence on which this science is built. My convictions about the broad significance of depth psychology may, therefore, seem fanciful to that still not inconsiderable number of skeptics who are inclined to look upon psychoanalytic therapy and research as a somewhat faddish and at any rate rather unscientific occupation.

I will not refrain, however, from developing now a specific speculative train of thought, even though I realize that, in doing so, I might well run the risk of exposing myself to the justifiable reproach that I am being unscientific, and am liable to increase the very prejudices against analysis that I am trying to reduce. Let me stress, however, that I do not seek the quick acceptance of my suggestions; I have only the wish that they not be rejected out of hand and that they be given some attention. My speculation concerns the nature of the phenomena which the psychoanalyst investigates or—to state my topic in traditional terms—the nature of the illnesses which he treats.

The arguments which I have been presenting up to this point are on the whole in harmony with the enlightened attitude that psychic disturbances are neither a sin nor a disgrace but are illnesses which ought to be cured. That this view is accepted by the professional psychotherapist goes without saying. I believe, however, that nowadays it is also held rather widely by broad, nonprofessional layers of the population—at least by the educated. I might be too sanguine in this judgment; the old prejudices are possibly still stronger than I think. But, be that as it may, there is no doubt that the view, which according to my optimistic assessment prevails today among the educated, deserves our full support: it is the expression of a progressive and enlightened attitude.

Still, attractive as these humanitarian views are for us, and much as they deserve our support within the framework of present social reality, I believe that the medico-therapeutic conceptualization of psychic disequilibrium on which they are based is too confining. I believe, in other words, that we need a broader outlook. Specifically, I would like to propose that psychological disturbance should not be looked upon as a disease—or at any rate not exclusively so—but as a way station on the road of man's search for a new psychological equilibrium.

Throughout the historical period, man has had to deal increasingly with the problems posed by a world which he himself has created. The simple drives which are his natural equipment have become less and less useful to him as the social environment in which he finds himself is growing more complex. His aggressivity, in particular, was once, in his animal past, indispensable for his survival—now, on the contrary, it has become the gravest threat to his existence: he must learn to control it if human life is to continue on earth.

But to suppress human drives can also be dangerous. The capacity of our biological and psychological equipment to adapt to change is limited, and the tension which the extensive suppression of our drives imposes on us becomes intolerable before long. Freud referred to this emotional burden, in a rather understated fashion, as "discomfort" or "discontent."[2] Man feels himself imprisoned by the demands of civilized existence and strives to escape. To let himself go, in orgies of lust and aggression, leads to disaster. Yet, the suppression of his drives—the meek acceptance of an ascetic existence—is a feat which is apparently also beyond his capacity, despite the two-thousand-year efforts of Christianity. Some of the gratifications from which man has obtained a modicum of relief in his predicament are slowly becoming unavailable. There are more people and there is less space. It is getting harder to find regions in which we can satisfy our need to roam about freely. Everywhere machines are doing the work of our muscles. And even the joys of parenthood will surely also have to be relinquished, at least by most, or else there will soon be standing room only on this earth.

Are these then, in the bitter words of the great Austrian satirist Karl Kraus, *the last days of mankind?* I do not think so. Football and boxing, to be sure, will not be our salvation—not even the enjoyment of nature

___

[2] The English rendition of the title of Freud's great essay *Das Unbehagen in der Kultur* is *Civilization and Its Discontents*. Actually neither the words "discomfort" nor "discontent" do full justice to the meaning of *Unbehagen*, although "discomfort," with its milder connotation of suffering and without the implication of resentment, is the closer equivalent.

in hiking and climbing. No, what is needed to ensure the survival of the human race—and this is the perhaps overly daring hypothesis which I announced earlier—is the intensification and, above all, the elaboration and expansion of the inner life of man.

I know that such an assertion will be offensive to many. Western civilization traditionally extols the man of action; it demands that the individual at least be engaged in activities. To contemplate one's navel, to give oneself over to inward-looking contemplation—these are attitudes which belong in different lands; and in our culture they are supposedly confined to a minority of eccentrics who cannot successfully adapt to the ways of the world.

Well and good—but let us not judge too quickly, and first let us look about us a bit. Let us, for example, consider the widespread attempts of the young people of today to obtain pleasures and satisfactions which are largely unrelated to external activity: by giving themselves over to the intoxicating effect of drugs and rhythmical music; by immersing themselves in Eastern philosophy; or merely by maintaining long periods of a wordless physical closeness, barely touching each other in some kind of ecstasy. I am not claiming that these practices are valid solutions of the great problems of human existence. I merely want to show that the rising generation is searching and exploring—specifically, that it is attempting to find sources of fulfilling gratification which are independent of external activity.

It is safe to assume that in the future man's external activities will have to be restricted even further. If, under these conditions, he wishes to continue to live proudly and contentedly—without the opportunity to fasten his interest upon the absorbing challenge of the conquest of new territories, without the engagement of his energies in battles and wars, and, last but not least, without the joys of being surrounded by the exhilarating play and laughter of his children—then man's originality, indeed his genius, will truly be put to the test. Under such circumstances the goal of maintaining human life, not only as livable but indeed as worth living, this goal can—and I do not discern an alternative—be reached only through the expansion and intensification of man's inner life.

But how do these reflections bear on the topic of the significance of the psychoneuroses? I believe that these psychic conditions which are generally conceived as diseases, and which are indeed the cause of much intense suffering and unhappiness, should in certain respects be understood as man's groping toward the enlargement and intensification of his inner life. I hasten to add that we are dealing here with attempts which have come to grief. Nevertheless, I shall be bold enough to assert that these miscarried attempts should be evaluated as more courageous, and potentially more creative, than some of the forms of psychic equilibrium that make up the area of emotional normality or health.

Mental health may be defined as the psychological condition which allows a person to respond actively to his environment and to obtain satisfaction from his encounter with the world. Freud described it as man's capacity to love and to work. Such a conception of psychic normality can remain unchallenged so long as we are referring to the world of yesterday and today, to man's position as we know it from the study of history and from our own experience. Within this familiar context we will surely consider it a desirable state of psychic health when a person reflects about the physical and social environment in which he finds himself and responds to it with a full range of emotions and effective actions: rejects it in courageous rebellion where he must; and embraces it lovingly where he can.

But what will be man's psychological task in the future? Let us assume that the dread of self-annihilation will prevent humanity from engaging in wars and that the condition of enduring peace will exert a wholesome, humanizing influence on people. Let us further assume that these psychological changes (coupled with the fear of civil disorders which might lead to uncontrollable wars) will bring about a modicum of social justice. Let us finally assume that reason and self-discipline will result in a worldwide agreement about the number of people that can be accommodated on this planet and will lead to the establishment of suitable safeguards that this number is not exceeded. What then?

I am fully aware of the fact that many readers will react with angry impatience to the foregoing considerations. It seems indeed so unlikely that the utopian conditions which I have just described are realizable that I might well be told to stop worrying about the welfare of mankind in a paradise which, after all, has no chance of ever becoming established. I could match such skepticism by the rejoinder that the future is unpredictable. And, in particular, I could point out that a worldwide overpopulation and a destructive potential of the magnitude of the unchained atom are factors which combine to bring about an unprecedented psychological situation—perhaps one in which people will act more reasonably than they have so far. The essence of our problem, however, has to be approached by a different road. If the development toward the establishment of a lasting peaceful equilibrium among people is to reach its goal, it must be maintained by the complementary cooperation of internal and external factors, i.e., more specifically, by the mutually complemental interaction between certain environmental changes and man's psychological responsiveness to them. Life in a peaceful environment—although apparently the ideal state—would not be without serious psychological problems. Such an existence would, on the one hand, lead to the withdrawal of the psychic energies from the battles and problems of the external world, demanding their new employment and thus necessitating an intensification of man's inner life. But, on the other hand—and this is the crucial point of my argument!—the most important precondition for mankind's approach to a state of external harmony and peace is a shift in man's psychological structure. If man could gradually withdraw from his present search for external sources of pleasure and instead would increasingly find contentment from the enjoyment of values which are in harmony with an intensification of his inner life, then he would pari passu be able to deflect his aggressive and libidinal drives from those dangerous aims which up to now have blocked the road toward the establishment of peace.

The work of the creative artist and performer and the psychological activities of those who are able to respond to art and to obtain pleasure from it should be regarded as the precursors of that ability to enjoy the pursuit of internalized interests of which I spoke. Consider, for example, the powerful psychological forces which music activates in those who can enjoy it. Here a whole universe of experiences is open to us which is hardly related to the realities of our everyday existence—a world in which we can reap satisfactions which are hardly related to those external goals which we traditionally strive to attain and for which we fight. But it is not only art that I have in mind here but also certain aspects of science. Thinking is trial action carried out with minute quantities of energy, says Freud's beautiful definition. Yes; but passionate reflection and mental conquest can more and more become satisfying purposes per se—and Freud himself is indeed an outstanding example of such an inward shift. Learning in order to know, reflecting in order to understand—not only to construct bridges or to organize excursions to the moon—such exercise of self-contained mental functions is a fulfilling activity for those who are adequately endowed in the intellectual and emotional sphere, allowing them to enjoy life and to consider their energies as satisfyingly employed.

Stated in the most general terms, my hypothesis is the result of the application of Darwinian developmental principles to a psychoanalytic sociology. There exist countless variations within the human race. Most individuals with their specific (and, within limits, fixed) abilities and disabilities are destined for extinction when a drastically changed environment ceases to sustain them. But within the legions there are a few—perhaps previously ill-adapted and weak—who will adapt to the new environment and will be able to survive, while all the countless others, the host of the formerly strong, will be destroyed.

Thus psychic disorders may be seen as a manifestation of man's attempt to achieve the intensification of his inner life: a developmental step which he must take in order to survive in his rapidly changing social environment. The neuroses as we know them have succeeded in bringing about a partial detachment of the drives from their primordial engagement with external reality; but the concomitant shift from action to thought and from the external object to the self has led here not to creative mental activity and to the enjoyment of one's self but to unsolved inner conflicts and psychic tension.

What is the relationship between the foregoing reflections and the central subject matter of this presentation, the question whether depth psychology is still relevant in the world of today? Does the conception of the psychoneuroses as man's attempt to shift his psychological energies upon his inner life throw new light on our evaluation of the importance of psychoanalysis as an investigative science and as a form of psychotherapy?

In most sciences there exists a more or less clear separation between the area of practical, empirical application and the area of concept formation and theory. In analysis, however, these two areas do not only form that partnership of active, reciprocal communication and mutual stimulation which prepares the soil for many important advances in other fields of knowledge—here they are merged into a single functional unit.

Psychoanalysis as an investigative science is inseparable from analysis as a form of psychotherapy. Not only does the therapeutic situation supply unparalleled opportunities for the systematic empirical observation of psychic processes in breadth and depth, but the aim of psychoanalytic therapy is in essence identical with the aim of science: to extend the reach of consciousness and to enlarge the ego's domain of knowledge and freedom.

A well-conducted analysis, therefore, which has been brought to a proper conclusion, provides the analysand with more than the diminution or disappearance of his painful and disturbing symptoms—there exists in him now a certain psychological openness, perhaps even a spark of that playful creativeness which turns toward new situations with joyful interest and responds to them with life-affirming initiative. Such a person may yet continue to be more easily traumatized than one who has learned to maintain a reliable yet restricting psychic equilibrium. But he will also be more perceptive and responsive than the rigidly normal.

Yes, depth psychology is still young and its achievements are limited. The psychoanalyst has, however, no reason to be either ashamed of the past performance of his science nor pessimistic about its future contributions. Not only can he maintain that the venerable injunction on Apollo's temple in Delphi, "Know thyself!," has nowhere in history found a more strict obedience than in the sphere of his activity, but perhaps he can also claim that he is the only scientifically systematic, yet understanding and respectful observer and helpmate in man's attempt to achieve a new psychological equilibrium which will be in harmony with the changed social environment of the future.

I have now come to the end. Throughout I have tried to refrain from offering simplistic solutions, from painting in black and white. And I have always attempted not to obscure the doubtful. Still, I will admit to the hope that I have not been unsuccessful in the support of my deep conviction that the continuing study of the inner life of man within the framework of depth-psychological treatment and investigation is an important, a valuable undertaking. To expand the realm of man's consciousness and thereby that of his self-control and creative responsiveness—during a historical juncture which confronts him with new and difficult tasks—is a goal which calls not only for the analyst's fullest effort and devotion but also for the support of his work by an understanding community.

Sigmund Freud
Centennial Lecture

ROBERT WAELDER

The hundredth birthday of a great man is one of the external landmarks which we use from time to time as an opportunity to look back in order to gain whatever perspective is possible. Time is a strange critic. Things that have been written some time ago show varying degrees of obsolescence. Many are no longer read because they are like yesterday's newspaper; they are stale, like yesterday's bread. Some obsolesce in a month, a year, a generation, while others have kept their freshness over hundreds and thousands of years. On this hundredth anniversary of Freud's birth, about half a century has passed since his main works were written. Half a century is not very long, but it is something, particularly in a time of rapid change like ours, and I think one can say when one reads Freud's work today that, with very few exceptions, it is as fresh as if it had only just been written. The degree of obsolescence of Freud's work in fifty years has been extremely small. There may be two radically different reasons why older things hold little interest for us. One, as mentioned before, is that they

The occasion was the Centennial of the birth of Sigmund Freud. This lecture was presented by the late Robert Waelder on Saturday afternoon, May 5, 1956, at the El Rodeo School in Beverly Hills, California. Dr. Ernst Lewy as President introduced Dr. Waelder in the name of the Los Angeles Institute for Psychoanalysis and the Los Angeles Psychoanalytic Society. ·

I do not know why this material was never published. Among Robert Waelder's papers I found typed material which seems to have been a transcript of what was recorded at that meeting. In Robert Waelder's own hand there was a fair amount of editing, apparently to smooth it out for the reader. Some additional editing work has been necessary.

I found this to be a beautiful lecture which, after these years, is even more worthy of publication.

Samuel A. Guttman, Ph.D., M.D.*
Professor of Psychoanalysis
Thomas Jefferson University
Jefferson Medical College
Philadelphia, Pa.

* This material was made available to me, as Literary Executor of Robert Waelder, by Elsie M. Waelder, Executrix.

are stale. But sometimes there is the opposite reason: that a work that once was accepted is now taken for granted. Schopenhauer once said that truth is but a brief holiday between two long and dreary seasons; during the first it was rejected as sophistry and during the second it is forgotten as commonplace. Freud's work, as far as I can see, is neither dated nor, indeed, yet commonplace; on the contrary, it is strangely alive.

Perhaps we may consider for a moment the essential ideas that Freud advanced in the last few years of the nineteenth century; he made many more contributions, but I want to point out the fundamental ones. There was, first of all, the idea of the so-called dynamic theory of human behavior, or, if you like, the idea that human behavior is ordinarily the outcome of conflicting inner tendencies. That thought is still very fresh. Even today, in books written by good authors, in the practices of our law courts, or in our political discussions, we more or less assume that a person, by and large, follows one goal at a time. The idea that in the ordinary course of events men are not single-minded, that what they do is the outcome of an inner strife, that their behavior does not prove that they had willed that all the time, but merely indicates that there was an edge—perhaps only a slight edge—for one group of motivations over another group of motivations, which often might have been shifted to an opposite behavior by a minor change in the weight of the inner vote: that is an idea which has not yet become common property.

The next great concept was that these inner conflicts are not always solved by a decision in favor of one or the other inner tendency, or by a compromise, but that we sometimes escape the necessity of deciding between alternatives by sweeping the disagreeable problem under the carpet, so to speak, by driving it out of our consciousness. We call that "repression." And as a result the motivating force has not become invalidated, but has become unconscious. This is the great concept of the power of unconscious motivation. And then comes the idea that neurosis is due to such inner conflict, which has not been solved but is merely evaded by driving it underground—a tremendous new concept. Before this, as much as psychiatry had looked out for the psychological reasons for mental disturbance, it had always sought them in external pressures.

Freud's new idea was that we get sick not from external pressures, great though they may be, but from not being at one with ourselves, i.e., from inner conflicts, and that the role of external frustrations is limited to that of a possible stimulus for arousing inner conflicts. We shall see that this idea, far from being stale, has as yet not been generally accepted, even by psychoanalysts.

Finally, the next two concepts hold that there are two weak spots in the organization of the mind, two areas in which man may easily fail in the solution of his inner conflicts, and in which, therefore, repression and its pathological consequences may easily occur. The first of these weak spots in our mental organization has to do with a specific type of challenge, viz., with the sexual challenges. It is in dealing with our sexual drives that we may show ourselves inadequate, unable to adapt, unable to reconcile inner and outer conditions, and therefore much more likely than in other areas to escape the problem by repressing it. Our sexual drives are the troublemakers because they are less capable of adjustment than other tendencies.

Then too, there is a period of time in which we are particularly vulnerable, viz., childhood. It is a time of a temporary weakness in our mental organization, and conflicts occurring in this period are more likely to remain unsolved than the conflicts of a later, mature time. These last two concepts constitute the sexual and infantile genesis of the neuroses. There are many more ideas and theories in psychoanalysis, but the four propositions mentioned may be said to be the fundamental ones. If a holocaust should destroy all our libraries and all people with psychoanalytic learning, it is quite possible that from these few basic propositions psychoanalysis could, in good time, be reconstructed.

It is not easy for us to imagine how tremendously difficult it was for Freud to arrive at these propositions, which ran strongly against common sense and against deeply imbedded prejudices of the time. But it is necessary to remember that the time of Freud's youth and of the most creative period of his manhood was the Victorian Age, in which the attitude of man toward his sexuality was one of denial. Sexuality was not talked about in civilized society, except at stag parties, and then with an air of lugubriousness. It was thought to belong to animal aspects of human nature, i.e., to a subhuman part of man which was not to be faced frankly and honestly. Of course, that does not mean that man in the Victorian Age did not express his sexual urges, but in polite society they could not be faced. Perhaps not often in history has there been so great an alienation of man from his biological roots as in just this era.

Two examples may illustrate the Victorian attitude toward sexuality. The first occurred not so long ago. At the outbreak of the First World War in 1914, the British War Minister, Field Marshal Earl Kitchener, gave the order of the day to the British army, which every British soldier had to carry with him at all times. He said—I do not quote literally—"During your operations you will be exposed to some temptations of wine or women. You must resist both temptations absolutely and unconditionally. While you have to treat all women with perfect courtesy, you must absolutely avoid any intimacy." Thus, only a little more than forty years ago it was considered to be a practical policy to ask soldiers going into battle that they should live in complete abstinence. You see how much has changed since that day; not so much perhaps in the behavior of soldiers, as in the attitude toward it. Another example shows how impossible it was for Victorians to admit that the higher and the lower aspects of man could have any relation with each other. About half a century ago, William James suggested in his classical book on pragmatism that the ideas of philosophers may be conditioned or influenced by their temperament. That seems to us to be quite a rather innocuous idea, probably true, but nothing to get excited about. Yet James found himself constrained to apologize for suggesting that something as dignified and as high as a philosophical system could have anything to do with things as low as emotions or temperament, and, even as late as 1935, F. M. Cornford, the English classicist, philosopher, and poet, while quoting that passage from James, still felt that the idea that philosophical thought might be influenced by temperament had been advanced by a "breezy American." Such attitudes account for much of the opposition and disparagement that Freud found in his earlier years.

Whenever a man has conceived great new ideas, it is interesting to ask how these ideas grew in his mind, how he got them along his way. There is a positivistic myth of the scientist, according to which a scientist is a purely receptive person who has no preconceived, guiding ideas, who observes what comes along. But that is a myth. If we study the history of thought, we get an entirely different idea. We find that the nuclei of the mature thoughts of great scientific creators existed in their minds early, for reasons unknown, long before they made their first observations. And it looks as if they set out in the world to find the proof for these embryonic ideas. I cannot prove to you that this is true of Freud. But I can give you a little detail which might be suggestive. We have a letter that Freud wrote shortly after his seventeenth birthday; he has just passed the "Matura," the much-dreaded graduating exam in classics and in mathematics, with which a boy finished the gymnasium and qualified for entry in a university. The letter, written to a slightly older friend, is a report on what happened in the exam and how he did in it. It is a delightful letter, showing great sense of humor and remarkable maturity for a boy just past his seventeenth birthday. Let me quote a few sentences that seem to be characteristic of the man that Freud was to become. Freud's letter is an answer to a letter from the friend, and we can only surmise what the friend may have written. Says Freud:

You brush aside too easily my worry for the future. You try to comfort me by suggesting that he who is afraid of mediocrity is thereby saved already. Saved from what, may I ask? Certainly not safe from being mediocre. What does it matter, after all, whether one is afraid of a thing or not? Is not all that matters whether what we feel is real or not? True enough that stronger minds have been afflicted with doubts in themselves, but does that prove that everybody who questions his worth is a strong mind? He may be a weakling in spirit, but an honest man; Honest through education, habit, or sheer self-torture. I do not want to persuade you to pitilessly analyze your feelings in moments of doubt, but if you do, you will find how little certainty you have in yourself. The magnificence of the world lies in this vastness of possibility, but unfortunately there is no solid ground for our knowledge of ourselves.[1]

[1] I find that this quotation is from a letter Freud wrote to Emil Fluss dated Vienna, at night, June 16, 1873. Waelder must have had access to the original letter in German and this is probably his own translation, which differs somewhat from the one which appeared, four years later, as Letter 1 on page five in *Letters of Sigmund Freud*, selected and edited by Ernst L. Freud (New York: Basic Books, 1960).

(S. A. G.)

We can find in these few lines the germs of some of the ideas that Freud shaped in later years. There is, for instance, implied in Freud's words the possibility of a "pitiless analysis" of one's feelings. There is also implied the idea that a thing may not be all that it seems to be on the surface—that is, honesty may not always be the result of education but may have its root in self-torture. There is implied the idea that something valued very highly, like honesty, may have its basis in something valued very lowly, a neurotic habit. Here you see in a seventeen-year-old, who had never seen a psychiatric patient and never knew that he ever would, an attitude of mind which made it possible for him to be the founder of the science of human personality.

The position of Freud, of course, has been unique in the field of psycho-analysis. Very nearly all that we have comes from Freud's own work. The contributions that we, the disciples of Freud, have made are relatively negli-gible. There are few examples in science in which a discipline has been so completely created and dominated by one man. The closest example that I know of would be the position which, for a much longer time, Euclid had in the history of geometry. Although his principles of geometry were written around 300 B.C., even up to the present time elementary geometry is taught in our schools according to textbooks only slightly different from Euclid's original book.

In the case of Freud this unique situation has given vent to a great deal of criticism. There are those analysts and near-analysts who say that we disciples of Freud are the members of a religious sect who swear to the words of the master, that we have closed our minds to scientific progress, and that they, unhampered by dogmatism, are now the only ones to uphold a progressive outlook. They are for advances in psychoanalysis; they empha-size new ideas, such as, e.g., the influence of culture on the neurosis of the individual, which Freud is said to have overlooked. They substitute for the libido theory the broader concepts of what they call "interpersonal relations." This widespread school of thought and its advocacy of progress against our own "reactionary orthodoxy" is well known. Are we Freudian analysts really opposed to new ideas? Are we people who wish to freeze the progress of scientific development in the molds of what one man has thought? I would not say that this is impossible; it takes all kinds of people to make a world, and devotees of conservation can be found everywhere. But, on the whole, if I look among the circle of men who I knew were close to Freud, I think I can honestly say that we had no greater desire than to see scientific progess, that we were looking out for new ideas and were not only ready to welcome them but eagerly desirous for them, hoping that perhaps it would be vouchsafed to any one of us to produce a new idea of importance that would carry our science forward.

But when we are confronted with the supposedly new ideas of the pro-gressive analysts, we feel impelled to reject them. We do so because they are not new ideas, but merely a return to the old pre-Freudian concepts.

As we have seen, one of the fundamental innovations of Freud's was the idea that an inner conflict rather than external frustration causes neurosis, and that sexuality and childhood have specific significance as the vulnerable areas of our development. If the new progressives come and tell us that the pressure of culture is responsible for neurosis, i.e., not inner conflict but outside pressure, they have returned to the pre-Freudian viewpoint. If they tell us that not sex but rather the more liberal and broader concept of interpersonal relationships and insecurities is the thing to look at, again they have thrown out of the window the Freudian theory that pathology comes about because of the human difficulty in adjusting to the exuberant growth of specifically sexual challenges; if they say that childhood has been overemphasized, they have thrown that aspect of Freud's theories out of the window too. In other words, they simply discard Freud's concepts wholly or partly. Let there be no doubt that I do not criticize them for so doing. It is their inalienable right to have their own ideas, and if they think that the Freudian concepts are wrong, it is indeed their duty to say so and to say it loudly and repeatedly. Science must be free, and we all, regardless of how strongly we may be convinced that we are right, may yet be wrong. But the question in our minds is why the critics who wholly or partially reject Freud's concepts and return to the pre-Freudian ideas, do not frankly say that this is what they are doing; why do they represent their views as a progress in, rather than a retreat from, psychoanalysis? Their intellectual ancestor, Alfred Adler, was clear about what he did. He held that psychoanalysis was mistaken, and he gave to his own system a different name. As to his present-day successors, we cannot help feeling that they are rejecting Freudian ideas while at the same time trying to retain the prestige value that has meanwhile come to be attached to the name of psychoanalysis. It is perhaps this element of disingenuousness which has aroused some emotionalism in our response.

I should like to give an example from the history of science to suggest that similar things have occurred before in comparable situations. Copernicus published his work on the heliocentric system in 1540. It was heatedly discussed for generations. It was not proved at that time: there were strong arguments against the idea that the fixed stars should have parallactic involvement, i.e., should give the appearance of rotary movement in a small yearly circle if the observing astronomer traveled around the sun. No such parallaxis was observed, though it does exist, because it exceeded the prevailing limits of observation. Those who opposed the Copernician system, however, must not be thought of as merely narrow-minded. When Kepler, in 1608 or 1609, found the three laws of planetary motion which were based on the heliocentric assumption, that was an important argument in favor of the heliocentric theory, though it was still not real proof. Later again in 1670, or a hundred and thirty years after Copernicus, Newton could show that Kepler's laws, which were based on the heliocentric hypothesis, could be explained by laws of gravitation that were equally suitable to explain the

31

fall of bodies on the earth. It was then that the discussion came to an end and the heliocentric theory was generally accepted. But perhaps the case was not scientifically closed until the discovery of the parallaxis of the fixed stars. In that more than a century in which the struggle was on, there was at one point a compromise suggested between the heliocentric and the geocentric philosophy, which gained many adherents. It was proposed by Tycho Brahe. According to this compromise proposition, all planets, with the exception of the earth, circled around the sun, but the whole solar system circled around the earth. This system, which could be made mathematically consistent, was widely accepted in the first decades of the seventeenth century.

It seems to me that much of the present so-called progressive psychoanalysis is comparable to the system of Tycho Brahe, which compromised between the new ideas and the old habits of thought. The progressive analysts tell us that Freud was somewhat right about inner conflicts, but not quite right, because they are really more a matter of cultural pressures. He was right about the importance of childhood, but not quite right, because it is not really so much the childhood. He was somewhat right about the unconscious, but the unconscious is really not quite so unconscious after all. But perhaps the case is not yet scientifically closed, as it was with the discovery of the parallaxis of the fixed stars. The progressive school of thought must of course have the freedom to propagate their ideas, but we Freudian psychoanalysts may be forgiven if we are unwilling to accept concessions to popular prejudice as the manifestation of scientific progress.

That, of course, leaves us with another question which I think is quite appropriate to consider on this anniversary: namely, in what direction can real progress be expected to come about? We cannot countenance the idea that no matter how great the achievements of Freud have been, his work should have been not only the beginning but also the end in the development of psychoanalysis. Where can further scientific development be expected? It seems to me that there is an immense difficulty in psychoanalysis regarding its further progress, and that is the tremendous difficulty of transmitting knowledge, insight, and experience from one person to the other, from teacher to pupil. There is a difficulty of language, of communication. It is already quite difficult even to explain the structure of a case to our colleagues. It works all right in a group of analysts who work together in close cooperation. But in meeting analysts from another circle, one has some difficulty in describing a particular psychic structure in a way that really communicates the idea that one wants to convey.

So formulated, it would seem that this difficulty in psychoanalysis is not unique. There has been a great deal of discussion and speculation about the question why the so-called scientific revolution of the seventeenth century had not already occurred in antiquity, in the Hellenistic Age, which was already a sophisticated, secular civilization. Perhaps it can be considered most concretely if we look at the history of Greek mathematics. The Greeks had a splendid period of mathematical development between approximately 400 and 200 B.C., in which a number of outstanding men, two of whom are known to everybody, Euclid and Archimedes, created among themselves practically the whole of what we call today "elementary mathematics." Archimedes came close as a hair's breadth to inventing the calculus that Newton invented almost two thousand years later and which was the prerequisite for the development of mechanics, dynamics, or physics. Then the development of Greek mathematics came to a stop; for 400 years there is no important mathematician, there is an isolated figure in the second century A.D., and another isolated figure in the third century A.D., and then it ends. One of the most likely causes is that the Greek mathematics was geometric and not algebraic. That means that there was no language or symbolic formulae through which they could express their ideas in a way that would be understood by everybody. They had to describe what they meant in plain words of ordinary speech, and it is extremely difficult to understand a geometric proposition that is explained in common language. Hence, dissemination of the theory was dependent on mouth-to-mouth contact from teacher to pupil; it could hardly be understood from mere reading. Such is the situation in psychoanalysis today, where the continuation of psychoanalysis is still dependent on person-to-person contact and preceptorial tuition. It seems to me that the main bottleneck for the progress of psychoanalysis today is the question of communication, the possibility of transfer of ideas from one to the other.

Thus, if psychoanalysis has not progressed very much beyond Freud, this is, in my opinion, not because Freud had finished his work and left little to be done by his successors, nor is it due to a lack of talent among Freud's followers. Rather, it seems to be due to the fact that psychoanalysts have to devote most of their lives to trying to rediscover for themselves what Freud already knew. Science progresses best and most rapidly when every idea is quickly disseminated and widely understood by a great number of people. We have not reached that condition. Also, there is in our field an immense waste: many of the most experienced and able psychoanalysts carry ideas in their minds which they have not completely been able to communicate to their students and which disappear from the earth when they die, as was apparently the case in other sciences at earlier stages, before more convenient and less subjective means of transmitting knowledge had been found. In fact, what many older psychoanalysts do at the present time is to instill, almost hectically, into a limited number of students as much as possible of the knowledge that they themselves have accumulated, lest it may disappear from the earth.

A very similar condition existed, to use an example closer at home, in the history of medicine before the laboratory, when experience at the sick bed was the only source of knowledge. There were, through the centuries, a number of apparently great diagnosticians, but they were individual men who had achieved in their own experience the ability to evaluate minute symptoms and from them form a diagnosis of illness. Little of their knowledge could be transferred to their students. So knowledge appears and disappears again in a tremendous waste of nature, while, of course, an electrocardiogram or a blood-pressure measurement can be transmitted to somebody else regardless of his talent or experience. I presume that if and when in psychoanalysis means are found to supplement clinical observation by other methods less dependent on individual intuition and experience, and if and when methods describing our results are found that are more precise and more easily disseminated, the progress of psychoanalysis will become very rapid.

I have so far spoken only about Freud's life work, psychoanalysis, and have said nothing about Freud's person. I am probably influenced myself by Freud's own attitude in this matter, his own reluctance to have his person be considered a matter of public interest. Freud thought people should be interested in psychoanalysis, but he didn't like it if they became personally interested in him. He felt that he as a person was not important. I have no doubt that this was his opinion. The story of Freud's personal intolerance is a myth if I ever heard one. The Freud whom I knew was indifferent to things done or said against his person; his interest was in the field. This supposedly very intolerant man had once come to a break with one of his students, not on account of a scientific controversy, but on account of some action by the disciple which Freud thought was detrimental to the position of psychoanalysis, precarious as it already was. The same man some few years later wrote a potboiler biography of Freud that was quite critical of him. Later again, for reasons of his own, this man wished to return to the fold, and Freud received him without the slightest difficulty. He felt no resentment over any personal injury. The only thing of which the Freud that I knew was really intolerant was intellectual dishonesty; there he knew no compromise.

It is not easy to convey any picture of Freud's person, partly because it has been so much distorted by legend. It is difficult to convey an idea of his princely generosity, of the penetration and depths and relevance of his remarks to any major or minor problem, and of his mellowness. I should like to relate one personal experience of the last time that I saw him. It will be eighteen years ago, in three days (May 8, 1938). It was in Vienna, under the Nazi rule; my family and I had just received our passports and permit to leave and wanted to leave right away, as one was in jeopardy every moment. The Freuds still had to wait another four weeks for their passports. I went to say goodbye to Freud. Practically all Viennese analysts of my generation had a signed photo of Freud. Though I, on occasion, had asked for Freud's signature on an etching or a photo for somebody else, I was always inhibited at asking this favor for myself. Now was the last opportunity, and I pulled myself together. I owned no etching of his, and there was no possibility of getting one under the circumstances. I happened to have an unmounted photo that the late Dr. Paul Federn had once given to me, so I took it up and Anna Freud mounted it in an improvised fashion on a piece of cardboard, and I asked Freud to sign it. This is what he wrote under the picture: "Behalten Sie mich lang in guter Erinnerung," which in English would approximately mean, "Keep long a good memory of me." If Freud had only said "keep a good memory of me" without that word *long*, I think it would have been a superfluous appeal. There wasn't any chance that I would forget him, or cease loving him until my last day. But what I find so immensely touching is the qualifying word "long." By writing this word "long," he implied that he did not expect me to do that for the rest of my life but only for a long time. He took it for granted that the day might come in my lifetime in which I would either forget him or no longer think well of him. I don't know whether I can convey my own feelings, but what is so immensely touching is, now that we have made a full turn and are back to the passage in the letter of the seventeen-year-old, the quiet acceptance of the transience of human loyalties and of all things human, an acceptance entirely without bitterness. The fact that he felt everything was temporary and transient didn't mean for him it was any less valuable while it lasted. He wrote a fine little paper on this entitled "On Transience."[2] I understand that the feeling of awe before the infinite and the humble awareness of our own nothingness has been called by many people the essence of "religious experience." Freud in one passage said that his humbleness before the vastness of the world and the awareness of one's own insignificance is not a religious but a par excellence irreligious experience, because, as he used the word, religion is merely the wish-fulfilling escape from the facts. That's a question of semantics which I will not enter but, however you call it, Freud had this sentiment in the greatest possible degree. In his relation with others there was therefore something which I might express best in the words of a poet. He had what W. H. Auden said about Shakespeare's Prospero: "The power to enchant that comes from disillusion."

[2] On Transience (1915). *Stand. Ed.*, 14:303–307. London: Hogarth, 1957.

II

PSYCHOANALYTIC THEORY AND DEVELOPMENTAL PSYCHOLOGY

Psychoanalysis and Theory Formation

MICHAEL FRANZ BASCH, M.D. (*Chicago*)

Introduction

Whether or not psychoanalysis is a basic science, the psychology underlying psychiatry (Freud, 1916, p. 21) that Freud believed it to be, remains an oft-debated and still unsettled issue. Rather than review and evaluate individually the numerous criticisms and defenses of psychoanalysis as a science which have appeared in the professional literature, I will attempt to clarify some of the questions involved by applying the tenets of scientific philosophy to Freud's concept of theory formation.

The nature, manner of acquisition, and validation of scientific knowledge was a controversial issue until progress in theoretical mathematics and mathematical physics in recent times resolved problems that had previously existed in philosophy. The search for absolute and absolutely certain knowledge that preoccupied so many metaphysicians and epistemologists in past centuries has been shown to be an unfruitful and perhaps an impossible quest. Scientific theory is valuable insofar as it permits verifiable predictions to be made; more cannot be expected from it.

My thesis is that the division of psychoanalysis into clinical and metapsychological theories, the former being considered empirical and inductive, and the latter speculative and deductive, is neither philosophically correct nor functional. In addition, consideration must be given to revising the assumption that metapsychology is abstracted from clinical theory.

Examination of some of the concepts involved will lead to the following suggestions: (1) There are inductive and deductive theories, but these are not to be equated with inductive and deductive inference. (2) Deductive theory is not solely the product of deductive inference, nor is inductive theory formed exclusively through inductive inference. (3) All so-called empirical or natural science is composed of inductive theories. (4) Inductive theories can be further divided into classificatory and explanatory theories; these are not on a continuum but run side by side and never meet, though

39

they complement one another. (5) Classificatory theory is formed through *abstraction from* observation, while explanatory theory is composed of hypotheses *about* observations. (6) Psychoanalysis is an empirical though not a biological or physical science and, therefore, is composed of inductive theories. (7) The division of psychoanalytic theory into clinical and metapsychological theories is untenable since it is neither functional nor epistemologically correct. (8) The proposed division of psychoanalytic theory into classificatory and explanatory forms cannot be understood in terms of the presently accepted division of psychoanalysis into clinical and metapsychologic theories; it represents a conceptual revision, not a transposition of terms.

More will be said about each of these aspects of theory formation. It may then be seen that the problems of psychoanalytic theory are in part due to the fact that scientific philosophy has failed to provide a sufficiently comprehensive framework which could encompass the data of psychoanalysis and in part created by some epistemologic errors committed by psychoanalysis. Regarding the latter point and anticipating once again what will have to be spelled out in greater detail: (1) Freud was in the habit of utilizing bridging terms which spanned two different forms of theory; (2) he reified descriptions, confusing them with hypothetical causes; and (3) he assumed that observed phenomena mirrored their origins. The above premature summaries may at least serve to give a hint of the tangle of problems confronting anyone who hopes to make even a beginning in reexamining the theoretical structure of psychoanalysis. Also, by pointing out the scope of the task they may implicitly serve as an excuse for the length of the exposition that follows.

Theory Formation: General Considerations

It has been a common but mistaken assumption that inductive theories are composed of observations while deductive theories are created by inferential reasoning. This leads to a false distinction between the two forms of theory, namely, that inductive theory enumerates facts while deductive theory consists of speculations or hypotheses. The epistemologic confusion involved here is a failure to clearly differentiate inductive and deductive theories from inductive and deductive reasoning or inference.

Deductive theory, as Russell (1912) has explained, deals with symbolic relations devoid of content. The assertion "two plus two equals four" does not warrant the question "two what and two what make four what?" On the level of symbolic or deductive theorizing two plus two equals four because it cannot equal anything else. This is what is meant by the self-evidence of the premises of deductive theory. Similarly, on the level of symbolic logic, i.e., a logic of symbols and not of content, *A* cannot be

A and *not-A* at the same time; this is a self-evident law of symbol manipulation. Deductive theory always deals with the vicissitudes of symbols as such and, properly reasoned, its conclusions are self-evident because they are already implied by self-evident premises.

When it is said that deductive theory proceeds from the general to the particular, what is meant is that deductive theory takes for its premises the general or self-evident truths of symbolic systems, not the generalities arrived at by enumeration of observations. Knowledge obtained through deductive theory is called "analytic" because it comes from analyzing the implications of the premises, and, since the premises already contain the conclusions, analytic knowledge is sometimes called "empty" knowledge. One should not be misled, however, into thinking that analytic knowledge is obvious just because it is self-evident. Both syllogistic logic and theoretical mathematics come under this heading, and certainly neither one is simple nor immediately apparent. "Self-evident" refers to the fact that the basis of proof for a deductive theory is logic itself, as opposed to proof by observation. Neither is it proper to say that analytic knowledge is "empty," if by that is meant that it conveys nothing new. Though it adds no new perceptual content, it can inform us about the vicissitudes of relationships within a system which are an essential aspect of knowledge.

An inductive theory is one based on the perceptual evidence derived from sensation and introspection. Since its conclusions are not logically necessary (i.e., to deny them involves no contradiction) but are synthesized from the premises, the knowledge generated by inductive theory is called "synthetic." All so-called natural or empirical sciences are, therefore, representatives of inductive theory, and it makes no difference whether these sciences are physical, chemical, biological, or psychological.

There is a widespread belief that observations are the product of the direct contact between brain and environment as mediated by the sense organs, and that inductive (scientific) theory consists of their collection and generalization. However, no such phenomenon as pure observation exists. Everything we claim to perceive or know from sensory evidence involves inferences that have been made about the sensory input. Indeed, that we are sensing rather than imagining is already an inference, i.e., a hypothesis or speculation albeit unspoken and usually not recognized formally as such. Therefore, no inductive theory is free of inferential reasoning.

The fear of theorizing or speculating still extant in scientific circles is unwarranted. Hypothesizing is not equivalent to mysticism, nor is speculation the antithesis of science. Hypothesizing is in itself neither scientific nor unscientific; the manner in which inferences are made and validated determines that issue.

Though no scientific endeavor can proceed without both inductive and deductive inference, it is important to examine each aspect of an inductive theory and determine which portions are arrived at through inductive inference and which through deductive inference. It is not that one method of reasoning is "more scientific" than another; one needs to differentiate the two because their credibility is tested differently. Inductive inference leads to statements which assert something about sense data and abstractions from sense data. The proof of such statements lies in the evidence that they describe some aspect of perception accurately. Deductive inference establishes relations between statements in the framework of an ordering process symbolized by various systems of verbal logic or mathematics. The legitimacy of deductive inference is established by demonstrating that the reasoning process employed has proceeded according to accepted rules, i.e., that the conclusions are properly derived from the premises. Inductive and deductive inference do not represent opposite ends of a continuum; they are complementary and together express symbolically the transformations carried out by the brain in its function of signal processing. Inductive inference may be thought of as being either true or false, i.e., in keeping with or contrary to perceptual evidence. Deductive inference is neither true nor false, but valid or invalid, i.e., properly or improperly reasoned according to the standards of the symbolic system accepted as representing order in a particular instance.

The attempt to distinguish scientific theories on the basis of their origin in either inductive or deductive *inference* is pointless, since no theory can be constructed without both forms of reasoning. However, to distinguish between types of inductive *theories* according to their function or purpose is both valid and useful. The terms "classificatory" and "explanatory" applied to inductive theory indicate the two separate functions that scientific theory is called upon to perform.

Classificatory theory organizes and systematizes data. It has mistakenly been equated with descriptive theory by epistemologists, but classification is not description. Classificatory theory is composed of an interlocking hierarchy of definitions which forms a schema or system believed to be both useful and in keeping with the facts. The Linnean classification is the best-known example of this form of theory whose goal is the promotion of understanding, i.e., the experience of comfort that accompanies the establishment of an order satisfying to the individual(s) concerned.

There are two factors involved in every explanation, and there are therefore two forms of explanatory theory based on whether the causal or the descriptive aspect of explanation is being postulated. Causal explanations seek to answer "why?," descriptive explanations, "how?" Both of these aspects are equally significant for scientific explanation; one cannot be subordinated to the other, neither can they be equated nor combined in a unitary theory.

Causal explanatory theories explain why what is observed to happen happens, by postulating a relationship of exceptionless repetition (Rapoport, 1954) between the observed and its hypothesized origins in events postulated as giving rise to the observed. It may be looked upon as a vertical hierarchy in which the events of underlying systems are seen as the necessary conditions for the occasion of events in the more superficial ones.

Descriptive explanatory theory regards the phenomenon to be explained as part of a horizontal system whose relationships the theory seeks to postulate. Such relationships are sometimes called the "sufficient cause" in philosophy. For example, we tend to say that bacterial pneumonia is caused by one of the varieties of pneumonia bacilli, yet it is a well-known fact that many individuals can harbor the "cause," i.e., the bacilli, without suffering from the clinical manifestations of pneumonia. The pneumonia bacillus is, in the classic terminology, a necessary but not sufficient cause of the illness. To explain how an individual harboring these bacilli develops pneumonia, the relationship of the system as a whole to the invader must be taken into consideration. Descriptive explanatory theory illustrates its postulates symbolically either through mathematical equations, through graphic isomorphisms such as maps, or linguistically through metaphor and analogy. The laws of science are descriptive explanatory theories; they account for what happens and will happen in the future on the basis of generalizations based not on why but on how a given set of circumstances is related (Toulmin, 1953).

In outline my proposed conceptualization of theory formation looks like this:

  I. Deductive theory
 II. Inductive theory
     A. Classificatory theory
     B. Explanatory theory
        1. Causal explanatory theory
        2. Descriptive explanatory theory

Instead of following the usual differentiation of psychoanalytic theory into clinical and metapsychological forms, a distinction based on the discredited antithesis between observation and speculation, I will apply the aforementioned division of scientific theory into classificatory and explanatory branches and seek to demonstrate that this is an epistemologically correct and practically useful categorization.

Theory Formation: Application to Psychoanalysis

The classificatory theory of psychoanalysis subsumes Freud's organization of what his patients told him in the analytic situation. Such terms as "Oedipus complex," "repression," "transference," "primary," and "secondary process" are shorthand for observations organized according to a significance they had for the innovator of the technique called "free association." The question of whether or not Freud really followed a method of "pure" observation is easily answered. No scientist ever did so, and it is no discredit to Freud that he began his researches with some hypotheses as to what he might find, etc. A scientific investigation presupposes dissatisfaction with existing theory and speculation about it and its potential resolution (Northrop, 1947). Equally pointless is the question of whether psychoanalytic classificatory theory is inductive or deductive. As was mentioned, it is, of course, inductive, as is every theory that does not take for its premise a self-evident law of mathematics or logic, i.e., a pure symbolic construct (Russell, 1912). What is incorrectly implied by that question, however, is that if hypothesizing has been used to arrive at conclusions the result cannot be an "inductive" or "empirical" theory. However, all thought content that we are aware of involves speculation, i.e., "if so . . . then so" kinds of reasoning. Indeed, all statements about perceptions involve at least the implicit inductive inference "if my brain is functioning properly then I am confronted by the following stimuli." Classificatory theory does make use of hypothetical reasoning in the form of inductive inference, and is no less an empirical theory for it. The notion that empirical science consists of the enumeration of observations which then terminate in certain useful generalizations begs the question of how that result comes about.

It is significant that the assertions of classificatory theory in psychoanalysis do not depend primarily on the formalities of logic but on the accuracy of observation. Every aspect of classificatory theory can be traced back to observation—this does not mean it is correct; it only means that the premises of the theory can be checked observationally or by empirical experiment. If the truth of the premises is born out, then the properly reasoned conclusions of such a theory are accepted as true also.

Classificatory theory originates in perceptual experience, namely, in what was sensed, felt, thought, or imagined, etc.

Psychoanalytic classificatory theory is based on observations obtained through the method of free association, which is, so far, the most effective manner of permitting a comparatively undistorted view of the early stages of abstraction from sense data.

The data which serve as the premises of what I propose to call the classificatory theory of psychoanalysis have been verified in their essentials innumerable times by trained observers, i.e., psychoanalysts. Where observational data indicated the need for change or addition Freud and others amended the theory appropriately, and analysts today continue to do so. No further proof of a classificatory theory is necessary. This is often overlooked and misunderstood by both psychoanalysts and their critics, who fail to realize that terms used to order clinical data are akin to categories in biology like "mammal," "reptile," etc.; i.e., these terms are nominal entities devised by Freud to classify particular observed events and their setting. They are abstractions, not postulated hypothetical entities (MacCorquodale and Meehl, 1948).

An analytic encounter in which the patient is observed to display toward the analyst the affectionate demands that at one time he made on his mother is considered to be a manifestation of the relationship called transference. It is futile to ask "Is this really transference?" or "Is there such a thing as transference?" Transference means only what Freud said it meant, and the described situation is one covered by his definition. Likewise, in mathematics two plus two equals four only because mathematicians say it must, and, since they can use such conventions to describe relations between observable events that can be consensually validated, science acknowledges the legitimacy of the system. To establish the scientific nature of terms such as "defense," "Oedipus complex," "transference," "anal stage," "penis envy," "castration anxiety," and so on, Freud had only to demonstrate that the phenomena or relationships that the term is said to define could be empirically validated, given the appropriate situation and a suitable observer. It should also be noted that the extension of the findings of psychoanalysis to human mentation generally is based on observation. The studies of dreams, jokes, and parapraxes in the general population as well as research into the verbalizations of psychotic and organically brain-damaged patients established empirically that the psychoanalytic classification of mentation was universally applicable.

At this point I would imagine that the reader, even if he agrees with me, might well think that what I call the classificatory theory of psychoanalysis is identical with what has been called clinical theory and might doubt the necessity of introducing a new term into the literature. However, considering the derivation and function of classificatory theory, much in psychoanalysis that has been thought to be "metapsychological," i.e., explanatory, belongs to classificatory theory. For example: Freud's division of thought into conscious, preconscious, and unconscious content is an abstraction from the clinical observation that thought content varies in the ease with which it can enter subjective awareness. Likewise, the division into primary- and secondary-process thought is a classificatory theory, since it too is a division based on abstraction from thought content; i.e., some thoughts can be seen to follow those rules formally codified by logic while others do not seem to do so. Freud's (1905) theory of human sexual development was also based on ordering observations made in clinical analyses and correlating these with the overt behavior of children and perverts, and the sexual behavior of average adults.

The delineation of Freud's clinical findings in terms of various organizing classificatory schemata creates a theory whose origin is directly related to psychoanalytic observation and whose proof depends on the verifiability of those observations. Therefore, as will be discussed in greater detail below, primary process, infantile sexuality, unconscious thought, etc., need no longer be accounted for through the postulation of such highly questionable concepts as the mental apparatus, psychic energy, and instincts.[1] In this

---

[1] E. Peterfreund's recently published monograph (1971) examines the failure of many of the long-established so-called "metapsychological" concepts of psychoanalysis to meet scientific criteria and includes an extensive bibliography of corroborating literature.

sense the term "classificatory theory" implies a fundamentally different orientation to psychoanalytic findings than that subsumed by the concept of "clinical theory."

There are those critics who would deny scientific standing to the classificatory theory of psychoanalysis on the grounds that psychoanalytic data is derived from the observation of events originating within the subject, i.e., memories, ideas, and feelings, rather than from externally stimulated, so-called objective, reality. This is the position of "naïve realism" which overlooks the fact that epistemologists have for centuries demonstrated that our seemingly immediate acquaintance with the external world and its objects is a belief or convention. The physical objects with which we populate our world are private constructs and the result of our capacity for abstraction from sensory stimulation (Korzybski, 1933). Neurophysiologic experiments corroborated this conclusion when it was demonstrated that external stimulation of one sense organ gives rise to exactly the same electrical activity in the afferent nerves as does the stimulation of any other sense organ. The qualitative differentiation into information regarding color, sound, taste, etc., and all the variations within each of the sensory modalities, occurs as the result of the activity of the portions of the brain in which the respective afferent nerves terminate (Hayek, 1952). There is, therefore, no qualitative code transmitted to the brain from the outside which informs it of the nature of the sensory input; redness, for example, is a function of the nervous system and has no existence outside the brain. Thus the sensory qualities and the objects into which we combine them are exactly like thoughts and feelings in that they represent the activity of the brain, and no more. It is an error to assert that external stimuli create a reality more credible than that which arises from internal stimuli, or that in some way mental representations which we project to the world outside have a validity that images projected to a location somewhere within our heads do not possess. Equally erroneous are those philosophic systems which assign a higher trustworthiness to self-conscious thought content and disdain the information obtained from environmental stimuli. "Reality" is independent of the origin or nature of the stimulus to sensation; the "real" is that which can lead to valid predictions.

However, prior to Freud there was no way in which internal stimuli and their vicissitudes in depth could be subjected to scientific observation and classified, and so, from the operational point of view, it was true that science was limited to inference based on the study of external stimuli and their effects. It was precisely one of Freud's achievements that his observational technique and the systematization of the results of that technique enabled the study of some intrasubjectively stimulated action to take place on the empirical level. In this, Freud must be acknowledged as having established a new branch of natural science.

Toulmin (1953), using examples from physics, calls attention to the fact that what we call "principles" and "laws" do not fit into the classic types of theory. The law of conservation of energy, the law of gravity, Boyle's law of gasses—all these are not classification of phenomena on the order of the Linnean classification in biology, nor are they explanations in the sense of giving reasons for what is observed in terms of a more fundamental order of existence. Though we say an apple falls "because" of the law of gravity, we do not mean "because" in the same way we mean that ice forms *because* of particular vicissitudes of motion among molecules of water. In the latter case we are explaining a phenomenon on the basis of the activity of an underlying system, but in the case of the law of gravity we are not really giving any reason for the phenomenon but a description of the apple's relationships and postulating what will happen to all apples in similar situations in the future. We call such a description an explanation, but what it explains is how, not why, certain events occur. Unfortunately, the word "description" is misused in everyday conversation, where it has a connotation of superficiality and is used to indicate what is better termed "expression," i.e., "the presentation of an idea, usually by the proper and apt use of words" (Langer, 1962, p. 78). A tale is not a description; novelists do not describe scenes and events—they express them. Description should mean delineating, tracing the outlines of something, finding the clarifying connecting threads that make what happens comprehensible in terms of the units involved and their relationship. General systems theory (Bertalanffy, 1968) concerns itself with such explanations, formulating mathematical equations which describe the behavior of a system focusing not on its content but on the relational process of the elements of the system in interaction. Similarly, symbolic logic is not concerned with the content meaning of words and statements but regards words as units inter-acting according to laws and principles which transcend their immediate significance.

Both in scientific and everyday discourse the inability to accommodate what I shall call "descriptive explanatory theory" has led to problems. These theories explain but they do not follow the rules for the formation and proof of causal explanatory theories. A descriptive theory does not postulate causality. As Toulmin points out, laws and principles are symbolic constructs which function as maps, guiding us and enabling us to predict what we will find or might expect to happen. All descriptive theories are arbitrary ways of looking at particular *relationships* for the purpose of formulating predictions involving these relationships only.

The so-called genetic and dynamic viewpoints of psychoanalytic meta-psychology fall into this category. The genetic point of view embodies an ordering and interrelating of psychoanalytic observations along a time axis and has led to lawlike generalizations regarding psychological develop-ment. Likewise, the inferences that make up the dynamic point of view are lawlike deductions about observation, i.e., abstractions organizing the experimental data and showing that memories and associations are not static constructs but represent changing relationships indicative of underlying

47

forces (Freud, 1916, p. 67). Neither the genetic nor the dynamic point of view in itself postulates causality; both are descriptive explanatory constructs which establish some of the operational laws through which human behavior can be understood.

Since the genetic and dynamic viewpoints are descriptive explanations, there is no need to advance causal hypotheses from other fields, like "instincts" from biology and "energy" from physics, in order to give them credence by making them seem to be causal explanations.

Another, but less successful, attempt at a descriptive explanatory theory was Freud's postulation of a mental apparatus. As in all sciences when the units in question are not exactly definable and mathematical treatment is not possible, metaphor and analogy are used to clarify and explain. A metaphor like the "mental apparatus" is a map whereby the processes in question are graphically described. Freud made clear, and analysts have always known, that neither the topographic nor the structural theories were meant to represent entities but were intended to describe processes. I will discuss two errors which have interfered with the proper use of the concept of a mental apparatus, namely, (1) the unwitting confusion of its descriptive explanatory function with a causal explanatory one; (2) Freud's belief that clinical observations mirror the processes giving rise to them.

Freud initially looked upon his hypothesis of a mental apparatus, in Chapter VII of *The Interpretation of Dreams* (1900, p. 536), as a tentative diagrammatic abstraction with which he could clarify his empirical data—or, as he later said of his models generally, their only reason for existence was their capacity to order the findings of psychoanalysis (1916–17, p. 296). He was scientifically entitled to construct such models, but used in this manner they belong to descriptive explanatory theory and not to causal explanatory theory. Also, none of these models represents mentation as a whole, which is what "models of the mental apparatus" seems to imply. It would be more accurate to call them "models of psychic conflict." They are ad hoc constructs for diagrammatic clarification of the particular aspects of mentation that Freud was examining psychoanalytically at the time of their respective construction, and, valuable as they are for the practicing psychoanalyst, they can hardly be said to depict a "mental apparatus." Freud specifically eliminated the fundamentals of mentation from consideration when he explained in the *Introductory Lectures on Psycho-Analysis* (1916, pp. 60–61) that he was not interested in the perceptions and thought processes as such that stemmed directly from organic events. For his purposes he chose not to call these "psychologic events"; only those secondary phenomena which had meaning in terms of psychologic conflict and could be investigated psychoanalytically were taken as psychological.

Nevertheless, though Freud intended them to be only descriptive schema, the topographic and structural theories were not limited by him to that function, since he also included them in his metapsychology and used them, as they are still used today, as causal explanations for mentation. In the

Introductory Lectures (1916, pp. 20–21), he seems to justify his approach to mental life by pointing to the absence of any relevant information about these processes in the field of physical science. The implication was, therefore, that causal psychological explanations were to substitute for the missing organic causal explanations of mental processes. The various divisions of the "mind" in Freud's writings are not nominal, abstracted entities as he intended them to be, but postulated, substantive entities, and they are used in the latter fashion throughout his works. For example, the *System Ucs.* and later the id are the entities upon which instinctual impulses impinge; the *System Pcs.* and then the ego are entities wherein secondary-process thought takes place, and psychic energy is transferred between all the divisions of the mind. Used in this way the divisions of the mind are imposed on observations as provisional causal explanations. Freud implicitly recognized this when he said that, though it was hypothetical, his construct of a mental apparatus probably approximated the facts (1916–17, p. 296), implying thereby the as-yet-unknown organic substrate of mentation. He apparently believed that his construction of a mental apparatus was justified by his clinical observations, for he asked rhetorically whether the postulation of a region of the unconscious could be questioned in the face of the evidence for the existence of unconscious thought (1916–17, pp. 277, 294).

The mistaken notion that clinical theory and the metapsychology used to explain it are opposite ends of a continuum and that the latter is an abstraction from the former is still current in psychoanalysis; see, for example, the influential article on the subject by Waelder (1962). However, theoreticians of science have repeatedly made it clear that no hypothetical theory can be abstracted directly from observation. For example, Albert Einstein says: "there is no logical bridge between phenomena and their theoretical principles," and in another essay, he states that "concepts have reference to sensible experience, but they are never, in a logical sense, deducible from them" (1934, pp. 4, 63).

Freud and other analysts confused abstraction and postulation, believing that they were only ordering their findings when actually they were creating hypothetical entities to explain their occurrence (MacCorquodale and Meehl, 1948). However, an explanatory theory cannot be proven true by the occurrence of the very observations it seeks to explain. In concretizing phenomena in the service of letting what is observed be its own explanation, Freud "begged the question" by assuming what needed to be proven. To say, as Freud did, that unconscious thoughts must, of necessity, stem from a *System Ucs.* does not indicate what the nature of such a system might be or wherein its power to create such thoughts lies; it tells us no more than we knew before from observation alone, namely, that unconscious motivation exists.

The postulation of hypothetical causal entities is a perfectly legitimate scientific exercise, but it does require at least the possibility of an indirect or direct demonstration of the empirical existence of the postulated entity.

Having stated that the mental apparatus was not to be equated with the brain and had no empirical existence, Freud inadvertently put himself in the position of having postulated not a hypothetical entity like the atom but rather a bogus or pseudo-entity, i.e., one whose potential existence can never be proven or disproven. From the viewpoint of scientific theory such entities are scientifically meaningless, and any theories based on such premises are equally meaningless. Therefore, the topographic theory and the structural theory of psychoanalysis based on the mental apparatus concept are meaningless theories insofar as they are used to account for thought processes. No science has been spared such mistakes in its development; the valid progress made in the name of such meaningless theories is made in spite of, not because of, them and eventually turns out to have a different explanation.

The confusion engendered by the hypostatization of the mental apparatus has been compounded by the implicit assumption of psychoanalytic theory that the observed mirrors its origins. Freud emphasized that though the technique of psychoanalysis was purely psychological, the origin of the phenomena so studied was in the brain's reaction to external and internal stimuli (1940 [1938], p. 144) and that some day the content of psychoanalysis would have to be placed on its organic foundations (1916–17, p. 389). In one sense this is a truism, but it also carried with it Freud's unwarranted conclusion that psychological observations reflect the processes that are their origin, i.e., that a study of conscious content will lead quite directly to an explanation of the processes giving rise to that content.

Freud's first attempt at a causal explanation of thought processes was the "brain" theory of the *Project for a Scientific Psychology* (1895). Here Freud assumed that, since we become conscious of words and images, thought processes operate with similar elements, the highest form of thought being the verbal form. However, like believing that a phonograph record must store sounds or that there are pictures in the television tube, this is a phenomenalistic fallacy.

The experimental evidence has shown that sensory qualities, images, and words are not the building blocks of thought processes. Thinking is a biochemical and electromagnetic process which periodically and in small part may be translated into the form of subjective awareness. Becoming conscious is an activity of the brain signifying a brain state which occurs when a particular, as yet unknown, relationship obtains within that organ (Smith, 1970; Langer, 1967; Ryle, 1949).

Subjective awareness or the phenomenon of consciousness is divided by us into sensory qualities, images, words, etc., but this is not the process of thinking, though usually it is mistakenly believed to be that. It should be noted that the study of clinical phenomena can demonstrate neither the falsity nor the truth of the causal hypotheses put forth in the "Project" or any other theory of brain functioning. Such theories are speculations in the realm of neuroanatomy and neurophysiology and can only be tested by devising appropriate empirical experiments in these areas that will test the truth or falsity of the conclusions to which such theories lead.

When in 1900 Freud tried to divorce himself from explanations based on brain anatomy or physiology and devised the concept of a mental apparatus, he did not abandon the belief that psychoanalysis constituted an investigation of the origin, vicissitudes, and nature of thought processes. For example, Freud observed that the meaning of behavior could be conscious, preconscious, or unconscious, but he then equated this with thought processes supposedly conscious, preconscious, and unconscious. Likewise, he observed that the meaning of the thought content involved in dreams, errors of everyday life, and neurotic ideation could only be deciphered if the laws of syllogistic logic were disregarded and order based on relationships of contiguity, simultaneity, and similarity of appearance was adopted. But then this discovery led to the unwarranted conclusion that this must represent thought processes of a "primary" and "secondary" nature, and so on.

Though Freud at times indicated that he knew in principle that we could not know anything of the nature of thought through the psychoanalytic method (1923, p. 90), in practice his theories were attempts at formulating a causal explanation of the processes underlying conscious experience. This concern with brain function or with the function of the "mental apparatus" was misplaced, since it could not lead to an explanation of what he wished to clarify, namely, the variation in intensity and effect of thought. Intensity and effect of thought refer to the meaning of thought, to its symbolic significance, which shapes behavior, including the further brain behavior termed "thinking."

Conclusion

Theories that can be based on psychoanalytic exploration deal with the origin of beliefs and expectations both in and out of awareness; they explain the disposition to behavior, not the neurophysiological processes that make the implementation of intentions possible (Freud, 1916, pp. 20–21). All that one may infer from a psychoanalytic examination of free associations is a deeper understanding of a patient's total behavior in particular situations. From such knowledge lawlike pre- and post-dictions can be made regarding the significance various experiences have had and may have for others in the future. The patient's participation in this work enables him to understand (classify) his beliefs and expectations, explain them dynamically (descriptively), and, most important, gain or regain a degree of control over them and their implementation through liberation of the creative aspect of the symbolic function.

Psychoanalysis provides a causal explanatory theory for the ends, not for the processes, of the brain events called thought. It is in the uniquely human aspect of behavior called "symbolic" that psychoanalysis can make its major scientific contribution. Confusions about the structure and purpose of scientific theory have hindered the development of psychoanalysis as a basic discipline and obscured the function it can perform for science at large.

BIBLIOGRAPHY

Bertalanffy, L. von (1968), *General Systems Theory*. New York: George Braziller.
Einstein, A. (1934), *Essays in Science*. New York: The Wisdom Library.
Freud, S. (1895), Project for a Scientific Psychology. *Standard Edition*, 1. London: Hogarth Press, 1966.
———— (1900), The Interpretation of Dreams (2d part). *Standard Edition*, 5. London: Hogarth Press, 1953.
———— (1905), Three Essays on the Theory of Sexuality. *Standard Edition*, 7. London: Hogarth Press, 1953.
———— (1916), Introductory lectures on Psycho-Analysis. *Standard Edition*, 15. London: Hogarth Press, 1963.
———— (1916–1917), Introductory Lectures on Psycho-Analysis (Part III). *Standard Edition*, 16. London: Hogarth Press, 1963.
———— (1923), New Introductory Lectures on Psycho-analysis. *Standard Edition*, 22. London: Hogarth Press, 1964.
———— (1940 [1938]), An Outline of Psycho-Analysis. *Standard Edition*, 23. London: Hogarth Press, 1964.
Hayek, F. A. (1952), *The Sensory Order*. Chicago: University of Chicago Press.
Kolakowski, L. (1966), *The Alienation of Reason*. Garden City, New York: Anchor Book edition, 1969.
Korzybski, A. (1933), *Science and Sanity*. 3d ed. The International Non-Aristotelian Library Publishing Company, 1948.
Langer, S. K. (1962), *Philosophical Sketches*. New York: Mentor Book edition, 1964.
———— (1967), *Mind: An Essay on Human Feeling*. Vol. I. Baltimore: Johns Hopkins University Press.
MacCorquodale, K., and Meehl, P. E. (1948), On a Distinction between Hypothetical Constructs and Intervening Variables. *Psychol. Rev.*, 55:95–107.
Northrop, F. S. C. (1947), *The Logic of the Sciences and the Humanities*. New York: Meridian Book edition, 1966.
Peterfreund, E. (1971), Information, Systems and Psychoanalysis. *Psychol. Issues*, VII: Numbers 1/2, Monograph 25/26.
Rapoport, A. (1954), *Operational Philosophy*. New York: Harper and Brothers.
Russell, B. (1912), *The Problems of Philosophy*. New York: Oxford University Press, 1969.
Ryle, G. (1949), *The Concept of Mind*. New York: Barnes and Noble, 1968.
Smith, C. U. M. (1970), *The Brain: Towards an Understanding*. New York: G. P. Putnam's Sons.
Toulmin, S. (1953), *The Philosophy of Science*. New York: Harper and Row, Harper Torchbooks edition, 1960.
Waelder, R. (1962), Psychoanalysis, Scientific Method and Philosophy (book review). *J. Amer. Psychoanal. Assn.*, 10:617–637.

The Instinct Theory
in the Light of Microbiology

THERESE BENEDEK, M.D. (*Chicago*)

This essay is an epilogue to the discussions of the papers republished in the volume, *Psychoanalytic Investigations* (Benedek, in press). Since they are supplements to the original publications, what motivates or justifies further elaboration of the problems discussed there? Several of my papers demonstrate Freud's second instinct theory (1920, pp. 7–64), according to which fusion and defusion of opposing instinctual forces—libido and aggression—motivate psychological processes. This left psychoanalytic instinct theory in limbo and necessitated a new overview, which may gain a great deal from a confrontation with the results of microbiological investigations.

Studying Freud's writings, one cannot fail to recognize his reluctance to accept the concept of an instinctual force natural to man that would be destructive.[1] Freud arrived at a general conceptualization of aggression when he viewed both libido and aggression divested of the affective potential of their motivational power. On this level of abstraction, libido and aggression are on equal footing, partners in the process of living. Why, then, and wherefore the concept of death instinct, a theory the usefulness of which as an explanatory theory Freud doubted, a theory which he deprecated since he had arrived at it, not by observation and analyzing psychological phenomena, but by speculation. At the same time he pursued it with the determination of a researcher who feels that he is on the right track but does not have the means to reach his goal.

[1] Throughout his earlier writings Frued viewed aggression predominantly as a manifestation of sadism. In *Three Essays on the Theory of Sexuality* (1905, pp. 135–243) he viewed it as a component of sexual instincts. In Section 4 of the second essay, he recognized the original independence of the aggressive impulses. "It may be assumed that the impulses of cruelty arise from sources which are, in fact, independent of sexuality but may become united with it at an early stage. The independent sources were traced to the self preservative instincts." In Section 2 of the third chapter of the "Little Hans" case history (1909), Freud wrote, "I cannot bring myself to assume the existence of a special aggressive instinct alongside of the familial instincts of self preservation and of sex and on an equal footing with them" (Editor's Introduction, *Civilization and Its Discontents* [1930], p. 61).

In the essay published in 1921, "Group Psychology and the Analysis of the Ego," Freud's attention was focused on the organization of the group. The manifestations of aggression in the group were in the service of life. Freud's only reference to the death instinct is relegated to a footnote. The next major contribution was *The Ego and the Id* (1923), which gave psychoanalysis a new dimension. In this work he developed "the structure of the mind." Since the stockpile of psychoanalytic investigation illustrated that the incorporated aggression of the parents participates in the unconscious process by which the superego develops, the role of aggression in the personality organization was an easily accepted theory. In this context Freud equated the aggression incorporated in the structure of the superego with the "dangerous death instincts" which "to a large extent undoubtedly continue their internal work unhindered (1923, p. 54). It is via the repressed Oedipus complex that the superego evolves and exerts its power by the circuit of repetition compulsion: "The more a man controls his aggressiveness, the more intense becomes his ideal's inclination to aggressiveness against his ego" (p. 54). Indeed, one is inclined to assume that Freud was thinking of the spiral of feedback process. It is in "The Economic Problem of Masochism" (1924) where Freud extrapolated from the superego the moral principle and defined it as "the conscience at work in the ego which may then become harsh, cruel and inexorable against the ego which is in its charge" (p. 167). In *Civilization and Its Discontents*, Freud discussed the psychological processes by which culture, internalized in the superego, may render primary instinctual processes survival negative (1930, pp. 64–145).

Since Freud considered Kant's "categorical imperative" a developmental adaptation to instinctual processes, we have to stop and ask—what is instinct? Are survival-negative instincts conceivable? The word "instinct" (as substantive and as adjective) is such an ingrained symbol of our world-view that it became an explanatory concept long before biology began to understand the universality, the extent, and the limitation of the term. The usage became a mental habit. Because it fits our intuition, what is instinctual seems in some sense already explained. Before the word was the observation. Initially, this might have been man's preconscious awareness of his body and its functionings, its feelings of pleasure and pain. From projections of feelings man draws his awareness of the world around him; he has learned to observe and "understand" the repetitions and regularities of living and nonliving objects around him.

Traditional doctrine defined instinct as an innate characteristic of the species which evolves spontaneously and functions without correction by intelligence. Since it was assumed that instinctual behavior cannot coexist with intelligence, it was assumed that man does not possess instincts. Such a concept, defended by the authority of the Church and embedded in the naïve narcissism of mankind, found its support in the sweeping scale of Darwin's theory of evolution (1829).

Darwin's epoch-making investigations mobilized interest in individual behavior. Early investigators, relying on their "macroscopic" observations of psychological phenomena, narrowed the gap between man and subhuman creatures. With expanding knowledge, the anthropocentric view of instincts fell away. From this viewpoint it is interesting to cite William James. In his *The Principles of Psychology* (1890), he defines instinct: "The faculty of acting in such a way as to produce certain ends, without foresight of the end and without previous education in the performance," and he adds, "Instincts are the functional correlates of structure. With the presence of a certain organ goes, one may say, almost always a native aptitude for its use" (James, as cited by Fletcher, 1957, p. 30). James considered the instinct experience to be based upon a perception or a sensation which contains an element of cognition of the "inner tension."

It is this cognitive element, this primary awareness of the significance of some object in the environment, which together with subsequent experience of memory, makes possible the gradual acquisition of a foresight of ends and of an awareness of the relevance of certain action as means of achieving these ends [1890, p. 31].

Here James attributes to animals the ability of anticipation. How very close this description of the instinctual process could fit a modern psychological model!

The scientific period of instinct theory began with the discoveries of physiology. It followed two different pathways; one was the investigations of physiologists, the other of psychologists, especially Freud and other psychoanalysts. It was in the physiological investigations of ethologists and the later discoveries of psychosomatic medicine that psychology and physiology met again. (But by then the term "instinct" had been almost excluded from the vocabulary of scientists.) It is interesting to note that Cannon's theory of homeostasis was published in the same year as Freud's fundamental theory of the psychodynamics of instinctual processes, "Instincts and their Vicissitudes" (1915).

Cannon's great contribution was the discovery of the physiological organization by which homeostasis is maintained (1953). He attributed these processes to the function of primary instincts; he differentiated sexual instincts as secondary; they develop with the maturation of the organism. Sexual instincts coordinate preparatory acts and the act of copulation; they organize the process of childbearing and the functions which concern the survival of the offspring. (My investigation of the female sexual cycle demonstrates the unconscious representations of primary instincts in the motivation of psychological processes accompanying the phases of the sexual cycle.)

Darwin's theory of evolution and the gold mine of his particular observations remained the background of the scientific world-view. Based on the assumption of the survival of the fittest, his theory was so pervasive that it took more than a hundred years (from the publication of *The Origin of the Species* to Haldane's *The Causes of Evolution*) to call attention to its epistemological mistake. J. B. S. Haldane pointed out that, "Natural selection will always make an organism fitter in its struggle with the environment," since only those who survive can be studied (1932, p. 119). Natural selection favors "reproductive success of a population and nothing more." More recent critics point out that "reproduction always requires some sacrifice of resources and some jeopardy of physiological well-being which . . . may reduce fitness in the vernacular sense of the term (Williams, as cited by Bakan, 1968, p. 26). With hindsight, one could say that on the basis of the structure of the superego and its role in man's individual and collective socialization, Freud discovered a "survival-negative instinctual process." Psychopathology gives ample evidence of the survival-negative influence of the process, just as culture and ethics show its integration in processes of survival.

But is that survival-negative component of life "innate"? This was the problem which Freud wanted to solve. Individual survival-negative mechanisms cannot be demonstrated in healthy, living organisms. Everyone knows that every living thing has to die, but no one knows why. As a physician, Freud knew many of the survival-negative mechanisms which lead to illness and death, but he was searching for instincts, by which he meant a force which "if we are not to abandon the hypothesis of death instincts, we must suppose [them] to be associated from the very first with life instincts" (1920, p. 57).

The knowledge about instincts per se seems to be more or less a by-product of investigations undertaken for other projects or with other purposes in mind. Freud could fit his early findings about psychic processes into the frame of the dualism: self-preservation versus preservation of the species. He conceived of instinct "as a concept on the frontier between the mental and the somatic, as the psychic representative of the stimuli originating from within the organism and reaching the mind, as a measure of the demand made upon the mind for work in consequence of its connection with the body" (1915, pp. 121–122). This insightful definition explained the manifold microscopic and macroscopic interactions between mind and body. It satisfied the requirements of the psychodynamics of the psychoanalytic process. Five years after this publication he surprised the world of psychoanalysts with the slender volume, *Beyond the Pleasure Principle*, which argued for the concept of the death instinct. The concept was alien to psychoanalysts. They conceived of instinct as a source of positive energy which integrates processes of growth and maturation. Here Freud argued for a conservative instinct which overcomes life. However, it was not so much the theoretical objections that caused the resistance against the concept of death instinct as the fact that the idea resisted empathic understanding.

The dynamic and economic principles of psychoanalysis are based on Fechner's "principle of constancy," according to which the function of the nervous system is to keep the "intracranial excitation constant" (1873).

I assume that in practical psychoanalysis the "reality principle" was the agent of interpersonal psychological processes long before Freud undertook this correction of his metapsychology.

Freud deposed the pleasure principle under the compelling influence of the compulsion to repeat. But his supporting evidence for the compulsion to repeat is remote from anything that biology deals with—although not quite. Memory is universal; it is not an attribute of Homo sapiens only. Remembering a traumatic event in an anxious dream, however, is probably a function only of the human psychic apparatus. For Freud such psychic events demonstrated that non–wish-fulfilling dreams facilitate the reorganization of painful memories toward a better balanced psychic condition. This is the function of the transference phenomena in which the "repressed unconscious," repeated and remembered, has a curative effect. But these repetitions are all in the service of survival. Whether it is a child's game which by repetition overcomes the pain of separation, or the mastery of a task accomplished by repetition, or even the behavioral manifestations of sexual instinct and procreation, they all belong to the same category. They all represent manifestations of the instinct of self-preservation and the instinct of survival in the offspring.

Freud was correct in saying, "Enough is left unexplained [by the pleasure principle] to justify the hypothesis of a *compulsion to repeat*—something that seems more primitive, more elementary, more instinctual than the pleasure principle which it overrides" (1920, p. 23; italics added). He then termed the compulsion to repeat "the source of the death instinct."

For Freud the repetition compulsion meant the manifestation of the natural law expressed in the tendency of living organisms to return to an earlier inorganic state. Knowing that his data did not support the evidence of a death instinct, he asked, "How is the predicate of being instinctual related to the compulsion to repeat?" (1920, p. 36). Psychoanalysis was not able to answer his question then, nor can it do so now, but his answer to his own inquiry should be quoted in full:

At this point we cannot escape a suspicion that we may have come upon the track of a universal attribute of instincts and perhaps of organic life in general which has not hitherto been clearly recognized or at least not explicitly stressed. *It seems, then, that an instinct is an urge inherent in organic life to restore an earlier state of things* which the living entity has been obliged to abandon under the pressure of external disturbing forces; that is, it is a kind of organic elasticity, or, to put it another way, the expression of *the inertia inherent in organic life* [p. 36; latter italics added].

Freud was aware that the term "instinct" was, at least, "strange," as he applied it as "an expression of the conservative nature of living substances" (p. 36). But he supports his concept by examples from animal life which "seem to confirm the view that instincts are historically determined" (p. 36). He cites the migration of certain fish species at spawning time, the migratory flights of birds, and he concludes:

The most impressive proofs of *there being an organic compulsion to repeat* lies in the phenomena of heredity and the facts of embryology. We see how the germ of a living animal is obliged in the course of its development to recapitulate (even if only in transient and abbreviated fashion) the structures of all forms from which it is sprung, instead of proceeding quickly by the shortest path of its final shape. This behavior is only to a very slight degree attributable to mechanical causes. . . . So too the power of regenerating a lost organ by growing afresh a precisely similar one extends far up into the animal kingdom [p. 36].

Indeed, all the examples which Freud cited and many others he could have collated proved only the universality of repetition compulsion which serves the instinct of the survival of the individual organism and its species. Yet Freud adhered to a concept which could not be logically proven, though it was an inexorable fact. Why did he cling to the term? Was it because of his ingrained dualism? Since there was an instinct which organized the process of living, he assumed an equal and parallel force which "silently" works toward "natural death" in every living organism. Was it that he was so imbued with the philosophy of conflicting forces that he conceived of "libido and aggression" as conflicting forces, such as love and hate in our human psychology, or was it a stroke of his genius that led him to believe beyond doubt that the compulsion to repeat is that biological law of living which finally conquers life in the individual organism and leads it to its earlier inorganic state? This was his scientific conviction. In spite of the paucity of biological data, he believed in science, in biology. As the closing statement of *Beyond the Pleasure Principle* he says:

Biology is truly a land of unlimited possibilities. We may expect it to give us the most surprising information and we cannot guess what answers it will return in a few dozen years to the questions we have put to it. They may be of a kind which will blow away the whole of our artificial structure of hypothesis [p. 60].

A half century has passed since Freud wrote those lines. The impressive progress of the basic sciences—physics and chemistry—has answered the question, "What is life?" And since biology has taken up the torch in the second part of this century, it is fitting to ask what answers biology can give to Freud's question: what is repetition compulsion, how does the concept "instinct" relate to the compulsion to repeat? What then is death? In spite of some implied confirmation, Freud probably would have been disappointed in the answer. Death is indeed innate to life, but there is no death instinct.

It was after the publication of the theory of the death instinct that a few psychoanalysts tried to connect the concept of instinct with the physical laws of living systems. Most significant was Bernfeld's publication, written in collaboration with the physicist Feitelberg: "The Principle of Entropy and the Death Instinct" (1931). More up to date is the study by Thomas Szasz (1952) who by that time could apply Schrodinger's hypothesis to explain the function of the second law of thermodynamics in open systems.

Biologists as well as physicists have shown that the phenomena of life can occur only in open systems. The physical condition of such systems appears to contradict the second law of thermodynamics, which states that every physical or chemical process that takes place in nature proceeds in such a way that the total entropy of the whole system increases. This would mean increasing randomness and disintegration of the living system. This so-called, first paradox of organismic life was explained by Schrodinger, a physicist, and two biologists, Needham and Lotka.

In the decade around the turn of the century, the problem stood in the foreground of scientific interest. Attention was focused on the fact that any living system receives a flood of energy from the environment. Through experiments, it became clear that the crucial characteristic of living matter consists in the ability to avoid decay by taking energy from the environment. Organisms take in air, water, sunshine; the more highly organized the organism, the more complex are the chemical compounds that constitute its nourishment. The digestion or metabolization of these sources of energy "costs" entropy, i.e., creates negative entropy which balances the positive entropy; thus order and organization is maintained. Schrodinger tellingly condensed the result of his investigations in his famous statement, "What the organism feeds upon is negative entropy." In a more complete statement he says, "The device by which an organism maintains itself stationary at a fairly high level of orderliness (= fairly low level of entropy) really consists in continually sucking orderliness from its environment" (Shrodinger, as cited by Szasz, 1952, p. 32). To this Szasz adds, "On the basis of the foregoing biological consideration, we would have to conclude that the ability of living matter 'to *suck* negative entropy from the environment' . . . must be regarded as the primary manifestation of the life instinct" (p. 32; italics added). The primary aim of instinct is to keep the life processes in operation by drawing negative entropy from the environment. This biophysical process, however, does not help to answer Freud's question: is "repetition compulsion" an instinctual process and does it lead to "natural death of living organisms"?

About a half year ago my attention was called to a book with the fascinating title, *Chance and Necessity*, written by the French Nobel laureate, Jacques Monod (1971). My enthusiasm for this work and what I have learned from it should not overcome the necessary boundaries of my aim, i.e., to deduct from the objective data of microbiology, which did not exist even two decades ago, those facts which could clarify the general theory of psychoanalysis. This essay cannot be a review of Monod's magnificent condensation of the biological research of twenty-five years. I intend to concentrate on those points which, in my opinion, are referable to the psychoanalytic instinct theory. At the outset, it should be mentioned that the "chance" of life in the biosphere is not pertinent to this essay, but the concept of necessity is, and it refers to the "repetition" enclosed in the process of life.

In order to keep in touch with what has been discussed before, I cite an experiment by Monod which illustrates that the invariant multiplication of simple (monocellular) living organisms is compatible with the second law. The experiment was set up in calorimeter; one millimeter water with some sugar and mineral salts which contain the essential elements of the constituents of living organisms. In this medium one bacterium, Escherichia coli (length, 2 microns), was set; thirty-six hours later the medium contained several billion bacteria. Nothing unexpected happened. The bacteria converted 40% of the sugar into cellular constituents; the remainder had been oxidized into carbon dioxide and water. The entropy of the system increased just a little more than the minimum prescribed by the second law. But, "Something unfailingly upsets our physical intuition as we watch this phenomenon. . . . We see very clearly that this process is bent or oriented in one exclusive direction, the multiplication of cells" (Monod, 1971, p. 20). One may say that one sees in the rushing, tumbling proliferation of the cells the goal of life, the invariant reproduction accomplished by the division of the cell as the bacteria utilize the thermodynamic laws with maximum efficiency "to carry out the project" and bring about the "dream" (as François Jacob put it) of every cell, i.e., to become two cells. This experiment illustrates not only that the thermodynamic debts in correspondence with the chemical process in the system (bacteria + medium) were duly settled, but also that in the process the bacteria multiplied several billion times. The experiments compellingly show that when life is incited, its very definition implies the compulsion to reproduce itself. Only by "becoming two cells" is the order-"negative entropy" maintained within the single cells. Indeed, as one imagines the rushing, tumbling cells, one also sees the excited biologist who, projecting his intuition, anthropomorphizes the cell, and Monod, by describing it, brings the excitement of the laboratory to the reader.

The metaphor of Schrodinger, as well as that of the biologist Jacob, gives us food for thought. The scientists could have been satisfied with the factual description and the proof of the discovery, but they used metaphors, active verbs—"sucking, dreaming"—to remind us of human experiences with which we can empathize. It seems not only that the concept "instinct" is on the border between the mental and physical, to paraphrase Freud's definition, but also that the investigator is on the border between observation and feelings. Irrelevant as this statement may appear at this point, it indicates one of the difficulties which investigators may find in conceptualization of instinctual phenomena.

Monod is deeply aware of the "animistic" tendencies in the psychology of human beings, from primitive man to the sophisticated scientist of today. Just as primitive man could see his *Umwelt* only in the awareness of his psychic and bodily sensations, scientists similarly may be taken in by their own projections onto the systems which they investigate. This is a special liability when one deals with a universal characteristic of life such as instincts, life force, etc. For whatever term we may attach to that *ultima ratio* which guides life on earth, man cannot avoid observing the order of events in his immediate surroundings and in the biosphere. Probably man's inborn need for security directed his attention to the movement of the "heavenly bodies," to the changes of seasons, to the mating seasons and other behavior of animals. It seems that the first abstraction which men drew from observations was the regularity and repetition of natural events.

Physicists and microbiologists discovered that repetition and regularity dominate the "microscopic world" of minerals as well as living organisms. Monod introduces this world by acquainting us with the microscopic dimension normally expressed in angstroms, a hundred million of which equal one centimeter.

The origin of life does not concern us here. It might have happened in a great variety of places by the same or a similar combination of atoms and molecules, but that minerals—those hard, solid, stony things—have faculties which are parallel to primary qualities of living substances, astounds us. Natural objects never present geometrically simple structures. Crystals are exceptional or unique among the lifeless objects of nature, since crystals, unlike other objects formed by natural forces, present exact symmetry, regular forms. Characteristics of crystals are (a) regularity, (b) repetition. The regularity of the macroscopic crystal comes about through the repetition of the microscopic structure of atoms or molecules constituting them. "A crystal, in other words, is the macroscopic expression of a microscopic structure" (p. 6). The words "regularity" and "repetition" remind us of instincts. There is another quality of crystals which renders crystals unique among the known inorganic substances. Certain chemicals in supersaturated solution do not crystallize unless the solution has been inoculated with crystal seeds. In cases of a chemical capable of crystallizing into two different systems, the structure of the crystals appearing in the solution will be determined by that of the seed employed. It is uncanny. The principle of "invariant reproduction" appears in the inorganic world of crystals. Indeed, in crystals, as in living substance, the structure of the assembled molecules itself constitutes a "source of information" for the construction as a whole. The process of information is the same as in living matter. Crystalline structures, however, in their molecular composition, are inferior to the simplest living organism known; therefore, they represent a lesser quantity of information from one generation to another.

It is a long exciting journey which unfolds from the prebiotic assemblage of protein molecules through the organization of the microscopic machine of a cell to envisage the billions of years of evolution and the myriad forms of life. When all this seems to have been accomplished, Monod demonstrates one more phenomenon beyond the accumulated evidence of research. He states, "The miracle stands 'explained'; it does not strike us as any less miraculous" (p. 138). It is the artist in the scientist that enables his readers to grasp the miracle of the molecular mechanism in the single cellular organism and in its variations through the vast sweep of organismic life.

The growth and multiplication of all organisms require the accomplishing of thousands of chemical reactions whereby the essential constituents of cells are elaborated. The precise adjustment and high efficiency of this enormous, yet microscopic, chemical activity are maintained by a certain class of proteins and enzymes, the latter functioning as specific catalysts.

The enzyme in combination with the protein which it activates forms a *stereospecific complex* and activates a reaction within the complex, a reaction which is *oriented* and *specified* by the structure of the complex itself. Here is the most elementary level at which structural information is created and distributed in living organisms: the enzyme possesses in the structure of its specific receptor the information which prescribes the next step in the biochemical process. Thus the stereospecific complex is the basic model of intersystemic information. It is this primary structure of proteins that holds those cognitive properties which, like Maxwell's demons, animate and build living systems.

The microscopic events form the fundamental miracle of life; the results of their repetition pervade all forms and levels of life, from the simplest living substance to the complex mental life of man. All those performances which, in our terminology, would be considered instinctual, rest in the final analysis upon so-called stereospecific properties, the ability of the protein molecules to "recognize" other molecules (including other proteins) by their shape and attract those which fit. The shape, of course, is determined by the molecular structure. Quite literally, a microscopic discriminative (if not "cognitive") faculty is at work here, achieved by the protein activated by a specific enzyme.

There are different proteins; among them the so-called globular proteins are particularly significant. Globular proteins form strands constituted by the segmental polymerization of amino acids. These strands fold upon themselves in a complex manner, thereby giving these molecules a pseudo-globular shape. But not all such structures are "chosen" to survive. Those so favored are recognized by the densification of their structure, corresponding to the expulsion of the maximum number of water molecules. To the unfolded or loosely folded fiber, any number of conformations are open, but the densified structure constitutes a stable, unalterable form. Its consisting molecules are locked and cannot be unlocked by any influence. The densified globular structure has functional properties, one of which is stereoscopic recognition, i.e., the capacity to form larger units of cell organization. In the physiology of normal medium, in aqueous phase, the bundled state of the protein is thermodynamically more stable than the unfolded one. It is a complex process of many phases and levels of structuration by which molecular ontogenesis evolves, maintained by cybernetic interaction between the intracellular and extracellular components. The closer description of the globular structure shows its submolecules (polymers, oligomers), which are arranged in symmetry so that symmetrical parts rotate. These are veritable crystals.[2] This intracellular movement in its regularity appears like the paradigm of a physical compulsion to repeat. Thus life begins. Globular protein even in its molecular level is a veritable microscopic machine, but only when its basic structure is established does it escape randomness. This is life, and from then on it must go on reproducing itself, exactly as the built-in memory of its species dictates, from the simplest unicellular organism to man himself. I cannot resist the temptation to quote Monod's analogy: "Randomness caught on the wing, preserved, reproduced by the machinery of invariance and thus converted into order, rule, necessity" (p. 98). Folding, i.e., structure formation, indicates negative entropy, the characteristics of living beings which make them appear to escape the fate spelled out by the second law of thermodynamics.

Much before molecular biology could help physicists solve this problem, James Maxwell, a nineteenth-century physicist,[3] attributed the function of "intra- and intercellular cognition" to a microscopic demon. This imaginary gatekeeper of microscopic size could choose to allow molecules to pass from one side of the gate to another in a way which permitted that in two enclosed spaces, originally of the same temperature, one grew hotter, while the other grew colder, all without any consumption of energy. The experiment, imaginary as it was, caused physicists no end of perplexity, for it did seem that through the exercise of his cognitive function, the demon was able to violate the second law.

The fantastic experiment was not only ingenious; it revealed the fundamental law of biology. It is applicable to the distribution of intra- and intersystemic information. The similarity between the function of the stereospecific property of proteins and Maxwell's demons lies in the circumstance that both sets of observations invite the hypothesis that the phenomena are guided by the exercise of a somehow cognitive function. The riddle was solved by Leon Brillouin who, drawing upon an earlier work of Szilard, demonstrated that the exercise of the demon's cognitive function is not gratuitous; it comes about at the expense of a consumption of chemical potential which, on balance, precisely offsets the lessening entropy within the system as a whole. Whether the laws of thermodynamics in the chemical system or the distribution of information in a biological system concerns us, the information is in equivalence to negative entropy. This theorem, central in modern science, originated—if not exclusively—in these two areas of experimentation. The ultima ratio of all "instinctual," i.e., teleonomic

[2] Some molecules of the globular structure "constitute real microscopic crystals." They belong to a special class which Monod calls "closed crystals, for contrary to ordinary crystals . . . they cannot grow without acquiring new elements of symmetry while usually shedding some of those they have" (1971, p. 82). These symmetrical pairs of crystals acquire functional properties.

[3] James Clark Maxwell, British physicist (1831–1879).

performances of living being is encased in the polypeptid fibers ("embryos") of the globular protein which in biology play the role that Maxwell assigned to his demons a hundred years ago. "It is at this level of chemical organization that the secret of life lies. . . . The miracle is the chemical organization" (p. 95).

"The organism is a self-constructing machine. . . . It shapes itself autonomously by dint of constructive internal interactions" (p. 46). The constructive interactions are microscopic and molecular; the molecules involved are essentially, if not uniquely, proteins. Proteins channel the activity of the chemical machine and assure its coherent functioning; one may say, proteins put the machine together. The microscopic, molecular level of cybernetic processes represents the model of the evolution of pluricellular organisms which evolve by coordination between cells, tissues, or organs. The epigenetic processes therefore consist essentially of the overall stereo-specific, spontaneous assembling of their protein constituents. Order, structural differentiation, acquisition of functions—all these appear out of a random mixture of molecules, individually devoid of any activity, any intrinsic functional capacity other than that of recognizing the partners with which they will build a structure.

At each stage, more highly ordered structures and functions appear; each results from the spontaneous interaction between products of the preceding states which thereby necessarily reveal the latent potentialities of the previous level. The structure (whatever it may be) gives the *ne varietur* order to the next step of the nonvariant production. In macroscopic structures, the interacting occurs, not between molecular components, but between cells. In pluricellular organisms, the coordination between cells and tissues or organs is guaranteed by specialized systems; not only the nervous and endocrine systems, but also direct interactions between cells serve that function. The overall scheme (plan) of a complex multimolecular edifice is contained in posse in the structure of its constituent parts, but only comes into actual existence through their assembly. "The epigenetic building of a structure is not a *creation;* it is a *revelation*" (p. 87). All the activities that contribute to the growth and multiplication of a cell are interconnected and intercontrolled, directly and otherwise. On the basis of the replication and multiplication of those microscopic processes, "It becomes possible to grasp in what very real sense the organism does effectively transcend the physical laws—even while obeying them—thus achieving at once the pursuit and fulfillment of its own purpose" (p. 80).

Today we know that from the bacterium to man, the chemical machinery is essentially the same, both in its structure and functioning. From the crystal's closed system through the nervous system of different organisms in the biosphere, repetition of the same processes asserts the epigenesis of the form and structure prescribed in the genes. The thesis is that the principal processes which maintain life are repeated in every organism and are the same from the single cell to the most differentiated and most complex

macroorganism, including man. They are repeated not only with every species and with every individual organism, but they are repeated also in the
same organism during its whole lifetime. Indeed, if Monod wishes to talk
in terms of instincts, he could conceive of repetition compulsion as a life
instinct, just as Freud saw the source of the death instinct in repetition
compulsion.

Monod does not talk about instinct, which we learned to view as innate
patterns of behavior in the service of the propagation of the species, universal
in its aim and varied only in the structures and behavior patterns by which
the aim is achieved. In contrast, Monod demonstrates the universal characteristics of living organisms by comparing them to a "project" programmed
into a computer. In this way he demonstrates that the computer functions
with absolute precision, revealing what was programmed by evolutionary
biology through billions of years. Yet, at the same time, he is aware that
his favored concept for presenting the innate goal-directedness of life en-
dangers what he considers most significant, the objectivity of science.
"Project" is a timely way of expressing the miracle of life which, for untold
generations, has awed men: the unalterable quality of all natural processes
that appear with a regularity and seem to be understandable only by assumption of a supernatural power. Now science can explain it.

The universal principles which we may consider parallel to psychoanalytic
instinct theory are conceptualized in the terms of (1) teleonomy, (2) autonomous and spontaneous morphogenesis, (3) invariant reproduction.

The word "teleonomy" is derived from the Greek word *telos,* which
means aim, distant goal, such as the central aim of life. Thus the term "teleonomy" expresses the goal-directedness of organismic life. All living organisms are endowed with a purpose which they exhibit in their structure and
carry out in their performance. Every activity, every artifact (such as the
nest) which they produce, is in the service of this central aim of self-preservation and the preservation of the species. Every activity which supports
teleonomy is called the "teleonomic structure," which is species characteristic.
The concept of teleonomy implies the oriented, coherent, constructive activity which serves the central telos of survival. This complex organization
evolves through thousands of chemical reactions, organized along divergent,
convergent, and cyclical pathways. A certain class of proteins, the enzymes,
play the role of specific catalysts; other elements function as regulatory
proteins which act as detectors of chemical signals. While the organism
is an autonomous machine, cybernetic systems govern and control its
activity.

The second characteristic of a living being is that its structure, from
its overall shape down to its tiniest detail, is the result of morphogenetic
interactions within the organism itself. Through the autonomous and spontaneous character of morphogenic processes that build the microscopic structure of living beings, one can say that living beings are self-constructing
machines; the word "machine" suggests the cybernetic processes which

take place within and between the cells for that aim. The third characteristic of living systems is the ability to reproduce themselves.

The macroscopic characteristics of all living systems—teleonomy, autonomous morphogenesis, and invariant reproduction—are terms which fit well the categories of the traditional theory of instincts. Teleonomy is represented in the manifestations of the instinct of self-preservation and in the preservation of the species; autonomous morphogenesis is the same plus the physiology of growth and maturation. With the maturation of the organism the sexual instinct takes over the coordination of functions which guard the preservation of the species through invariant reproduction. Invariant reproduction fits the concept of sexual instinct—another level of teleonomy. Men have long wondered about nonvariant reproduction and have created myths and fairy tales about it. How is it possible? Are there minuscle chicks preformed in the egg? Today, probably any high-school boy could answer, "Of course, it is the genetic code; the DNA sends the message." He probably does not realize that fifteen years ago scientists worked hard but hardly imagined that the key to the code would be found. I assume that Monod would not disagree with my assumption that the genetic code is the key which justifies his statement: "To biologists of my generation fell the discovery of the virtual identity of cellular chemistry throughout the entire biosphere" (p. 103).

The miracle of invariant reproduction has been solved by the translation of the genetic code. Regarding invariant reproduction, the question is: what is the source of information and what is the information? The existing structures represent a considerable quantity of information. The source of information expressed in the structure of living beings is always another, structurally identical object; thus information presupposes a structure. Thus, as we have seen, the third property of living beings is the ability to transmit *ne varietur* information corresponding to their own structures. This body of information describes the organizational scheme or plan which is transmitted from one generation to another.[4]

Teleonomy, autonomous morphogenesis, and reproductive invariance are closely interconnected properties of organisms, but they are not of the same standing. Teleonomy and autonomous morphogenesis can be generalized in terms of instincts; they can be intuitively understood. Genetic invariance is different; it is inaccessible to direct observation; it reveals itself only through autonomous morphogenesis of the structures that constitute the teleonomic apparatus. Teleonomy and invariance are characteristic properties of living beings; spontaneous morphogenesis could be considered a mechanism. It may intervene in the elaboration of teleonomic structures and in the reproduction of invariant formation. Darwin saw in this paradox the dilemma of evolution, the internal necessity of adaptation. "The distinction between teleonomy and invariance is more than a logical abstraction. It is

---

[4] The information necessary to reproduce a highly ordered structure can be defined in units of information termed the "invariance content."

warranted on the grounds of chemistry. Of the two basic classes of biological macromolecules, one, that of protein, is responsible for almost all the teleonomic structures and performances; while genetic invariance is linked exclusively to the other class, the nucleic acid" (Monod, 1971, p. 17).

This gradual disclosure of the universal "form" of cellular chemistry seemed . . . to render the problem of reproductive invariance still more acute and more paradoxical. If chemically the components are the same and are synthesized by the same processes in all living beings, what is the source of their prodigious morphological and physiological diversity? . . . We now have the solution to this problem: the universal components—the nucleotides on one side, the amino acids on the other—are the logical equivalents of an alphabet in which the structure and consequently the specific associative functions of the proteins are spelled out [pp. 103–104].

With each succeeding cellular generation, it is the *ne varietur* reproduction of the text written in the form of the DNA sequence that guarantees the invariance of the species. It was Mendel's discovery that the gene is the unvarying bearer of hereditary traits; Watson and Crick discovered the structural basis of the reproductive invariance of the genes. These two facts established the certainty and full significance of the theory of natural selection.

In the normal organism, the microscopic precision machinery confers a remarkable accuracy upon the process of the translation of the code. The translation mechanism is strictly irreversible. Information is never seen being conveyed in the opposite direction from protein to DNA. The upshot of this is "that there is no *possible* mechanism whereby the structure and performance of a protein could be modified. . . . Hence, the entire system is totally, intensely conservative, locked into itself, utterly impervious to any 'hints' from the outside world" (p. 110).

Physics, however, shows "that—save at absolute zero, an inaccessible limit—no microscopic entity can fail to undergo quantum perturbations whose accumulation within a macroscopic system will slowly but surely alter its structure" (p. 111). Here again from the laws of the physical world comes the hint that death is inevitable.[5] Living beings, despite the perfection of the machinery that guarantees the faithfulness of translation, are not exempt from this law. Organic pathology as well as aging in pluricellular organisms is partly accounted for by the piling up of accidental errors of translation. But "accidental errors" brought about by external forces which cause mutations do not qualify as instincts. Instincts are universal organizers of living processes. Mutations might result in "telic decentralization," a term used by David Bakan to characterize "instinctual processes" which do not correspond to the teleonomic structure and tendency in a human being.

[5] Psychoanalytic investigations give reason to speculate about psychological "perturbations" which may influence basic adaptive processes and the "genes" of the next generation. Since my investigation of diabetes, several studies have pointed in the same direction.

In formulating my answer to Freud's quest in *Beyond the Pleasure Principle*, on the basis of his investigation, I have to say that his closing paragraph of that work was superfluously modest. Biology did not "blow away," but confirmed, Freud's intuition about the all-encompassing power of the compulsion to repeat normal and pathological processes, psychological as well as organic. But he did not consider that force an "instinct." The term "repetition compulsion" might even be misleading, since the term "compulsion" is pre-empted by a special form of psychic pathology. Freud was aware that he was dealing with a force, unconscious and relentless in its function. But why was he reluctant to consider it an instinct or even a "death instinct"?

Freud considered repetition compulsion a universal phenomenon, manifest throughout the organismic world, in plants as well as in animals. Although he attributed to it a "demonic force," he did not consider it an instinct because of its conservative and regressive characteristics. Freud's knowledge of Darwin's theories shows in his statement: "Both higher development and involution might well be the consequences of adaptation to the pressure of external forces; and in both cases the part played by instincts might be limited to the retention . . . of an obligatory modification" (Freud, 1920, p. 41). Without knowing the structure of genes, Freud throught of inheritance as less concrete, but just as pervading a factor in repetition as modern biologists do. His intuitive insight regarding repetition has been proven. Although he considered repetition compulsion the source of death instinct, this hypothesis did not clarify the concept of the death instinct since he was stubbornly set to keep the two concepts apart.

It would be a repetition of what has been discussed earlier to restate the seeming paradox of the thermodynamic law in open systems. Whether the pre-biotic state of a protein-enzyme compound or the structure of any form of its epigenesis throughout the biosphere is investigated, the thermodynamic balance is maintained by the same process. Like any "work," be it metabolism on the macroscopic level or the "microscopic cognition" of Maxwell's demons, information is always "work" because it drains energy (chemical potential) into the process which it executes. The consumption of energy offsets the surplus entropy caused by the process and thus keeps the entropy balanced in the system as a whole. One may say that the physical condition which makes life possible also sets its limits.

Biology has shown that the inevitability of death is rooted deeper than the biological system. It is rooted in the physical system of inorganic matter from which it emerged and to which it strives to return through life. Putting it this way, of course, we just reformulate or put in another frame of reference Freud's repeated statement about the tendency of living organisms to return to their former state of existence. Since Freud conceived of this as an unconscious "striving" which is a characteristic of all instincts, he did not feel the necessity of abandoning the concept of instinct. Human intuition is, however, against the concept of death instinct, since it contradicts the natural inclination to attribute instinct to the process of life as its organizer. Biology, while proving that repetition is the sine qua non necessity of life, offered one more argument against the concept of death instinct; it revealed that death itself (sui generis) cannot have psychic representations. Death is absolute; it is not on the frontier between mental and somatic. Repetition is somewhat different. On the basis of the microbiological evidence, we may paraphrase Freud's definition. Repetition as an ongoing biological process is on the frontier between living substance and nonliving matter. This primary biological process was discovered by Freud in its most distant epigenetic manifestations, in the psychological processes of man.

It is difficult for us who are used to interpreting repetition in the context of what is repeated—memories, experiences, fantasies, actions—to conceive of it as an abstraction indicating the thermodynamic laws of open systems. Of course, on a higher level of organization, one may relate it to mechanisms, since the teleonomic apparatus affords the physiological structures which are the channels of the repetition. The repetition is beyond perception and awareness. Repetition, even the human "repetition compulsion," has no psychic representations. This is easier to assume about "repetition" than about death. After all, no one feels "repetition" as a biological necessity.[6] The statement that death has no primary psychic representations may be unbelievable since there is an abundance of symbols, symptoms, rituals, and personal experiences which represent psychological elaborations of the concept of death, which in itself cannot be imagined.

When I wrote the paper "Death Instinct and Anxiety" (1931) on the basis of the psychoanalytic study of phobic and acutely anxious patients, I assumed that anxiety was the psychic representation of the death instinct. The closely interrelated hormonal physiology of anxiety and aggression, however, revealed that anxiety is not the representation of the death instinct, but the manifestation of the defense structure that is mobilized against the fear of death. The primary, psychic representation of death is the fear of death. Every organism is equipped with signals and structures to defend itself against the danger of death. It seems paradoxical to illustrate the universality of the defense against death with the bacterium which multiplies in order not to die in consequence of entropy.

If all instinctual processes are in the service of survival, what is the epistemological value of the concept of death instinct? Does it enhance our understanding of human life? Does it help us to understand "normalcy," or its opposite, pathology? Several books could be written in attempting to answer this question. Here, however, some general statement should suffice. Freud formulated his thesis of repetition compulsion and death in-

---

[6] The compulsion to repeat actions, which is a frequent symptom in compulsion neurosis, is an analyzable phenomenon and is not the same as that which Freud described as repetition compulsion; just as the wish to die in a depressed person is not the same as the universal death instinct.

stinct soon after the First World War. For years afterward, he was preoccupied with the role of aggression in intrapsychic processes. The intrapsychic controlling system, the superego evolving from the child's relationship with his parents, may turn it to an "individual-survival negative" instrument, charged with hostility toward the self. This "macroscopical" intrapsychic organization is in continual communication with "microscopic" defense structures. Several of them are known as defense mechanisms of the ego. But there are psychosomatic defense mechanisms which, developing early in life, may cause predispositions for psychic and organic pathology.[7] These are just hints of a steadily expanding field of research which, I hope, will substantiate my opinion of the value of the derivatives of the concept of death instinct.

"Death instinct" was a misnomer, since "instinct" is applicable only to living beings. Repetition compulsion is validated by the primary (fundamental) biological process that holds the mystery of life. Psychoanalytic theory relinquished the concept of death instinct and with it, it seems, forgot about Freud's great biological discovery. This is, however, a loss only in regard to the philosophy of our science, since only the process which is repeated is accessible to psychoanalytic investigation, not the repetition per se. What has remained from the concept of death instinct?

Aggression as a source of affect—anger, hostility, antagonism—seems to be an opponent force to libido, but on this level it refers to the psychology of object relationship, to the developmental theory. The concept of "fusion and defusion," however, refers to another level, to another system of psychobiological processes. Structure formation, as well as decomposition of structures and replacement of them, occurs in the silence of biological and physiological processes. It is the same with psychobiological structures. The fusion and defusion of minute occurrences which add up to superego, or to a hysterical symptom, are not accessible to experience. This assumption implies a more basic change in psychoanalytic theory than is generally recognized.

Freud formulated his dualistic instinct theory to explain the concept of "conflict" and its psychodynamic consequences. For the conceptualization of a conflict, he always needed two arms of a scale to weigh the contrasting forces. The psychic manifestations may have been very different, but actually they belonged to the same psychological systems. On the level of psychological symptom formation, the manifestations of the libidinal and the aggressive factors are accessible to analysis.

The concept of "fusion and defusion" is of another order of abstraction. At the same time that Freud adhered to the idea that death instinct originates in a source which is in contrast to that of libido, he proposed a unified

---

[7] After the investigation of Selye on the effects of physiological stress in "diseases of adaptation," the interaction of psychological and somatic factors were investigated by many. For a concise survey of the basic psychological factors in organic illness, see Engel's *Psychological Development in Health and Disease* (Philadelphia: W. B. Saunders, 1962).

instinct theory with the concept of "fusion and defusion" of psychic energy. On the basis of psychoanalytic studies, Rangell formulated that libido and aggression are not antagonists but partners in living (1968).

Structure formation consists of repetitions of primary processes, fusions and defusions, not only on the biological level but also on psychological levels.[8] Fusion represents the balance of a system, but defusion is the necessary step for the new integration. Thus both integration and disintegration play a role in any process of growth and development as well as in decomposition, illness, and aging.

A unified instinct theory is the logical consequence of Freud's instinct theory. Instinct for Freud represented a manifestation of energy which instigates and motivates the functions of an organism. Working on the manifestations of this force in and via the human mind, he might have thought that the instinct theory is our mythology (1933), but actually he never treated it as such. He never considered "instinctual energy" as a transcendental "life force" (Bergson) or its structure formation as a manifestation of "entelechy" (Driesch). Every developmental process with all its variations was motivated by the innate and environmental factors which could be accounted for. Freud was a natural scientist and created in psychoanalysis a "natural science" of the human mind. But like many great scientists, he was caught by his earlier discoveries.[9] He too adhered to his earlier concept even when he was discarding it. Freud held on to the dualistic instinct theory even with the concept of the death instinct. It may be that without his vision fixated on the final end, he could not have formulated the conviction which has been proven by molecular biology, that with the onset of life begins a process which is repeated on every level, in every process and structure formation through which it leads, through aging, to death.

BIBLIOGRAPHY

Bakan, D. (1968), *Disease, Pain and Sacrifice*. Chicago: University of Chicago Press.
Benedek, T. (in press), *Psychoanalytic Investigations: Selected Papers*. New York: Quadrangle/The New York Times Book Co.
—— (1931), Death Instinct and Anxiety. *Internationale Zeitschrift für Psychoanalyse*, 17:333–343.
Bernfeld, S., and Feitelberg, S. (1931), The Principle of Entropy and the Death Instinct. *Internat. J. Psycho-Anal.*, 12:61–81.
Born, M. (1971), *The Born-Einstein Letters: The Correspondence between Albert Einstein and Max and Hedwig Born*. New York: Walker & Co.

[8] The fusion and defusion of instinctual processes are probably comparable with the prebiotic, protein-enzyme compound.

[9] As an example, see the correspondence between Einstein and his pupil Max Born (Born, 1971).

Cannon, W. (1953), *Bodily Changes in Pain, Hunger, Fear and Rage: An Account of Recent Researches in the Function of Emotional Excitement.* Boston: Branford.

Fechner, G. T. (1873), *Einige Ideen Zur Schopfungs–und Entwicklings-geschichtkte der Organismen.* Part XI, Suppl. 94.

Fletcher, R. (1957), *Instinct in Man.* New York: International Universities Press.

Darwin, C. (1829), *The Origin of the Species.* London: *Thinker's Library.*

Freud, S. (1915), Instincts and their Vicissitudes. *Standard Edition* 14:117–140. London: Hogarth, 1957.

––––– (1905), Three Essays on the Theory of Sexuality. *Standard Edition,* 7:135–243. London: Hogarth, 1961.

––––– (1920), Beyond the Pleasure Principle. *Standard Edition,* 18:7–64. London: Hogarth, 1955.

––––– (1921), Group Psychology and the Analysis of the Ego. *Standard Edition,* 13:68–143. London: Hogarth, 1958.

––––– (1923), The Ego and the Id. *Standard Edition,* 19:13–66. London: Hogarth, 1961.

––––– (1924), The Economic Problem of Masochism. *Standard Edition,* 19:167–189. London: Hogarth, 1961.

––––– (1930), Civilization and Its Discontents. *Standard Edition,* 21:64–145. London: Hogarth, 1961.

––––– (1933), New Introductory Lectures on Psycho-Analysis. *Standard Edition,* 22:81–111. London: Hogarth, 1964.

Haldane, J. B. S. (1932), *The Causes of Evolution.* London: Longman.

James, W. (1890), The Principles of Psychology. New York, Macmillan.

Monod, J. (1971), *Chance and Necessity,* trans. Austryn Wainhouse. New York: Alfred A. Knopf.

Rangell, L. (1968), A Further Attempt to Resolve the Problem of Anxiety. *J. Amer. Psychoanal. Assn.* 16:371–404.

Schrodinger, E. (1945), *What is Life?* New York: Macmillan.

Szasz, T. S. (1952), On the Psychoanalytic Theory of Instincts. *Psychoanal. Quart.* 21:25–48.

Williams, G. C. (1966), *Adaptation and Natural Selection: A Critique of Some Current Evolutionary Thoughts.* Princeton: Princeton University Press.

Psychoanalysis and Science: The Concept of Structure

SAMUEL A. GUTTMAN, PH.D., M.D. (*Philadelphia*)

Some fields of science, such as molecular biology and high-energy physics are moving ahead very rapidly, while others, including psychoanalysis, are not. Slower progress is not necessarily due to the complexity of the subject matter or the difficulties of learning or teaching it, since advances seem to come from those fields demanding a high level of intellectual activity. It is significant, too, that we are perhaps better acquainted with the political, economic, and social possibilities and consequences of nuclear theory and research than with its relevance for theory construction. Yet to find the object of scientific knowledge we must go to its theoretical assumptions.

My concern here is not with the success of psychoanalysis as it is practiced but rather with the problems of formalism: what this science means and what it implies. Although today scientific truths can be tested by experience, the Greeks, in contrast, presupposed the existence of a definitive, all-embracing idea which would serve to explain all observable phenomena. But the results of modern science do not lead me to believe that this is possible, now or in the future. We think, we work, and we discover new phenomena. But what we find tomorrow will not necessarily fit in with our current theoretical constructs. In a beautiful paper, "The Need for New Knowledge," Oppenheimer (1959) discussed the fact that new knowledge opens up endless choices and is ennobling in its union of simplicity and truth. But though such new knowledge generally also engenders fear or anxiety, hope, suspicion, and cynicism, we see in the recent *Symposium on Basic Research*, of which Oppenheimer's paper was a part, how a group of most distinguished scientists bravely refused to confine their interest to any one area of man's creative life. In essence it seems to me that a psychoanalyst, if he is to be a scientist, must be a person who is not only involved but

Presented at the 24th International Psychoanalytical Congress in Amsterdam (1965).
    Professor of Psychiatry (Psychoanalysis), Jefferson Medical College, Philadelphia, Pa.

73

is really committed to a broad program of creative scholarship in its deepest sense.

I will not focus on content or special problems but rather will attend to more general issues. In psychoanalysis, as in any other science, the creative core of the discipline is intimately related to the intellectual efforts of the times. Great issues are qualitative, and public evaluation is not essentially important. A personal measure of one's own scientific abilities is crucial, and the ability to remain problem-oriented, rather than merely method-oriented, is essential in order to avoid constricted scientific achievement. There is a tendency to distrust abstractions, yet it seems that more and more abstractions are invented. Particularly in psychoanalysis, we have the great problem of maintaining scientific knowledge independent of the role of the psychoanalyst as "knower." In psychoanalysis the making of observations presents special problems of an ontological nature; here the subject matter must be seen as independent of its relation to the perceiver.

The newness of psychoanalysis may be compared to the revolutionary approach of quantum mechanics. Quantum mechanics is a rather new set of ideas which has reproduced, very well, and with great accuracy, observed facts of atomic behavior. It also has opened up new avenues of understanding in its explanation of phenomena not understood before, events which can be seen from the viewpoint of simple electric attraction and repulsion between atomic nuclei and electrons, which may then be reduced to simple electric forces. Quantum mechanics provides for many more stable states of matter than classical mechanics could. Psychoanalysis, too, is a rather new formalism. Our fundamental notion for the understanding of a great variety of phenomena can be reduced to conflict (struggle between forces) with resultant inner fear or danger—anxiety. Just as quantum mechanics contains the concept of probability at the most fundamental level, making it necessary for certain statements to remain, in principle, inexact, we must realize that, when we employ the psychoanalytic situation for investigation, there is only a relatively fair degree of certainty and probability.

At this time I will consider one particular area which is relevant to theory construction in psychoanalysis. In a recent overview (1965), I have maintained as one thesis that there is nothing arcane about psychoanalysis and that there is much we can learn from others. Each and every thing is always related, in different ways, to the environment and the times. The arts and sciences are not only influenced by the fashion of the epoch of which they form a part but also are related to one another. It is this principle which I have singled out to discuss. In science, every historical period needs, seeks, and devises a paradigm. I use "paradigm" here as defined by Kuhn (1962): "a widely recognized achievement that for a time provides model problems and model solutions to a community of practitioners of a science."

Today, the almost unbelievable advances in technology have no doubt played a role in fostering a separation between the natural, scientific, or rational, and the artistic, aesthetic, or irrational. According to the Greek concept, the gods, or man and his intelligence, created form. This unity was essential, as was the unity of matter. There was no possibility that anything had more than one matter, or more than one form. Living as we do in the midst of this particular cultural time, it is difficult for us to see general resemblances. In this age of specialization, we tend to see only marked distinctions, not likeness. Generally, our personal experiences are too fragmented, and knowledge tends to remain too solidly within disciplines, each with a rapidly expanding private language. The accessibility of only one area or body of knowledge is, unfortunately, too prevalent today.

Biology and other sciences have taught us that knowledge of living man will inevitably flow from so-called basic studies of elementary structures and reactions of fragments derived from living things. The concept of structure is the ordering principle of every area of creative thinking and doing in our time; it is a key concept for current creative work in the arts and sciences. It seems to me that the crucial unsolved problem we have to face in psychoanalysis is related to this same concept of structure. It is essential that we try to understand the nature of the cohesive, or organizing, forces which maintain man in an integrated state so that he can relate successfully to his environment. Is not this problem of structure what Nunberg addressed himself to in his 1930 paper of Synthetic Function?

It is almost a platitude to state, in these simple terms, that every science proceeds more or less explicitly from hypotheses of greater or lesser generality. From these hypotheses particular consequences are deduced, which can be tested by observation and experiment. As it advances science does not rest with simple generalizations from observable facts, but organizes these general hypotheses at a higher level into a hierarchical deductive system. In the area of contemporary physics, for example, abstract mathematical entities serve to make an elaborate theoretical system. It is true that the mathematics employed is difficult and can only be understood after long training. But to understand how the mathematics is used requires no special mathematical ability. What is necessary is an interest in, and an ability to explore, modes of thinking as well as the way scientific language and symbolism are used in the expression of a scientific theory.

The function of a science is to establish general laws covering the behavior of the empirical events or objects with which the science is concerned. When a science is in a highly developed state, the established laws form a hierarchy in which special laws follow a smaller number of highly general laws expressed in a very sophisticated manner. If a science is in an early state of development, what is sometimes called its "natural-history stage," the laws may be merely generalizations that order things into various classes. However, to emphasize the establishment of general laws as a function of a science is not to overlook the fact that in many sciences the questions to which the scientist attaches the most importance are those that deal with the causes of particular events rather than with general laws. The statement that some particular event is the effect of a set of circumstances involves the insertion of a general law; to ask for the cause of an event is always to ask for a general law which applies to the particular event. Though we may be more interested in the application than in the law itself, a law must be established.

The fundamental concept of science is that of scientific law, and the fundamental aim of a science is the establishment of such laws. In order to understand how a science works, and the way in which it provides explanations of the facts which it investigates, it is necessary to understand the nature of scientific laws and what it is to establish them.

There is a tendency when a question is raised, or an issue discussed, that relates to a matter of theory, to move at once to a historical summary of the concept. I will not do this, but suffice it to say that structure as a concept began to play a role in the thinking of Western man around the turn of the century. Hertz (1894) showed his understanding of the concept in logics and mathematics, although he did not use the term "structure." Russell and Whitehead (1910) elaborated on the concept and its meaning. The concept has as its only objective the idea of a changing pattern of relations; its philosophy is monistic, relational, precise, and potentially comprehensive.

It is no quibble to separate the notion of structure from such related concepts as order, form, function, organized complexity, whole, system, process, or Gestalt. Each historical era seeks and needs a central idea for understanding. Structure, as a concept, seems central to our time. As old connections crumble away, our creative efforts inevitably seek out new ordering principles to replace the old. In different fields, for different reasons, the new ordering relations are being accepted as fundamental. We recognize that the key properties of different materials are determined according to the way in which atoms, the basic building units of nature, are joined together, rather than, as once assumed, according to the elemental stuff of the material. The differences among solid, liquid, and gaseous states are explained by the patterning of their atoms and the relative closeness of their molecules.

From inorganic structures to plants and animals, from the movements of animals to their social behavior patterns and to human relations, structure is central. A sharp focus of structure awareness extends from the molecular structure underlying the genetic mechanism on to living forms. Thus, a built-in program of growth and development is provided for an infinite variety of unfolding living structures.

The concept of structure is also important in the theory of understanding. Studies of perception and cognitive processes by Gestalt psychologists show that psychological events occur not through the accumulation of individual elements of sense data, but through the coordinated functioning of clearly patterned networks of sensation determined by structural laws.

Creative exploration in the arts has yielded significant parallels with scientific investigation. Early twentieth-century painters, hoping and attempting to embrace the complete vista of contemporary conditions, looked for structural principles in art. Instead of aiming at an illusory rendering of what they could see around them, they invented images and patterns. Clear, unmodulated surfaces, abstract shapes, simple basic colors devoid of emotional overtones were used as building blocks. Passionate involvement with an image-building process had its great ancestor in Cezanne, whose many successors build consistent, legible pictorial structures from the direct data of inner sensibility.

Neither can genuine architecture be viewed in pieces or parts, each of which is autonomous and exists alone. A fragment of architecture is no more than a mutilated object. Contemporary architecture—like painting and sculpture—is most absorbed with structure. The ever increasing size of buildings has brought the problem of structure to the forefront. It has assumed such formal importance that it has become the central feature of architectural design. In structural architecture the forces of compression and tension foster a pattern for the neturalization of stress. This is visible and comprehensible and is demonstrated by the properties of the materials with which the forms are executed.

In the arts the knowledge of structural laws of nature can aid us in creating forms. The world as a set of structural systems is not, should not be, divided into two territories—scientific knowledge and artistic vision. A search for possible common denominators in our contemporary scientific, technological, and artistic achievements presents a very great challenge. There is so very much to know, and one's experience is necessarily limited and fragmented. Communication problems exist, and there is a scattering of knowledge in many self-contained disciplines. Each seems to have its rapidly expanding private language. We are moving away from a simplicity to a modern concept of ordered complexity. This, however, is not a rigid framework for a schematized reality, but a way of ordering elements which have a hierarchy of relationships and interrelationships. The position of structure—as a concept—may be defined in a specific way or in a more general fashion.

The concept of structure has also played an important role in molecular biology. The discovery of the actual pattern of the coiled intracellular protein molecules which are the physical basis of heredity, is remarkable. We see that the infinite variety of the individuality of organisms is dependent on the permutations and combinations of some twenty-odd amino acids. At another time and in another context Lucretius said: "'tis thus by bodies unseen that nature works her will."

Let me give a trivial example from another area—the study of language. We use the twenty-six letters of the English alphabet. These are structures. The way they connect and relate to one another permits word formation. This, then, is followed by sentence formation, and so on. Actually, it is possible to express the whole of human knowledge in this manner—a very remarkable state of affairs.

In a paper presented to the New York Psychoanalytic Society in January,

1965, David Beres showed how "structure" is used in many ways in the psychoanalytic literature. Understandably, he states that in the "biological sciences structure refers to morphology and function to physiological activity, both of which can be directly observed. With psychological phenomena the interrelationship is not as easily demonstrable."

In this paper Beres devotes considerable attention to "structure" and the "structural theory," with particular reference to the works of Gill, Glover, Hartmann, and Rapaport. He raises many questions about the work of Gill and Rapaport, in particular. In brief, what Beres objects to is this: "It is precisely the designation of mechanisms and processes as structures or structural concepts which I question." Hartmann [1963] has said that: "Every semi or relatively stable formation (in the mental apparatus), is called a structure and in a structure, as Rapaport said, the rate of change is lower than in process." For Freud (1923), the ego, superego, and id were the mental structures. The concept of structure as viewed by Hartmann is consistent with the key concept in current theory construction in the arts and sciences. The discovery of the formed interconnections of structures, which we view as a whole, is a system. If there is a fundamental validity to the idea that the concept of structure *is* the "key" to our contemporary view of theory construction in psychoanalysis, as it is in all other intellectual endeavors, then structures have a place in all of our "meta" points of view.

We are in the midst of continuing developments in psychoanalytic theory construction. There will be advances with examination of differing ideas. The ultimate value of any one notion will be determined by its usefulness for further theory construction and its relationship to advances in explaining ambiguities of man and his behavior.

We need broad and unambiguous communication for the continuing development of psychoanalysis. What is important is to find shared areas of concern and areas of unsolved problems. What are the important unsolved problems in psychoanalysis? We have seen that the attention of all scientists—including psychoanalysts—has been moving from the simple toward the complex. It seems that the prevailing idea of structure is in some ways replacing the older concepts of atomism and form. Atomism, broadly speaking, involves according to Whyte: "reduction of complex data to finite numbers of fixed unit factors." Yet Whyte states that: "the status of physical atomism is uncertain . . . I believe because it is in the course of being transformed into a theory of structure with structural rather than atomic laws in the traditional sense." Form, on one hand, is the overall shape of line, surface, or volume, or, more accurately, the ordering of the parts which determine these shapes. On the other hand, structure "is form seen inside, as a definite arrangement, static or changing, of localizable parts." Structure must be at least partly ordered or it is lost in chaos. The crucial matter—and I cannot stress this too much—is that the essence of structure as a concept is not on the terms or elements themselves, but is on the relationships and interrelationships.

Some colleagues involved in the education of psychoanalysts have become increasingly concerned with the quality of the psychoanalytic understanding of the candidates and recent graduates. I will touch on only one aspect of this important and complicated matter. What I have to say is purely impressionistic in nature, but I mention it now because it is a matter of practical importance and warrants continuing attention and study. A notion and concern in some quarters has centered about the candidates' considerable interest in and attention to theoretical abstractions of a higher and higher level. Concepts of structure do afford us a greater opportunity for the ordering of observational data. A language of concepts has a tendency to go further and further away from the subject of our work and original interest: man and his feeling, thinking, and behavior. The language departs from that ordinarily used for communications about everyday thoughts, ideas, feelings, and actions. A recent experience is interesting. At the annual scientific meetings of the American Psychoanalytic Association (May, 1965), advanced candidates and recent graduates from the Institutes of the Affiliated Societies participated in discussion groups which were clinical conferences. Here material from an adult or child in psychoanalytic treatment was presented. There was no screening of participants; each institute made application forms available to its own advanced candidates and recent graduates. In all, seventy-five wished to participate in these clinical conferences. Three clinical conferences were set up on adult cases and one on a child case. The chairmen were some of our most experienced and respected teachers. There was a significant feeling of surprise, voiced independently, by each of these teachers. The young colleagues, who came from almost all of our institutes, were able to discuss the material at a high level. I was told: "They made sense, they seemed to understand—they ought to make good analysts." One colleague wanted my assurance that these were not a group of post-postgraduates. "You mean to say," I was asked, "they are just advanced students and recent graduates?" It is evident to me that continuing experiences and observations of this kind are warranted. In psychoanalysis, even more than in any other science, it is imperative to use clinical material, consistently and persistently. This is certainly not a novel idea, yet there is a tendency to think that, since psychoanalysts generally spend most of their working time with patients, they may feel bored or uninterested in meetings devoted to a discussion of clinical and theoretical matters. A theoretical matter illustrated with a clinical vignette is generally of greater interest. For some years now, in the didactic portion of the curriculum of my institute, we have had a continuous case seminar for students in all years, including the first. Beginning in the second year, and continuing in all other years, there are also clinical conferences.

Wisdom is a matter of picking out what is important. Scientific communication is more than a description of facts or reporting of news. We can best communicate through channels of shared experience. This is most important because with higher and higher levels of abstraction, a natural state of affairs in the historical development of all sciences, knowledge tends to relate less and less to human experience and often goes beyond aspects of human grasp.

There is a breakdown of communication between the scientist and the humanist, and when this occurs concepts are not, or cannot be, related to human experience. Scientific knowledge tends to go away from human experience, and scientists, if they want to communicate, must return to the original basis of their work.

Scientific abstraction, a most powerful tool, must somehow or other be used in a fashion similar to that of the artist who exploits complex relationships. Somehow we must be able to put things together. This is our great task in psychoanalysis—to understand more actions and interactions between structures or units. The possible combinations which exist cannot be computed. We must, consistently, in our work, consider at least in part, the relationships between structures. These exist as a result of the individual's maturation and development, and of his evolutionary history, which determines any and all complexities of nature and of man, in particular.

Man's enjoyment of the different qualities of chemical and building materials, art, sculpture, etc.—understood today in terms of composition, interatomic forces, and structure—has played a role in developing his intellectual awareness, giving him some confidence in dealing with his environment and himself.

In the past, the scientist has tended to depend on rather subtle abstractions which related the whole to its parts. Now we must relate parts with the whole—with the whole system and subsystems, too. We must aim for significant understanding of wholes—the whole person in relation to himself and the world we live in. Our understanding must be precise enough to be called scientific and communicable enough to be taught.

The use of structure as a concept permits fuller understanding of complex fields. As the scientist explores further complexities, his area of interest and approach will move in the direction of the humanist. It seems to me that psychoanalysis may be subjected to less and less attack over the next decades (at least from scientists or philosophers). At the outset the psychoanalytic method of investigation and psychoanalytic theory naturally were addressed to a very complex field. Other scientists, only more recently, have devoted their energies and talents to areas of equivalent complexity. Now science may once more blend more successfully into a broader range of human activity. Structural laws aid us in creating forms—aesthetically as well as intellectually. Understanding comes best from a point of view which scans greater areas with variations in attention. In all areas of intellectual pursuit man's concern is with systems of greater and greater complexity.

In closing I will use an example from the history of science in order to convey the essence of the concept of structure. In 1858 August Kekule came up with the idea that six atoms of carbon might arrange themselves in a closed ring. This, of course, had an importance in itself. There was something of greater moment behind this idea, but Kekule, as well as others, remained unaware of this. In recent years, because we are less concerned with what something is made of, our main focus has shifted to how it is put together. Today it seems obvious to us that the alignment of the rings determines the properties of solid carbon. If these rings are laid flat, one on top of the other they tend to slide. In this way we have graphite. If the rings are interlocked a diamond is formed. The interlocking makes for the most solid union.

We need to develop further principles, not of simple isolated or relatively isolated parts but of the interconnections and interactions of very complex structures with parts interacting on one another. The interactions take place on all levels with a hierarchy of substructures continuing to form interacting superstructures.

An intellectual approach such as this can readily be related to a study of man. I refer to ordinary man—one who sees wholes and is able to perceive and enjoy sensed relationships which defy detailed breakdown into small parts. We must try to avoid an ever-present danger, a danger which may tend to increase. We must not assume that those things and events which can be intellectually understood, in some cases scientifically computed, are the ones of greatest significance.

BIBLIOGRAPHY

Beres, D. (1965), Structure and Function in Psychoanalysis. Presented at the New York Psychoanalytic Society, *Internat. J. Psycho-anal.*, 46:53–63.

Freud, S. (1923), The Ego and the Id. *Standard Edition*, 19:3–66. London: Hogarth Press, 1961.

Guttman, S. A. (1965), Some Aspects of Scientific Theory Construction and Psychoanalysis. *Internat. J. Psycho-anal.*, 46:129–136.

Hertz, H. (1894), *Principles of Mechanics.*

Hartmann, H. (1963), Ego Psychology. Princeton Conference No. 45, Center for Advanced Psychoanalytic Studies, Princeton, N.J.

Kuhn, T. S. (1962), *The Structure of Scientific Revolutions.* Chicago: University of Chicago Press.

Nunberg, H. (1930), The Synthetic Function of the Ego. In: *Practice and Theory of Psychoanalysis.* New York: International Universities Press, 1955, pp. 120–136.

Oppenheimer, J. R. (1959), In: *Symposium on Basic Research,* ed. Dael and Wolfle. A.A.A.S. Publication No. 56. Washington, D.C.

Russell, B., and Whitehead, A. N. (1910), *Principia Mathematica.* Cambridge: Cambridge University Press.

Symposium on Basic Research (1959), Edited by Dael and Wolfle. A.A.A.S. Publication No. 56, Washington, D.C.

Whyte, L. L. (1965), Atomism, Structure and Form (A Report on the Natural Philosophy of Form). In: *Structure in Art and in Science,* ed. Gyorgy Kepes. New York: George Braziller.

Notes on
"Psychoanalysis and Science: The Concept of Structure"

HEINZ HARTMANN, M.D.

There was a time when in analysis one looked askance at questions of concept formation, at the specific concern with their clarification, also at the changes concepts have undergone in the course of analytic development, and at methodology in general. The first attempts in this direction did not find much interest among psychoanalysts. The situation has considerably changed in this respect.

Papers in this field of analysis are not rare today. It has been repeatedly made the central topic of panel discussions in the last years. The whole field has been recognized as a legitimate part of analysis. The development of some of the analytic concepts—like the ego, repression, structure, and some others—has been the object of special studies. Here belongs also the comprehensive work of the Concept Group under the guidance of Dr. Nagera at Anna Freud's Hampstead Child Therapy Clinic.

The concentration on such questions has various aspects. One can treat them historically or in a more strictly methodological sense. Both aspects are important; also, the one cannot be substituted for the other. The history of a science can be an approach to methodological questions, but it does not mean that it can always answer them.

Beyond this, there is, of course, also the question of the position of analytical thought in the history of ideas, about which Dr. Guttman has spoken just now. About cultural factors that had an influence on Freud much has been said, in particular of course from the point of view of the development of psychoanalysis. But, as to scientific method, we remember also

The greater part of this article was read at the 24th International Psycho-Analytical Congress in Amsterdam (1965), as a contribution to the discussion of a paper of this title presented to the Congress by Dr. Samuel A. Guttman. Reprinted from *Hoofdstukken uit de hedendaagse psychoanalyse*, 1967.

that he had emphasized himself—regarding the methodological problems he had to face—how often he had to start from scratch, because a methodological framework, hallowed by experiment and by tradition, as it exists in the natural sciences, did not exist in his field. His work is revolutionary in this sense, too. This would lead us to the development of "paradigms," a concept introduced by Kuhn and also mentioned by Dr. Guttman.

On the other hand, it is also true that Freud formed some of his concepts after the model of those that were current in the sciences of his time (physiology, physics, chemistry). The use of such models has proved fruitful in many areas. But I have discussed that elsewhere and don't want to repeat it here. What is decisive, is which changed meanings such model concepts take on in the factual and theoretical milieu of his new science and what the reach of these concepts and the criteria of their application have become in analysis.

One may ask what the turning to this aspect of analysis means, and what we can expect of it. The discussion of the methodological questions which analysis poses often serves the purpose of proving its character as a science; and, with adversaries of analysis, of denying its character as a science. But obviously such studies have also, beyond these questions, a broad importance for analytical theory.

It is necessary clearly to differentiate in analysis where it has the character of a historical study, and where the historical material which analysis recovers serves the formulation of laws in the sense of natural science. Some comparisons of analysis with archeology that Freud used have led to the overvaluation of the intimacy of connections between analytical and historical research. I think a more detailed examination, not only of some occasional comparisons in Freud but of all those passages that relate to this topic, demonstrates that the aims of his research quite preponderantly coincide with those of natural science. A particularly interesting field is certainly also the comparison of analytic concepts with analogous concepts in other sciences, of communalities and differences. This is, indeed, one of the more important aspects of Dr. Guttman's paper. It can be very fruitful, where it is specific. It presupposes a clear knowledge of concept formation in analysis and of its particular characteristics, and makes specific methodological studies necessary. It is only on the basis of such a comparative study also that we can objectively compare, e.g., the rate of progress in analysis with that in different fields referred to by Dr. Guttman.

The role of observable facts and of hypotheses formation is in analysis the same as in natural sciences. There is in analysis the same difference in levels of theoretical discourse. There is one mainly descriptive aspect, then there is a level still relatively close to observation but really, in this or that one aspect, transcending it. Then another one, which is the theoretical discourse proper. Theories or hypotheses connect the constructs of psychoanalysis with the observational data (Hartmann, 1958, 1959; Waelder, 1960). The concepts of psychoanalysis are to a large extent not descriptive but explanatory. Here methodological studies inside of psychoanalysis have led to a greater clarity of differentiation. It hardly happens today, as it commonly did in the past, that unconscious mechanisms, or let's say, libidinal cathexes, are being described as data of observation. It is particularly the presentation of analytic knowledge in the case histories that makes this differentiation so important. That the lawlike propositions worked out in analysis for explanatory purposes are used there, too, is natural enough; but it often happens that papers that are presented as clinical in nature are, in fact, primarily meant to prove or to illustrate an hypothesis. Or, what is basically a clinical observation is presented on the level of precocious abstraction as a theoretical paper. Observations in our clinical literature are, of course, also fruitful as validation or invalidation of analytical hypotheses. But when these hypotheses are presented as clinical findings, misunderstandings are unavoidable. It is my impression that this has happened less frequently lately.

The fact that most tenets of psychoanalysis are formulated at a considerable distance from both overt behavior and immediate experience is well known by now. Still the place of this among the characteristic features of psychoanalysis as a science is not always correctly understood. This difficulty is enhanced as a consequence of a prevailing lack of clear differentiation of the analytic hypotheses as to the degrees to which they have been confirmed. One important difference, which is rarely sufficiently and systematically emphasized, is the validity of clinical inference developed in the psychoanalytic situation versus the validity of inferences developed in applied psychoanalysis. To give another example of the same: There was a time when Freud's clearly speculative ideas, for instance, about the life and death instincts, were treated, in a way, as if they were on the same level as clinical hypotheses. This too has become not so common today, probably thanks to an increase in methodological clarity, which has been established.

About the special position among analytic hypotheses of the death instinct, as compared to the psychology of instinctual drives, which are a part of clinical experience, see Hartmann, 1939, and Lampl-de Groot, 1956, who even asks for a terminological differentiation between the two.

If we speak in analysis of the dynamic, economic, structural, adaptive—and maybe genetic—points of view, this does not indicate the preference of the analyst for highly complex conceptualizations, but a necessary consideration of the complexity of the subject matter, which every approach will have to face that seriously endeavors, as does psychoanalysis, to formulate statements on the total human personality. One may single out for specific study one point of view—structural in the case of Dr. Guttman's paper—though we know that analysis yields the full amount of what it can contribute toward an explanation of man only by considering also the other points of view and the interactions of all the categories of data to which they refer. The few spotlights on methodological problems I have just introduced are essential for the whole: but every study, even of a single aspect, has to take them into consideration.

If one considers the complexity not only of the analytical material but also of the concepts and the necessary connections with other fields, one will agree with Dr. Guttman that "a psychoanalyst, if he is to be a scientist, . . . must be . . . really committed to . . . creative scholarship in its deepest sense."

Trying to understand the structural concepts of analysis, one is confronted with the difficulty that this term is used with very different meanings. We are speaking of the structure of a science (Rapaport's best-known book has the title *Structure of Psychoanalytic Theory*); the term is, however, also used in logic, in linguistics, in related fields; we speak of economic, of social structure, and so on. According to what I said before, we have to try to denote which of the many elements contained in the various concepts of structure may find a place in the structure concept of analysis— and vice versa.

To Dr. Guttman, the concept of structure is a key concept, not only in analysis, but also in the development of many other sciences today, and he also traces it, courageously, in contemporary art. He has some interesting things to say about the role of "structure" in a great number of different disciplines, like physics or molecular biology.

A comparative study of the various meanings of "structure" in various disciplines is imperative. Also, the concept of structure, as Dr. Guttman correctly states, is to be separated from such related concepts as order, form, Gestalt, and others. This is work in progress, but to a large extent work still to be done. "The essence of structure as a concept is not on the terms or elements themselves, but is on the relationships and interrelationships"—this sentence is quoted from Dr. Guttman's paper. Elsewhere, speaking of psychoanalysis, he mentions the cohesive organizing forces and considers what Freud calls the synthetic function as "the counterpart of the whole problem of structures." Though we use the term "organizing function" (besides "synthetic function"), the relation is still not completely clear.

Of course, the concept of structure in psychoanalysis has been repeatedly studied. From recent years I mention only Gill, Arlow and Brenner, and Beres. Some of the points these authors make are discussed in Dr. Guttman's paper. Freud's tripartite structure of personality—ego, id, superego—is *part* of what he considers structure. It is a part that is comparatively easily understood. What beyond this can be called structure in analysis is not as easily decided. I have (1939) widened the concept by including in it aspects of the ego, like automatisms, and studied the relationship between flexibility and automatization. I spoke of the latter as characterized by the "relative stability," which, however, should not be misunderstood as absolute rigidity or immutable stability. A concept similar to this one, structuralization as relative stability, has then also been used by Rapaport and others.

This problem has been stated in more detail recently (by Beres). The definition I suggested is, according to Dr. Guttman's paper, consistent with what he calls "the key concept in current theory construction."

I do not want to go into the question discussed by Dr. Guttman how far a common denominator can be found between the development of the structural point of view in psychoanalysis and, e.g., certain features of modern art. Much preliminary work will have to be done before we can venture to answer this question without equivocation. Also, it would lead me too far to attempt a reasoned approach to the problem whether or not the world as a set of structural systems should be divided into two territories, "scientific knowledge and artistic vision." That such a division is widely accepted, there is no doubt. Whether it *should* exist—this is a preference judgment: we may individually accept or reject it, but our decision on this matter does not rest on psychoanalytic thinking.

That, as Dr. Guttman asserts, the use of the structural approach may bring the scientist closer to the humanist, I personally consider possible. It is a complex question and, in the context of what Dr. Guttman says at that point, I may introduce another consideration. We should not forget that in analysis all the essential concepts are rather far removed from both everyday discourse and immediate experience, and structure is no doubt one of these concepts. It is true that in analysis knowledge often tends to grow beyond human grasp (Dr. Guttman also rightly states this as a general trend in science).

Still, we try to understand and explain "wholes," the whole being in analysis, the whole personality, and this is quite naturally a subject to which Dr. Guttman turns at the end of his paper. The contrasts between analysis and those schools of psychology whose best-known representative is Gestalt psychology have often been investigated. Without going deeper into this subject here, I only want to say: while we probably all agree that psychoanalysis more than any other branch of psychology deals with the total personality, still, methodologically, it is clear that it differs widely from what one often calls a "wholistic" approach. Or, to state it differently, although we speak in analysis often of the whole personality, the concepts we use in dealing with it are not *wholistic*.

BIBLIOGRAPHY

Arlow, J. and Ch. Brenner (1964), *Psychoanalytic Concepts and the Structural Theory.* New York: Int. Univ. Press.
Beres, D. (1965), Structure and Function in Psycho-analysis. *Int. J. Psychoanal.* 46.
Gill, M. (1963), *Topography and Systems in Psychoanalytic Theory.* New York: Int. Univ. Press.
Hartmann, H. (1939), *Ego Psychology and the Problem of Adaptation.* New York: Int. Univ. Press, 1958.

——— (1958), Scientific Aspects of Psychoanalysis. *The Psychoanalytic Study of the Child*, 13.

——— (1959), Psychoanalysis as a Scientific Theory. In: *Psychoanalysis, Scientific Method and Philosophy. A Symposium. Ed. S. Hook*, New York: New York Univ. Press.

Lampl-de Groot, J. (1956), Psychoanalytische Trieblehre. *Psyche*.

Waelder, R. (1960), *Basic Theory of Psychoanalysis*. New York: Int. Univ. Press.

Two Prevalent Misconceptions about Freud's "Project" (1895)

MARK KANZER, M.D. (*New York*)

There are two prevalent misconceptions about the "Project," Freud's important first draft of a mental apparatus, which first came to light, in the
sense of its publication in English, nearly sixty years after it was first drawn
up in 1895 (Freud, 1887–1902). The one regards it as "ostensibly a neurological document" (Strachey, S.E. 1:290), the other as "disavowed by its creator" (p. 293). Since these judgments are to be found not only in the
Standard Edition of *The Origin of Psychoanalysis* but in the original English
version edited by Kris *et al.* (Freud, 1887–1902),[1] the summary by Ernest
Jones in *The Life and Work of Sigmund Freud* (1953)—actually the first
official report of the Project in English—and in the early reviews by Erikson
(1955), Bernfeld (1955), and Brierley (1967) (in her comments on the
Standard Edition), it is not to be regarded as surprising that these opinions
are now all-but-established doctrine.

In challenging such authority, the burden must rest on the challenger.
Nevertheless, the task seems by no means insuperable, since we find the
evidence is obvious: 1) Freud, as we shall demonstrate, kept right on with
the Project after he is supposed (for inaccurate reasons) to have disavowed
it; and 2) the work was quite ostensibly a "psychology," Freud's own code
name as used repeatedly in his correspondence with Fliess, which included
the Project.[2] The distinction is important in that the neurological aspects

---

Elaborated from a paper on "Reality Testing in the Design of the Mental Apparatus,"
presented before the American Psychoanalytic Association on December 21, 1968.

[1] Because of the greater detail which it offers (for example, the fuller inclusion
of relevant letters from Freud to Fliess), we shall use the Kris version as our basic
source of reference. Nevertheless, constant cognizance will be taken of the Standard
Edition, which will be invoked directly when this seems clarifying.

[2] Only once, in fact, did Freud use the phrase "Psychology for Neurologists," and
that was in his very first reference to the Project, the letter of April 27, 1895 (1887–
1902, p. 118). Thereafter it was invariably "psychology."

were placed in the foreground by the early commentators, so that the real significance of the Project as a remarkably early statement of Freud's principal metapsychological postulates has been obscured. A correction of this distortion in stress will serve the purposes of portraying more accurately the history and meaning of psychoanalytic thought.

The misconceptions led the original commentators into contradictions and labored secondary revisions in their accounts of the Project itself. We may begin with the essentially correct depiction of the background of this work as provided by Jones, who tells how Freud became obsessively preoccupied early in 1895 with a scheme to devise the model of a "mental apparatus" which would explain observations on the unconscious that were being incorporated into the *Studies on Hysteria* that he was engaged in completing with Joseph Breuer (Breuer and Freud, 1893–95). After several hints about the plan in letters to Wilhelm Fliess, his confidante and unconsciously chosen analyst, he visited his friend in Berlin and, on the way home in September, began a written draft that was sent off on October 8. Thereafter, addenda followed, but on November 29, Freud declared in a much-quoted statement: "I no longer understand the state of mind in which I hatched out the 'Psychology' . . . it seems to me pure balderdash" (Jones, 1953, p. 383).

Our differences with Jones (and other commentators) begin at this point. Jones takes the statement at face value and sees in it a return to a normal state of mind after a temporary aberration: "We may regard the feverish writing of the 'Project' as a last desperate attempt to cling to the safety of cerebral anatomy" (p. 384), when confronted with the vast unknown of the unconscious. After November 29, however, the obsession was "all over," the futility of the regression to neuroanatomy and the associated influence of the Helmholtz school (with which Freud had long been associated) became apparent and the result salutary. Freud would have no choice thereafter but to develop the more autonomous line of thought that resulted some years later in Chapter VII of *The Interpretation of Dreams*, the usual point of departure for analytic theoreticians before the discovery of the Project.

Jones further strengthens the case for the repudiation thesis with the remark that "Freud never asked for the return of that interesting manuscript which had cost him so much trouble, nor apparently did he ever want to see it again. He had been relieved of an oppressive burden, and his attitude towards what he had given birth to rapidly changed (p. 381). The reader is further prepared for an attitude of repudiation on his own part when at last he is invited to examine for himself "what claims this curious document has on our interest" (p. 383). While Jones does point out that "nowhere in Freud's published writings do we find such a brilliant example of his capacity for abstruse thought and sustained close reasoning," this is made the occasion for an explanation that the work is atypical, lacking in a clinical foundation, and an exercise in deductive reasoning such as "one would have expected from a philosopher rather than a pathologist" (p. 384). The philosophic aspect apparently relates to the Helmholtz doctrines which regarded psychology as a purely natural science, and Freud is described by Jones as inspired by the attempts of his friend Exner the previous year to elaborate a psychological scheme on a neurophysiological basis. (Actually, Freud had been endeavoring, at least since his work on aphasia in 1891, to evolve a brain-mind model which differed sharply from prevalent notions among the Helmholtz group, including Exner.)

"After such a long preamble," Jones continues (the preamble covered some six of a total of fourteen pages devoted to the work), he finally offers an outline of the contents. In so doing, his stress on the neurophysiological aspects is epitomized by quoting approvingly the opinion of Strachey that the Project represents "a highly complicated and extraordinarily ingenious working model of the mind as a piece of neurological machinery" (pp. 386–387). In this view, Jones declares that the key concept "quantity," as a basic force in these operations, may be nearly equated with the physiological expression "sum of excitation" or with physical energy. Thus, "Freud distinguished between two sources of Quantity: that derived from the outer world and that from within the body" (p. 385). Jones then proceeds to treat the mental apparatus as the "neurological machine" which necessarily had to break down and be abandoned as Freud undertook to make it assume the complicated functions required by the clinical problems of depth psychology which absorbed him.

Here we must interrupt Jones's thesis to note the isolation, abbreviation, and casualness with which a most important datum is presented: the concept of "quantity" (later more frequently appearing in Freud's writings as "energy") and its basic formulation into a "principle of neuronic inertia," Jones tells us, "was born in his clinical observations of the psychoneuroses, from the notions of intensive ideas, of stimulation, substitution, discharge, and so on, and [that] he felt it legitimate to transfer it to the field of neuronic activity (which in its turn was to explain the working of mental processes)" (p. 386).

Since the origin of Freud's neurological propositions from his clinical observations seems so much more clearly and importantly expounded in the Project itself, and since the matter is so crucial in relation to whether we are being presented with a "neurological document," philosophically oriented, or a set of neurologically clad psychological propositions drawn from clinical observation and inductively developed, we should turn at this point to Freud's actual statements:

This [quantitative] line of approach is derived directly from pathological clinical observations, especially from those concerned with "excessively intense ideas." (These occur in hysteria and obsessional neurosis, where, as we shall see, the quantitative characteristic emerges more plainly than in the normal). Processes such as stimulus, substitution, conversion and discharge, which had to be described in connection with these disorders, directly suggested the notion of viewing neuronic excitation as quantities in a condition of flow [Freud, 1887–1902, p. 356].

Kris surmises, probably correctly, at this point, that Freud was proceeding beyond the language of contemporary psychology, to which Breuer wished to restrict him in accounting for the behavior of patients included in their *Studies on Hysteria*. However, like Jones, Kris does not draw the seemingly obvious conclusion: that Freud's "neurones" and the processes among them were hypothesized not from actual observations in neurology (though what little was known about neuroanatomy and neurophysiology at the time was certainly used) but from clinical data, and they were used to explain clinical data, not to explain neurological data. Freud's "neurones" are in fact inventions: they are "psychical processes" which are to be *represented* "as quantitatively determined states of specifiable material particles" and are "to be assumed" to be neurones (p. 355).

In his inductive plan to generalize his clinical observations on hysterical and obsessive ideas (which are henceforth equated with neurones that form associations, are cathected with energy, and bind or discharge it), Freud now promulgates a "principle of neuronic inertia": [cathected] neurones tend to divest themselves of quantity" (p. 356). This, in neurological language, is close to the "principle of constancy" which he had devised with Breuer in somewhat more psychological language and which was to remain in the latter form a fundamental postulate of all subsequent mental apparatuses. Actually, the principle of neuronic inertia is closer to the Nirvana principle of later years, and is recognizable in the concept of the death drive. (Jones himself inaccurately equates the concept of "neuronic inertia" with the more limited pleasure-unpleasure principles (1953, p. 386) which likewise began their careers in neurological raiment but evolved with little change of meaning into a psychological hypothesis. So, too, did the physical aspects of energy.)

From "neuronic inertia" (as from the constancy principle in later apparatuses) Freud proceeds to derive a reflex structure of the mind and differentiates two forms of energy, the primary and the secondary processes. These latter, as he repeatedly emphasized, constituted thereafter unshakeable theorems in psychoanalysis. To suggest that they were borrowed from any extant neurological teachings would be incorrect, and Freud pointed out their pragmatic origins forty years later with the statement that, "Behind all these uncertainties [with respect to the analytic concepts of energy] there lies one new fact, whose discovery we owe to *psychoanalytic research*. We have found that processes in the unconscious or in the id obey different laws from those in the pre-conscious ego. We name these laws in their totality the primary process, in contrast to the secondary process which governs the course of events in the preconscious, in the ego. In the end, therefore, the study of psychical qualities has after all proved not unfruitful" (Freud, 1940, p. 164; italics mine).

Thus again the independent and clinical approach of Freud to the "neurophysiology" and "philosophy" of the Project is confirmed, and Jones's account must suffer accordingly. A careful comparison of the apparatus of 1895 with Chapter VII of *The Interpretation of Dreams* will show how little is changed even in nomenclature. In the former, Freud proceeds to make basic postulates about "specifiable material particles" which are "assumed to be neurones" (1887–1902, p. 355). These are then divided into phi (perceptual) and psi (memory) systems (p. 360), culminating in a discharge apparatus. In Chapter VII, the reflex is still the model of every mental activity, and the "elements" are now constituents of "psi systems" of a hypothetical "photographic apparatus" (p. 536). The one is no more an exercise in neurology than the other is an exercise in photography. Both conform to the dictum that "we are justified, in my view, in giving free rein to our speculations so long as we retain the coolness of our judgment and do not mistake the scaffolding for the building" (p. 536). This, we contend, is what the early commentators did with respect to the Project.

Twenty years after the Project, Freud, in "The Unconscious," was still deriving economic aspects of the primary and secondary processes from clinical observations, tracing their "energic" courses among "elements" in topographic systems (1915, p. 186), cathecting "ideas" rather than neurones and declaring that in this way we attain "the deepest insight we have gained up to the present into the nature of *nervous energy* (pp. 186–188; italics mine). Another two decades and this outline has scarcely changed (1940). The "elements," still extended in space, have been arranged in structural systems (p. 198). Energy from the body fills the ego organization and is bound or dicharged in somatic innervations. Freud defends his scientific right to remain indefinite as to the nature of the instincts or of energy (p. 159) but still insists that his postulates about the mental apparatus have been pragmatically derived "by studying the individual development of human beings" (p. 145)—i.e., clinical observation.

Strachey, who in his introduction to "The Unconscious" refers to the Project as an "astonishing production" (S.E. 14:163), in turn makes the astonishing statement that its aim was to exclude any need to postulate "unconscious mental processes" and to achieve a "chain of physical events unbroken and complete" (p. 163). In a similar vein, he discounted elsewhere the really astonishing discovery of structural aspects in the Project with the explanation that "the Project is pre-id" and "there were bound to be similarities between a pre-id and a post-id picture of psychological processes" (S.E. 1:292). How, economically, the differentiation of the primary process or of the detailed operations of dream and symptom formation, as recounted in the Project, can be considered as "pre-id" and designed to eliminate the unconscious, seems unfathomable. On October 20, 1895, Freud, reporting the latest triumphs with his "psychology," declared that it made it "possible to see from the details of neurosis all the way to the very conditioning of consciousness" (1887–1902, p. 129).

For it was during his "obsession" with that work, and certainly in close connection with this creative turmoil, that Freud achieved his own, self-proclaimed, greatest moment of insight, the discovery of wish-fulfillment as the guiding force of the dream (July 24, 1895). This is introduced effectively, even dramatically, at the end of Part 1 of the Project and is followed up in Part 2 by the analysis of a hysterical symptom which shows the same basic mechanisms, discusses repression and the unconscious, and requires almost no trace of neurological machinery to describe them.

Though Jones and even Kris take the position that the discussion of dreams in the Project is so primitive that it is hardly worthy of their attention (Jones gives it two lines in the presentation of the Project itself, one of which refers to a brief and unenlightening reference elsewhere [1953, pp. 354, 390], while Kris considers this "first attempt at a theory of dreams . . . fragmentary in so many essential portions that it scarcely seems worthwhile to compare it in detail with *The Interpretation of Dreams* [Freud, 1887–1902, p. 400 n]), it is Strachey, surprisingly enough, who gives it due homage (apparently at an earlier period when he had not yet come under the influence of other viewpoints) (S.E. 1:293).[3]

In his introduction to the dream book, Strachey lists as the Project's early contributions: 1) wish-fulfillment; 2) the hallucinatory character of dreams; 3) regression; 4) motor paralysis during sleep; 5) the mechanism of displacement; 6) the similarity between dreams and symptoms; 7) the primary and secondary processes. Enthusiastically, he continues: "It is no exaggeration to say that much of the seventh chapter of 'The Interpretation of Dreams,' and indeed, of Freud's later 'metapsychological' studies, has only become fully intelligible since the publication of the 'Project'" (S.E. 4:xv). At this time, Strachey does not take too literally the "neurological machinery": While

> . . . the neurophysiological basis was ostensibly dropped, nevertheless—and that is why the "Project" is of importance to readers of "The Interpretation of Dreams"—much of the general pattern of the earlier scheme, and many of its elements were carried into the new one. The systems of neurones were replaced by "psychical' systems or agencies; a hypothetical 'cathexis' of psychical energy took the place of the physical 'quantity'; the principle of inertia became the basis of the pleasure (and unpleasure) principles" [p. xviii].

Strachey, quoting from Freud, comes to the conclusion that the latter was largely justified in a statement that the dream book "was finished in all its essentials at the beginning of 1896"—i.e., with the completion of the Project and a supplementary draft sent Fliess on January 1, 1896.

In Jones, the ego's role as an "organization of neurones" receives attention almost exclusively from a neurophysiological standpoint, largely isolated,

---

[3] Marjorie Brierley, reviewing the Standard Edition version of the Project, gave her readers the impression that "Freud himself thought so little of it and it is written in purely neurological terms" (1967; p. 325). Suzanne Bernfeld (1955) simply echoes Jones (1955).

except for defense, from functions of memory and thought occurring "between the various neuronic systems" (1953, p. 390). "Criteria of reality" noted by the ego are treated neurophysiologically without referring to their relationship to psychological concepts of reality testing and the reality principle, as Strachey and Kris do. How differently the same account can be envisioned we learn from the review of Heinz Hartmann (1956), who recognizes the obvious fact that the ego of the Project "in the language of physiology is a group of neurones and, where it is psychologically characterized, a group of ideas." The concept that is expressed there—the ego is an organization with constant cathexis, a pillar of subsequent structural psychology—applies in both senses. Hartmann goes on to say further that, "The idea of an ego characterized by its functions" (another pillar of structural psychology) "is presented here with the greatest definiteness." He includes reality testing and attention among these functions. Far from seeing in this work a mere exercise in neurophysiological mechanics with which Freud retreated from the wave of the future, Hartmann observes that "the three approaches to psychology which he was later to call the topographic, the dynamic and the economic" were already present, and he sums it up with the tribute that "The imaginativeness and, at the same time, the strictness of the hypotheses presented in this work is extraordinary indeed" (p. 427).

Later viewpoints that would distinguish genetic and adaptive viewpoints find expression in an early envisionment of the mother-child unity, which draws from Kris the comment that "in none of Freud's later formulations" was "the part played by object-relations in the transition from the pleasure to the reality principle . . . equalled or surpassed" (Freud, 1887–1902, p. 379 n). Strachey points out that the parallel drawn in this work between the forces at work in repression and in resistance was the "cornerstone of psychoanalysis" (S.E. 1:351), and we also find present among many other concepts of permanent value unmistakable delineations of hypercathexis, thought as experimental action and the signal theory of affects. Where Strachey concedes that "the Project, or rather its invisible ghost, haunts the whole series of Freud's theoretical writings to the very end" (p. 290), we would prefer the emendation that it continued to provide their blood and sinews.

It is rather obvious that such a work, containing the fundamentals of Freud's clinical and theoretical outlook, could not have been "repudiated," nor could its essence have been neurological. Erik H. Erikson (1955) has compared the correspondence with Fliess to the log of the voyage of Columbus to America, a justified analogy, especially when taken in the sense of the opening of a new world rather than a misguided attempt to reach India. The latter slant must create contradictions and embarrassment for a historian. Thus, the ghost of the Project appears to have pursued Ernest Jones (1953), for having declared on page 383 that the "curious document" was "all over" on November 29, 1895, he had to report "another curious feature of the story" on page 393: "We have told earlier how Freud soon cast aside this remarkable production as a thing of no value, of which he was almost ashamed." Nevertheless, "his revulsion in attitude, from elation to depreciation, did not proceed, as one might have supposed, from insight into the inherent incompatibility of the double task he had attempted to perform"—i.e., the construction of a common framework for neurology and psychology. "On the contrary, he continued for more than a year longer to bring emendations to his theory in the same terms of brain anatomy and physiology. It was not that he had appreciated the impossibility of the task, merely that he was dissatisfied with his endeavor to carry it out."

Freud's failure to share his own assessment puzzles Jones, and he admits that "one cannot, however, be quite sure on this point." He considers that the fault must be in the man himself. "As we saw earlier in connection with his seduction theory, Freud had a way of rather obstinately persisting with an idea even when he was uneasily half aware of being on the wrong track. To have to retrace one's steps is never pleasant" (p. 393). Perhaps Jones himself was struggling with a similar problem. The story, bracketed between two "undoing mechanisms" that accentuated its curious features, might have been more simply and positively told as an ongoing line of development attended by many doubts, including an emotional repudiation on November 29 (Jones himself tells of another in August), and one that was certainly being pursued productively in December, 1896, more than a year later. There was also a transparent motive, which we shall discuss later, for the aberrant state of mind of November 29.

It would indeed be difficult to say when Freud discarded the neurological framework. Little is heard of the mental apparatus after the end of 1896, when Freud became preoccupied with self-analysis and evolved the libido theory. The death of his father on October 23, 1896, certainly had a decisive influence on his life. Perhaps a letter to Fliess on September 22, 1898 (Freud, 1887–1902, p. 264), recounts as well as any other the slow withering away of interest in the neurological aspects of the "psychology," now called "metapsychology." He speaks apologetically, rather than with shame or repudiation, as he recounts that he had "no desire at all to leave the psychology hanging in the air with no organic basis. But, beyond a feeling of conviction [that there must be such a basis], I have nothing, either theoretical or therapeutic, to work on, and so I must behave as if I were confronted by psychological factors only. I have no idea yet why I cannot yet fit it together"—i.e., the psychological and the organic.

We find an echo of this viewpoint in Chapter VII, when Freud informs the reader that "I shall carefully avoid the temptation to determine psychical locality in any anatomical fashion. I shall remain upon psychological ground" (1900, p. 536). He still did not appreciate the notion that the task was impossible; he was merely dissatisfied with his endeavor to carry it out, for we find him succumbing momentarily to temptation and hopeful of future success as he interjects a few paragraphs further on that "a most promising light would be thrown on the conditions governing the excitation of neurones if it could be confirmed that *in the* [psychological] *psi systems memory and the quality that characterizes consciousness are mutually exclusive*" (p. 540; italics Freud's).

Erikson (1955, p. 7), in his commentaries on the Project, acknowledges that the work is "forbidden reading for all but a few" (see also Kris's Introduction, Freud, 1887–1902, p. 27), and thanks Jones for having "humanely offered a pre-publication memorandum" in return for which he accepts the thesis that the scheme was "recanted" on November 29. However, while he also accepts the view that it was a "neuronic golem" with "astonishing reasoning" which had the virtue of teaching Freud the futility of such "creative misconceptions," he also makes the crucial point that the neurones already "seem to do" what ultimately the more psychological apparatus accomplishes, suggesting (perhaps in some contradiction to the neurology-as-wild-oats theme) that without the neurological foundation, Chapter VII would not have been achieved; (see also Strachey, S.E. 4:xviii). (In view of the Hamlet-like aspects of Freud's mental state during the writing of the Project, as well as that of the reviewers, it might not be amiss to quote the obsessive Dane himself: "Seems, madam! nay, it is; I know not seems"). Nor is Erikson perturbed, after accepting the view that the Project had been "recanted," by the fact that a draft of May 30, 1896, though "still ascribed to different neuronic systems," already charts "the epigenetic character of human development, the erotogenic zones and the stages of libido" (1955, p. 9).

To the difficulties in understanding the Project which arose from its designation for a private audience of one, its terse phraseology, unfamiliar language, abbreviations, and baffling anticipation of ideas seemingly belonging to a future epoch (and which therefore tempted references to "nuclei" and "forerunners" of later formulations), Erikson adds another of great interest. Freud, it is well known, was chagrined at the reappearance of a correspondence long presumed destroyed, as promised, and opposed its publication. Though Jones applies this attitude to the Project, which Freud supposedly never wanted to see again and whose return he never demanded, there is every reason to suppose that Freud's distress was due to the personal side of the correspondence with Fliess, details of which may well be compared with the publication of an analytic session. (No reason can well be adduced for requesting the return of the Project, since it represented only a portion of Freud's ideas and was reformulated with each passing week). Though Freud's most intimate followers, while wishing to spare him pain yet carry out their obligations to science, delayed the publication of the correspondence more than two decades after the death of Fliess and more than one after Freud's (partly, however, for external reasons), Erikson surmises an aftereffect in "an attempt to limit the readership and to determine the use of the volume by suggesting that the material thus released 'contained nothing sensational' " (p. 11).

Perhaps the most scientific and unbiased approach to the Project and its meaning might be achieved by placing it in a longitudinal line of development among Freud's ideas and discarding the notion that it was a fit of fever, an aberration that others, as well as he himself, could not understand. The monograph *On Aphasia* in 1891 will be chosen as a logical starting point, for it was indeed among the last of Freud's truly neurological endeavors, yet already reflected growing insight into mental processes as derived from his experiments in cathartic therapy with Josef Breuer, to whom the work is dedicated. Siegfried Bernfeld rightly calls it the "first 'Freudian' book . . . with all the precious simplicity of style, lucidity of presentation, and tantalizing hiding of ideas, as if the reader were as passionate a detective as the writer" (1944, p. 357).

In this essay, Freud rejected the crude localizations of psychic function favored by the leading advocates of the Helmholtz school, including his former teacher Meynert. Drawing instead on the dynamic and evolutionary approach of Hughlings Jackson to both neurological and linguistic functions, he devised for an explanation of their interrelationships a unique "speech apparatus" which Stengel has called the "elder brother" of the mental apparatuses that were to come (1891, p. xiii). By means of this device, he wrested language functions from any crude relationship to brain processes and paradigmatically investigated slips of the tongue as an example of a speech disorder which could be multidetermined by organic factors, fatigue, or psychic causes. He even used empathy and self-analysis as investigative tools (offering an interesting vignette which does not seem to have received further mention in the literature), so that his patients emerge as human beings in sharp contrast to the "neurological machines" that they seem to have represented to other investigators on this subject.

As a result, he already felt "isolated" among his Viennese colleagues (Stengel, 1953, p. 17)—neither for the first nor for the last time—but was not too unhappy about this state of affairs, reporting with satisfaction to a friend that he had "crossed swords" with the luminaries of the neurological world and had been "fresh" enough to "scratch even the high-throned idol Meynert (Jones, 1953, p. 213). (The role of aphasia in marking a switch of allegiances, personally and ideationally, from Meynert to Breuer finds an echo in the Project which signifies a similar switch from Breuer to Fliess, with the dream book perhaps a termination of the latter transference.)

Jones points out that the paper on aphasia "was a stage in Freud's emancipation from the more mechanical aspects of the Helmholtz school in which he had been brought up" (p. 215). (We must construe otherwise than does Kris references by Freud to the organic substratum of mental functions, which the former interprets as still pursuing a strictly localizing approach (Freud, 1887–1902, pp. 359–360, 366). To indicate Freud's actual views on this subject (which to be sure do not always emerge clearly in his often fragmentary statements), we may cite a remark in later years that were there in fact localizing correlations, "[they] would at the most afford an exact localization of the processes of consciousness and would give us no help towards understanding them" (1940, pp. 144–145). We do not agree with Kris that a rejection of crude localizing theories by Freud in 1915 was inspired by the lack of success with the Project, where brain-mind functioning was rendered quite in accord with the principles enunciated in *On Aphasia*.

Another characteristic of Freud's presentations, as revealed in the work on *Aphasia*, might have given pause to anyone about to proceed with the assumption that he was regressing to the "safe" neurology of predecessors whom he did not hesitate to repudiate. Though he used neurological language in the 1891 study, Stengel brings out the fact that he was already lending the words a twist which alienated them from the prevailing contexts and fitted them into his own, beginning in this way a transmutation that would carry them increasing distances over the years. Thus projection, representation, associative pathways, retrogression, and cathexis were already well-advanced neuroanatomical and physiological concepts, which in the 1891 work were being equipped with more dynamic meanings so as to serve as scaffolds for the evolving Freudian structure.

There is also a self-description of the pragmatic meaning of the work on *Aphasia* that we might well heed in preparing ourselves not only for the Project but for fourteen officially labeled drafts that he was to send Fliess over the years (as well as many discussions worthy of such a label). "It is with a clear exposition of the problems that the elucidation of a scientific work begins" (1891, p. 104). The first draft, A, was sent to Fliess at the end of 1892 to apprise his friend of the current status of his work and, although a tantalizingly brief outline, represented a formal scientific memorandum. It continues to deal with the body-mind problem, but in relation now to the progress of Freud's clinical studies on hysteria. There are specific headings: Problems; Theses; Categories for Observation; Etiological Factors. Under the first, one already finds such a basic question (a point of departure for structural concepts more than three decades later) as whether anxiety arises "from the inhibition of the sexual functions or from the anxiety connected with their aetiology (1887–1902, p. 64), and, under "Aetiological Factors," one sees a beginning glimpse of infantile sexuality in a brief item on "sexual traumas dating back to before the age of understanding" (p. 66).

The succession of drafts constitutes a laboratory record from which the Project may be seen as emerging. Draft D in May, 1894, already involves such concepts as the principle of constancy, internal and external stimuli, and the "storing up of excitations" (binding) which will enter into the Studies on Hysteria, the Project, and beyond. As 1895 approaches, Draft G depicts a "sexual apparatus by means of which impulses from the testicles" (a forerunner of the erogenous-zone concept) proceed to successive borders between the body and the mind, culminating at last in a penetration of the ego boundaries and the attainment of consciousness. (It is not difficult to see in this delineation an outline of later descriptions of the course of the libido from the body to the id and, through a succession of censorships, to consciousness and motility—i.e., specific action.)

Freud further postulates in sketchy fashion in Draft G groups of "sexual ideas" which are apparently hierarchically extended from neurones to consciousness, forerunners of the later "complex," so that lesions at different levels will be manifested by different forms of neurosis. The pleasure and unpleasure principles find beginnings in the postulation of degrees of "voluptuous feeling" that are quite concretely related to the quantity of discharge of sexual substances. Draft H, which follows soon afterwards (January 24, 1895), approaches the neuroses from a more psychological and ego-functional standpoint and considers reality-testing in relation to projection and other defense mechanisms, leading Kris to comment that such "detailed discussion of projection and its employment in normal and abnormal psychical processes is only to be found in Freud's later works. . . . The emphasis on the concept of defence in this paper and the comparison of the effectiveness as defense mechanisms of the symptoms exhibited in different cases anticipates a good deal of what was to be stated thirty years later in *Inhibitions, Symptoms and Anxiety* (Freud, 1887–1902, p. 109 n).

The first clear-cut reference to the Project occurs on April 27 and indicates that the work has been under way for some time (perhaps since the beginning of the year, but more directly as a continuation of the final chapter in *Studies on Hysteria*, written in March, from which Freud was compelled, through differences with Breuer, to render some of his ideas only abortively). From the beginning, the references to the new psychology show Freud enthralled, perhaps as never before or later, by a need to achieve through thought and writing the realization of some inner vision. He spoke of being driven by a "tyrant," of the work as an "incubus" or a "superhuman task"—or, in more compliant moments, he described himself as heeding a "still small voice" from within. Apparently the opening up of vistas offered by insight into the unconscious had begun to penetrate in its potential meaning to his own inner self. Boundaries between the inner and outer worlds were being effaced and reformed in the first stages of an analytic process that was not yet under ego control (Kanzer, 1961).

The Project itself is remarkably free of the inner turmoil that attended its creation. Metaphors, such as we have mentioned, indicate another layer to the process and add dimension to our understanding of the "repudiation" that will follow. Thus, on June 12, he informs Fliess that he is not yet ready to send an outline of the "psychology" which he now mentions in every communication: "Saying anything now would be like sending a six-months female embryo to a ball" (p. 121). We may use the six-months estimate as possibly significant of the actual age of the Project (using Drafts G and H for orientation and also noting a disposition we ourselves have found in Freud to react to a new year with special empathy (Kanzer, 1969); Kris also surmises that the work began early in 1895 (1954, p. 25).

Why a female embryo? We cannot assume prophetic powers, but it was a fact that both Mrs. Freud and Mrs. Fliess were to give birth before the year was over, and these circumstances may well have been known already to the physician-fathers. It is in the letter of June 12 that Freud refers to himself as bearing a "superhuman burden"; (could Jones, in his suggestion that Freud, after writing the Project, "had been relieved of an oppressive burden, and that his attitude toward what he had given birth to rapidly changed" [1953, p. 381], unconsciously have been making connections that do not appear in his conscious account?).

On July 24, Freud had the famous Irma dream in which a diagnosis is being made on a sick woman by himself and other physicians. One of the details refers to the pregnancies of his wife and raises questions as to the responsibility for her conception. There also seems to be possible birth imagery in a report during August of difficulties with the Project which (as on other occasions) was impelling Freud toward doubt and repudiation: "I have surmounted the first foothills, but had no breath left for further toil." He was impelled at this time to depart for Venice with his younger brother Alexander, an event which we have related elsewhere to his well-known travel phobia, to the ritual significance of his annual southern travels as September—the ninth month—approached, and the particular reactions to the birth of younger siblings which his beginning analysis would be impelling him to work through (Kanzer, 1969). The manuscript of the Project was begun in September, written "in one breath" (Freud, 1887–1902, p. 125), and delivered to Fliess in October. In that month, he also revealed the intention of naming the child William, after his friend, if it was a boy (p. 130). By November 8, he was in a rebellious mood toward his "tyrant" and reported having "bundled the psychological drafts into a drawer, where they must slumber until 1896." It is difficult to escape the impression of a pregnancy-equivalent conveyed by these metaphors correlating the Project with the expected infant. The same letter ends with the causal remark, among some other items, that "Martha is already suffering pretty badly. I wish it were over" (p. 134).

There follows on November 29 the famous "repudiation of the Project," and on December 3 the happy news that the infant ("complete," though a female) had finally arrived. The very next letter on December 12 already begins to show a revived interest in the Project, and by January 1 (with the symbolic birth of the New Year) the work that was destined to slumber until 1896 appears with an important addition. It seems less than analytic to leave Freud's obviously emotionally charged "repudiation" of the Project on November 29 unadorned by other inferences except that his neurological guidelines had proved to be a failure.

The continued elaboration of the Project on January 1 revealed, according to Kris, a "conception of hallucinations" which "hinted at here is repeated in

[*The Interpretation of Dreams*] practically unaltered" (Freud, 1887–1902, p. 143 n). It is difficult to understand how a "hint," on practically unaltered repetition, becomes a full-fledged statement. On January 1 Freud was explicitly calling it a "new hypothesis" (p. 143) and quite correctly appraising its importance for the concept of mental functioning. Neither can we accept a suggestion put forward by Kris that "immediately after Freud had written the 'Project,' his interests were diverted to other problems. With his return to clinical work during the autumn, the theory of the neuroses moved into the foreground of his thoughts, and his principal discovery of the autumn of 1895 related to the distinction between the genetic factors in obsessional neurosis and hysteria" (p. 351).

Kris refers to "Letter 34" (p. 132) to substantiate the above contention, which seems to contrast so sharply with Freud's undiluted preoccupation with the Project through most of the autumn. Letter 34 remarks that Freud's clinical observations have "strengthened my confidence in the correctness of my psychological assumptions" (November 2). More likely Kris refers to the discussion of the origin of neuroses on October 16 (Letter 31) which expresses satisfaction that they will be explained "by the formula of infantile sexual shock and sexual pleasure" (p. 128). Here, remarkably, he adds that such discoveries afford him only a "flat satisfaction," since "real satisfaction" is associated with filling "the psychological gaps in the new knowledge" which "demand the whole of my interest" (p. 128). It is in any event part of a misapprehension to see the clinical and the theoretical aspects of Freud's work as dissociated: the drafts we have cited show over the years the constant oscillation from one to the other as new observations and inductive theory-making absorbed Freud's energies and drove him with irresistible force toward the charting of the unknown. At the end of the epochal dream book, he sees the new findings as merely a path leading to a greater understanding "of the normal structure of our mental instrument" (1900, p. 607).

Strachey also misses the essentials of the apparatus and its significance in the line of Freud's development when he dissociates the Project from its successors with the appraisal: "In the first place, it will be immediately obvious that there is very little indeed in these pages to anticipate the technical procedures of psychoanalysis. Free association, the interpretation of unconscious material, the transference—these are barely hinted at." He finds an "uncomfortable divorce between the clinical and theoretical significance of sexuality," since this instinct plays a large part in the clinical but not in the theoretical sections. The discrepancy "was only to be resolved a year or two later by Freud's self-analysis, which led to his recognition of infantile sexuality and to the basic importance of unconscious sexual impulses" (S.E. 1:291).

Had Strachey considered Freud's other mental apparatuses, he might not have singled out the Project's for such comments. Neither Chapter VII, nor the metapsychology papers, nor *The Ego and the Id* discuss technical procedures or clinical findings to any greater extent than the Project, for they are *metapsychological* conclusions drawn from the technical procedures and clinical findings. The preface to *An Outline of Psychoanalysis* states the guiding principles unmistakably: "The aim of this brief work is to bring together the tenets of psychoanalysis and to state them, as it were, dogmatically—in the most concise form and in the most unequivocal terms" (Jones's abstruse, deductive, and philosophic form of presentation). "Its intention is naturally not to compel belief or to arouse conviction. The teachings of psychoanalysis are based on an incalculable number of observations and experiences, and only someone who has repeated those observations on himself and on others is in a position to arrive at a judgment of his own upon it" (1940, p. 144). We have already seen, in Draft G, that Freud placed sexual impulses in a basic motivating position and that he did not require self-analysis to recognize infantile sexuality which, already on the horizon in Draft A at the end of 1892, was clearly enunciated (as we have pointed out) in Letter 29 on October 8, 1895—the very same letter that accompanied the sketch of the Project to Fliess in Berlin (1887–1902, pp. 125–126).

Strachey's reservations will call for more serious consideration if the question is raised as to whether Freud's early techniques and clinical knowledge made it possible to see in the Project conceptions that could serve to elaborate an analytical metapsychology. Here we do find ourselves in agreement with Jones when he states that the chapter on psychotherapy in the *Studies on Hysteria*, linked with the start of the Project, presented "a sufficient approximation to the future free association for it to be generally regarded as the inception of the psychoanalytic method" (1953, p. 244). Gedo and co-workers (1964) report, from a methodological scrutiny of the *Studies* that "even a partial list" of the ideas it embodies "is like a drum-roll of our most essential psychoanalytic tools" (p. 747). Moreover, "our tracing of the logical network within the book has shown the impressive tightness of Freud's inductive thinking, and his restraint in refusing to outdistance his evidence." This verdict may be compared with Hartmann's impression, which is worth quoting again, that in the Project, "the imaginativeness, and at the same time, the strictness of the hypotheses presented in this work is extraordinary indeed" (1956, p. 427). It cannot but serve the interests of analytic understanding to place this work of genius in its correct position as a fountain of Freudian thought which, in the words of Ernest Jones, "provides the student with a wealth of material for research" (1953, p. 383).

Summary

1. In 1895, Freud wrote—partly in neurological terms—an outline of a mental apparatus, known as "the Project." Inasmuch as it was a sketch to provide

the basis of a dialogue with his friend Wilhelm Fliess, with whom he corresponded, it was never included in his published works and did not come
to light until 1928 or reach the general public until 1950.

2. Two general misconceptions have attached themselves to this work
and are found predominant among the early commentators. These see the
Project as a "neurological document" and as "repudiated by Freud himself."
The origin of these erroneous opinions is traced in the present review,
and a picture of the apparatus as in fact a remarkably early and permanent
presentation of the basic postulates of psychoanalysis is left in their place.

3. Elucidation of an emotional turmoil which accompanied Freud's creative efforts during the writing of the Project assists in understanding his
ambivalence and the temporary repudiation that has disturbed the correct
perspective in which this first Freudian "mental apparatus" should be placed.

BIBLIOGRAPHY

Amacher, P. (1965), Freud's Neurological Education. *Psychological Issues*, [No.] 4.
New York: International Universities Press.
Bernfeld, S. (1944), Freud's Earliest Theories and the School of Helmholtz. *Psychoanal.
Quart.*, 13:341-362.
Bernfeld, S. C. (1955), Sigmund Freud: The Origins of Psychoanalysis; a Book Review.
Psychoanal. Quart., 24:384-391.
Breuer, J. and Freud, S. (1893-95), Studies on Hysteria. *Standard Edition* 2. London:
Hogarth, 1955.
Brierley, M. (1967), Book Review. *Internat. J. Psycho-Anal.*, 48:323.
Erikson, E. H. (1955), Freud's "The Origins of Psychoanalysis." *Internat. J. Psycho-
Anal.*, 36:1-15.
Freud, S. (1954), *The Origins of Psychoanalysis, 1887-1902*. New York: Basic Books.
—— (1891). *On Aphasia*. New York: International Universities Press, 1953.
—— (1900). The Interpretation of Dreams. *Standard Edition* 4-5. London: Hogarth,
1953.
—— (1915). The Unconscious. *Standard Edition* 14, 159-216. London: Hogarth,
1957.
—— (1923). The Ego and the Id. *Standard Edition* 19, 3-68. London: Hogarth, 1961.
—— (1926). Inhibitions, Symptoms and Anxiety. *Standard Edition* 20, 77-178. London:
Hogarth, 1959.
—— (1940). An Outline of Psychoanalysis. *Standard Edition* 23, 141-208, London:
Hogarth, 1964.
Gedo, J., Sabshin, M., Sadow, L. and Schlessinger, N. (1964), "Studies on Hysteria":
A Methodological Evaluation. *J. Am. Psychoanal. Assn.*, 12:734-751.
Hartmann, H. (1956), The Development of the Ego Concept in Freud's Work. *Internat.
J. Psycho-Anal.*, 37:425-438.
Jones, E. (1953), *The Life and Works of Sigmund Freud*. Vol. 1. New York: Basic
Books, 1953.
Kanzer, M. (1961), Freud and the Demon. *J. Hillside Hosp.*, 10:190-202.
—— (1969). Sigmund and Alexander Freud on the Acropolis. *Amer. Imago*,
26:324-354.
Kris, E. (1954), In: Freud, S., *The Origins of Psychoanalysis*. New York: Basic Books.
Stengel, E. (1953), In: Freud, S., *On Aphasia* (1891). New York: Basic Books.
Strachey, J. (1953-1964), In: Freud, S., *Standard Edition* 1, 4, 14, 23.

Comments on Some Instinctual Manifestations of Superego Formation

HANS W. LOEWALD, M.D. (*New Haven*)

In the following pages certain clinical observations during the termination phase of analysis are taken as the starting point for discussing some of the vicissitudes of superego formation. The termination phase, with its specific problems of separation from and relinquishment of a love object, can give insight into such vicissitudes inasmuch as the resolution of the transference neurosis and the resolution of the Oedipal conflict are intimately related to each other. Broadly speaking, the paper is concerned with the relations between instinctual drives and psychic structure. In this respect I hope to make a contribution to the much-needed rapprochement between what are loosely called "id analysis" and "ego analysis," or "id psychology" and "ego psychology." I explore certain instinctual manifestations, appearing in a group of patients during the termination phase of analysis, in their significance as drive representations[1] of superego formation. The emergence in male patients of passive-homosexual fantasies in regard to their male analyst during the termination phase will be discussed from the point of view of the resolution of the Oedipus complex. The appearance of such

Versions of this paper were presented in 1961 and 1962 at meetings of the Division of Psychoanalytic Education, Downstate Medical Center, State University of New York, of the Chicago and Philadelphia Psychoanalytic Societies, and of the Western New England Psychoanalytic Society. The revision for publication owes much to the discussions following these presentations. I am particularly endebted to the late Maxwell Gitelson and to Charles Kligerman and Theodore Lidz for their extensive and enlightening discussions.

[1] The term "representation," is used here in its broad sense and not in its narrower meaning of "idea" or "ideational representation" (the German *Vorstellung*). The noun "representation" here refers to what Freud has called a "representative" (in German *Repräsentant* or *Repräsentanz*), which is not necessarily ideational. Cf. Strachey's discussion of these terms (in Freud, 1915, pp. 111–112).

fantasies can be considered as a resumption of the task of resolving the negative Oedipus component, which leads to the relinquishment and internalization of this object-relationship aspect, and thus contributes to superego formation. But such passive-receptive strivings in the male will be further considered in their more fundamental significance as instinctual representations of internalization processes in general.

In the course of the terminating phases of analysis with male patients I have been impressed with the frequent appearance of direct, undisguised manifestations of such passive-homosexual strivings toward the analyst and of defensive struggles against these strivings. I have in mind wish fantasies of being the receptive partner in anal intercourse or fellatio practices with the analyst, impregnation and pregnancy fantasies, at times expressed or accompanied by somatic representations such as intestinal, stomach, or throat discomfort, bloated feeling in the abdomen, or nausea. Not infrequently such fantasies take the form of accusations against the analyst that he has aggressive designs on the patient. These may be pictured as frank sexual aggression or as a desire on the analyst's part to subject the patient to permanent submission in the form of unnecessarily prolonged treatment. Attempts to analyze the patient's expressed wish to terminate the analysis may be construed as demonstrations of the analyst's need for continued power over the patient, even in the face of the analyst's stated agreement on a termination date. It should be emphasized that the patients in question did not come to analysis because of homosexual problems or paranoid tendencies; nor has analysis in these cases revealed significant degrees of homosexual pathology (as distinguished from normal homosexual personality trends). While homosexual fantasies in the transference had appeared at times during the course of the analysis, they did not play a prominent part prior to the termination phase.

The analyst encounters a specific difficulty during the termination phase of any analysis. Both analyst and patient may become aware of signs or intimations that termination is approaching. If the matter is first brought up by the patient, the analyst will attempt to analyze what is involved in the patient's feeling or his wish to terminate. It may be nothing but a manifestation of resistance. But one may safely say that resistance of one kind or another always plays a role in the patient's urge to terminate. The uncovering of that factor, in and by itself, is not a valid argument against terminating the analysis. Our clinical judgment must be guided by an assessment of the balance of factors involved. We cannot, at this juncture of the analysis, remain completely wedded to the analytic process itself, which is by nature interminable, but must step out of it with one foot, as it were, to survey and assess also the extra-analytic reality of the patient's life. Our analytic as well as our more broadly clinical judgment must come into play. If meaningful advances have taken place in the inner reorganization of the patient's life, sooner or later his need for independence from the analyst and from analysis will assert itself, as will reactivated wishes for continued dependence; both will be present, in varying proportions. It frequently occurs that these contradictory tendencies reinforce each other. The more the patient becomes aware of his passive strivings toward the analyst, the stronger defenses against them may grow, leading to increased insistence on termination. On the other hand, a growing awareness and assertion of adult independence may throw the patient back in the direction of submissive-dependent attachment. At such a time the homosexual wish fantasies and defensive projections may come to the surface.

The question may arise whether it is the pressure of impending termination which brings about these homosexual manifestations, or whether it is the emergence of homosexual strivings in the course of the deepening analysis which pushes the patient toward termination, as a defense against them and as a resistance against their being analyzed. If such homosexual conflicts in the transference clearly appear in the context of an ongoing analysis as part of the unfolding analytic material, without apparent provocation by the reality factor of contemplated termination, it is likely that subsequent pressure from the patient for an early termination is an expression of resistance and not much more. It is likely, on the other hand, that the emergence or reemergence of such conflicts in the context of the termination phase represents their reactivation by the impending termination. This activation then needs to be analyzed in terms of the resolution of the Oedipus complex and of the transference neurosis and should be understood as part of the process of working through this problem.

Why does the Oedipal conflict become reactivated during the termination phase, and why in this form? Termination represents separation from and loss of a love object. We call the process of coming to terms with and working through such a loss the work of mourning. Mourning, properly understood, involves more than the gradual giving-up of the love object, the detachment of object cathexis. If brought to completion, the work of mourning encompasses the internalization of elements of the lost object-relationship. A partial narcissistic recathexis of the drive energies employed in the object-relationship takes place. Anna Freud some years ago reemphasized these two phases of mourning: "The process of mourning (*Trauerarbeit*) taken in its analytic sense means to us the individual's effort to accept a fact in the external world (the loss of the cathected object) and to effect corresponding changes in the inner world (withdrawal of libido from the lost object, identification with the lost object)" (1960, p. 58).

Mourning, in these respects, has its prototype in the resolution of the Oedipus conflict. There, too, a complex process of relinquishing and identifying with love objects takes place, involving the transformation of object libido into narcissistic libido. Such identifications lead to the formation of the superego. We may say that the first mourning, properly so-called, takes place in the resolution of the Oedipus conflict. In contrast to later mourning experiences at times of permanent loss of a love object by death or definitive separation, the mourning of the resolution of the Oedipus conflict takes place in the presence and often with the help of the external objects being mourned, i.e., the parents. If this help is not forthcoming, because of inadequacies in the parents or because of the early death of a parent, the normal resolution of the Oedipus complex is interfered with and subsequent mourning experiences are likely to show pathological characteristics. Recently there has been increased interest in the vicissitudes of the Oedipus complex in the one-parent child and in children who have lost a parent during significant periods of Oedipal development, including loss through death or divorce during adolescence (for a recent review of the literature, see Miller, 1971).

I have implied an answer to the question why the Oedipus conflict becomes reactivated during the termination phase of analysis. Insofar as termination means loss of or separation from a parental love object, it is not merely one of a number of mourning experiences but is, as the resolution of the transference neurosis, to be understood as a resumption or repetition of the first mourning, of the resolution and mastery of the Oedipal conflict. Not unlike the original resolution and its further elaboration during adolescence, the work of mourning during the termination phase takes place in the presence and with the help of the parental object being mourned. Frequently, the clinical picture during termination more closely resembles the adolescent than the original Oedipal phase. My earlier comments on the specific difficulty for the analyst in assessing the patient's urgings and readiness for termination apply—*mutatis mutandis*—in many ways to the parents' difficult position in regard to the dependence-independence problems of their adolescent child. The patients' conflicts over termination, sketched above, as well as aspects of their behavior, often are a good facsimile of adolescent conflicts and behavior. A mainly clinical discussion of the problems confronting us would have much to gain from detailed consideration of and comparison with the adolescent phase. However, in my opinion, predominantly metapsychological discussion gains more by having recourse to the model situation, the original Oedipus complex—at least at this stage of our knowledge.

My second question was why the Oedipus conflict would be reactivated in the termination phase of analysis in the specific form described above. To avoid misunderstanding, I emphasize that in this paper I focus on a particular aspect of the Oedipus complex, without any implication that it is the only aspect, the only representative of the Oedipus complex appearing during termination in these patients. I do believe, however, that the aspect under consideration here has unique, although by no means exclusive, significance for problems of termination and superego development. Why do passive-homosexual strivings, in the cases mentioned, come to the fore at that time, often for the first time with such clarity and persistence? To approach this question I will take a theoretical detour. It has become customary, often to the detriment of therapy and theory, to overemphasize the distinction between ego psychology and id psychology. Problems of object loss, of introjection, identification, and mourning are discussed as ego-psychological problems. The energy involved in ego functioning and in the cohesion of ego structure itself is said to be neutralized, desexualized, and de-aggressivized energy. It is no longer psychic energy as we know it from the object cathexes of instinctual drives. But the ego pathology with which our patients confront us is a manifestation of various kinds of faulty modification or transformation of drive energy. Equally, normal ego and superego formation and functioning are manifestations of modification and transformation of drive energy, ego autonomy notwithstanding. Seen from the perspective of ego psychology, on the other hand, instinctual conflict or instinctual manifestations have to be understood as drive expressions or drive levels of ego processes. In our daily analytic work we often find that we have a choice: to deal with a given issue, a dream, a piece of behavior, a transference manifestation, either from the point of view of the id or from the point of view of the ego. Which choice we make depends not only on the content of the material but also, and often more so, on the context in which the material is brought up, and especially on our assessment of the psychic level from which the patient is speaking or which he is tending to obscure or neglect.

When we speak of neutralization and desexualization, it is important that these terms do not become mere words, devoid of live meaning. Freud speaks of desexualization very graphically: "When the ego assumes the features of the object (by identification), it forces itself, so to speak, upon the id as a love-object and tries to make good the loss of that object by saying: 'look, I am so like the object, you can as well love me!'" And he continues: "The transformation of object libido into narcissistic libido which thus takes place obviously implies an abandonment of sexual aims, a process of desexualization; it is consequently a kind of sublimation" (1923, p. 30). The relinquishment of Oedipal objects and their "restitution" in the ego, as a precipitate or differentiating grade constituting the superego, is a process of desexualization of libidinal cathexis, so that object cathexis becomes transformed into neutralized, narcissistic cathexis. Prior to and during the course of achieving this relinquishment and this narcissistic transformation of object cathexis (and partly because of the impending relinquishment) the sexual-aggressive object cathexis may actually increase. This is a dynamic-economic description of the fact that the work of mourning is indeed an achievement in which rather violent and sudden cathectic shifts (often manifested in mood swings) may occur.

We may now give a partial answer to our second question. Insofar as the resolution of the Oedipus complex in the boy involves, among many other factors, the relinquishment of the passively loved father and of the boy's feminine attachment to him (the negative or inverted component of the Oedipus complex; (see Freud, 1923, pp. 28–34), it is easy to understand how the impending relinquishment may heighten passive-homosexual strivings. The resumption of resolving the Oedipus complex, culminating in the relinquishment of incestuous object relations and in their partial internal restitution during the termination phase (resolution of the transference neurosis), can lead to a heightening of passive-homosexual tendencies in the male patient, as a step toward relinquishing the relationship with the analyst as an incestuous love object. This increase would be part of the mourning process and of its pronounced cathectic shifts—a last stand, as it were, in the struggle to resolve the negative Oedipus component, presaging the reconstitution of aspects of this relationship in the superego.

But there is another, and more fundamental, aspect to the resurgence of the passivity conflict in men at the end of analysis.[2] It is of a more general nature than the negative Oedipus component, although perhaps related to and enhanced by it. I spoke of the passivity conflict in terms of passive-receptive, and in that sense feminine, strivings. The symptoms were fantasies or their equivalents of oral or anal intercourse and of impregnation by the analyst. These are incorporative fantasies. The introjective component of identification is a taking-in, a psychic incorporation. Incorporation, especially oral incorporation, has always been seen as the instinctual-somatic prototype of introjection; the term "introjection" is usually employed to denote the ego aspect of such processes. In the unconscious and for the unconscious, using primary-process mentation, introjection of an Oedipal object relation is an incorporation. The resolution of the Oedipus conflict, insofar as it involves an introjection of the relinquished object relationship, has aspects of a receptive, incorporating process. In keeping with the progressive genitalization of sexuality, the taking-in gets represented more in genital than in pregenital terms of receptivity. I mention in passing that to my mind the fantasies of oral and anal intercourse, in the group of patients under discussion here, bespeak a genitalization of orality and anality rather than a simple, direct regression to pregenital stages of libido development. That is to say, the fantasies are hysteric-obsessional in nature rather than schizoid or depressive-paranoid. Fantasies of the latter type are seen in the more severe character disorders, whereas the fantasies discussed here represent in the main regression up to but not beyond the phallic level.

The term "passive-receptive" (as the term "feminine" itself) is easily misleading. Incorporation, taking-in, is not necessarily passive if passive is thought of as the opposite of aggressive. Incorporation can be, and often is, an aggressive process; we only have to think of the devouring quality of many incorporative acts. And indeed the resurgence of what I called "passive-homosexual strivings" in these patients frequently shows, together with submissive feelings, such aggressive-devouring aspects. The term "passive," then, should be understood to mean the direction of the act, rather than to indicate necessarily the quality of gentle or abject submission to another object. Taking-in may occur in a variety of modes; the taker may incorporate the material actively, aggressively, or he may devour it destructively; he may "passively" submit or yield or surrender. The material, on

---

[2] Much of this discussion would be applicable to women patients as well, but the details of their psychosexuality are sufficiently different to warrant a separate consideration of their internalization processes.

the other hand, may be offered lovingly or grudgingly; it may be forced on the taker or be withheld and yielded to him only as a result of aggressive demands. These varieties of taking and giving, as we well know, determine the character of the superego to no small degree. Also, each mode of giving and of receiving exerts an influence on its counterpart. When Freud spoke of the superego as the representative of the id, he must have had in mind, too, the varieties of taking-in in introjection.

The emergence of receptive-homosexual strivings in relation to the analyst during the termination phase can be understood as an instinctual manifestation of the introjective elements of the work of mourning involved in the resolution of the transference neurosis. We are too apt to view the Oedipus conflict, and thereby the transference neurosis, in terms of instinctual and object-relation problems, without sufficient consideration of their implications for psychic structure building, that is, for superego formation. Sandler (1960) has commented on this issue in his illuminating paper on the superego. On the other hand we are apt to view psychic structure without keeping clearly in mind the instinctual-energic side of structure formation, i.e., the libido transformations and internalizations involved in psychic structure building.

Emergence of such homosexual strivings is emergence into consciousness. What remain to be brought to awareness are not the instinctual strivings themselves but their representational relationship to the ego problems with which the patient is struggling. What leads to expansion and enrichment of the ego, to the extension of the ego's reign, is not the emergence of the instinctual strivings into consciousness per se, but the understanding that the homosexual fantasies are, on one level, instinctual manifestations of internalization problems, of the work of mourning. And it is the understanding that the work of mourning and of internalization represents transformations of incorporative-receptive instinctual processes, which allows the id to play its necessary and living part in the reorganization of the superego.

Our question was why the Oedipus conflict and its resolution would be reactivated in the specific form described, during the termination phase of analysis. The question is not yet fully answered. I hope we have come to see more clearly why passive-receptive strivings, in the sense clarified above, are reactivated. But we need to comprehend more fully why they are expressed in phallic-genital terms, in terms of frank sexual fantasies and wishes rather than in the form of derivatives of higher-level representatives. The answer lies, I believe, in the retransformation of narcissistic-masochistic cathexis into object cathexis, a retransformation which is involved in the externalization of superego introjections.[3]

---

[3] The terms "narcissistic," "masochistic," "libidinal," and "aggressive" must be understood here as metapsychological, not as clinical terms. Insofar as the distinction between sexual and aggressive drives is valid, masochism (as a metapsychological concept) is the counterpart to narcissism; both are here understood as internalization modes of aggressive and sexual drives respectively. See my discussion of some of these issues in a previous paper (1962, pp. 491–493).

We know that introjected object relations which are elements of superego structure are comparatively easily reprojected into external relationships. We see this not only in paranoid conditions but to a certain degree in every analysis, when the analyst becomes an external embodiment of features of the patient's superego. Without such transference projection, subsequent modification of the now external Oedipal relationship in the transference, and, finally, reinternalization of aspects of the changed relationship, no real therapeutic change takes place. Expressed in metapsychological terms: the narcissistic-masochistic, internal relationships which constitute superego structure, and whose cathectic energies consist of (relatively) desexualized, deaggressivized energy, become deneutralized, are reconverted into sexual-aggressive cathexes in the process of transference projection. To put it somewhat differently again, and less abstractly: the revival, in the transference neurosis, of the Oedipal relationship with the parents, of the conflicts and libidinal-aggressive tensions inherent in them, and of the separation experiences and renunciations inherent in their resolution—this revival means repersonification, on the plane of external object relations, of what had become, to a greater or lesser degree, dynamic forces and interrelations of psychic structure during the original Oedipus resolution. If internalization of object relations or, as Freud would say, identification with the Oedipal object, implies desexualization and is, according to him, "a kind of sublimation," then reexternalization in the transference means resexualization and desublimation.

The specific task in the termination phase, where the separation from the analyst is to be worked through, is the resumption of the Oedipus-conflict resolution with its renunciations and internalizations—the restoring of the superego structure which had been partially dissolved. In primary-process thinking, based on or picturing the earliest bodily processes of incorporation, and becoming imbued with the later, progressively genital editions of them, such internalization is sexual. If the analysis has been effective, primary-process representations of internalization and of the work of mourning are activated. Expressed conversely: mourning becomes regressively transformed into the components of sexual relinquishment of and by the incestuous object, and sexual incorporation of the object, in predominantly phallic-genital terms, since this is the stage reached at the height of the Oedipus conflict.

An analysis, seen in oversimplified schematic outline, consists of two constantly intermingling and overlapping phases: a phase of rolling the infantile neurosis, in the reenactment of the transference neurosis, back toward its Oedipal and pre-Oedipal origins; and a phase of leading forward, from this dissolution of the infantile neurosis into its elements, by reworking the conflicts, to a healthier resolution of the Oedipus complex and to healthier ego organization. Following this scheme, the superego would be the first to be subject to a gradual dissolution, from the end point of infantile psychosexual development into its Oedipal-instinctual elements. At this stage, then, intrapsychic Oedipal relations constituting superego structure tend to be reconverted into Oedipal object relations as manifested in the positive and negative transference. In the termination phase reconstitution of the superego takes place, to the extent to which disorganization of this structure had occurred. And the task of internalization, to the degree to which repressions have been lifted in the course of the analysis, comes up in the concrete terms of id language, in terms of undisguised instinctual manifestations.

In sum: the homosexual attachment of the male patient to his analyst, while specifically expressing the negative Oedipus attachment, the "feminine" attachment of the boy to his father, is in a more general and fundamental sense an instinctual representation of his receptivity, by virtue of which he internalizes previously established object relations to become structural elements of his superego.

It is true, of course, that what we call here the boy's "feminine attitude" expresses itself also, to a greater or lesser degree, in his attachment to his mother. In fact, children of both sexes display passive-receptive ("feminine") attitudes toward their mothers as well as toward their fathers, and active-aggressive ("masculine") attitudes toward their fathers as well as toward their mothers. These are in part determined by parental attitudes and are responded to by mothers and fathers in different ways at different times. All this depends on a great variety of intrafamilial factors and on habitual attitudes of the individuals involved in such interactions. Direct identifications, i.e., identifications which belong to a genetically earlier stage than object relations and are not transformations of the latter, further complicate the picture. Freud has called attention to these intricacies in his discussion of the superego and the Oedipus complex in *The Ego and the Id* (1923, pp. 28–34).

When we speak of "bisexuality" in this connection (bisexuality of each parent as well as of the child), the term serves as a shorthand expression to indicate the following: insofar as the term "feminine" has come to be associated with receptivity and the term "masculine" with activity directed outward, both sexes, although often in significantly different proportions, show both attitudes. In this sense parents and children are bisexual; the question whether and to what extent such bisexuality is biologically or culturally determined is not at issue here. One might then speak of the "masculine" counterpart or object of the boy's "feminine" strivings, which counterpart may be, in a given case and at a given time, the father or the mother; just as mother or father may be the "feminine" counterpart to his masculine strivings. The same is applicable to girls and their masculine and feminine counterparts.[4]

---

[4] Perhaps it needs to be emphasized that I do not intend to minimize the decisive impact of the biological sex differences on psychological development. Nevertheless, familial-cultural factors decisively shape and modulate these biological determinants.

Viewing the resolution of the Oedipus complex as a process of mourning, we must say that to the extent to which the Oedipus complex is repressed the task of mourning has not been accomplished. While in repression drive energy is withdrawn from object relations (and in this sense the external object relationship is relinquished), it remains sexualized and is invested in unconscious, fantasy-object relations. The transformation of external relationships into internal, structural ones (narcissistic transformation of drive energy) has not been achieved in repression. Instead, relegation to the id has taken place.[5] In perversion—and the wish fantasies of the patients cited fall into this category—given components of the Oedipus complex return from or escape repression as well as structural neutralization and become available for direct expression in external object relations. In this light the homosexual, conscious fantasies of these patients can be seen as way stations on the road to either true internalization or repression. They may be regarded as equivalents of the polymorphous-perverse manifestations of childhood, which are equally way stations.

Freud has spoken of the "struggle against passivity" in men and penis envy in women as the bedrock we reach when "we have penetrated through all the psychological strata"; he understands "the masculine protest" and "the wish for the penis" as expressions of "the repudiation of femininity"— "this remarkable feature in the psychical life of human beings" . . . , "part of the great riddle of sex" (1937, pp. 250–253). Is not the great riddle of sexuality, of sexual differentiation, at the same time the great riddle of individuation, of becoming a separate biological and psychological entity? Freud speaks of the repudiation of femininity, the repudiation of receiving and yielding and surrender. But what about the repudiation of masculinity, the repudiation of self-assertion, of the isolation of independence, of the exposed position of separateness? Freud stressed the fear of castration and the wish for the penis—but what about the wish for surrender and for a womb? Our patients, I believe, show both. They may show us a way to understand the great riddle of sexuality and individuation in a less one-sided fashion. The development of an internal world[6] of psychic structure, an important share of which is due to internalization, might be a sign of man's affirmative acceptance of "femininity," no matter how much he may appear to repudiate it in his struggle for mastery of the external world and against receptivity toward men. The male's fear of castration and his struggle against passivity certainly must involve a wish for them, just as the female's tenacious wish for a penis must contain the opposite—penis fear. I believe there is clinical evidence to show that side by side with penis envy, and no less primary, there is repudiation of "masculinity" in women.

[5] For a more extensive discussion of this issue see Loewald (1973).
[6] Cf. Rapaport's distinction between the inner and the internal world (1957, pp. 696–697).

Addendum

In his searching discussion of this paper, when it was presented in Chicago in 1961, Maxwell Gitelson raised an important objection to my formulation in terms of reexternalization of superego elements or of retransformation of narcissistic into object cathexis, as an explanation for the appearance of the undisguised instinctual manifestations which are the starting point of my presentation. The narcissistic, internal relationships which constitute psychic structure and whose cathectic energies consist of desexualized, neutralized energy, Gitelson maintained, refer only to the ideal normal resolution of the original Oedipus complex. To the extent to which such ideal resolution has occurred, he claims, no resexualization and desublimation in the transference would occur. "We must consider," Gitelson said, "that the elements, dynamic forces, and interrelations of psychic structure in the patient have retained their original drive qualities and that re-externalization in the transference cannot mean resexualization and desublimation but rather explicit recapitulation in the transference of the original drive qualities of the Oedipus complex, which have survived as such in the neurosis and have been more or less successfully repressed and defended against."

Gitelson rightly emphasizes the distinction between what Freud (1924) has called the "dissolution" and the "repression" of the Oedipus complex. He maintains that my clinical data should be understood in terms of de-repression; accordingly, "the original drive qualities of the Oedipus complex, which have survived as such in the neurosis" under repression, through analysis would have returned from repression and appeared in consciousness. Reading the data in this way, we would not deal with a disorganization of true superego structure (if the superego—and I agree with this view—in its ideal normal form is the result not of repression but of dissolution of the Oedipus complex), but with a return from repression of component drives of the Oedipus complex which never had been adequately desexualized and neutralized. While the clinical data cited would be manifestations of drives which now, as the result of analytic work, are becoming available for narcissistic transformation and neutralization, these drives, in Gitelson's interpretation, had not been so transformed during the Oedipal period, due to neurotogenic object relations impeding true psychic structure formation.

The difference in our interpretations of these instinctual manifestations, however, is more than a disagreement about the specific genetics of the situation. The difference revolves around the question: is psychic structure (in the sense in which we use this term for a structure such as the superego) irreversible? To Gitelson, if I understand him correctly, there is no return from structural neutralization; what returns, returns from repression; true structuralization in his view is irreversible. With this view I disagree, especially when applied to superego structure. To put this problem in concrete terms: is the reactivation of the Oedipal struggle in adolescence, for instance, necessarily and only based on pathological solutions during the original Oedipal period, and is its revival in analysis necessarily a sign of pathology? Or is even an ideal normal resolution of the Oedipus conflict, ushering in the latency period, no more than a resolution *for the time being*, so that the issues involved will return inevitably, although on a new level of organization, during puberty-adolescence, demanding fresh solutions both internally and externally, since the adolescent is confronted with new integrative tasks? Whether and to what extent he is able to confront these tasks depends in great part, to be sure, on healthy resolution during the Oedipal period. But does this mean that the Oedipal struggle is not unfolded again or that his superego structure does not undergo fresh phases of disorganization, involving reexternalization and deneutralization of previously narcissistically transformed drive components—unless there was a pathological outcome of the Oedipal conflict, i.e., unless the complex had been merely repressed? (cf. Freud, 1924, p. 176–177).

There are, I believe, other stages in later life, among them the analytic situation, where internalization structures, especially superego structure, may and often do undergo phases of disorganization and reorganization. These involve what I would call the return from internalization of instinctual cathexes. The reactivation of Oedipal problems at such stages, to my understanding, is not necessarily and exclusively due to unresolved Oedipal problems left over from the past and repressed. Such reactivation may bespeak, rather, a healthy resiliency of the ego, undoubtedly based on earlier nonrepressive structure formation, which enables the individual to engage in a disorganization in the service of the ego, i.e., to undo, to an extent, former structural resolutions and to arrive at novel resolutions, at higher levels of organization. New integrative tasks, imposed by changing life circumstances or chosen by creative individuals, tend to trigger such reactivations. The normal adolescent revival of the Oedipus complex ushers in an *advance* in development; it is not simply a resumption of the old conflict because it had been repressed. There can be no doubt, however, that both factors, derepression and reexternalization, are most often intermingled and hard to sort out in a given case. The lines between so-called pathology and normality can never be neatly drawn, least of all in adolescence and in the psychoanalytic situation.

Gitelson's interpretation and mine therefore are not contradictory or mutually exclusive. The difference lies in our diverging views on the question of mutability or immutability of psychic structure.

BIBLIOGRAPHY

Freud, A. (1960), Discussion of Dr. John Bowlby's Paper (Grief and Mourning in Infancy and Early Childhood). *Psychoanalytic Study of the Child*, 15:53–62.

Freud, S. (1915), Instincts and their Vicissitudes. *Standard Edition*, 14:111–140, 1957.
––––– (1923), The Ego and the Id. *Standard Edition*, 19:3–66, 1961.
––––– (1924), The Dissolution of the Oedipus Complex. *Standard Edition*, 19:172–179, 1961.
––––– (1937), Analysis Terminable and Interminable. *Standard Edition*, 23:211–253, 1964.
Loewald, H. W. (1962), Internalization, Separation, Mourning and Superego. *Psychoanal. Quart.* 31:483–504.
––––– (1973), On Internalization. *Internat. J. Psycho-Anal.*, 54 (in press).
Miller, J. B. M. (1971), Children's Reaction to the Death of a Parent; A Review of the Psychoanalytic Literature. *J. Amer. Psychoanal. Assn.* (1973), 19:697–719.
Rapaport, D. (1957), A Theoretical Analysis of the Superego Concept. In: *Collected Papers of D. R.* New York and London: Basic Books, 1967.
Sandler, J. (1960), On the Concept of Superego. *Psychoanalytic Study of the Child*, 15:128–162.

Affects and Psychoanalytic Knowledge

ARNOLD H. MODELL, M.D. (*Brookline, Mass.*)

If one asks, what is it in psychoanalysis that corresponds to the raw data of other sciences, one discovers that there is not a simple or direct answer. Although science no longer accepts the Baconian notion that there are "facts" in nature isolated completely from the influence of the selective process of theory, nevertheless there is the unassailable belief that at bottom science rests upon a perceptual base. Whether that fact is a fossil bone, or a species of bird, or the swing of a needle in a scientific instrument, facts are sensuous. In archaeology and paleontology, historical sciences analogous to psychoanalysis, the data can be literally tangible; the bits of broken pottery and broken bones can be touched. As is true of psychoanalysis, and in contrast to the more advanced sciences, there are no instruments interposed between the perceiver and that which is perceived. But what does the psychoanalyst perceive? Is there something that corresponds to the tangible artifacts of the archaeologist? Or does the mind, in Sherrington's words, move ghostlier than a ghost? Are the fundamental data of psychoanalysis elusive and ineffable?

Hartmann has said that the data gathered in the psychoanalytic situation are primarily behavioral data—verbal behavior, silence, bodily movements, etc. (Hartmann, 1959). These data are then interpreted with reference to internal, that is, mental, and not behavioristic processes. But is this strictly so? Not all such verbal behavior constitutes psychoanalytic data. One has only to think of the attempts to "objectify" psychoanalysis by means of tape recordings. Without intending to depreciate the value of such studies, these procedures soon demonstrate that all of the patient's words are not data and that if all the recorded words were considered to be of equal significance one would soon become engulfed by this verbal flood. Words by themselves do not necessarily constitute the primary data of psychoanalysis. Consider those people who use words to communicate nothing, who use speech to create distance, to bore, and to distract. For this reason I believe that the attempt of a certain French school of psychoanalysts to view our science as a branch of linguistics (for example, the work of Lacan [1968], who was obviously influenced by Claude Lévi-Strauss) is not entirely convincing. What endows words and other bits of behavioral data with significance is the perception of the observing analyst that these bits of behavior are associated with affects.

It can be justly argued that when words are used not to communicate but to create distance, this too is a form of data, a form of data that is usually classified as a defense, presumably a defense against the closeness of an object relationship. This is unquestionably true, but in contrast to the ongoing psychoanalytic process, where affects are communicated, the patient is here in a state of withdrawal; there is a temporary cessation of the analytic process. Once having observed the nature of this defense, the data do not change and there is no further increment of knowledge. We would say that the patient's affects are the transmitter of data, and the transmission only occurs when there is an affect bond between the patient and the observing analyst. The analogy of the patient's mind as a transmitter was described by Freud (1912) as follows:

[The analyst] must turn his own unconscious like a receptive organ towards the transmitting of the patient. He must adjust himself to the patient as a telephone receiver is adjusted to the transmitting microphone [p. 115].

The perceptual organ of the psychoanalyst is that which permits him to perceive the affects of others. Such an organ is not so clearly identified as are the organs of sight, hearing, and smell. This fact has caused considerable confusion to philosophers and has accordingly interfered with the establishment of an epistemology of psychoanalysis. Because psychoanalysis cannot be fitted into any ready-made epistemology, as Ricoeur (1965) has so aptly said, "the understanding of Freudianism requires a new advance of thought." There is something very queer in the assumption, "I feel, therefore I know." It is Descartes' cogito turned upon its head. It is beyond my competence and the scope of this paper to pursue what is one of the leading problems of modern philosophy. It is clear, however, that the ancient separation of mental faculties of cognition and feeling is false. There are two recent works which have dealt extensively with this specific problem of the philosophical implications of psychoanalytic knowledge: the contributions of Ricoeur and of Yankelovich and Barrett (1970).

When we return to Freud's analogy of the patient's unconscious mind as a transmitter and the analyst's unconscious mind as a receiver, the analyst's unconscious may be correctly likened to a perceptual organ, but in this instance it is a perceptual organ that significantly influences that which is perceived, for not only will the analyst's unconscious influence that which the patient produces as data, but also the analyst's interpretations will produce fresh material. However, the perturbing effect of the psychoanalytic observer does not constitute an insurmountable obstacle to scientific objectivity. For an analogous situation exists in physics: Niels Bohr (1958) writes:

. . . the necessity of considering the interaction between the measuring instruments and the object under investigation in atomic mechanics exhibits a close analogy to the peculiar difficulties in psychological analysis arising from the fact that the mental content is invariably altered when the attention is concentrated on any special feature of it [p. 11].

If we take the analyst's unconscious perception of the patient's affects to be the fundamental perceptual instrument, this places the problem somewhere in the broad category of the analyst's "countertransference." This term is not ideal, for in its narrower sense it denotes the analyst's neurotic responses to his patient, but in its broader sense it connotes the sum total of the analyst's perception of his own affective responses. It is the analyst's preconscious perceptions of his affects that permit him to use the communication of affects as a perceptual instrument. It becomes a neurotic problem for the analyst, interfering with the analytic process, when his perceptions are under repression and remain unconscious.

That the countertransference is an observing instrument has long been known to psychoanalysts, for in 1926 Helene Deutsch observed that:

This internal experience of the analyst . . . established between him and the analysand a contact which is outside the conscious apparatus, even though this process itself is stimulated by a motor verbal discharge, on the one hand, and by a reception of the latter through the organ of hearing, on the other hand. However, that which takes place between the first stimulation of the senses, and the subsequent intellectual processing of this stimulus is a process which is "occult" and lies outside the conscious. Thus we speak of the analyst's "unconscious perception" [p. 136].

In this paper Deutsch first introduced the idea that empathy takes place by means of the analyst's partial identifications with the patient.

Deutsch further proposed a tentative differentiation of classification of this mode of unconscious communication. Her description has been clinically confirmed by Racker (1968), although these concepts are by no means familiar to most psychoanalysts. Deutsch differentiated empathy and intuition, which proceed from an identification with the patient, from another process which she termed "a complementary attitude." She states:

The essence of all intuition in general, indeed intuitive empathy, is precisely the gift of being able to experience the object by means of identification taking place within oneself, and, specifically, in that part of oneself in which the process of identification has taken place. This intuitive attitude, i.e., the analyst's own process of identification, is made possible by the fact that the psychic structure of the analyst is a product of developmental processes similar to those which the patient himself has also experienced. Indeed, the unconscious of both the analyst and the analysand contains the very same infantile wishes and impulses [p. 137].

Deutsch goes on to observe, however, that this countertransference is not limited to an identification of certain portions of the patient's ego, but also entails the presence of certain other unconscious attitudes which she would like to designate with the term "complementary attitude":

We know that the patient tends to direct his ungratified infantile libidinous wishes at his analyst who, thus, becomes identified with the original object of these wishes. This implies that the analyst is under the obligation of renouncing his real personality even in his own unconscious attitudes, so as to be able to identify himself with these *imagines* in a manner compatible with the transference phantasies of his patient. I call this process "the complementary attitude" in order to distinguish it from mere identification with the infantile ego of the patient [p. 137].

I would understand Deutsch's distinction as follows: knowledge through empathy is a kind of refinding of aspects of the self in the patient, whereas in the complementary attitude the analyst is acted upon by forces in the patient and may unconsciously be manipulated to recreate certain imagoes in the patient's past that are alien to his own character. It is as if the patient's unconscious is a stage director who assigns roles to the analyst with the entire process remaining outside of consciousness. Until the analyst becomes aware of what is happening, he might find himself tending to act in the direction of the role to which he has been assigned. In contrast to the act of empathy, which is apt to be pleasurable for the analyst, this complementary attitude is apt to be experienced as something unpleasant; instead of the pleasure of recognition there is the unpleasantness of being acted upon. The analyst is in a comparatively passive position until he has a conscious recognition of what is occurring.

This complementary attitude may bear some relationship to the process of projective identification that has been described by Melanie Klein and her students. Racker (1968) describes the process as follows:

The complementary identifications are produced by the fact that the patient treats the analyst as an internal (projected) object, and in consequence the analyst feels treated as such; that is, he identifies himself with this object.

Thus an analyst sometimes experiences unaccountable affects, affects that cannot be attributed to the process of simple contagion, although the analyst may tend to react to the patient's hostility with a corresponding affect (Rycroft, 1956) and may experience contagious anxiety and depression. The complementary attitude involves affects that are linked to imagoes belonging to the patient's past. This fact may remain outside the awareness of both the analyst and the patient.

Although these processes are by no means limited to any single diagnostic group, the observation of schizophrenic patients is useful, as the regression throws these issues into sharper focus and with greater intensity. For example, during one phase of my treatment of a schizophrenic girl I was unable to understand why I experienced intense guilt concerning the apparent lack of progress of the therapy. I knew that I did not have any exaggerated therapeutic expectations and therefore could not account for the guilt solely as a consequence of my having failed therapeutically. This guilt only became understandable when I recognized that I was experiencing something that corresponded to Deutsch's description of the complementary attitude. This patient believed that her father had driven her mother crazy and was responsible for her mother's own mental illness. What the patient believed had occurred between her parents was now reenacted in the transference, and I was assigned the role of the damaging, destructive father who was now driving the patient crazy. As a result of processes which are still unclear, I did in fact experience this unreasonable sense of guilt.

This passively experienced complementary attitude gives way to a more actively perceived understanding when the analyst succeeds in some degree with his own ongoing self-analysis. In this way what is experienced passively becomes transformed into something active and is mastered. Even in most well-conducted analyses the analyst may at times be thrown "off balance" in this way and go on to achieve a reintegration with the deepening of his understanding of the analytic process.

What Deutsch described as empathy is analogous to what Freud (1925) described for perception in general. That is, Freud stated that perception is always a re-perception, a re-finding of the object that has been lost. As such it carries with it a certain quantum of pleasure. It has been frequently noted that the analyst's empathy may be heightened by states of mild depression as well as states of mourning, states in which there is some longing for a lost object. This is in contrast, as I have said earlier, to the experience of the complementary attitude, where there is the unpleasant experience of being intruded upon.

Both the complementary and empathic countertransference which are first experienced unconsciously or preconsciously become worked over by the analyst's secondary intellectual processes. This is what Greenson (1960) calls "insight," in contrast to the more regressive affective response of empathy. Here the analyst's experience of insight entails some measure of recognition and categorizing of what he has first experienced unconsciously. In the experience of the complementary attitude some time may elapse before the analyst recognizes the source of his own affects and understands their origin.

To return to our original question, I hope that I have satisfactorily demonstrated that the fundamental data of psychoanalysis are the perception of affects and that this perception corresponds to the visual and tactile organs of other scientists. It is questionable whether affects are ever devoid of mental content, although Jones (1969) has described the hypothetical case of the infant who may experience affects prior to the development of ideational content—a state of affairs he described as "aphanisis." This description remains to be empirically demonstrated. The affects associated with transference are always embedded in the context of identifications with formerly loved objects or aspects of the self (Kohut, 1971). Whether the content corresponds to actual experiences with a loved object or the objects have themselves been created by the subject is immaterial. In this sense the objects have a historical dimension. We know that this historical dimension refers also to the self. It is not uncommon, for example, in the analysis of a narcissistic character for the analyst to begin to wonder about his own capacity to care for others. This corresponds to the mirror aspect of the transference that Kohut has described.

But there is another dimension to the affects that are experienced in the analytic situation, a dimension that corresponds to the present, that is, to the current, object relationship between the patient and the analyst. This distinction also can be related in the broad sense to the difference between transference and therapeutic alliance (see Zetzel, 1970).

The facts of an analysis consist of more than the affects of transference communications. The method of free association produces memories of the past, dreams, reports of current experiences, etc. Are these not also facts? I believe that whether or not an analyst can utilize such products of free association as facts depends upon the quality of the current object relationship between the analyst and the patient. If the patient is withdrawn and communicates without affect, it is as if the unconscious transmitter has been turned off, and the same communications may have to be re-heard at a later date if they are to be utilized as analytic facts. It is for this reason that, with the more disturbed patient, greater reliance is placed upon communication via the transference as compared to the use of memories of the past. Anna Freud (1969) has recently noted that the unique role given to the transference in the psychoanalytic process to the exclusion of all other avenues of communication is a major point of controversy in the analytic world today. It would appear that this controversy may reflect a different patient population where the maintenance of the constant object tie to the analyst cannot be taken for granted, a nosological group where affective withdrawal may assume major proportions. When this is the case, the analyst cannot make use of the patient's free associations as such: transference begins to occupy exclusively the center of the analytic process. The analyst is forced to use his countertransference as a perceptual instrument to observe shifts of engagement and withdrawal. Although some patients remain in the presence of the object, that is, the analyst, without severing object ties, they are actually in a state of unrelatedness. They describe this as the sensation of being trapped in a plastic ball or capsule. I have observed this as characteristic of certain borderline and narcissistic patients in a state of both withdrawal and extreme dependence upon the object (Modell, 1968). While this phenomenon is most commonly observed in borderline patients, where it may assume proportions of a characterological formation, it is not uncommonly observed in neurotic patients as well. It is still not yet clear whether all people possess this capacity of affective detachment or whether this phenomenon reflects a form of specific pathology. Nevertheless, when this occurs there is an interruption in the analytic process, an interruption in the flow of psychoanalytic knowledge. The transmitter, as it were, is turned off, and the analytic process itself remains in a state of suspension until affective contact is regained.

In many respects this phenomenon resembles the more familiar defense of isolation. But the motive for defense appears to be somewhat different, for the defense of isolation is mobilized by anxiety, which in turn is the response of the ego's fear of being overwhelmed by affects, while in the withdrawal that we have been describing the defense is directed primarily against the closeness of an object tie.

The capacity to know the affective state of another human being is a biological given. In a recent paper (Modell, 1971) I offered some speculations concerning the evolutionary significance of the communications of affects, with special reference to their possible function in ensuring the survival of the group. If these speculations are true, it would suggest that the capacity to know the affective states of another probably antedates the acquisition of language. This more primitive communication of affects becomes grafted onto verbal expression through the medium of the tone of voice and inflection. The phenomenology of this process is outside the realm of psychoanalysis and belongs to the area of psycholinguistics. But as I have attempted to show, the affective component may also be withdrawn from linguistic expression so that language ceases to be a source of psychoanalytic knowledge. I am suggesting that we are utilizing a form of innate knowledge in the psychoanalytic process. In this we are very much in accord with the recent contributions of Chomsky (1971) who proposed that our capacity to understand sentences may rest upon certain genetically determined structures of the mind. It is in the same sense that "facts" of psychoanalysis are perceptually and biologically rooted.

BIBLIOGRAPHY

Bohr, N. (1958), Light and Life. In: *Atomic Physics and Human Knowledge*. New York: Chapman and Hall.

Chomsky, N. (1971), *Problems of Knowledge and Freedom*. New York: Pantheon.

Deutsch, H. (1926), Occult Processes Occurring during Psychoanalysis. In: *Psychoanalysis and the Occult*, ed. by G. Devereux. New York: International Universities Press, 1970.

Freud, A. (1969), *Difficulties on the Path of Psychoanalysis*. New York: International Universities Press.

Freud, S. (1912), Recommendations to Physicians Practicing Psycho-Analysis. *Standard Edition*, 12:111–120. London: Hogarth, 1958.

—— (1925), Negation. *Standard Edition*, 19:235–239. London: Hogarth, 1957.

Greenson, R. (1960), Empathy and its Vicissitudes. *Internat. J. Psycho-Anal.*, 41:418–424.

Hartmann, H. (1959), Psychoanalysis as a Scientific Theory. In: *Psychoanalysis, Scientific Method, and Philosophy*, ed. by S. Hook. New York: New York University Press.

Jones, E. (1929), Fear, Guilt and Hate. In: *Papers on Psychoanalysis*. London: Baillere, Tindall and Cox, 1948, 383–397.

Kohut, H. (1971), *The Analysis of the Self*. New York: International Universities Press.

Lacan, J. (1968), *The Language of the Self*. Trans. by A. Wilden. Baltimore: Johns Hopkins Press.

Modell, A. (1968), *Object Love and Reality*. New York: International Universities Press.
———— (1971), The Origin of Certain Forms of Pre-oedipal Guilt and the Implications for a Psychoanalytic Theory of Affects. *Internat. J. Psycho-Anal.*, 51:48–58.
Racker, H. (1968), The Meanings and Uses of Countertransference. In: *Transference and Countertransference*. New York: International Universities Press.
Ricoeur, P. (1965), *Freud and Philosophy*. Trans. by D. Savage. New Haven: Yale University Press, 1970.
Rycroft, C. (1956), The Nature and Function of the Analyst's Communication to the Patient. *Internat. J. Psycho-Anal.*, 37:469–472.
Yankelovich, D. and Barrett, W. (1970). *Ego and Instinct*. New York: Random House.
Zetzel, E. (1970). *The Capacity for Emotional Growth*. New York: International Universities Press.

Symbolism and Mental Representation

PINCHAS NOY M.D. (*Jerusalem*)

In the course of my studies on the psychoanalytic aspects of art, I found it necessary to learn more about the concept of symbolism, a concept central to any theory dealing with the "nonlogical" functions of the mind, such as the phenomena of dream, fantasy, symptom formation, and art. The more I delved into the study of the concept, the more confused I found myself. I discovered that every author approaches symbolism from another angle and understands its meaning differently, so that no generally shared formulation and theory explaining symbolism exists. It is not surprising, then, that such a concept, which is used by so many disciplines, in science, philosophy, and art, is vague in its formulation and ambiguous in its meaning.

When the various meanings given the term in psychoanalytic and related literature are surveyed, three main approaches emerge:

1. There are authors who refer to symbolism as a mode of thinking, as a kind of mental process, which they call "symbolic thinking," "symbolic process," etc.

2. Others regard symbolism as a technique of mental representation. They speak of "symbolic representation," "symbol formation," and so on.

3. Many confine symbolism to the realm of communication only and approach the symbol as a means, aside from signs and signals, of communicating.

When examining the first approach, we see that the term "symbolic thinking" is used loosely, as synonymous with such terms as paleologic, dereistic, or archaic thinking, all of which are actually synonymous with the term "primary-process thinking." Since I do not know of any serious study which tries to isolate "symbolic processes" as distinct from what we know as "primary processes," I consider it irrelevant to continue to discuss this approach.

The third approach, which confines symbolism to communication only, does not really exclude the second one. Any system of communication de-

The preparation of this paper was supported in part by the Harry Leon Roth Memorial Research Fund of the Israel Institute for Psychoanalysis.

pends on processes of mental representation, since it is only possible for one human being to transmit to another some cues signifying a whole experience and not the experience itself. Thus, from the psychological point of view, the study of any system of communication has to begin with an understanding of the techniques by which experience is encoded into messages by the sender and is decoded again by the receiver—i.e., the techniques of mental representation.

In this paper the second approach will be adopted, and an attempt will be made to use the up-to-date knowledge of psychoanalysis, cognitive psychology, and communication to reformulate the psychoanalytic concept of symbolism and to explain the unique ability of the symbol to represent and express the deeper, unconscious levels of the human mind. Symbolism will be approached only as one of the techniques used by the mental apparatus for mental representation. In addition, an attempt will be made to show that there is no specific mode of "symbolic thinking"; the technique of symbolism may be used to represent any kind of mental material, regardless of the mode of thought processes according to which it has been organized. The theory to be presented here relies heavily on the writing of five authorities, each of which has contributed, from his own particular point of view, to the understanding of symbolism: Freud (1900), Jones (1916), Rycroft (1956), Gombrich (1965), Arieti (1967). The reader acquainted with their writings will certainly discover that their ideas pertain to every part of this study.

In order to give an exact description of the mechanism of the techniques of mental representation, I feel the need to begin with a general description of the organizing processes, those processes which organize mental raw material into meaningful schemata which may then be represented by any of the available techniques. This paper, therefore, will be divided into three parts: the first will deal with the organizing processes in general; the second will study the techniques of mental representation; and the third will discuss the relationship between the representational technique of symbolism and the unconscious.

I. The Organizing Process

The term "organizing processes," suggested by Hartmann (1947), will be used here to cover a wide range of ego functions: synthesis, integration, discrimination, coping, regulation, problem solving, adaptation, assimilation, etc. All of these processes, although fulfilling different functions of the ego, are in some way related to the *organization* of raw mental material or the *reorganization* of previously organized material.

In a study of the organizing processes, the functioning of the computer may serve as a useful explanatory model. The advantage of this model is in its ability to aid in explaining the mechanism of the organizing processes, an issue hitherto hardly investigated. The danger, however, of using such a mechanistic model is in its inability to deal with the dynamic aspect of mental organization, i.e., everything related to the dynamic interplay of psychic forces, such as drives, defenses, aspirations, etc. Therefore, keeping this limitation in mind, I will use the computer model only to the degree to which it may help in elucidating the structure, mechanism, and modes of operation of the mental processes.

The mental apparatus may be compared to a computer in that it receives input from various sources: from the outer world through the sense organs; from within the body through inner sensory receptions; and from the vast reservoir of memory. Taking into consideration the difficulties in studying the inner sources of input, I will confine myself in this study only to the best-known source of input—the perception of outer stimuli, which I will use to elucidate the mental processes by which input is organized.

The tremendous amount of information pouring into the apparatus is incessantly meaningless to the receiver until the data are processed and organized into meaningful schemata which can be identified by matching them up against corresponding schemata stored in memory. Almost any one of the two various mental functions, such as perception, memory, orientation, or assimilation, can be carried out only after the raw data of input have been organized into some kind of meaningful and identifiable schemata.

The human computer, like any computer, processes its input according to given programs. Following Miller, Galanter, and Pribram (1960), the term "plan" will be used here for the human counterparts of the computer programs. Such a plan acts as a set of instructions, prestored in the apparatus, according to which new data are processed, organized, and constructed into some fixed schemata. Characteristic of the human computer is the multiple processing of the input by numerous plans, so that any new information is simultaneously processed in several ways. Each such plan processes its data according to a different category of organization, so that any raw data fed into the apparatus emerge as multiple and differing outputs. Each plan has a twofold function: first, to pick out a group of data from the mass of raw data making up the input, according to a given criterion; and second, to process, organize, and arrange this data according to a given set of instructions "written" on the plan.

For example, let us see what happens in a routine activity such as reading a book. The input is compounded of information regarding the many aspects of the book—its title, the author's name, its content, aesthetical value, educational significance, etc. Various data are "attacked" by the apparatus, to be concomitantly processed by several plans. In accordance with each plan, a specific group of data is picked out from the input to be processed together with the other data originating from other perceptual sources, or from memory. Every single bit of datum will enter into the processing of several different plans. All the formal elements, such as color, shape, size, etc., will be organized into a scheme to make up the inner image of the book as an object. The title will be organized with related information regarding other, similar books, under the plan of, let us say, "children's literature." The name of the author will be organized under the plan of "modern writers," and the book's style, its educational value, etc., will be similarly processed. Many elements will certainly be related to the reader's personal experiences and will thus be processed, each one of them, with the appropriate memories. The title may remind the reader of one of his birthdays, when he received, as a gift, a book bearing a similar title, and so on. The various elements, therefore, will be organized by objective criteria that treat the book as a phenomenon in reality as well as by subjective criteria that are based on what the book means to the reader.

This simple example demonstrates how every new group of data presented to the apparatus is immediately broken down into its components, and how each bit of information is "picked up" by several plans to be processed together with related information originating in other sources.

Let us try to classify the various organizing categories into their main groups of criteria:

1. The first group of organizational criteria is the objective one. Accordingly, data are organized into schemata corresponding to patterns existing outside, in reality. Such "patterns" are: (a) physical objects existing in reality. To construct an inner image of an object, data from various sensual sources are organized into a "gestalt," in an attempt to duplicate the object as it supposedly exists in reality. For example, an object image like "car" is compounded of all the visual, auditory, and tactile data originating from the object. But the inner image of such an object includes more than its mere physical qualities, for it has to include all the bits of information related to it, such as its name, function, value, etc. (b) Abstract objects which have a kind of "objective" existence in reality although they do not make up a physical entity. For example, a symphony by Beethoven, although it never exists physically in any place, is regarded as a kind of "materia" bearing an independent existence. (c) A regular sequence of events occurring in reality, such as the laws of nature (the rain following the accumulation of clouds), human activities (walking, speaking), the rules of language, etc.

In all these cases data are processed according to plans that organize them into images, gestalts, or patterns of events which are supposed to reflect similar patterns of organization existing outside the individual and independent of his personal view. The central criterion uniting all the organizing categories of the group is outer reality. I therefore suggest calling them *the objective categories*.

2. The second group of organizational criteria is the conceptual one. According to this mode of organization, any of the various qualities included in the objective schemata are taken out of their context and transversely organized into new groups. For example, many different objects possess the sensual visual quality of the color red. All the qualities of the many

objects are reorganized into the concept "red." A red apple, a red flower, or red blood do exist in reality, but the concept of the color red, not denoting any particular object, does not exist in reality and is only a creation of the human mind.

The organizing categories of this group consist of the various conceptual (e.g., color), functional (e.g., speed), or ideational (e.g., value) qualities. This second mode of organization, therefore, intersects the first objective mode, and, if we imagine it graphically, is perpendicular to it. This mode of processing is based on reality even though it does not reconstruct objects or objective events as they exist in reality. It reflects the human striving for orientation in reality in its attempt to comprehend reality through a second dimension—the qualities and attributes of the objects and events.

Since concepts, according to this mode, are created with regard to the various qualities of the objects, I would suggest calling the categories lying at the base of the organizing plans *the conceptual categories.*

Both groups described are similar in their attempt to organize information into schemata which correspond to a reality existing outside the individual and independent of him. I would therefore unite both groups under the term *reality-oriented categories.*

3. The third mode of processing is based on plans that include non-reality-oriented categories. Besides its function of processing information in terms of reality, the mental apparatus also has to assimilate and integrate any new information so that it can become part of its body of experience and memory. Thus new data bearing some personal significance is processed together with similar material from memory or material aroused by the influence of the drives. Almost any newly perceived information has several attributes which bear significance or some other relation to inner states of feelings, wishes, drives, expectations, attitudes, or past experiences. The data belonging to these attributes have to be processed together with, and against, the concomitant material belonging to this inner state, a kind of processing which requires the use of entirely different plans from those of the reality-oriented mode of processing.

We have seen in the case of reading how many elements of its content may impinge upon the reader's states of feeling or may remind him of various events he has experienced in the past. These elements are processed to be assimilated with related feelings and memory schemata. The organizing categories, in this third group, are all subjective, without reference to outer reality. The criterion underlying all these categories is the *self* in its various states of present and past feeling and experience. Therefore, I would suggest calling them the *self-oriented categories.*

The classification of the organizing processes into three modes is obviously an artificial one, because in practice the mental apparatus does not function according to three distinct sets of processes. Although we conceptualize the mental apparatus as a three-dimensional model, the activity of processing in fact proceeds in all possible directions. The distinction suggested above, of three modes of processing, is nothing more than an attempt to abstract from this three-dimensional space its three main perpendicular axes. The first two modes, which process data in terms of reality, may be conceptualized as the two *horizontal axes*, width and length, and the third, which processes data in light of inner experience, as the *vertical axis*. For the sake of simplicity I will refer, in this paper, to the horizontal and vertical axes as if they were two distinct modes of processing, but I will ask the reader to remember that they are no more than two extremes on a continuum which includes the entire range of all modes of processing.

The difference between the two horizontal modes and the vertical one, considering their dependence on outer reality, also determines their relation to consciousness. The plans based on the reality-oriented categories, which process data horizontally, organize data into schemata which reflect events, objects, or isolated qualities existing in reality. Such a mode of processing requires a constant contact with reality, to check the organizing activity and to match its results against the continuous perceptive input from outer reality. Experimentation with sensory isolation has proven repeatedly that the regular function of the reality-oriented organizing processes is dependent on the continuous influx of data from the outer world (Goldberger, 1961).

In my paper dealing with the theory of the primary processes (Noy, 1969), I brought some evidence to show that reality-oriented processes also require a constant flow of feedback. In other words, these processes are monitored and their regular function is maintained by the process of constantly perceiving the results of their own functioning. Thus, both functions, the one of constant perception of reality and the second of feedback perception, are mandatory for the regular operation of the reality-oriented processes. The continuous process of matching these two streams of information monitors the apparatus and safeguards it from any deviation of the inner functions from the requirements of reality.

The regular function of the reality-oriented processes requires the "tuning" of the apparatus to perceive sensory and feedback information, an activity which requires a considerable amount of attention cathexis. The more complex the reality-oriented activity is the greater the requirement for attention cathexis. Such sharp attention is achieved only in states of consciousness, since only under the light of consciousness is it possible to direct attention to perceive input information on all its details. This is the reason why a considerable part of all reality-oriented activity is performed under consciousness, and this is especially the case with those activities which require originality and adaptation to novel situations.

The "vertical" organizing activity, as compared to the horizontal one, is relatively independent of reality. The categories lying at the base of the organizing plans are all subjective, so that the processing of information in this mode scarcely requires any "tuning" to reality. This mode of processing, therefore, may continue to function even while the apparatus is shut off from any incoming stimuli and feedback information, a state which normally occurs during sleep or some other state of relative unconsciousness or "decathexis" of attention. This means that whether mental processes are conscious or unconscious depends, among other factors, on the degree to which consciousness is required to enable them to function regularly. It may be that many processes remain unconscious not because they are kept out of consciousness by some mechanism of repression, splitting, and so on, but simply because they do not require consciousness in order to function regularly. For reasons of mental economy, consciousness, which is a rather limited ability of the mind never able to cover more than a thin segment of mental activity, has to be spared for those functions which demand it most. In most cases those are the reality-oriented functions involved in the daily task of encountering the ever-changing environment.

Since the horizontal processes are able to operate regularly only while the apparatus is open and tuned to reality, they cease to function when contact with reality is lessened or blocked, as in sleep, unconsciousness, or experimental sensory isolation. The vertical processes, on the other hand, being independent of such contact with reality, can keep on functioning in all states of disconnection with reality. This explains the diurnal fluctuation in the pattern of processing. During states of wakefulness both modes are active so that all data that are processed multiply according to both. However, since it is the horizontal, reality-oriented processes which mainly determine expressive behavior, they "cover up" the vertical modes. The last, scarcely observed directly in behavior, can be observed only by the method of introspection in such "secret" activities as feelings, fantasies, planning, contemplation, etc.

During sleep the activity of the horizontal processes is reduced until a state is reached where the vertical ones "take over" and acquire dominance. Their function is expressed mainly in the dream, an activity predominantly organized by these processes. But the shift from one state to another is not only confined to sleep. The dynamic fluctuations between states of behavior dominated by horizontal modes and states where vertical modes "take over" are also characteristic of regular waking activity. In states such as contemplation, fantasies, or day dreaming, attention to outer reality is reduced, and a shift of dominance from the horizontal to the vertical modes of processing occurs.

Kubie (1966), although he used different terms, expressed a similar idea.

It is my thesis that both awake and asleep, there is a constant asymbolic (imageless) preconscious stream of central activity. . . . this activity consists of a continuous preconscious (subliminal) processing of experience . . . the ensuing flow of processing always represents a condensation of the near and far, the past and present, plus their extrapolation into the future . . . This preconscious processing of data goes on unceasingly throughout all life.

The question which I am sure many readers have already asked themselves is: How does the distinction between "horizontal" and "vertical" modes

of mental processes suggested here differ from the accepted distinction between the secondary and primary processes?

I purposefully have limited my use of these terms until now, because
some meanings attached to them in psychoanalytic literature do not fit
the theory presented here. The primary processes are regarded by many
theoreticians as primitive and infantile, and less differentiated or "refined"
in relation to the secondary ones. This view implies that the mental apparatus
is composed of several hierarchical layers of processes which differ qualitatively one from another in their operational aspect. The processes lying
in the higher layers are superior to those lying in the lower layers in their
organizational power, functioning efficiency, and the quality of their
product.

Neisser (1963) approached the problem from a different vantage point
and, using the computer model, assumed that primary and secondary processes are two distinct kinds of processes. In his opinion, the secondary
processes are analogous to the sequential processes of a computer, while
the primary are analogous to the multiple processes.

The opinion expressed in the present paper is that there is no qualitative
difference between the various processes. The mental apparatus does not
possess different organizing processes which differ in their stage of development, refinement, differentiation, efficiency, etc. All mental processes are
identical in all these aspects. Nor can the opinion of Neisser be accepted
because, as was shown above, the mental apparatus operates only in accordance with the principle of *multiple processing* on all its levels. The
difference is not in the *processes*, but in the *plans* according to which they
operate. What I have here called horizontal and vertical modes are only
different kinds of plans—i.e., different sets of instructions according to
which the various processes select different mental material and organize
it in different ways. The material processed by the horizontal plans is predominantly *information*, while the material processed by the vertical plans
consists of *feelings, wishes, and states of experience.*

Since the horizontal modes process information, they deal mostly with
conscious material. The vertical modes, however, dealing with feelings,
wishes, and experience, always involve unconscious material as well in their
processing. This is due to the fact that practically any feeling or wish
is in one way or another connected to unconscious material.

In a paper that revises the psychoanalytic theory of the primary processes
(Noy, 1969), I have defined the primary and secondary processes according
to their functions only. The secondary processes are defined as all those
processes serving the ego's function in its encounter with reality, i.e., reality
perception, orientation, communication, and reality-directed behavior. The
primary processes are defined as all those processes serving the ego's function
in maintaining its self-sameness and continuity, assimilating new experiences
into the self-system, integrating of present events with the past, and adjusting the ever-growing self to the encounter with the changing reality so

that it may be able to cope, master, and adapt to the demands reality imposes upon the self. Here the secondary and primary processes[1] are defined not according to drive cathexis, relation to consciousness, degree of development or refinement, but only according to their function, the secondary processes being *reality-oriented* and the primary processes being *self-centered*. In other words, all mental processes serving reality-oriented functions are called secondary, and all processes serving self-centered functions are called primary.

If the definition of the primary and secondary processes is limited to the point of view of their functions, then their relation to the different modes of mental processes becomes clear. The concept of primary-secondary processes refers to the various *functions* the processes fulfill, while the concept of vertical-horizontal modes describes the different *forms* in which the processes operate. To formulate: the primary processes operate according to vertical modes, the secondary processes according to horizontal modes.

II. Mental Representation

The mental apparatus, in its various cognitive functions like thinking, reasoning, memory, and communication, scarcely operates on the raw data of input, but rather on the various schemata constructed by the organizing processes. These schemata are the object images, ideas, concepts, structured events, memories, wishes, expectations, etc., which participate in the various mental operations. If we compare the raw data to "atoms," then these schemata are the "molecules" of which the mental material is composed. These molecules may be composed of only a few atoms or some hundreds or thousands of atoms. Try to imagine how many data are included in a scheme such as "the human body," or "Beethoven's Ninth Symphony." To utilize these "heavy" schemata in the various mental operations is a clumsy and difficult task. Therefore, some "shorthand" device must be developed, some method by which overflowing schemata can be represented in mental operations by only a few single cues, while all other data belonging to the scheme can remain at rest. It is only the ability of the human mind to develop such economy of mental representation that has enabled it to evolve to the highest levels of achievement and to handle efficiently a practically unlimited amount of information, in such functions as thinking, reasoning, and communication.

Conscious thinking and reasoning usually operate with only some cues or "memory traces" (see Rapoport, 1954) to represent the schemata, which

---

[1] It must be remembered that the meaning of the term "processes" as used for primary or secondary processes is not the same as the term "processes" used today in the computer model. In the first instance it would be better to replace the term with the term "functions" and to speak about "primary or secondary functions."

133

are almost never totally retrieved. The ability to operate with mere "traces" enables thinking to save the energy and time which would have had to be expended if it were to operate with full schemata, thus enabling men to think swiftly and effectively. But, if thinking and reasoning were to depend mainly on mental representation for their efficiency, communication, without the availability of an effective means to represent the images, ideas, or concepts which have to be transmitted, would hardly be possible.

In this section, the two main techniques used in mental representation—the sign and the symbol—will be examined. Both of these techniques are used, depending on need, in the various mental operations requiring representation, such as memorizing, thinking, reasoning, and communication.

A. THE SIGN

A sign is any single datum or group of data within a mental scheme which may represent the whole scheme. If only a single datum is used as a sign, then it must be a central one so that the whole will be identifiable by it. For example, in a scheme like "car," data like the word car, a known brand name, the voice of the horn or the engine, a picture of a steering wheel, or an outline of its form all may serve as sufficient cues to signify the car. If less recognized data are used to serve as a sign, then several of them will be needed to represent the whole. A windowpane, for example, will not suffice in representing a car unless it is presented along with the entire door, and the same for the paint, fuel, etc. The rule is that *every* datum or group of data out of the "circle" of data composing the whole scheme may serve as a sign, on the condition that the whole may be identified through it. The number of data required to be included in the sign is therefore dependent on the degree to which they are recognized by all people sharing the same system of communication.

The question is whether a datum not belonging to the scheme to be represented may also be used as a sign. In my opinion this question is irrelevant, since every datum, even if it is once arbitrarily connected to a given scheme, becomes a part of it. As shown above, the "circle" of data comprising a scheme includes all bits of information related to the object, idea, or concept. The "circle" of an object, therefore, includes not only its physical attributes, which make up an inner visual, auditory, or tactile image, but also everything known about its function, its relation to other objects, etc. Of course, the various names by which the object is marked also belong to such related information. A scheme is not a closed entity, but an ever-growing construct in which all new information learned about an existing scheme is automatically added to the circle of data. Thus, any word or cue which may be arbitrarily selected as a sign to represent a scheme will serve its purpose only after it is known as belonging to the given scheme, i.e., after becoming a part of it.

The technique of representation by a sign is biologically rooted. An animal manages to avoid danger, to find its mate, or to get its food because it is able to foresee a train of events or the presence of another animal by one or several cues of information associated with this event or animal. The ability to use signs, which originally developed in biology as a means of survival, was further developed by human beings to enable them to use their highest mental functions and to create the most efficient system of communication—language.

The advantage of the sign as a technique of representation lies in its economy, since it allows the mental apparatus to spare the energy required for the reconstruction of the whole scheme which is needed in thinking or communication. However, its limitation lies in its ability to represent only those mental schemata which are common to all individuals using a given system of communication. This last statement requires some words of explanation.

The numerous plans stored for the usage of the apparatus differ one from another in their degree of *endurance*. There are plans which, once created, persist forever and become part of the permanent stock of organizational plans. For example, once we have developed the plan to combine various perceptual data from the environment into the scheme of a man, from then on every sight, touch, smell, voice, action, movement, etc., belonging to the concept of "man" will automatically be processed along with all other data to compose the inner image of "man." Only in extreme cases, such as drug intoxication, fatigue, or disease, may such a basic plan be undermined so that the various data carrying information about men will be processed by "wrong" plans to produce different and bizarre meanings.

At the other end of the continuum of endurance lie those plans which are created only for a specific situation, used once, and then cast off—for example, a plan created for the solving of a problem in a chess game or a riddle which is never used again once the problem has been solved.

Between these two extremities lie many plans of different degrees of endurance, from the lifelong stable plans to the numerous plans created for the solving of novel, everyday problems.

The second difference between the various plans is their degree of *universality*. Some plans are used and shared by all people belonging to a given culture, while others are individualistic and exist only for the use of one man. Most plans active in the reconstruction of objective schemata are common to all the people who live in the same environment and are confronted by the same objects and events in reality. The same is true for a great many of the concepts which are created by abstracting the various qualities or functions belonging to those objective schemata. Such concepts, because they are so universally used and shared, tend to achieve an existence of their own, a kind of status as a "general truth." People who use sensual concepts like "warmth" or "softness," or abstract concepts like "beauty," "faithfulness," or "success," refer to them as if they really possessed some objective existence of their own, apart from the human mind that created them.

In contrast to the horizontal plans, which tend to be universally shared, the vertical plans serving the self-centered functions tend to be more individualistic and personal. The "inner life" of the individual is so influenced by his unique history, experience, and idiosyncratic ways of response to new impressions that the vertical plans are individually tinged and vary from one person to another. The more universal and socially shared plans in this mode are those centered around the generalization of feelings and emotions and are more of the nature of what Miller, Galanter, and Pribram (1960) call "metaplans." These are "plans for generating plans," which consist of a general set of rules or a formula according to which temporary plans, adapted to a given immediate situation, can be created. A concept like "happiness," for example, refers to a universal and socially shared concept, but as a processing category it can only serve as a metaplan. The meaning this concept holds for each person and the way he associates his personal experience with it differ so widely one from the other that each must create his own individualistic way of processing experiences and memories related to this emotion, i.e., each must create his own plans.

The first limitation of the sign as a technique of representation is, according to the above discussion, its ability to represent only the schemata whose forming plan possesses both characteristics—endurance and universal shareability. These plans are found mainly among the horizontal processes, but scarcely ever among the vertical ones. This limitation is actually experienced by anyone who attempts to express his personal feelings and experiences by using the signs of language. He will certainly feel the great discrepancy between the relative ease with which language conveys objective information and the difficulty and clumsiness with which it expresses feelings and subjective experience.

The second limitation of the sign as a technique of representation is its need to refer to the whole scheme in all its components. A sign is actually an "all-or-nothing" phenomenon. If recognized, the scheme as a whole is immediately retrieved; if not, the scheme will not be presented, neither as a whole nor in any of its parts. For example, the word "table" automatically brings forth the entire group of data composing the inner image of this object; the word "hero" includes all the qualities included in this concept.

Moreover, the signs of language refer not to any given single scheme, but rather to the generality of the scheme. The word "table" refers to all tables in the world, or the concept "desire" refers to any kind of desire a living creature may feel. Language may refer to the individual case only in a roundabout way, by reaching the singular through a train of generalities. For example, I want to refer to this particular desk on which I am now writing. When I say it is a desk, I thereby refer to all desks in the world. I then have to qualify it as being brown, but thereby I refer to every brown table in the world. I therefore have to continue and describe it as "this brown desk in the room . . . ," i.e., I must add another generality—"room"—and so on, until, from this train of generalities, the one single desk emerges.

This characteristic of the sign, its reference to the whole, becomes practically an invincible hindrance when the need arises to emphasize and stress only a given attribute of the whole. In regular communication it is not enough to be able to transmit a concept, image, or idea. In many instances a particular part must be qualified in some way, emphasized, or lessened. For example, I may want to emphasize David's strength or to qualify how strong he is and not merely say that he is strong. If a scheme is compared to a circle of data, the sign always refers to the whole circle. What can we do if we are interested in singling out only one particular datum from this circle? How can one single link in the chain be isolated from the whole? To achieve this end the technique of sign representation is not sufficient; another technique of mental representation is required.

B. THE SYMBOL

A symbol is a technique of mental representation used to emphasize, isolate, or qualify a certain link in the circle of data comprising the whole scheme with the aid of a second scheme. The two schemes must have at least one datum in common, which is, to use the term suggested by Von Domarus (1964), the "identical predicate" common to both schemata. If we imagine a symbol graphically, it will appear as two circles of data placed adjacently, one to another, with their edges overlapping. Thus, in the sentence "The girl is sweet as honey," the attribute "sweet" is the identical predicate common to both schemata—girl and honey—or, graphically, the area in which both circles overlap.

The "identical predicate," or, in other words, the attribute common to both ideas or images, does not have to be explicity presented, as, for example, in the phrase presented by Jones (1916): "John is a lion." Here the common attribute "brave" is missing from the sentence. The word "John" is a sign referring to the whole circle of data that comprises all the attributes belonging to a given man, and the word "lion" is a sign referring to all the attributes that qualify a lion. Since each sign retrieves the whole scheme, in all its components, the attribute common to both circles automatically gains a "double weight," and therefore it is not necessary to present it explicitly.

The power of the symbol to isolate a single attribute out of the circle of the symbolized is only one of its functions. Its main function is to qualify this isolated attribute by giving it a specific meaning. This meaning is derived from the meaning that the "identical predicate" bears in the context of the second circle. If, in the symbol "John is a lion" the aim were merely to isolate the common attribute "brave," many other mental schemata possessing the trait "brave" could have been chosen as well. The reason for this choice was certainly the symbolizer's intention to describe a specific kind of bravery, in this case an elementary, animalistic bravery of someone prepared to fight and tear his enemy apart, even with his bare hands and

137

teeth. If, for example, another symbol like "John is like a Kamikaze pilot" is used, the emphasizing effect of the attribute "bravery" would still be the same, but the meaning of this particular kind of bravery would be understood quite differently.

The ability to specify one of the attributes of the symbolized, to give it an accurate and delicate meaning in addition to the meaning derived from the regular context, is the unique power of the symbol. The efficiency and elegance of the symbol lies in its ability to convey such a meaning in the shortest possible way, sometimes in only one or two words. To convey the same meaning by using the signs of language would certainly require a full sequence of sentences.

If we call the symbolized circle A and the symbol B, the law of symbolism would be formulated thus: "Symbolism is a technique of mental representation by which a certain attribute belonging to the mental scheme A is qualified with the aid of another mental scheme B. The qualified attribute is an identical predicate common to both schemata, and the specific meaning it gains in regard to the other attributes composing A is derived from its specific meaning in the context of B."

The "identical predicate" common to A and B may involve a single, isolated attribute or a group of several attributes common to both. For example, compare the two sentences "this woman is like a child" and "this woman is like a flower." Women and children have many attributes in common, and the meaning of the symbol may therefore be any one of the alternatives or all of them together. The woman may be small, infantile, ignorant, weak, charming, or innocent like a child. Women and flowers, on the other hand, share only very few common attributes, so that here the common meaning can only be "this woman is charming like a flower." Graphically then, in example I the two circles, A and B, overlap over a great area so that a full group of attributes emerges as common to both. In example II, only the edges of the circles overlap, delineating only one or two common attributes.

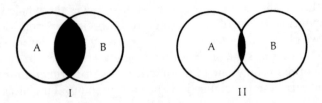

In some symbols the overlapping is so minimal that not even a whole attribute is involved—only a part of it. As an example, let us examine the phrase presented by Jones (1916) "as wise as a serpent . . . " on which he wrote: "Serpents are, in fact, not wiser than most animals, and the false attribution of wisdom to them is secondary and due to a process of true symbolism . . . " (p. 185). There is actually no "false attribution"

here. The aim of this symbol is not to qualify the adjective "wise" in general, but to specify and stress a specific variant of "wisdom," the serpent's particular wisdom in getting out of trouble, in "twisting" himself and slipping away from any apparently inescapable situation. To stress this particular point a symbol is chosen which shares with the symbolized only the attributes of "twisting" and sliding, but not "wisdom" in general. It is in these cases, where a technique is required to convey exact, delicate, and specific points of meanings that the advantage of the symbol over the sign becomes evident.

The advantage of the symbol is both qualitative and quantitative. Every technique of representation strives for economy, the ability to express maximum meaning with the aid of minimum cues. From the quantitative aspect, the symbol is the most economic technique available, since it has the ability to convey a whole array of meanings with merely a single word. However, this advantage is also a qualitative one, since the one word used as a symbol may convey the meaning better than a whole sequence of descriptive sentences. When the poet in "The Song of Songs" described his beloved, what better description could he have found than the symbol "As the lily among thorns, so is my love among the daughters"?

Let us now examine several other "technical facilities" of the symbol, which will give us some idea of the wide range of application of the technique. In all the examples presented up to now A, the symbolized, and B, the symbol, are both present. However, this condition is not a mandatory one. Occasionally, only B is present, while A is not mentioned at all. These cases do not nullify the law that for any symbol both A and B are necessary. For the sake of economy, however, A need not be presented explicitly, since in many cases it can be easily deduced from the context. When the prophet Amos addressed himself to the people of Israel and said, "Hear this word, ye kine of Bashan, that are in the mountain of Samaria . . . ," he did not need to make the symbolized explicit because every one could understand from the context that he was not speaking to the cows of Bashan but to the men of Israel. The same would be true if a poet said, for example, that "the door opened and a flower entered." It would be clear from the context that he was referring to a beautiful woman.

In regular language symbols are widely used without any reference to the symbolized; it is an implicit assumption that what is symbolized is self-evident in the context. We say, for instance, that we must curb "galloping inflation" without explicitly comparing "inflation" to a galloping horse: or we may say "fishing for compliments"; "embracing a belief"; "weighing an alternative"; or "a whistling wind."

This technical device of symbolization, presenting B alone while assuming that A can be deduced from the context, can be used in an interesting way. Since many times the context is ambiguous, several different A's may be derived, so that B can be used to convey several different meanings at the same time. This is one of the main characteristics of the symbol—its power to convey multiple meanings. This device is used deliberately by writers and poets who possess the artistic skill to construct a story or poem that conveys multiple meanings. Kris (1952) termed this phenomenon "aesthetic ambiguity." The symbol implanted into such a poem or story acquires different meanings, according to the level of meaning to which it is related. To use Freud's term (1900), such a symbol is overdetermined, i.e., it may express several meanings.

If we conceptualize an artistic creation as a multilevel matrix bearing a different meaning on each of its levels, the symbols interwoven in it are like nodal points which cut through all the levels of meanings. They are like links which integrate different levels into one artistic unity and serve as a junction through which the reader may shift his attention from one level of meaning to another.

We saw that the symbol B can fulfill its function without being presented together with the symbolized A, thus relying on the ability of the mind to deduce A from the context of the train of thought or the communication. This ability may be used in some "tricky" way as well: A symbol B may be presented in isolation, without any meaningful context which may even refer implicitly to A. This "trick" misleads the perceptive apparatus to look for some nonexistent meanings. Practically every word, phrase, or description that appears out of context in a chain of communications is treated as if it were a symbol. For example, if someone tells you that he sat in his room, the door opened, and a pole entered, you will certainly understand that since poles cannot walk, he is using the word as a symbol referring to a tall and slender fellow. Similarly, anything which appears as illogical in the context of a communication is supposed to be a symbol and therefore acts as a kind of "invitation," which forces the perceptive apparatus to look for a possible symbolized meaning disguised somewhere in the context. If such a disguised A is not found, the receiver will certainly find some explanation of his own and will be sure that "that is certainly what he meant." In cases where no symbolized meaning is explicitly or implicitly presented, the receiver tends to *project* onto the communication a meaning of his own. In some cases he may be aware that the meaning he is projecting is his own, but more often, he will not even be aware of it, and may believe that it is really the "right" meaning. In this "tricky" way the receiver is stimulated to activate his imagination and to project his own unlimited ideas, feelings, and memories.

This technique, not widely used in ordinary communication, is one of the most common means used by art to "invite" the reader or spectator to become involved intellectually and emotionally in the artistic experience. A. Stokes (1965) called this effect "the invitation in art." In literature, and particularly in poetry, symbols are often interwoven into some metaphysical context which bears no reference to the symbolized or to any realistic context from which the symbolized may be inferred. The reader, being eager to understand "what the writer really means," is forced to use his imagination in order to participate in the creative experience of the search for meaning. This activity, the "stirring up" of the inner world of imagination, is exactly the effect the artist is interested in producing. Arieti (1967) presented a fine example when he cited Blake's beautiful poem which tells about a rose destroyed by an invisible worm. In the poem no reference is made to what the rose might symbolize. Arieti analyzes this short poem to show how many meanings can be attached to this sick rose, so that every reader may project onto the poem the meaning that best fits his own feelings. One may "understand" the rose as a symbol representing a beautiful woman inflicted by illness, while another "understands" it as representing the eternal struggle between beauty and evil, and so on. The aesthetic value of such a poem stems from the fact that it can be understood as conveying not only any one of these meanings, but all these meanings together, each on a different level of abstraction. The two symbols, the rose and the worm, make up the junction from which different directions may be taken toward many possible interpretations.

The various ways in which the symbol can be used to express meaning, as described so far, can be arranged along a continuum based upon the strictness of meaning they convey. On the one end are those symbols which Langer (1948) called "discursive symbols." They appear mainly in regular language, their meaning is a strict one, and for any symbol B there is only one symbolized A, which is either presented explicitly or is easily referrable from the context. At the other end are the highly overdetermined or "nondiscursive" symbols which are used mainly in art. Their meaning is ambiguous and changes according to its context. Such a symbol is placed on so loose a matrix that numerous symbolized A's may be referred to or projected onto it. Of course, between these two extremes many possible transitional phases bearing different degrees of "strictness" or "looseness" of meaning are to be found.

The discursive symbols are usually schematized, redundant, universal, and well integrated into the body of regularly used language as fixed tokens of the language. The artistic symbols, on the other hand, are usually original, not widely used, and newly created for each instance. The former, therefore, may be used by anyone who masters a given language, while the latter, if they are to be skillfully used, require a "touch" of creativity and a special talent for the technique of symbolic representation. Indeed, one of the main criteria which determines the "greatness" of a writer or poet is his talent in choosing those "elegant" symbols which, although simple and short, are capable of conveying maximum levels of meaning, each appropriate to a different state of mind of the reader.

In conclusion let us contrast the formulation of symbolism as presented in this paper with other formulations in scientific literature:

1. The symbol is traditionally defined "as something that stands for something else" (Spiegel, 1959), as "a representative or substitute of some other

idea" (Jones, 1916), as "a cathected presentation standing in the place of some other, less neutral idea directly connected with drive aims" (Holt, 1967), etc. This is only a sample of the many formulations that conceptualize the symbol as a *substitute* which replaces the symbolized. The formulation presented in this paper sharply differs from this view. It approaches the symbol as a *dual unit* composed of both elements—the symbol and the symbolized. While a sign is a cue representing or substituting for a mental scheme (idea, object, concept, etc.), the symbol always conveys meaning by linking together at least two different mental schemata. And, if it seems as though one scheme substitutes or replaces the other, it only appears so because the one being "replaced" does not have to be explicitly presented and may be left to be deduced implicitly from the context.

2. Jones (1916) regards the symbol as being "characteristically sensorial and concrete . . . more primitive, both ontogenetically and phylogenetically, and represent[ing] a reversion to some simpler and earlier stage of mental development." Many authors share this view, which treats the symbol as a primitive form of representation according to which abstract ideas and concepts are represented by concrete and sensorial (mostly visual) images. Although most symbols use concrete images, this can by no means be regarded as the rule. According to the technique of symbolism, the mental scheme *B*, used to qualify a certain attribute belonging to scheme *A*, may be chosen from any available ideas, object images, concepts, and so on, on all possible levels of abstraction. No rule confines this choice to any particular kind of scheme. Since most symbols have to be simple, universally understood, socially shared, and must have the ability to best illustrate the intended meaning, it is only natural that they would be chosen from the world of concrete images common to all men, such as the many animistic images used symbolically in language. But many times, especially in art or religion, abstract ideas and concepts are used as symbols. The choice of the symbol depends upon the kind of attribute it is meant to qualify. If the aim, for example, is to qualify an attribute belonging to one of the sensual qualities of an object, then it would be done best with the aid of a concrete symbol. But, if the attribute is spiritual or aesthetical, an abstract symbol might do the job much better. For instance, the poet telling about a rose and a worm uses, in this case, concrete animistic symbols to convey some abstract meaning, but when he speaks about the struggle between beauty and evil, for instance, he uses abstract symbols to convey his ideas.

3. What is the relationship between the symbol and language? Language is defined by many authors as a system of signs, by others as a system of symbols, and by some as a combined system of both signs and symbols. The view presented here is that the unit of language, the word, is always a sign, and if it is used as a symbol, it is done so secondarily. The word is a cue or a code which refers to a mental scheme; it is always only one datum out of the circle which makes up the whole scheme. However,

the whole scheme represented by the word-sign may be used as a symbol. For example, in the phrase from "The Song of Songs" quoted above, the word "lily" itself is only a sign referring to an object image, a flower. But the flower as a mental scheme is used in this phrase as a symbol to qualify one attribute of the beloved woman. Ordinary language is full of symbols which are used to convey the more delicate meanings requiring greater exactness of expression than a sign can attain. The symbols are never the words themselves, but only the objects, concepts, or ideas signified by the word.

4. Symbolism is regarded by many psychoanalysts as *the* technique for the representation of unconscious material. Jones (1916) discriminates between the process of symbolism as understood in general and "true symbolism" as conceptualized in psychoanalysis. He wrote: "Representation of unconscious material—this is perhaps the characteristic that most sharply distinguishes true symbolism from the other processes to which the name is often applied" (p. 139).

I will try to show here that, although the symbol is often the best available means for representing unconscious material, this cannot be regarded as its main or only function. Symbolism is a generally applied technique for mental representation which may be used by the mental apparatus in all operations where representation is required, and I first discussed the various ways the symbol is used in conscious and preconscious mental representation in order to stress this point. But, its special characteristics—its ability to represent an isolated attribute out of a whole mental scheme, the overdetermination of its meanings, and its faculty to be utilized as a junction for the shift of attention from one level of meaning to another—make symbolism a particularly efficient means for the representation of unconscious material: indeed it is the best available technique for this purpose. To describe this special "affinity" of symbolism for the unconscious, I will have to further analyze the characteristics of the unconscious and vertical modes of processing and the special difficulties involved in the representation of unconscious material.

III. Symbolism and the Unconscious

The problem of the representation of the "deeper" levels of the mind is actually the problem of how the output of the vertical modes of processing may be encoded and represented. In order to study the techniques by which this representation is achieved, it is necessary to first examine, in more detail, further characteristics of the vertical modes, beyond those presented in the first section of this paper.

The study of the vertical modes is rather difficult since it is extremely hard to demonstrate them in action. In regular mental activity, they are usually obscured by the reality-oriented, horizontal modes of processing, and their products pass, as a rule, a process of "secondary elaboration" (see also Breznitz, 1971). The natural condition where this interference of the horizontal modes is at a minimum, though never completely absent, is in the *dream*, where islets of "pure" products of vertical processing may be seen.

Among the induced mental states where horizontal activity is reduced to a minimum, free association as practiced in psychoanalysis creates an additional, suitable condition for study of the vertical modes *in situ*. Psychoanalysis, as a technique of exploring the depths of the mind, relies mainly on these two states—dreams and free association—to reach the unconscious. The clinical examples chosen in this chapter to demonstrate the characteristics of the vertical modes and the technique of their representation have therefore been taken only from these two fields of mental activity.

To get a closer look at outputs of the vertical mode of organization, let us take a banal example from a typical analytical hour. The patient in his free associations presents various memories from his near and far past, among which, at first glance, no logical relation is evident. He tells about his friend, about a boss, about a teacher he had in elementary school, an uncle of his, etc. Only with time does the analyst realize that a common denominator unites all these seemingly unrelated memories. In this particular instance they are all related to interpersonal experiences in which the patient felt himself humiliated and ridiculed by a person who, in every confrontation, always succeeded in emerging with the "upper hand." It was revealed that the patient, at present a grown-up man holding an eminent academic position and known for his "self-confidence," was rather anxious about the forthcoming visit of his elder brother, who has lived abroad for many years. Far away, in his remote childhood, it was this brother who was always the dominant, the stronger, and the cleverer, who knew how to manage, while the patient's repeated experiences in competing with him resulted only in feelings of humiliation and defeat. Through the years, though he became independent and successful, he never overcame this childhood trauma. The associations presented in the many analytical hours expressed his repetitious attempt to work through this traumatic experience presently aroused by the forthcoming arrival of the brother.

This example demonstrates the inner structure of what we may call loosely a "vertical circle." It is composed of various fragments of memories, information, feelings, etc., all related to a certain state of feeling, wish, experience, or idea, which serve as the organizational category of the circle. Such a "circle," therefore, could be imagined graphically as a necklace in which the string is the central organizational category and the threaded beads are the numerous bits of mental material related to this category.

On the plan forming the circle are written instructions, according to which the mental material relevant to a given category is selected. In the above example, the plan included instructions to select and retrieve from the store of memory all relevant material related to the feeling of "humilia-tion by a person in a position of seniority." After selection, the material is then processed in many ways which vary according to the problem in question and the aim to be achieved. The various bits of memories, wishes, information, etc., are put one against the other, compared, matched, frag-mented, assimilated, and so on—all the various mental operations are included in what is called "working through," "problem solving," "mastering," "as-similation," etc. As a result of this processing the material is constructed as a scheme whose inner structure certainly varies, depending upon the specific way the material is processed.

Our knowledge concerning the structure of the vertical schemata is so limited that scarcely anything can be said regarding the various structural patterns of such schemata. However, any thorough analysis of a dream or a piece of art shows how every single content is inlaid into the whole scheme, not only by its relation to the central organizing category, but also by numerous meaningful associations which connect it to any of the other contents. If we could reconstruct a given vertical sheme in all its parts, including the unconscious ones, it would certainly emerge as a com-plex matrix, all parts of which are connected to one another by numerous threads of meaning and are together connected to one central category. Analysis of dreams reveals, again and again, that neither the presence of any given content, nor its place among all other contents, can be explained as trivial; dreams are always the outcome of complex rules of structuraliza-tion, most of which are still unknown to us (see also Ehrenzweig, 1967). For example, a patient, after reporting a dream in which a certain boy, who was her classmate in her first year at elementary school appeared, noted: "Why the hell did exactly this boy appear in my dream? I scarcely knew him, had nothing to do with him, and haven't really thought of him for some twenty years." By means of association it was revealed how every attribute of this image, his given name, family name, address, the place where he sat in the class, etc., were really meaningfully connected to other contents of the dream, until finally, we could both be only as-tonished at the ability of the "dream work" to find, among the millions of images stored in memory, the one which so perfectly fit into the dream matrix, like a piece completing the construction of a complex jigsaw puzzle.

The point to stress is that the vertical mode is a kind of processing which, being in the service of the self-centered functions, is subjected only to inner laws of organization. Therefore, since it is free from the requirement of taking reality into consideration, all its components are presented only to the extent required by the organizational demands of the vertical mode. The self-centered functions are not obliged to organize their material into schemata which would correspond to models existing in reality, such as objects, chains of events, etc., and so their products are also not required to be identifiable by the conscious mind. This allows for the economy of presentation, so characteristic of the vertical mode, which enables it to present only the few relevant aspects of a given object or idea without any need to reconstruct the whole reality-oriented scheme.

For example, if I have trouble with a certain person because of his loud voice, which irritates me, in reality-oriented thought I would have to reconstruct the entire scheme of the man, in all its parts, even though nothing but his voice is relevant to my problem. However, in a dream, where I am free from this compulsion to restore whole objects, this man may be represented simply as a noisy loudspeaker. Everyone working with dreams cannot but wonder about this capacity of the dream to express ideas in the shortest and most efficient way, without the wasteful necessity of adding details not directly relevant to the issue. Let me demonstrate this economy in the means of expression with a dream of my own.

In the dream I was walking down a street trying to catch the last bus, which was leaving at five minutes before midnight. The bus station was located near a building which stood alone in an empty street. Since I had returned from a funeral of a close relative the evening before, I could easily discover in the dream a preoccupation with death, like the idea of the bus leaving five minutes before midnight. Thus, after several associations the meaning of all the parts of this dream became clear to me except for one—the building near the bus station. I knew the building, but I could not remember anything connected with it. Moreover, the building was located in the dream in a city and on a street that had no meaning for me in reality, and while the city and street turned out to be connected with associations meaningful to the ideas of the dream, the building did not. Also, near the building in the dream I saw a colleague who was in reality under my supervision. He is a very creative fellow and, like many creative persons, he often says things which at first seem totally "out of context," only to be later discovered as interesting and original ideas. I felt that his presence should be understood as a hint given by the dream to look for a meaning of the building which was "out of context" to the general context of the dream. When I arrived at this idea, I suddenly realized that during the entire time I had been lying in bed uncovered and actually half-frozen because my blanket had fallen down while I was asleep, which was assuredly the reason for my having awakened. Then the meaning of the building became clear to me as I remembered that in its basement a workshop for the "repair and renewal of blankets" is located. In the formation of this dream, therefore, two independent trains of thought came together: one aroused by the attempt to cope with the revival of some death anxieties, and the second aroused by the present feeling of coldness. The interesting question is why were the feeling of coldness and the falling blanket responsible for the image of the building where the workshop was located rather than any other image which would perhaps have better represented the blanket as an object?

The story is that several weeks before the occurrence of the dream I had given my daughters' blankets to this workshop in order to have them widened, since they were too narrow and always fell down at night while they were sleeping. Thus the building where the workshop was located did not merely represent the blanket in general, but "highlighted" one particular aspect of it—its annoying tendency to fall down at night. For the dream, which on this occasion dealt with the feeling of being cold, only this one aspect of the blanket was relevant, and therefore, from among all the possible images which might have represented the blanket, only this one was selected.

This economy in the meanings of expression and the independence from the reality principle, as exemplified here, make the self-centered vertical mode of processing so efficient in handling the various stimuli which the self is required to cope with. These stimuli originate from two sources: (a) drives and wishes originating from within; (b) new perceptual experiences. These two sources are actually interdependent, because drives usually give rise to wishes which strive for gratification through objects and experiences in reality, while new perceptual experiences affect the self which is forced to cope with them, particularly when they are related to a drive or impinge upon a wish.

The point is that the self seldom has to cope with perceptual input organized into reality-oriented schemata; usually it has only to deal with those isolated perceptual elements which are in some way relevant to the self, such as those attributes that relate to wishes, impinge upon conflicts, or correspond to states of feelings. The vertical mode, therefore, hardly ever deals with whole objects or concepts, but only with some of their attributes. For example, let us consider the act of becoming acquainted with a new neighbor. Certainly an internal scheme, including all you get to know about him, will be formed. Perhaps nothing in his appearance or behavior arouses any emotional response in you except for his particular manner of smiling, which reminds you of someone you once knew in your childhood, though you are unable to even remember who it was. After you have met this neighbor, if you continue to be preoccupied with thoughts about him, they will only be related to his manner of smiling, and perhaps you may even have a dream the following night in which various smiling faces may appear.

The reality-oriented scheme formed of the neighbor in this example is an outcome of the horizontal modes of processing, while the "working through" of the ideas related to his manner of smiling is in the vertical mode. The vertical circle here originates from one of the attributes out of the horizontal circle, the only quality of this man which becomes for some reason relevant to the self. This is generally the nature of every vertical circle—it always originates from one attribute out of a horizontal circle. If several attributes of a given horizontal circle are relevant to the self, then certainly numerous vertical circles may originate from the one horizontal circle. To imagine it graphically, the vertical circle hangs down from one of the links in the horizontal circle, or numerous vertical circles hang down, each one from another link in the horizontal circle. This particular link, i.e., the attribute out of the horizontal circle which, owing to its relevance to the self, arouses vertical processing, I will call the "key attribute" of the vertical circle.

This *key attribute* holds a unique position among all the other attributes of the vertical circle for the following reasons:

1. It may be the stimulus which arouses the whole vertical circle. This happens in a case where a certain attribute out of a horizontally processed scheme bears a particular personal significance or arouses an emotional response sufficient to recruit the self-centered functions to cope in some way with it. In such cases the key attribute is identical or closely related to the central organizing category of the vertical plan.

2. In most cases, it is not the key attribute alone which arouses the vertical processing, but the drive, wish, conflict, or any other internal state of mind aroused by this stimulus. The key attribute acts, in these cases, only as a kind of catalyzer that arouses an internal state which forces the self to cope with it by its vertical modes of processing. It holds, then, among all other attributes of the vertical circle, the unique position of "starter," the stimulus which initiates the processes resulting in the formation of the whole circle.

3. The vertical modes, whose function it is to process mental material according to internal criteria, always involve, in their processing, the unconscious levels of the mind. Almost any wish, conflict, or emotional experience has its roots deep down in the unconscious, since it is always associated with early memories covered by the amnesia of childhood and is usually related, in some way, to one of the "forbidden" unconscious wishes. As a rule, therefore, a considerable part of any vertical circle is unconscious; frequently only the upper part of the circle remains conscious. The key attribute, because it belongs to a horizontal circle, is mostly conscious, and very often it is the only single conscious attribute in the vertical circle.

This short discussion of the main qualities characterizing the vertical mode of processing will enable us to deal with the central issue of this section of the paper—the means for the representation of the vertical circles. As was previously shown, representation of a circle is done by the presentation of only one or several data out of the circle. If a datum is a central one and is identifiable as being part of the circle, it alone may represent the whole circle; but, if it is a less identifiable datum, several of them will have to be presented in order to represent the whole circle. We have already seen that in the horizontal circles most often numerous data are sufficiently identifiable to be used, each by itself, as signs to represent the whole. In the vertical circles, the case is different; most of its data are unconscious, and therefore unidentifiable. Even if they are presented, the forces of repression, which act upon most unconscious contents, will actively prevent us from comprehending their meaning. In addition, the conscious data of the circle, if present at all, are usually unsuitable for representing the whole, if the temporary existence of the vertical circle and its highly individualistic composition is taken into consideration.

There remains only one datum out of the circle—the key attribute—which may be solitarily used to represent the whole, owing to the fact that it is conscious as well as central enough to be identifiable. Moreover, since the key attribute was, from the beginning, the stimulus or the "starter" which aroused the processes to form the vertical circle, every renewed presentation of it may again retrieve the whole circle. Thus, the key attribute may act either as a sign to represent the still existing vertical circle, or as a "starter" to arouse the vertical modes of processing to form such a circle anew. If other data, besides the key attribute, are used to represent a vertical circle, several of them must usually be presented, because an additional single datum which may alone suffice in serving as a sign to represent the whole circle may seldom be found.

As an outcome of this discussion my first assumption emerges. Two different techniques are used by the mental apparatus to represent vertical circles: (1) representation by one central datum out of the circle, a datum which is mostly the "key attribute"; (2) representation by a line of peripheral data, which are chosen mostly out of the less important ("second-grade") data. I would call the first technique *central representation* and the second *peripheral representation*. In analyzing these two techniques I am aware of the fact that they are perhaps not the only techniques used for representation of outputs of the vertical mode of processing and that further research may reveal additional techniques. At present, these techniques are simply the only ones whose operation I feel able to demonstrate and analyze.

My second assumption is that in both cases the data chosen to represent a vertical circle, whether single or multiple, and whether central or peripheral, are always represented by the technique of *symbolism*. To prove this last statement allow me first to describe and discuss the two techniques, each of which will be demonstrated by a dream.

A. CENTRAL REPRESENTATION

A colleague who was under my supervision once told me a dream of one of his young female patients; in it she drew a car which was stuck on a "huge, round, hard wooden electric pole." The dream occurred at night while she was sleeping with her friend, a married man, twice her age, after they had enjoyed hours of intensive sexual activity. She told the therapist: "I played with his penis for hours and did all sorts of crazy things with it." The therapist, who immediately realized that the pole was a symbol representing the penis, asked me a question which, I am sure, generations of teachers have been asked during supervision or dream seminars: "Why does the dream have to disguise a content and represent it by a symbol if there is nothing unconscious or forbidden about it?" In this case, after hours of actually dealing with the penis, why could it not be blatantly represented in the dream? In answer to this question I suggested that perhaps the pole did not represent the penis as an object at all, but only "highlighted" one particular quality of it, its taut and unyielding hardness. I suggested, therefore, that he explore further what this aspect really means to the patient. In the following sessions her anxieties concerning the penis were revealed. She regarded it as a dangerous instrument which could surely hurt her and destroy her from within. The therapist learned that her "crazy play" with the penis was a kind of compulsive preoccupation aimed at mastering her anxieties in an attempt to convert this dangerous and frightening instrument into a familiar and "innocent" plaything, an attempt at mastery which was also reflected in the dream. Actually, then, the dream intended not to represent the penis in general but only its one, single quality that was relevant to the unconscious, anxiety-arousing conflicts.

In this example, the penis, in all its attributes, is the horizontal "circle," while the collection of images, feelings, and memories related to the idea of the hard instrument threatening to tear and destroy her from within make up the vertical "circle." The quality of unyielding hardness which is the one link common to both circles is the key attribute, which was the only one that appeared in the dream to represent the vertical circle. All other parts of this vertical circle were revealed only after several additional hours of analysis.

The noteworthy fact is that the key attribute, which is the sign representing the circle, was presented by the technique of *symbolism*. Two horizontal circles—circle *A*: the penis (the symbolized) and circle *B*: the electric pole (the symbol)—were used to delineate the common attribute of "unyielding hardness." Only after this attribute was isolated from the horizontal circle to which it belongs could it be used as a sign to represent the vertical circle.

This description must give rise to some new thoughts about the whole issue of the meaning of symbols and their interpretation in dreams. The electric pole in this dream is evidently a content alien to the context of the dream material. According to the classical interpretation, the function of such symbols is to serve as substitutes to disguise the "real" contents. However, according to what has been presented here, the symbol in the dream has a much more general function, beyond its function of deceiving the "censor." It is a technical device to represent the contents of the dream and is therefore an integral component of the language of the dream which is also used when there is nothing to be disguised.

With regard to the interpretation of the symbols in the dream, most analysts, because they approach the symbol as merely a substitute for some disguised content, regard it as sufficient to detect the hidden material that is symbolized. It seems to me that this task, usually a relatively easy one, has to be regarded as only the first step in the process of the interpretation of the symbol. The next question we must always ask ourselves, after we know the meaning of *A* symbolized by *B*, is "Why exactly was this particular *B* chosen from among all possible *B*'s?"

As an example, let us remember what Freud wrote in *The Interpretation of Dreams* (1900): "It is highly probable that all complicated machinery and apparatus occurring in dreams stand for the genitals (and as a rule male ones . . .). Nor is there any doubt that all weapons and tools are used as symbols for the male organ: e.g., ploughs, hammers, rifles, revolvers, daggers, sabres, etc. . . . " (p. 356). We may add to Freud's list symbols like towers, scissors, water hoses, balloons, knives, poles, etc., which may all be used to symbolize the penis. If we examine these symbols we will see that each one represents an entirely different aspect of the penis: the tower—its length; the water hose—its ejaculating capacity; the knife—its penetrating power; the balloon—its erective quality, etc. Therefore, it is in no way a matter of pure chance what B is chosen to represent the penis, but it is certainly a function of the specific aspect of the penis that the dream refers to. The dream, as a self-centered activity, is never concerned with the penis as a real object but only with those aspects of it which are in some way "problematic" for the self, and which therefore, according to the rule of economy, will be represented in the dream. The answer, then, to the question "Why exactly this B . . . ?" may therefore indicate the specific aspect the dream deals with, and by this reveal the key attribute of the vertical circle which makes up the framework of the dream.

Taking into consideration the fact that the various aspects of an object may also reflect different stages of development, the finding of the particular aspect the symbol refers to may indicate the specific developmental state to which the dream has regressed. For example, the penis in the anal period bears the meaning of an excretory organ, while in the phallic period, that of a penetrating instrument. Repetition of various symbols in consecutive dreams referring to the same stage may even indicate the point of fixation in the specific developmental stage to which the patient has regressed in this period of his psychoanalysis.

B. PERIPHERAL REPRESENTATION

This technique of representation is essentially the one described by Freud (1900) in the chapter "The Work of Displacement" in *The Interpretation of Dreams*. According to this technique, a vertical circle is represented by an overdetermined symbol which refers to an attribute common to a whole group of data out of this circle. This attribute is often one which, although common to all the data, has no meaningful relation to the organizing category uniting them, such as a word, quality, or formal feature which is only coincidentally common to this data. To quote Freud: "What appears in dreams, we might suppose, is not what is important in the dream-thoughts but what occurs in them several times over." Let me demonstrate this technique by a dream of one of my patients.

In the dream the patient was in a room where in one of its corners a girl was lying on an iron bed. He wanted to look at the girl but felt ashamed to do so. In his associations the word "iron" reminded him of a friend whose family name is "Barzel" ("iron" in Hebrew, the language of this patient, is "barzel," a word used also as a family name in either its nominative form or in its declension "Barzelay"). A day before the occurrence of the dream he met his friend, who was known as a "happy bachelor," strolling near his house. He imagined him as surely being on his way to visit a new girlfriend living in the neighborhood, but in spite of his *curiosity* to know who the girl was, he was *ashamed* to ask. When I asked for further associations he replied that nothing meaningful came to his mind "but only various people bearing the same name as my neighbors 'Barzelay,' a teacher I had in childhood also named 'Barzelay,' and an attorney named 'Barzel.'" After I pressed for further associations regarding these people, it came out that his neighbors, an elderly couple living opposite him, are always *curious* to know what is going on in his home and use every opportunity to come in and look around. The teacher mentioned was his music teacher in elementary school, who was known only by his family name; and the children had always been *curious* to find out his first name. The attorney, who had become famous some years ago for revealing personal scandals about known people, always aroused his *curiosity* as to how he succeeded in "peeping into people's private lives and uncovering their dirty business."

When I suggested that the dream dealt with his childhood curiosity to "peep" into his parents' bedroom, he suddenly remembered an additional association which shed light upon the entire dream. The kitchen of the neighbors called "Barzelay" has a common wall with his and his wife's bedroom, and many times, when he wanted to take an afternoon nap, he could not fall asleep due to the noise of the dishes coming from the other side of the wall. At night, being with his wife, the idea occurred to him that, just as he could hear his neighbors making noise in the kitchen, they could probably hear what happened in his bedroom.

Thus the vertical circle, making up the framework of this dream, is composed of the various ideas and memories related to the infantile curiosity to "peep" into his parents' bedroom and is represented by the symbol "iron bed." This symbol has one attribute, the word "iron" ("barzel'), which is common to several links in the vertical circle. To imagine it graphically, if the components of the vertical circle' are like beads strung on a ring, the symbol *B* is a second ring placed so that it cuts through the edges of several beads (A_1, A_2, . . .). In this technique the symbol *B* is used

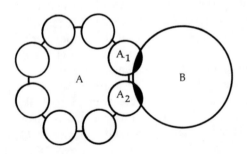

only as a mean for "marking' several A's, in a number sufficient to signify the vertical circle, so that its real power to isolate and qualify the attribute common to it and the various A's is not utilized at all.

In other dream samples using the technique of peripheral representation, it can be proven that the symbol is further utilized in all its capacities. The isolated common attribute of B and the various A's may be, in these cases, a key attribute which gives rise to a secondary vertical circle, in which case further analysis would prove, for example, that the attribute "iron" gives rise to its own vertical circle. The dream is a complex matrix composed of sequential levels of meaning, so that every link in one vertical circle may give rise to secondary circles, and so on. Actually, every interpretation of a dream may be continued to reveal these additional levels, but for the purpose of the present discussion such further analysis would be superfluous. The purpose of presenting the dream examples here was only to demonstrate the main techniques of representation.

In the two dream examples presented, the signs for representing the vertical circles were presented by the technique of symbolism. As stated above, it is my assumption that this is always the case. What is the reason for this? Why does the mental apparatus always use a symbol for the representation of a vertical circle? To explain this phenomenon, we have to remind ourselves of some of the processes characterizing perception.

The mental apparatus in perception, the so-called "perceptual apparatus," tends to organize any raw input into meaningful schemata. In other words, it "catches" any input by its horizontal modes of processing and organizes it into a reality-oriented, logical fabric. This organizing function, essential for the orientation and adaptation to reality, also acts as a defensive barrier by creating a kind of protective network to prevent any unorganized material from penetrating into the deeper layers of the mind (see also Ehrenzweig, 1953, 1967). Our perceptual apparatus is ever active in its attempt to "understand" everything we perceive, and it resists being overflooded by mere experience. What we are unable to understand logically, we tend to treat as "nonsense" and simply reject. This is really what happens to the dream that gets rejected as "illogical," whose meaning is not understood by either the dreamer or by the untrained listener.

The result of the horizontal organizing activity is that every isolated cue presented to the perceptual apparatus is immediately processed with other data to be included in one of the objective or conceptual schemata or is treated as a sign to retrieve such a scheme. For example, if an attribute like "unyielding hardness" is presented, it would certainly retrieve such objective schemata as "steel," "wood," or even "penis," but it is unlikely that it would retrieve a vertical circle which includes the unconscious memories regarding childhood fantasies and fears of bodily mutilation by hard instruments.

The problem, then, is how to reconcile the tendency of the perceptual apparatus to automatically "catch" any isolated data and process them into the horizontal network of objective and conceptual schemata, with its requirement that the one or several data representing a vertical circle should appear as isolated in consciousness? The best and, indeed, the only way to overcome this "interference" of the horizontal modes of processing is to cooperate with them and to take advantage of them. This is made possible by the technique of symbolism.

The symbol, which is a technique derived from the horizontal modes of processing, and which works with horizontal circles, succeeds in a simple and ingenious way to utilize the tendency of the horizontal modes to organize any isolated data into schemata in order to get the opposite result—the presentation of isolated data. This isolated data, singled out of a horizontal circle by the technique of symbolism, may then be used to represent any given vertical circle.

The conclusion to be derived is that the techniques of mental representation, at least so far as we know at present, are always based on the horizontal modes of processing. We may assume that no technique can ignore, bypass, or overcome the basic tendency of the perceptual apparatus to organize any material through its horizontal, reality-oriented modes. This is why symbolism, if used as a technique for the representation of vertical circles, must always use horizontal schemata as auxiliary means, even if they are out of context as to the contents the vertical mode is dealing with. For example, the electric pole, in the above-mentioned dream, has no relation to any of the ideas making up the material of the dream. It appears in the dream only as an auxiliary technical device to single out the one quality required to represent the given vertical circle. Similarly, most of the symbols used in dreams, art, and in the other media representing unconscious contents are actually not a part of the contents they express, but are "out-of-context," horizontal schemata presented only for technical reasons of representation.

This brings us to the last problem to be dealt with—symbolism and the communication of the unconscious. Until now we have seen how unconscious material may be represented via the vertical mode of processing. Albeit no communication can proceed without the processes of mental representation, such representation alone does not ensure communication but is only a necessary condition for it. As shown in section II, mental representation, as one of the central functions of the mental apparatus, is necessary for most of the "higher," inner mental operations that do not involve communication. The dream, for example, which is a medium hardly bearing any communicative value, uses processes of mental representation widely. The very fact, therefore, that symbols are used to represent unconscious contents cannot yet be regarded as proof of their ability to communicate those contents.

The whole issue of "unconscious communication" deserves some words of clarification: the rule of communication requires that the information encoded by the sender into a message and transmitted by any of the available media, can be decoded by the receiver to reproduce the exact same information. The efficiency of any set of communications is generally measured by the degree of its accuracy in transmitting information from a sender to a receiver. Many authors, who assume that such a process as "unconscious communication" does exist, tend to apply the same rules to the unconscious as well. In formulations expressing this view, which are particularly found in professional literature on the psychology of art, one may find such statements as "the direct communication between the unconscious of the artist and the unconscious of the public," "the unconscious conversation between the creator and the listener," etc.

It seems to me that the fallacy underlying such an approach is that a fallacious analogy is made between conscious and unconscious communication. The basic rule of conscious communication, which requires accurate transmission, can in no way be applied to unconscious communication. Although the sender may express unconscious contents in his communication, and the receiver may respond with the arousal of unconscious contents of his own, the aroused contents will seldom be identical to the contents expressed, so that no "transmission" of ideas will really occur. Even if an artist succeeds in expressing his sorrow or happiness in art, and his message arouses within me a similar emotion, it will always be *my own* sorrow or happiness which will be aroused—never *his*. "Unconscious communication," therefore, is not a process of an exchange of information transmitted from one unconscious to another, but a process by which out of the unconscious mental activity of the one, messages are emitted which, when perceived by the other, may arouse *his own* unconscious mental activity.

The communication between the expressed unconscious states and those who are aroused is usually confined to the general tone of feeling, the kind of wish aroused or the central conflict involved, while the content of ideas and memories attached to these states remains highly personal and bears no resemblance. A public of hundreds attending a play or concert may react to a given piece of art with similar emotion. All may express deep sorrow, for example, but if asked what they are imagining at this particular moment, a hundred different stories will certainly be reported.

The question whether the symbol can be used as a mean for unconscious communication must therefore be confined only to the question of "does the symbol have the power to arouse the receiver's unconscious?" The exact outcome of this arousal, however, will always be determined only by the subjective state of the receiver.

In order to study the symbol from this aspect, it is best to concentrate upon the symbol as used in art. Art is regarded by most psychoanalytically oriented authors as *the* medium of communication whose function is to arouse the reaction of the unconscious of the receiver. In a forthcoming paper I intend to analyze art from the point of view of communication (see also Noy, 1968, 1969, 19672), to show that most of the formal elements of art are, in essence, intricate and ingenious techniques aimed to bypass, evade, or penetrate the logical, reality-oriented protective layer, to directly arouse the deeper levels of the mind via the vertical processes. The symbol stands out from among the many techniques used in art as one of the cardinal means of achieving the goal of arousing and stirring up the deep processes of the mind.

The comprehensive study of the symbol's function in art is certainly beyond the scope of the present paper, and we will therefore survey only the main characteristics which make the symbol one of the best means used to communicate with the unconscious. Because such a survey will only repeat things already said, this may serve as a good opportunity to recapitulate the main points of the problem of symbolism and the representation of the unconscious and to conclude this paper.

1. The way to arouse unconscious material is always via the action of the vertical modes of processing. It is only when an organizing plan based on a self-centered category is "called" into action that all unconscious bits of information, wishes, states of experience, feeling, and memories related to this category are retrieved to enter into the action of processing alongside the conscious ones.

2. The vertical modes of processing are activated by any input bearing some personal significance, i.e., arousing drives or wishes, corresponding to an internal state of feeling, or impinging upon an internal conflict.

3. Although any element of input, even if already organized into the network of the horizontal mode of processing, may arouse vertical processing if it is loaded with "heavy" personal significance, isolated cues, singled out from the network of horizontal processing, have a better chance of arousing such processing. Such isolated cues may arouse vertical processing and form vertical circles, even if their personal significance is so low that, if they are presented as a part of a horizontal network, they would remain "neutral."

4. Symbolism is the best-known technique for singling out elements from existing horizontal schemata. It achieves this end by working in line with the horizontal, reality-oriented, organizing tendencies of the perceptual apparatus and by taking advantage of them. It therefore arouses the resistance of the protective layer of the perceptual apparatus relatively less than any other technique used in communication.

5. In order to hold such resistance to a minimum, the symbol, as used in art, does not usually present any "dangerous" content blatantly. In most cases only "innocent" ideas or images are presented, which are at times totally out of context in the communication and which at first sight appear as meaningless. The symbol never imposes itself, but rather delivers its message only to the mind which is ready to decipher its meaning actively. The perceptual apparatus is therefore free to "take it or leave it," and if it takes, it may only take those meanings relevant to it, thus being free to reject the rest. The way people respond to symbols in art is similar to the way they respond to jokes. Those who cannot allow themselves to respond simply "do not understand," and for them the symbol remains

meaningless. Others, although able to understand, can only do so after a lapse of time, when their logical thinking has managed to "explain" the meaning. They may be able to interpret, analyze, and even discuss professionally "what the symbol means," but they remain well protected against the danger of getting its deeper meaning. Those who are free to grasp the symbol are able to get its deeper meanings, to react with the arousal of their own imagination and wishes, and to absorb its message as a total experience. The symbol, by not saying anything directly, enables anyone to take only the exact amount of meaning which he is able to tolerate, i.e., to reach the limits set by his own defenses.

6. As stated in points 2 and 3, a perceptual stimulus which arouses the vertical modes of processing has to fulfill two conditions: it must bear a personal significance for the receiver, and it must be presented as a unit singled out from the horizontal network. The mere presentation of isolated cues would not suffice to arouse vertical processing if their meaning remains "neutral." The deep meanings of the symbols used in art are indeed never neutral. They generally refer to those human feelings, experiences, memories, and conflicts, many of them unconscious, shared by all mankind or at least by most men brought up in the same culture. We confront again and again in art symbols related to such universal themes as Oedipal love, sibling rivalry, prohibited aggression against parental figures, castration fears, and the conflicts aroused by growth, maturation, and death. The specific power of the symbol in art lies in its reference to the central problems which any human being has to cope with endlessly, whether consciously or unconsciously, throughout his lifetime.

7. The effect of the symbol in arousing the vertical mode of processing depends, to a large extent, on its freshness and novelty. Any symbol used redundantly tends to become a schematized token of language and loses its power to evade the resistance activated by the protective layer of the perceptual apparatus. Art as a medium never sinks into stagnation, and forever renews its means of expression, thus maintaining its power to arouse the unconscious of the receiver. In any work of art, new symbols are created which, by their originality, succeed in perplexing the perceptual apparatus, penetrating its protective layer, and reaching the deepest, most guarded layers of the mind.

BIBLIOGRAPHY

Arieti, S. (1967), *The Intrapsychic Self*. New York: Basic Books, Inc.
Breznitz, S. (1971), A Critical Note on Secondary Revision. *Internat. J. Psycho-Analysis,* 52:407–412.
Ehrenzweig, A. (1953), *The Psychoanalysis of Artistic Vision and Hearing*. London: Routledge & Kegan Paul, Ltd.
——— (1967), *The Hidden Order of Art,* Berkeley and Los Angeles: University of California Press.

Freud, S. (1900), The Interpretation of Dreams. *Standard Edition*, 4 & 5. London: Hogarth Press, 1953.

Goldberger, L. (1961), Reactions to Perceptual Isolation and Rorschach Manifestations of the Primary Process. *J. Project Tech.*, 25:287–302.

Gombrich, E. H. (1965), The Use of Art for the Study of Symbols. *Am. Psychologist*, 20:34–50.

Hartmann, H. (1947), On Rational and Irrational Action, in *Psychoanalysis and the Social Sciences I*. New York: International Universities Press.

Holt, R. (1967), The Development of the Primary Processes: A Structural View, in *Motives and Thought: Psychoanalytic Essays in Honor of David Rapoport*. New York: International Universities Press.

Jones, E. (1916), The Theory of Symbolism. *Papers on Psychoanalysis*. London: Tindall & Cox, 1920.

Kubie, L. S. (1966), A Reconsideration of Thinking, the Dream Process and "the Dream," *Psychoanal. Quart.*, 35:191–198.

Kris, E. (1952), *Psychoanalytic Explorations in Art*. New York: International Universities Press.

Langer, S. (1948), *Philosophy in a New Key: A Study in the Symbolism of Reason*. New York: Rite and Art, Penquin Books.

Miller, G. A., Galanter, E., Pribram, K. H. (1960), *Plans and Structure of Behavior*. New York: Henry Holt & Co.

Neisser, U. (1963), The Multiplicity of Thought. *Brit. J. Psychol.*, 54:1–14.

Noy, P. (1968), A Theory of Art and Aesthetic Experience. *Psychoanal. Rev.*, 55:623–645.

———— (1969). A Revision of the Psychoanalytic Theory of the Primary Process, *Internat. J. Psycho-Anal.*, 50;155–178.

———— (1972), About Art and Artistic Talent. *Internat. J. Psycho-Anal.*, 53:243-249.

Rapaport, D. (1954), On the Psychoanalytic Theory of Thinking. In: *Psychoanalytic Psychiatry and Psychology*, ed. R. P. Knight & C. R. Friedman. New York: International Universities Press.

Rycroft, C. (1956), Symbolism and Its Relationship to the Primary and Secondary Processes. *Internat. J. Psycho-Anal.*, 37:137–146.

Spiegel, Rose (1959), Specific Problems of Communication in Psychiatric Conditions In: *American Handbook of Psychiatry*, ed. S. Arieti. New York: Basic Books, Inc.

Stokes, A. (1965), *The Invitation in Art*. New York: Chilmark Press.

Von Domarus, E. (1964), The Specific Laws of Logic in Schizophrenia. In: *Language and Thought in Schizophrenia*, ed. J. S. Kasanin. New York: W. W. Norton & Company.

Action: Its Place in Psychoanalytic Interpretation and Theory

ROY SCHAFER, PH.D. (*New Haven*)

The theoretical advances of recent years have made it both possible and legitimate to question the proposition, binding on psychoanalysts for so long, that being a Freudian analyst means adhering faithfully to the fundamental assumptions and concepts of Freud's metapsychology. We are now in an early phase of the revision of these fundamental assumptions. This revision is unlike those attempted during earlier phases of the development of psychoanalysis, in that it entails no discarding or devaluing of Freud's clinical methods and the findings amassed by means of this method. My basis for making this claim is the slow, steady increase in the Freudian literature of the number of discussions which not only present fundamental critiques of metapsychology but go on to outline or at least point to new modes of conceptualization. These new modes have often centered on the concepts *experience, meaning, choice* (or *decision*), *intention*, and *reasons*, and they derive at least some of their stimulation from the writings of modern phenomenologists and existential analysts. I mention all this not as a prelude to a critical review of these developments but as a way of placing this paper in its correct historical context.[1]

The Third Fenichel-Simmel Memorial Lectures, delivered, in slightly different form, before the Los Angeles Psychoanalytic Society and Institute, November 17 and 18, 1971. Preliminary and partial versions had been presented earlier to the Philadelphia Association for Psychoanalysis, and the Washington and Western New England Psychoanalytic Societies. To all I am indebted for helpful critical discussions. This work has been supported by the Old Dominion Fund, administered through the Student Mental Hygiene Division of the Yale University Health Service, and the Foundation for Research in Psychoanalysis.

[1] Without pretending to give a complete or satisfactorily annotated bibliography in support of this proposition, I refer the reader to the following authors: Home (1966), Rycroft (1966, 1968), Apfelbaum (1966), Guntrip (1967), G. S. Klein (1967, 1969), Hayman (1969), Grossman and Simon (1969), Applegarth (1971), Prelinger (1972), and Schafer (1968a, 1968b, 1968c, 1970b, 1970c). Preliminary or preparatory contributions have been made, in effect if not by intention, by Gill (1963), Schafer (1964, 1967b), Holt (1967), Rangell (1969), and Sandler and Joffe (1969). Set primarily in a philosophical context, and not without serious limitations and biases, but nevertheless searching in their critiques and stimulating in their suggestions, are the contributions of Binswanger (1936, 1946), Sartre (1943), Hampshire (1959), and Ricoeur (1970).

It is my purpose in this paper to set forth a new systematic mode of conceptualizing Freudian psychoanalysis. This mode centers on the concept *action*. I do not mean action in the usual sense of motor behavior that has some visibility in, if not impact on, the real environment; I mean it in the much broader sense which in psychoanalytic discussions has usually been rendered by the word *activity*. The rationale of my choice of term, as well as the amplification and application of my proposal, will be presented below in section II. There I shall attempt to show how psychoanalytic interpretation is essentially interpretation of action and how it leads to the replacement of what I call "disclaimed action" by claimed and integrated action. The psychoanalytic process and the nature of psychoanalytic interventions will be examined within the framework of the action concept.

But before embarking on that conceptual expedition I believe it necessary to develop further certain aspects of the general critique of Freudian metapsychology. By metapsychology I refer to the set of interrelated concepts and propositions concerning dynamic, economic, structural, adaptive, and genetic aspects of mental functioning that constitutes the traditional Freudian model of mind (Rapaport and Gill, 1959). Specifically, I shall focus first on the anthropomorphism which both pervades and artifically sustains metapsychology. I shall try to show that this anthropomorphism is a consequence of the mechanistic foundations of Freud's model of mind (see also in this regard the excellent contribution by Grossman and Simon, 1969). And I shall go on to argue that the growing appeal of such concepts as *ego autonomy*, *identity*, and *self* represents a reaction against mechanistic theory, although it is typically a reaction that miscarries owing to persisting employment of mechanistic-anthropomorphic modes of thought. All of which is to pave the way toward the action model I shall then propose for consideration. That model makes it possible to deal consistently and logically with issues ordinarily dealt with unsystematically in metapsychological discussion. (Adequate presentation of the proposed new model requires a book-length effort—which is in progress.)

I. The Mover of the Mental Apparatus

Let us turn first to that most difficult subject, metapsychology. If I could make it entertaining, simple, or at least short, I would. But I can't. Metapsychology is a serious matter because orderly thinking is a serious matter, and thus far metapsychology has been our one reliable guide to orderly psychoanalytic thinking. Metapsychology is complex because people are complex, and thus far it is Freudian psychology, of all the psychological approaches to human beings, that has resisted most effectively the inevitable and strong pressures toward simplification. And my discussion must be long because metapsychology has a long history during which many good thinkers have both contributed to it directly and used it in making various clinical and "applied" contributions. Metapsychology cannot be dealt with in a perfunctory way.

I have, however, already set forth in recent years and at some length my critical views on this subject (Schafer, 1968a, 1968b, 1968c, 1970b, 1970c). Although these publications make up the general background of this paper, it is simply not possible to summarize them even briefly here; nor, in my opinion, is it necessary to do so, for as my theme is action I think it legitimate to confine my remarks to certain general aspects of traditional metapsychology. As my title indicates, I shall be emphasizing its anthropomorphic aspects in particular. I shall, however, add to the timeliness of this discussion by attempting to derive from some of my conclusions an explanation of the growing popularity of such terms as *ego autonomy, identity, and self*, and by presenting a critique of these terms as well. Although manifestly I shall range far from the action model of psychoanalytic interpretation and theory, fundamentally I shall still be developing the case for that model.

CONCEPTUAL DIFFICULTIES IN FREUDIAN METAPSYCHOLOGY

First of all, Freudian metapsychology. The terms of Freudian metapsychology are those of natural science. Freud, Hartmann, and others deliberately used the rhetoric of forces, energies, functions, structures, apparatus, and principles to establish and develop psychoanalysis along the lines of a physicalistic psychobiology.

It is inconsistent with this type of scientific rhetoric to speak of intentions, meanings, reasons, or subjective experience. Even though in the first instance, which is the psychoanalytic situation, psychoanalysts deal essentially with reasons, emphases, choices, and the like, as metapsychologists they have traditionally made it their objective to translate these subjective contents and these actions into the language of functions, energies, and so forth. In this way, they have attempted to formulate explanations of action in the mode—actually it is only one of the modes—of natural-science explanation. They have suppressed the intentionalistic, active mode. In line with this strategy, reasons become forces, emphases become energies, activity becomes functions, meaningful thoughts become representations, affects become discharges or signals, deeds become resultants, and particular ways of struggling with inevitable diversity of intentions, feelings, and situations become structures, mechanisms, and adaptations. And, in keeping with the assumption of thoroughgoing determinism, the word *choice* has been effectively excluded from the metapsychological vocabulary. Action, if it is not used in the sense of acting-out, is understood merely as behavior with respect to the so-called external world (Hartmann, 1947).

It is curious, to say the least, that practitioners of a discipline that is so specifically concerned with human subjectivity and action should have continued to devote themselves to the impersonal, mechanistic rhetoric of natural science. It is all the more curious in view of the close parallels between this language and what I shall discuss later under the heading "disclaimed action" (e.g., "My unconscious made me do it, so don't blame me!"). Analysands and metapsychologists sound strangely alike.

There was something about this discrepancy between practice and theorizing that seemed to trouble Freud. We are all aware that Freud did not adhere consistently to the scientific model on which he had pinned his theoretical hopes. While using it, he "anthropomorphized" it. In doing so he made some of his most memorable statements—for example, when he spoke of the superego as the heir of the Oedipus complex, and of the ego's serving three masters, or letting itself die, or deforming itself. Freud often spoke in this way of the psychic structures, the topographic systems, the primary and secondary processes, the great principles, and the instinctual drives and energies—he spoke of all of these as if they were purposive, meaning-creating, choice-making, action-oriented entities, which is to say, as if they were minds within the mind, or homunculi.

Was this anthropomorphizing mere carelessness or indifference on his part, or metaphorical embellishment, or inevitable conceptual impurity retained in the process of developing a new field? I do not think any of these characterizations is exact. I would emphasize, rather, that Freud felt his powers of understanding to be too confined by the natural-science model. It is as if he sensed that this model excluded something essential, something it had to exclude owing to its internal logic, and yet something that psychoanalysis could not do without, namely, the purposive agent, the experiencing human being, the active self, the "I," or whatever one chose to call it. To put the matter in terms of Binswanger's (1936, 1946) later discussions, Freud must have sensed that natural-science theorizing necessarily reduces that personal "I" to a clinically unwieldly or unsuitable thing, organism, or apparatus; or in Buber's (1923) term, to an "It."

When Freud was not being self-consciously theoretical, he spoke a different language—a purposive or intentionalistic language, or, in my terms, a rudimentary action language. Consider, for example, these two excerpts from his stunning papers on technique:

It must be understood that each individual, through the combined operation of his innate disposition and the influences brought to bear on him during his early years, has acquired a specific method of his own in his conduct of his erotic life—that is, in the preconditions to falling in love which he lays down, in the instincts he satisfies and the aims he sets himself in the course of it [Freud, 1912, p. 99].

The more plainly the analyst lets it be seen that he is proof against every temptation, the more readily he will be able to extract from the situation its analytic content. The patient, whose sexual repression is of course not yet removed but merely pushed into the background, will then feel safe enough to allow all her preconditions for loving, all the phantasies springing from her sexual desires, all the detailed characteristics of her state of being in love, to come to light; and from these she will herself open the way to the infantile roots of her love [Freud, 1915, p. 166].

Consider, too, this excerpt from "Beyond the Pleasure Principle":

What psycho-analysis reveals in the transference phenomena of neurotics can also be observed in the lives of some normal people. The impression they give is of being pursued by a malignant fate or possessed by some "daemonic" power; but psychoanalysis has always taken the view that their fate is for the most part arranged by themselves and determined by early infantile influences [Freud, 1920, p. 21].[2]

"A . . . method of his own"; "preconditions . . . he lays down"; "she will herself open the way"; "their fate is for the most part arranged by themselves"! Thus Freud the clinical analyst, a striking contrast to Freud the scientist. Yet, as I have mentioned, Freud the clinical analyst had his say in the theory through his anthropomorphic rendition of his metapsychology.

Let us move on now to that most excellent theoretician, Robert Waelder. He, too, could not escape this difficulty in conceptualization. Consider, for example, the following passages, which, by the way, despite their awkward construction, I, along with many others, count among the theoretically most suggestive and clinically most useful statements in the psychoanalytic literature:

According to this principle of multiple function the specific methods of solution for the various problems in the ego must always be so chosen that they, whatever may be their objective, carry with them at the same time gratification of the instincts. However, in the face of the dynamic strength of human instinctual life this means that the instincts play the part of choosing among the possible methods of solution in such a way that preferably those attempted solutions which also represent gratification of the dominant impulses will appear and maintain themselves. . . . In a situation of conflict each method of solution which perceives an experience as coming from the outside and itself passively surrendering to these outside forces, is an attempted solution for certain problems, is gratification of love and hate relationships, defense reaction and others such [Waelder, 1930, pp. 56–60].

Notice how Waelder was driven to anthropomorphize what he calls "methods of solution." According to him, these methods maintain themselves; they perceive experiences and perceive themselves; and they passively surrender. In this passage, in a similar but less obvious anthropomorphizing vein, Waelder also indicated that instincts have preferences and make choices. I think it fair to say that Waelder was trying not to see that there are more things in heaven and earth than can be spoken of in the natural-science rhetoric of Freudian metapsychology, and that, as a consequence, he was resorting to anthropomorphizing of mechanistic concepts.

What of Heinz Hartmann? He did make extensive efforts to deal with

[2] Although Freud went on in this connection to begin arguing for some principle "beyond" the pleasure principle, or, as it turned out, antithetical to it, he nowhere modified his assertion that, clinically, the analyst may look at normal and neurotic lives as actively chosen or "arranged."

this problem systematically. First, he explicitly devoted himself to purging metapsychological discourse of anthropomorphism. He did so particularly by working out refined conceptualizations of functions, psychic energy, and intrasystemic heterogeneity, and by his consistent application of these conceptualizations. Consider, for example, the following contrast. On the one hand, Freud (1928) had spoken of the ego's submitting itself masochistically to a tyrannical superego, with both ego and superego playing son and father simultaneously in that interaction. On the other hand, Hartmann, together with Loewenstein (1962), tended to speak of interactions between certain ego functions and superego functions; he proposed that each function was fed by and expended libidinal and aggressive energies of varying degrees of neutralization; and he further proposed that the proportions of pleasure and pain in the interaction could be accounted for by the types and degrees of energy discharge involved in these mutual influences. The difference between the two approaches is plain enough. Hartmann certainly seems to have succeeded in eliminating Freud's anthropomorphism from metapsychology. (However, that he still retained it in a subtle, yet central, way will soon be made plain.)

But Hartmann was too wise and conscientious a thinker to drop the matter there. As his second contribution in this respect, he attempted to find a place for whatever it was that the anthropomorphism was supposed to have informally retained in the theory. He did this in several steps. One step is represented throughout his writings (Hartmann, 1939, 1964) in his emphasis on higher-order, central-regulating, and organizing functions. These are the functions that differentiate and synthesize mental processes and contents, and also control other functions by setting aims, establishing rank orders of functions, and controlling expenditures of the neutral and neutralized energies that are freely available to the ego for carrying out its activities. For example, these are the functions that suspend certain rational and defensive functions in "adaptive regressions." Essentially, they constitute what Hartmann (1939) termed, in his great monograph on adaptation, the "intelligence" of the organism. But, although he placed these functions at the top of the hierarchy of functions, Hartmann never amplified this conceptualization in proportion to its obviously central strategic significance. It is a most striking gap in his theorizing!

The second step Hartmann took to recast Freud's anthropomorphic formulations was this: he acknowledged intentionality as a human characteristic and classified it as an ego function (1952, p. 173); however, he defined intentionality quite narrowly as one function among others—a direction-setting function—and he did not discuss it at length. Moreover, according to my reading of his somewhat ambiguous discussion, he seemed to be restricting intentionality to the defining of *conscious* intentions. This view of it, which does not violate the logic of natural-science theorizing, is considerably more restrictive than the one derived in part from Brentano and Husserl and their modern followers according to which intentionality is the defining feature of every psychological act. For psychoanalytic psychology, then, it is a universal; it defines our subject matter. In any case, Hartmann's including so shrunken a version of intentionality in psychoanalytic theory could not go far toward dealing with problematic anthropomorphizing.

In a third step, Hartmann emphasized functions of primary and secondary autonomy. This step seemed to allow recognition of apparently "free" or conflict-free behavior without any compromise of the natural-science, deterministic model of explanation. Two points must be noted here: (1) if "autonomy" is to retain any meaning, designating these functions "autonomous" amounts to stating that they are or can be self-activating and self-regulatory; (2) to speak of "relative autonomy" is, though it represents hedging to the point of self-contradiction, still a way of ascribing freedom to functions. I shall return to autonomy concepts soon.

Although Hartmann seemed to have considered taking a fourth step against anthropomorphic theorizing, he never quite took it. This step would have been a full discussion of the problem of meaning. He referred to *meaning* in a number of places, but he discussed its concrete application only in one place and there only briefly (1955, pp. 217–218). He merely stressed that *meaning* was an unclear concept, and he suggested that the established metapsychological concepts, such as the functions and regulating principles, were the appropriate and adequate ones to deal with its referents. In another place (1959, p. 346), he said "that the same manifest action, attitude, fantasy may have different 'meanings' (that is, may be the result of the interaction of different tendencies)." Here, in equating meaning with the resultant of forces, he took the position he had worked out long before (1927) and was never to depart from. This is the position that psychoanalysis is and must be a mechanistic theory cast in terms of forces and energies—a position in consequence of which "understanding," "meaning," "reasons," and suchlike are to be regarded merely as subjective mental contents, not yet "objectified" in the language of scientific causality. I believe that had Hartmann explored the idea of meaning, he would have had to confront the fact that mechanistic theory is merely an option, not a necessity, for psychoanalysis (Schafer, 1970b); and he might have moved toward the type of mixed economic-experiential conceptualization most recently attempted by Ricoeur (1970).

Hartmann's treatment of this central problem of meaning may be interpreted in the following manner. He wrote as if he had seen, correctly, that a full, direct consideration of meaning would require a theoretical model radically different from the traditional natural-science model, and as if he had concluded that, for the sake of consistency in his own (and Freud's) systematizing efforts, it was best never to get deeply into it. He committed himself to Freud's model.

I have sketched Hartmann's efforts systematically to expunge anthropomorphic formulations from metapsychology, and I have indicated that as a natural-science theoretician he was both exactly right to set this as his aim and impressively consistent in his pursuit of it. But was he really successful? Did he really rid metapsychology of its anthropomorphic heritage? As I have already indicated, I believe that he did not succeed. I believe that in the relatively undeveloped concepts of intelligence, central regulating and organizing functions, autonomy, and intentionality as one ego function among others, there remain many residues of this problematic anthropomorphism. I suggest that Hartmann implicitly ascribed intentionality and choice to the central functions and the autonomous functions. How else can we understand functions that set aims, rank order other functions, or discharge their own noninstinctual energy? In being represented as self-activating and self-regulating, autonomous functions are being implicitly portrayed as independent, symbol-utilizing minds that can make themselves up. There is no way around this anthropomorphic implication.

Despite his sticking to the impersonal language of energy and functions, Hartmann placed in "the ego" a center of actions that only a mentally intact human being might engage in. In the very terms of his own argument, intentionality could not be, as he said, one direction-setting ego function among others; nor could it be restricted to consciousness. Nor could *meaning* be set aside as mere experience or mere content waiting for its scientific conceptualization. Intentionality and meaning were coterminous with ego itself. There was a person loose in the apparatus, a mastermind working the mechanism—what in a general way Ryle (1949) in his brilliant book, *The Concept of Mind*, called "the ghost in the machine," and what, in my adaptation of his argument to this particular problem, I shall call "the mover of the mental apparatus."

In this light, it is possible to understand why Hartmann's conceptualization of intersystemic relations was so awkward: he had to limit himself to speaking of noncognitive "influences" of id and superego on ego functions because he could not attribute perceiving, knowing, and choosing to the id and superego without having to face the problem of anthropomorphism all over again—and the problem of meaning as well. Without these limits, the structures would have begun to sound too much like people in relationship to each other—as they do in Fairbairn's (1952) theorizing. And yet what sense does it make to speak of noncognitive influences in mental functioning? How can "the superego" influence what it does not know? How can it even choose to exert influence? Who or what activates the superego? How can it be activated? Who or what receives the signal or knows its meaning? Surely, Hartmann was not setting forth a conditioned-response, simple reflex-arc, nonsymbolic neurological theory. In these respects, the purity of Hartmann's natural-science rhetoric rests on an incomplete analysis of the conceptual field.

On the basis of these considerations, I come to this conclusion: however much Hartmann eliminated blatant anthropomorphic thinking from Freud's metapsychological formulations, in certain critical respects he did not succeed in resolving the problems latent in them. His efforts were incomplete, insecurely founded, and unconvincing. Incorporated in them were problems they were meant to solve. Further, I believe that *in principle* a mechanistic model of human psychology, so long as it is an attempt to deal with fundamental and complex phenomena and relations, must in the end turn into an anthropomorphic model. Hartmann had to fail in this respect. He had to hide a mover in the mental apparatus, for an apparatus cannot move itself; nor can it, like the human mind, move the world. It cannot, for example, invent psychoanalysis. We shall identify that hidden mover before we are through.

What follows from this? Most generally, I suggest that we may take the state of theoretical affairs I have described in this brief review of Freud, Waelder, and Hartmann as an indication that it is now time to try out radically different conceptual models. These models should be tried out with all due regard for their internal logic, just as Hartmann tried out the natural-science model with all due regard for its logic. The rationale of engaging in these attempts is simply that we have yet to find a home for the sense in Freud's unabashed metapsychological anthropomorphic theorizing. After all, Freud's *Ich* is not just ego and self: it is also "I," the agent, the subject who must always be assumed in any psychological proposition. This agent is psychoanalytic theory's greatest embarrassment, for the theory can only reduce him to anthropomorphized ego functions. Hartmann (1950) and also Jacobson (1964) attempted systematic differentiations of the concepts *ego* and *self-representation*—the established metapsychology could accommodate both of these terms—but where is the "I" (and the "over-I") that Freud could not do without?

The "I" or agent must remain outside the natural-science rhetoric. It should not, however, be left in limbo. Analysands often try to leave it in limbo, as when they insistently disclaim responsibility for action. But in the course of our analytic work we analysts try to restore an unthreatened sense of activity to the analysands and to enhance it as well as preserve it for ourselves against the analysands' assaults and seductions. But we have no theory to formalize and guide this defining aspect of our work. Our general theory serves other purposes. Up to now it has been left to the existential psychoanalysts to develop this theory of agents—persons defined by their intentions, choices, and actions—but it is also true that up to now these analysts have been distorting and discarding so many of the essential Freudian contributions to the understanding of human existence that I, at any rate, cannot consider them psychoanalytic.[3] Be that as it may, we encounter here serious gaps between our clinical interpretations and our theorizing, as well as gaps between our general theorizing and our theorizing

---

[3] For example, the existential psychoanalysts rely heavily on interpretation of manifest content; moreover, this content is often gathered outside a psychoanalytic treatment situation, perhaps from creative writing or letters or Kraepelinian observation of patients from afar. Infantile sexuality is often ignored or its significance minimized.

about the therapeutic process. Some vexing issues in psychoanalytic discourse have developed in and around these gaps. The gaps themselves, it should become evident, reflect shortcomings of the mechanistic model of mind.

SIGNIFICANT GAPS BETWEEN THEORETICAL AND CLINICAL PROPOSITIONS

I shall now discuss some of these gaps, and the issues they imply, under the following headings: (1) the adaptive ego; (2) identity; (3) self; and (4) the theory of the psychoanalytic process.

(1) *The adaptive ego.* By introducing adaptational considerations into metapsychology, Hartmann appears to have provided an opening for confused theorizing. Through this opening many authors have by now attempted to reintroduce the central agent, the embarrassing "I," into metapsychology. The adaptive ego or ego functions, or the autonomous ego functions, have been used to include just what the decorum of natural-science conceptualizing is designed to exclude, namely, the sentient, self-determining, choice-making, responsible, active human being. In natural science that human being must be made into an object of observation, a mechanical object, and thus an object of an order different from that of the free observer. It is only on the surface that this use of "autonomy" remains functional and impersonal. Often, it is merely a pseudo-orthodox way of saying "he" or "she"—or, possibly, since analytic self-esteem has gotten hooked up to being autonomous or "having" autonomy, the adaptive or autonomous ego may be a covert way of saying "I," that is, the author himself. It can be an instance of the observer's exempting himself *as observer* from deterministic propositions.

Additional problems have ensued in this regard. To accomplish their mission fully, the adaptive ego-ists have tended to slip into simple, unsubstantiated assertions that this or that function *is* autonomous and the corresponding behavior adaptive. They do not trouble themselves with noting that they lack clinical evidence to support their assertions. They do not seem to remember that this evidence would have to be collected during clinical analytic investigation of the implicated functions and behaviors (Schafer, 1967a). Some of the comments included in the recent panel report in the *International Journal of Psycho-Analysis*, "Protest and Revolution" (Francis, 1970), demonstrate all too well this cavalier attitude on the part of analysts who should know better.

Surely, from all we do know as analysts, we should be especially cautious and should be armed with qualifications and question marks when speaking of autonomy and adaptiveness. Freud dealt a great blow to human narcissism when he showed how illusory were many or most of mankind's claims to conscious functional autonomy and adaptiveness. He showed that the conscious unitary will was not all, and often not much. He dealt another blow when he showed how limited and misleading are impressions of motivation gained through informal social observation and conscious, directed report. Freud struck these blows through his clinical method, not through common-sense observation of social behavior supplemented by what we may call "wild ego analysis." In these times of psychosocial variables, psychohistorical explanations, and a widespread professional rage to be relevant—all of which require radical, untested, and highly questionable assumptions about ego autonomy—wild ego analysis may be a greater threat to Freudian analysis than wild id analysis.

It is not Hartmann's conceptualization of adaptation itself that is at fault here. The reason for this theoretical "return of the repressed" is this: the anthropomorphic formulations no longer being acceptable, it has become necessary to provide new forms of expression for the irrepressible theme of action, that is, of human beings doing things for specifically human reasons. Anthropomorphism in metapsychology is the archaic representation of the theme of human action. It is ironic that these new forms have been developed at the center of Hartmann's rigorous conceptualizations. There they violate both the decorum of Hartmann's theorizing and the exacting demands of Freud's psychoanalytic method. I did, however, point out earlier that, careful as he was, Hartmann could not purge his own formulations of anthropomorphic implications.

(2) *Identity*. Some Freudian analysts have tried to use Erikson's (1950, 1956) concept of identity to reintroduce the active person, the "I," into metapsychological as well as clinical discourse. They speak of identity as being, doing, requiring, and effecting various things. In one way this usage makes a new thing or apparatus of identity. Identity becomes something one has or loses or searches for. In this respect identity is being used the way "*the* ego" is used by many analysts as a machine with a single, central intelligence. Theoretical advance is blocked by this mechanistic reification.

But in a deeper way, this use of identity is only a breath away from saying "the person" or "the agent." Moreover, I believe it to be true that, as Erikson uses it, identity is more phenomenological and existential-analytic than Freudian-metapsychological. Identity is very similar to the existential-analytic concept of *being-in-the-world* in that both are used to attempt a basic thematic characterization of a person's way of creating, arranging, and experiencing his life. Identity is the theme of his actions. Although Erikson retains Freudian drives, defenses, identifications, superego dictates, and stages of development as components of the concept of identity, he tends to view them in the context of life themes and to explain them by reference to these themes. Thus, like the existentialists, he reverses the Freudian priorities which require explanations to move from content to formalistic concepts. Hartmann's translating "meaning" into "the result of the interaction of different tendencies" is an instance of what I mean by the Freudian priorities.

I submit, then, that as a concept identity is phenomenological, existential, and intentionalistic at its core. Contrary to the argument of Rapaport and Gill (1959), identity is not in the same realm of discourse as Hartmann's adaptation theory, which is natural-scientific and mechanistic; consequently, the two cannot be reconciled with each other. Erikson has contributed to this confusion by mixing mechanistic with existential concepts in setting forth his ideas.

Let me also suggest in this regard an explanation of the wide professional appeal of Erikson's writings. I believe that this appeal stems from the fact that Erikson has helped the psychoanalytic therapist to feel that it is all right once again to think about himself and others as people who do things rather than as organisms or apparatus with functions—and while yet retaining Freudian insights! This is the same dynamic as the one that has led so many otherwise thoughtful analysts to accept uncritically Freud's anthropomorphizing of mechanistic variables as respectable theory. It seems that, in the final analysis, the important thing is that the person be alive and well in the impersonalized theory, that there be a mover—now called "identity"—hidden in the mental apparatus.

I conclude that identity seems to help bridge the gap between traditional theory and practice more than it in fact does. Actually, it introduces a second kind of theory without discarding the first. Ultimately, this mixing of forms of theory is more obstructive to psychoanalytic conceptualization than the many loose, ambiguous, repressive, and regressive purposes to which the term "identity" is currently being put. Nevertheless, identity may be seen as a move toward new theoretical models suitable for human beings and their actions.

(3) *Self.* Self is the third of the problematic "bridge" concepts I shall discuss. For the most part, Hartmann steered clear of self in his systematic writings. As he used it, it was roughly synonymous with the whole biological person or organism. He meant to differentiate self from self-representation, and to emphasize the latter when clarifying and amending Freud's fuzzy conceptualization of the relation between narcissism and ego. From the point of view of traditional theory, *self*-representation is merely mental content; though a necessary concept, it is not central.

In contrast to Hartmann, another excellent Freudian theoretician, Heinz Kohut, has become deeply embroiled with self in his recent explorations of narcissism (1966, 1971). He uses the term to refer to a new dynamic and structural entity as well as to a life theme. This usage seems to be in the service of bridging the gap between theory and practice while both avoiding anthropomorphism and preserving the mechanistic metapsychology. Like identity, however, Kohut's "narcissistic self" mixes two different types of discourse in that it represents an attempt to inject the person as agent into a natural-science model of mind.

Additionally, Kohut's weighty and ambitious use of self encounters a problem I could as well have mentioned in connection with identity. The problem is this: descriptively and dynamically, Kohut's narcissistic self overlaps and is confused with the tripartite structure of the mental apparatus. Specifically, Kohut attributes to the narcissistic self features of both the so-called id (e.g., exhibitionism, grandiosity, drive urgency, demands on the ego, and libidinal energy seeking discharge) and the so-called ego (e.g., ambitions, affect signals, and self-feeling). That he treats this self as a new psychic structure, characterized like the others by its independence, is evident in his statement beginning, "The interplay between the narcissistic self, the ego and the superego . . . " (1966, p. 256). At this point, then, Kohut's generally careful and informed conceptualizations suffer from his attempt to mix a phenomenological, experiential, representational concept with the traditional structural-energic metapsychological entities.

Kohut's sophisticated difficulties are all the more apparent when, in one of his central propositions, he says, "At the risk of sounding anthropomorphic, yet in reality only condensing a host of clinical impressions and genetic reconstructions, I am tempted to say that the ego experiences the influence of the ego ideal as coming from above and that of the narcissistic self as coming from below" (1966, p. 250). Again, he mixes experiential and traditional metapsychological terms; now, however, he adds to his difficulties by thinking of his argument merely as risking anthropomorphism, and then by suggesting in vain that richness of clinical connotation can eliminate the risk of "real" anthropomorphism. Clearly, against his better judgment he is caught up in conceptual conflict.

Consequently, and despite his most illuminating discussion of the phenomenology and dimensions of narcissism, by being tied to the ideas of the narcissistic self and by retaining mechanistic implications, Kohut has put himself in great theoretical difficulty. The mechanistic and the experiential rhetorics simply do not mix. Nevertheless, although it does not seem to be his intention to do so, Kohut may yet be contributing to the development of a new theoretical language for psychoanalysis. Like Erikson's "identity," Kohut's "self" seems to be a move toward the model of active persons. To regard Kohut's theoretical contributions on narcissism as transitional to new modes of psychoanalytic conceptualization is to make more comprehensible the unsatisfactory construction of many of his formulations. The same type of difficulty occurs in a paper on the self by Levin (1969) and in the use of "experiential" and "nonexperiential" by Sandler and Joffe (1969).[4]

Outside the realm of Freudian theorizing, the concept "self" has enjoyed—or suffered?—wide popularity and usage. Neo-Freudians and existential psychoanalysts seem to like the term because it is so well suited to their generally humanistic, intentionalistic rhetoric. It is obvious, however, that they have used "self" as an all-purpose term. Like "identity," which they also favor, "self" refers at different times to personality, person, mind, ego, life theme, "I," and subjective life in general. Used this loosely, "self" is of little use in the quest for clarity of thought.

---

[4] In some places Kohut (1971) indicates his appreciation of these difficulties, yet he continues to employ such formulations as that the grandiose self makes demands on the ego. His transitional position is also evident in his tending (in footnotes) to suggest some new interpretation of libido whereby it is equivalent to experience or meaning.

Furthermore, in these neo-Freudian and existential writings we often encounter the term "self" as "*the* self." Like the thing-ness and agency attributed to identity, "*the* self" concretizes or substantializes a term that is primarily subjective or experiential and whose force is primarily adverbial and adjectival. Moreover, in some of its usages, such as "self-actualization," "*the* self" is set up not only as the existential referent of behavior but as, all at once, the motor, the fuel, the driver, and the end point of the journey of existence. It is ironic that self as *the* self has become an It: the shadow of natural-science theorizing has fallen on humanistic conceptualization.

As *the* self, self is also a vague affirmation of the unity of the personality; like "*the* ego" and "*an* identity," it implies a natural state of personal unity and harmony. In its unqualified form, however, that implied affirmation is based far more on hope than on evidence or reasoned argument. A major consequence of this affirmation is that we all quickly become, in Laing's (1969a, 1969b) popular phrase, divided selves, when it would be much closer to the truth to say that the undivided self is at best a possibly useful theoretical fiction and at worst a manic dream of fusion or a new version of the old psychoanalytic dream of perfect and total genitality.

It is perhaps related to this fantasy of undivided subjectivity that self has often been invested with a sentimental glow, if not a quasi-religious halo. Take, for example, Harry Guntrip (1967, 1968): he has written extensively and with much sophistication on a number of the crucial theoretical issues I have been taking up, and we have much to learn from him; yet he is so sentimentally concerned with the need for a humane theory of self and others that he argues in more than one place the superiority of his version of object-relations theory—*on humanistic grounds!* He proceeds as if kindly theory is better theory, or a kindly theoretician a better theoretician. In my view, his theoretical formulations are implicitly in the service of his aiming to give moral support to the taxing work of deep psychotherapy with schizoid patients. But this is to repeat the same error as that made earlier by Sullivan, Fromm-Reichman, and their followers. Empathy is not theory.

In any case, many writers have been projecting considerable warmth, humaneness, and dignity into the idea of a naturally unitary self shattered by an injurious world. One is made to feel that it is callous and dehumanizing to think about people in other terms. In fact, one is discouraged from thinking very much at all in this regard. As I suggested earlier, you will find an outstanding example of this anti-intellectual romanticizing of self in the writings of R. D. Laing (1969a, 1969b).

No doubt, all the current enthusiasm for self-concepts as well as autonomy and identity concepts will have to be explained by an intellectual historian of the future. Meanwhile, however, looking at it simply from the standpoint of problems inherent in Freudian theory, I propose that, like autonomy and identity, self is the center of some necessarily unsuccessful Freudian efforts to imbue a mechanistic, natural-science theory with experiential excite-ment—or, from a related vantage point, of necessarily unsuccessful efforts to bring theory closer to good therapy.

(4) *The theory of the psychoanalytic process—and "the mover" revealed.* It remains to consider one more gap between interpretation and general theory. We encounter it in a problematic aspect of the theory of the psy-choanalytic process. It is this: the person as human being rather than mecha-nism, the one addressed by the interpreting psychoanalyst, lurks in the shadows that surround such familiar and useful concepts as the reasonable or rational ego, the observing ego, the ego core, emotional insight, the thera-peutic alliance, the working alliance, the mature transference, higher levels of organization, and growth tendencies. Sooner or later, these concepts are used, they have to be used, to imply an agency that stands more or less outside the so-called play of forces, the so-called interrelations of functions, the so-called field of determinants. They have to be so used because they express attempts to avoid making manifestly anthropomorphic formulations, but without rethinking the fundamental conceptualization of psychoanalysis. There is the gap: between the person on one side and natural-science ap-paratus on the other. This split-off agency that makes psychoanalytic work possible is somehow specifically human in that it makes specifically human experience possible and communicable, and specifically human goals de-finable, maintainable, and approachable. Implicitly, this relationship-forming agency is a whole person. The psychoanalyst cannot think about his clinical work without using concepts of this sort. He cannot think that some of his analysand's ego functions have formed an alliance with some of his ego functions—not, that is, without being anthropomorphic about functions!

We can now identify the mover of the mental apparatus. He is the psy-choanalytic clinician's projection of himself into the model of mind. The clinician rightly insists on remaining in the act. It is he who is irrepressible. He never really regards himself as an apparatus or his work as the resultant of forces or the interplay of functions. Though he may pay homage to Freud's metapsychology by using these mechanistic terms when discussing the psychoanalytic process, to himself he remains an agent, a person who chooses what to do and does it, and who can detect when he has chosen wrongly or acted inappropriately, and who can then do something about that. He is the one who invented the machine. He turns it on and off. He tinkers with it.

The clinical psychoanalyst does not even really regard his analysand as an apparatus, except perhaps sometimes when thinking of his psychopathol-ogy, for psychopathology gives all the appearance—but only the appear-ance!—of being the resultant of forces and defective apparatus. It is a curious kind of isolating or splitting to regard one's analysand as an existen-tial person with mechanistic psychopathology. I hope I have been successful in showing that that splitting is necessary only so long as we adhere to the mechanistic model of mind. To be internally consistent, the evolving theory of the psychoanalytic process requires a completely nonmechanistic model of mind. The action model which I will now present is a model of that sort.

II. Claimed and Disclaimed Action

It is to a certain emphasis in Fenichel's ever-rewarding monograph on technique (1941) that I am particularly indebted for a large part of the inspiration of Part II of this paper. I am thinking of his repeated reference to ascertaining the activity that lies behind apparent passivity. He said, for example:

> *How does interpretation work?* We do not want to differentiate at this point between interpretations of resistance and interpretations of instinct, but to ask about the factors common to both. The answer in general is this: the attention of the ego is drawn to a "preconscious derivative." How does this take place? (*1*) What is to be interpreted is first *isolated* from the experiencing part of the ego. This preliminary task drops out when the patient already has some critical attitude towards that which is to be interpreted. (*2*) The patient's attention is drawn to his own *activity: he himself* has been bringing about that which up to now he has thought he was experiencing passively. (*3*) He comprehends that he had motives for this activity which hitherto he did not know of. (*4*) He comes to note that *at some other point*, too, he harbors something similar, or something that is in some way associatively connected. (*5*) With the help of these observations he becomes able to produce less distorted "derivatives," and through these the *origins* of his behavior become clear [pp. 52–53; Fenichel's italics].

In brief, the strategy of interpretation is this: to identify a network of intelligible actions where none was thought to exist, thereby expanding the range of acknowledged activity in the patient's experience of his life, and to develop a history of this life as intelligible activity. Although this search for activity has not been conceptualized explicitly and systematically, and indeed has often been lost sight of altogether, it is presupposed in the guiding strategy of psychoanalytic work, namely, the analysis of transference and resistance. We regard transference and resistance as activities. The beneficial change we help bring about in the way our analysands lead their lives may be seen especially clearly in the light of this strategy of interpretation.

I am going to examine some of the essential aspects of the passivity-activity ambiguity as we encounter it in clinical work. After examining this aspect of analytic material and the changes it undergoes, I shall direct your attention to similar ambiguities in the fundamental rule we present to analysands and in our interpretations. My discussion of these major aspects of the analytic situation should pave the way toward a radical reconceptualization of the psychoanalytic method and its theory. According to this reconceptualization, psychoanalysis will be more clearly recognized to be the study of human action viewed along certain lines. I shall attempt to show that what Fenichel presented as merely an empirical strategy implies a basic model for rendering human events intelligible and thereby amenable to rational and orderly therapeutic influence. Far more than a technique, it is a language that is distinctively psychoanalytic. You will understand, I hope, that I can only touch on highlights of this broad and as yet incomplete reconsideration of our concepts.

I shall begin with a brief clinical example. A middle-aged professional man had been unable to work for a number of years following the breakup of his marriage. He presented himself as the victim of a faithless and cruel wife, a very disadvantageous divorce settlement, and the animosity of his children, who had inexplicably turned against him. He stressed that he had been doing nothing for some time—staying at home and sleeping all day, and letting his business affairs, his personal relations, and his professional reputation suffer badly. It is not surprising that during the course of treatment we established that (for the most part unconsciously) he had played an active, intelligible part in bringing about and maintaining this entire state of affairs. He had, for example, offered himself up as a sacrifice to his wife's narcissism and sadism just at the point during the divorce proceedings when he could have easily and rightfully developed his case against her. He had nursed his feeling of having been betrayed and abandoned by family, friends, and colleagues. He had, in fact, regressed to a position modeled after one he had occupied during childhood, when he had had to mother and father himself and had succeeded against great odds in developing and sustaining considerable ambition and interest in intellectual and esthetic matters. Needless to say, he had chosen his wife largely so that he could masochistically enact a repetition of his infantile situation; apparently the crippling divorce settlement had been a climactic consummation of this repetition. We also established that, far from his having been doing nothing during his inactive period, he had been reading voraciously (I use the word advisedly) all night long, thereby extending his intellectual range even further, and he had slept by day both in order to get his needed sleep and to cultivate the conscious and public image of being a derelict. Many other, easily anticipated kinds of details emerged during this investigation.

The point I want to emphasize by citing this example is this: in order to set in motion a specifically psychoanalytic therapeutic process, I assumed and then sought to establish that, while apparently "doing nothing," this man had remained active all along. He had been doing something important, something ultimately understandable, something that constituted an affirmation, a maintaining and developing of strength. I had to see his passivity as being the most determined activity; his doing "nothing" as doing a great deal. (Psychoanalysts know how that is in their own "doing nothing"—their seeming inactivity in their work.) I shall say more about the specific rationale and advantages of this approach shortly.

As to technique in a situation of this sort, I will mention in passing only one of a number of useful measures. What was particularly significant here was to point out the activity implied in his energetic and emphatic efforts, conscious and otherwise, to prove to me that he was a beaten-down, worthless, hopeless, unreliable wreck. In other words, I had to help him acknowledge how actively he was trying to initiate another repetition of abandonment, this time within the transference. Both the harsh judgments he passed on himself and his need to prove anything at all implied that he still maintained aspirations, he cared what he made of himself.

No doubt the situation I have described represents one instance of the kind of thing Fenichel had in mind when he wrote the passage quoted above. I may mention, again only in passing, that the principle of establishing the activity within apparent passivity is nowhere more urgent and fruitful, when patiently implemented, than in work with psychotic problems. This point seems to me to be better appreciated in certain respects by analysts in the so-called English school than by those Freudians who maintain the traditional emphasis on a weak ego passively overwhelmed by a strong pregenital id. But, in any case, psychological therapy with psychotics, when it is fruitful, seems to entail establishing that psychosis, too, is intelligible activity. One instance of what I mean is the increasingly common view of psychotic regression as a kind of adaptation—a protection of a true self by a false self as well as a collusion with the desperate needs of family members.

Now, in our daily lives as well as in our clinical work we are surrounded by less extreme instances of masked activity. It is to these that I shall now turn. For reasons to be advanced later, I shall refer to them as "disclaimed actions." The identification of disclaimed action, though it has been conceived in other terms, is central to, if not the very center of, the psychoanalytic study of human existence. To make my point I shall discuss three ideas which can be fully understood only in relation to the concept of disclaimed action: *slip of the tongue, mind,* and *conflict.*

SLIP OF THE TONGUE

If one looks at the idea *slip of the tongue* from the standpoint of disclaimed action, one notices several facts immediately. First, it is being maintained through the use of this locution that it is the tongue, not the person, who has slipped—as if the tongue regulates its own activity. Second, it is being maintained that what has happened is accidental—a slip—and not a meaningful, intended action. (To refer to it as a *Freudian* slip of the tongue, as people do in everyday life, often involves a third disclaimer to the effect that attributing significance to a slip is optional or else that not oneself, but only someone else—a Freudian—would think that the utterance in question had some special significance.)

In psychoanalytic practice, we do not accept these disclaimers. We do not believe that there has been an accident. We do not believe that the tongue has anything fundamental to do with the occurrence. And we do not believe that the attribution of significance is optional. We treat the phenomenon as an action. To us, it is something the patient has done, something that is intelligible in terms of actions he wishes to perform and the conflicts he experiences in this regard. In effect, in interpreting a slip the analyst affirms the following proposition: while with the help of repressive action, the speaker thought he was intending to say only one thing, he was actually saying two; or, even though he might have been aware of warding off inclinations to say something different or contrary, he nevertheless *did* also say something else that *was* different or contrary. Nothing "slipped out." Words are not furtive entities, nor do they move from one place to another; if spoken, they make public what would otherwise remain private. In a slip, then, the speaker simply does two things at once. A two-sided action, and both sides his responsibility![5]

More than once I have heard the introduction of a speaker contain the following slip: "It is now my great pleasure to *prevent* our distinguished guest." (I have, by the way, also heard these two words put the other way around: "With only two days left before your vacation, there is not enough time to *present* a catastrophe.") But to return to the "introduction" slip: it is an instance of what I mean when I speak of someone's saying two things at once—the consciously intended statement which we may for the moment believe to have been sincerely intended, and the interpolation of the idea "prevent" with its equally sincere implication of envy, let us suppose, or rivalry. In short, we might interpret that the introducer was ambivalent and that he acted on both thrusts of this ambivalence. The slip is not a disrupted action; it is a special kind of action in which two courses of action are represented simultaneously.

If is, of course, wrong to think that the unconscious, latent, or implicit course of action is what the speaker "really" wanted to say, for it was also what he wanted *not* to say. Furthermore, there *was* something else he *did* want to say. It is just that as he worked it out he had to give some overt sign of his dilemma. His defensive attempt, his conciliatory striving, his wretched substitute action—for the psychoanalyst all are equally real; they are to be understood as facets of one action.

To return to the man who presented himself as a do-nothing failure, he made the following slip during the analysis of his self-destructive inactivity: "There was nothing I could do that wouldn't make things work—er—worse."

THE CONCEPT OF ACTION

Before going on to speak of the ideas of *mind* and *conflict*, I should clarify the sense in which I am using the word *action*. By action I do

---

[5] The issue is, of course, much greater than simply that of responsibility in the usual sense, though it is also true that in the realm of judgments of responsibility, which includes unconscious as well as conscious guilt, we encounter disclaimers of the utmost urgency and desperation in psychoanalytic work as in everyday life.

not mean voluntary physical deeds only. In this model, action is human behavior that has a point; it is meaningful human activity; it is intentional or goal-directed deeds by people; it is doing things for reasons. There is nothing the psychoanalytic system of thought can deal with that is not action as here defined. For example, to think of something is to do an action; to see or remember something is to do an action; to be silent or otherwise inactive is as much an action as to say something or to walk somewhere. It is one kind of action to say something and another kind to think it and not say it. The propositions I am advancing are not descriptive, empirical propositions; they are definitions that establish the logic of this psychological model. According to this model, those human phenomena that are not actions are bodily changes, motoric or otherwise, that take place essentially as normal or pathological neurophysiological processes. They involve no mental aim or directionality, no choice, no synthesis of interests, courses of action, and skills. They are devoid of symbolic content. They have no reasons.

I could have chosen the word *behavior* instead of *action*. Actually, both words are unsatisfactory in that ordinarily both imply motor action. However, by using *action* I call attention to the analyst's strategic emphasis on activity within apparent passivity or inactivity. Alternatively, I could have used the word *activity* instead of *action*. However, as I am trying to avoid the ambiguities of traditional activity-passivity discussions (Schafer, 1968c), I prefer the less encumbered and less equivocal *action*. I realize that my choice is less than entirely satisfactory.

But there is a matter far more important than the choice of word. It is the methodological recognition that, in principle, there is no limit to the number of vantage points from which an action may be regarded, and therefore no limit to the number of ways in which it may be defined or described. Psychoanalysts have not always been sufficiently self-conscious about the fact that they look at their material from only certain points of view and perhaps only on certain levels of abstraction; consequently, they sometimes mistakenly consider their mode of understanding to be the only possible or true psychology—and a complete one at that! Elsewhere (Schafer, 1968a), I have discussed how this is the case with respect to motives.

Consider, for example, a student said to be reading a book. His action may also be described as studying, doing his homework, preparing for a test, competing with classmates for recognition and advancement, complying with his parents' wishes, sublimating voyeuristic tendencies in intellectual pursuits, making rapid and discontinuous eye movements over a page of print, adhering to the norm of his class, and so on and so forth. Clearly, what we call an action, how we name it, and the temporal and other boundaries we set for it, depend on the kind and level of descriptive or explanatory context we are trying to establish and maintain. There is no one description of the action that is the only true one, though there are an infinite number that may be false. Indeed, "the action" can refer only to a set of possibilities rather than a unique denotation. To the extent that we discard simplistic notions of fact and truth, we accord proper importance to considerations of consistency, coherence, and usefulness within a systematic approach to reality.

As for the reader in my example, there is at least one description of what he is doing under which he may be said to know what he is doing. If we take into account unconscious knowing, we may say that there must be more than one such description. But we cannot say that he knows, in any useful sense of "knowing," all the possible descriptions of his action. This means, too, that the agent cannot know all the possible implications and consequences of his actions. In psychoanalysis, therefore, connections and other interpretations do not always deal with repressed material. The "unconscious" is not omniscient. Psychoanalytic interpretation does uncover the sense in which the agent knows what he has chosen to do: that is, it establishes just what his action is to him. But it does a lot more than that. It also teaches him to see actions in a new light, to be alert to implications, interrelationships, and consequences of actions that he never dreamed of, as the saying goes. In this way, interpretation opens up to the analysand a whole new world of possibilities—evaluations, goals, and strategies. The analysand's position as historian of his life is extended and made more efficient; he is more aware that he has been making choices all along and that he now has more and different choices to make (Schafer, 1970a). Of course, his need for this assistance is itself a consequence of defensive actions and must be so interpreted throughout the analysis.

It would require at least an entire paper to survey the ways of looking at actions that are distinctively psychoanalytic. For the time being, let me merely mention the effort to understand action as manifesting or implying the unconscious repetition in current life of infantile patterns, with all their physically sexual and aggressive, magical, anxious, guilty, defensive, reparative, regressive, and progressive aspects.

I have not forgotten that there are resistances, that is, actions taken by the analysand to block or retard the progress of the analysis. But let me add that not all the analyst's facilitation of progress consists of clearing away resistances through interpretation. As I have mentioned, he is also teaching his analysand a way of looking at his own life and understanding it—as action. This way of looking at one's life has coherence, consistency, and therapeutic effectiveness; that is why the analyst fosters it. I know that in saying this I seem to be laying the analyst open to the familiar charge that he does indeed brainwash his analysand. Whatever else that charge might be (political attack, self-defense, etc.), it is certainly philosophically naïve; it misses the point that unless there is some way of looking and understanding, there can be no way of studying any aspect of life whatsoever. "Life" has to be thought; it is an abstract idea. What passes for ordinary everyday understanding of mental life is a mishmash—which means the person is free to conceptualize as he pleases, but too often he is only conceptualizing in line with unresolved conflict.

Thoughtful psychoanalytic understanding is a way out of this confusion. It is not a carte blanche approach. It is an arduous discipline distinguished by the cogency of its questions; the affective impact of its content; the patience it requires in the sorting of material for hypotheses, evidence, and explanations; and the respect it implies for the desperateness of the human condition, a desperateness that gives rise to a fundamental hatred and mistrust of change and usually precludes even the comprehension of deep change. Through the analytic conceptions of this material that he imparts to the analysand, the psychoanalyst helps give form to the material that is disclosed to him.

I have attempted to explain my conception of action and to indicate some of its implications. To explain further, I would have to go into the concepts of choice, intention, motivation, and the like; regretably I must defer that discussion for a future paper.[6]

MIND

On, now, to *mind*—the second term I have selected to discuss from the standpoint of disclaimed action. We are familiar with the great variety of locutions according to which the mind is a place, an autonomous thing, or a part-aspect of one's existence. For example, as to mind-as-place, people say, "I must have been out of my mind," "Suicide entered my mind," "I put that out of my mind." As to mind-as-autonomous-thing, people say, "My mind refused to think about it any further," "My mind is racing," "My mind plays tricks on me." And as to mind-as-part-aspect-of-one's-existence, we encounter the following types of locutions in which the "I" and the mind are thought of as two separate and independent entities: "I am of two minds about it," "I didn't keep my mind on my work," "I wish I knew my own mind."

All such locutions state or imply that there is a subject or agent who exists or can exist apart from his mind. Accordingly, he can observe his mind, comment on it, put it to work, inhabit it, be betrayed by it, limit its scope, and so on. This way of thinking (which, as we have seen, characterizes Freudian metapsychology) has many implications, but what concerns us here is its function in disclaiming action. The analyst may very well take it as disclaimed action when he hears an analysand split off or split up his mind in these ways. He may rightly assume that the analysand is feeling anxious or guilty. Depending on the direction of his psychoanalytic slant, he might think of the event as a defensive splitting of the ego, a regression to primary-process concreteness of thought, or a projective cre-

---

[6] For some background discussions of action and related concepts, I refer the reader to Aristotle's *Ethics*, Ryle (1949), Anscombe (1956), Austin (1956), Hampshire (1959, 1962), and Williams (1956). My discussion of action follows from, but does not follow exactly, these and other writings on the subject.

ation of persecutors. In any case, if he takes up this locution at all, he will implicitly or explicitly interpret it as an action—an action that disclaims action. He does so, for example, when he responds to "I must have been out of my mind" with such a comment as, "You feel so guilty about what you did that you refuse to think that you were capable of doing it." I do not mean that traditionally analysts have thought of these interventions in terms of disclaimed action. I do mean that the relevance and effectiveness of these interventions stem in significant measure from their treating such comments by analysands as disclaimers. Traditional Freudian conceptualization has obscured this fact.

The late Dr. B. D. Lewin recently took up this very subject of mind and its metaphoric treatment (1971). Although both refreshing and informative in his comments on archaic conceptions of mind, his presentation had serious flaws, for he was, among other things, wrongly encouraging us analysts to use a piece of primary-process thinking both in teaching our theory of mind and in our clinical interpretations; one might say that he was encouraging conceptual acting-out instead of analyzing (see especially pp. 21–22). Mind is not a room or a suite of two rooms; there is no man or maniken looking in or looking on, or guarding doorways against entities at once mechanical and furtive in their actions. For theoretical purposes, it can be said that mind is an abstract designation of the sense we make of human existence or action; depending on one's approach, it may include among its referents desires, intentions, aims, reasons, meanings, and cognitive functions or performances such as perceiving and remembering. It has never been helpful to *systematic* explanatory thinking or teaching to resort to these anthromorphic, spatial, and mechanical metaphors, although I would not question that it has been helpful to *preliminary* explorations, like Freud's, or that it has been comforting to all of us to have them readily available like old friends or dependable escape hatches. As for the usefulness of the two-room and manikin model of mind in clinical interpretation, I shall argue below that the *progress* of an analysis is marked by diminishing use of it or any of its variations.

In keeping with the action model of interpretation I have been developing, I would say that mind is something we do, not something we have, and not something we are or are not related to or in possession of. And this, I submit, is the sense in which we do interpret mind to our analysands, even though we may obscure our action by using the inexact words of everyday speech.

CONFLICT

I turn now to the third concept, *conflict*, the discussion of which should develop my point about psychoanalytic interpretation further. Here is a clinical example. An obsessional analysand keeps interrupting what he is saying in order to report still another "intruding" thought. These thoughts, he declares, prevent him from getting to the point. He insists that he wishes it were otherwise. I remark on his viewing these thoughts as not his own. He responds that he does think of it as another person inside him who won't let him finish what he's saying. He goes on spontaneously to reflect that he knows that he is thinking all these thoughts, but that it is impossible to think of himself as doing two contrary things in this way. (Allow me for the moment to pass over the indication he gives of an introject fantasy as part of his obsessionality. I passed over it at the time, too.) I now remark to him that the tempo of interruptions increases whenever he is telling me something that might be exciting, such as the topic of the preceding moment, which had been a sexual encounter with a girl, and that, in keeping with his previously avowed policy of carefully controlling everything, he controls his mounting excitement by interrupting himself frequently. As he had been complaining earlier in the hour of increased obsessional fragmentation of thinking in connection with some research he was doing, I add that I suppose he found doing the research exciting, too, and so had had similarly to control that excitement by stepping up the tempo of his interruptions. He confirms the feeling of excitement but quickly goes on to minimize the significance of what I have said, declaring that he has been clear about this much all along; in fact, it is what he has been telling me. He then goes on to some further fruitful elaboration of the interpretation. I then point out that characteristically he first has to minimize what I say because he finds it exciting when I speak to him and because minimizing is his way of controlling that excitement; once he has it controlled, he can work with the idea I have presented. After some further minimization, he acknowledges that I am right about that. Here my account of this incident ends—but not the struggle, obviously.

What is the struggle? Whatever content we ascribe to it, we would all agree, I think, that it is a manifestation of what we call intrapsychic conflict. But we must not forget how we arrive at that idea. We must start from the observation that throughout this interchange this analysand is continuously engaged in action. Simultaneously or in alternation, he is attacking and protecting, or, if you will, defying and complying, castrating and being castrated, soiling and being retentive, seducing homosexually and being seduced homosexually, and so on and so forth. On what basis, then, do we say that he is expressing conflict? Not really on the basis that he "has" "conflicting impulses," for a formulation in terms of impulses, rather than being naïvely descriptive, can only express an a priori commitment we have made to speak in the mechanistic language of forces and energies; it is as if we had decided in advance that *impulse*, because it has more of an "inside" and "prior" ring to it, was more profound or primary than *action*, which sounds outward, superficial, behavioristic, merely a sign of something else or a resultant of "forces." The fact is, however, that we speak of conflict because we observe the analysand to be engaged in contradictory actions. He conveyed his incipient recognition of this very point when he himself raised the question of his engaging in two contrary actions simultaneously. He could not just then experience the act of interrupting as his own, but for the moment it did at least make sense to him that, looked at as a form of control of excitement, it was the kind of act he would engage in under these circumstances. It was a beginning of a new understanding.

Later in the analysis, I could expect that we would get to the interrupting introject he had hinted at. But what, in the end, is an introject? Isn't it a piece of disclaimed action, a fantasy created and invoked by the analysand, a fantasy he takes to be a real event which he experiences passively? I have discussed this frequently misunderstood issue at length in a somewhat different connection in my book on internalization (Schafer, 1968a), under the heading of "The Power of the Introject." There I tried to demonstrate that that power could only be the subject's own. In the present context my point is that the introject is the fantasied embodiment of one action that the analysand is disclaiming; as such the action can be neither integrated nor rejected by him in a basic way. Indeed, considered by itself, the introject experience is itself an action, though an odd and well-disguised one. It is an action open to someone already engaged in conflicting actions. What the analysand does not allow in speech or other public action, he may allow in a sort of projective fantasy.

My obsessional patient is both telling me and not telling me exciting things. He is both interrupting and protesting his interruptions. He is claiming some of his actions and disclaiming others. In this respect, which of course is not the only one of significance for his analysis, the introject experience constitutes his disclaiming strategy. He is constructing or reviving a projective fantasy, and, through regression, treating it as real. Thereby he is avoiding the conscious experience of personal conflict. And yet all we really have to work with analytically as observations or evidence are conflicting actions and a hint of a fantasy about some of these actions.

There is more to be gained by considering the conceptualization of this example a bit longer. In this instance, it may be said that the analysand's initial action is his interrupting himself. This action seems to be modeled in some respects on his sense of having been frequently and meaninglessly "interrupted" by his parents. The introject corresponds to the parents in some of its details. By representing his interrupting as his being interrupted, he is attacking these parents as well as controlling them (and me, in the transference). It is an undercover attack, an instance of what another analysand, in another example of disclaimed action, called "sneaky motivations." The fact that it is undercover, that it is represented as the action of an internal presence, indicates the conflict between acting destructively and acting protectively. Being a disclaimer, it also indicates the conflict between consciously acknowledging and denying that in every important detail of his present behavior he is active rather than passive, creator rather than creature, an intentional person rather than a defective apparatus which happens to be under close observation.

Any of you might disagree with certain details of my partial analysis of this introject experience, but you would not, I think, disagree that it is in the nature of the psychoanalytic outlook that interpretation must culminate in formulations that are cast in terms of personal activity. Like slip of the tongue, mind, and conflict, an introject is not something a person has or something that happens to him; it is something he thinks, which is also to say, something he does. The same must be said of any identification.

Conflict, then—to return directly to our starting point—may be conceptualized in the following way. As a psychological event, it involves a minimum of three actions. The agent engages in two actions which, in a third, he believes to be incompatible with each other. For reasons which have to be established in each clinical instance, he continues doing both, despite his belief in their incompatibility. He may or may not acknowledge consciously that he is doing both, that the actions are incompatible, or that he cares whether they are or not; these important variations reflect additional defensive actions, beyond the disclaiming itself, that the agent might take with respect to the conflict.

You might object, now, that conflict can exist when no action is being taken, as for example in the struggle to resist temptation or to control an impulse. I say that this is a matter of conceptualization and not brute fact. I am suggesting that this situation be regarded not as a struggle between impulses or systems or substructures, but rather as an instance of the person's acting more effectively in one respect than another. The successful resisting of temptation—what we might call inhibition—is one action through which a person has succeeded in stopping another; at least he has stopped the *public* action, for he may still carry out the action in fantasy. An impulse is an action that is not being carried out, and its not being carried out may be due to other actions one has engaged in to that very end. An impulse is an action a person would do were he not effectively preventing himself from doing it.

Impulse is not logically or psychologically prior to, or more internal than, action. We do not, as is commonly said, inhibit impulses; we inhibit actions, and "impulses" are the results of these inhibiting actions. Nor does one act on impulse, though one might think so, owing to his awareness of the effort entailed in restraining actions he would otherwise engage in. In this view, thought is silent speech (Ryle, 1949). I should say *silenced* speech. I am not as far from Freud's basic concepts or Fenichel's formulations as I might seem to be at this point. I remind you that Freud conceptualized thought as experimental action, and, though he did not develop an action model of psychoanalysis, he was ever conscious of delay of action as the foundation of psychical development and functioning; however, in keeping with his mechanistic model of mind, he tended to speak in terms of delay of *impulse*. In his terms, the secondary process regulates the primary-process tendency toward immediate discharge; in action terms, one type of action is used to stop another. And, with regard to Fenichel (1941), is there after all a great difference between demonstrating that unconscious defense is activity, as he proposed, and asserting that defense is an action taken unconsciously to stop another action?[7]

I hope that by now I have made clear the view of interpretation I am developing. As I said, I believe it to be the view that all analysts implicitly share. I think that by remaining loyal to Freud's metapsychological ideals we have obscured our recognition of this fact and have blocked the development of its crucial systematic possibilities. I chose to discuss *slip of the tongue, mind,* and *conflict,* because I believed that in these instances I could easily show the implicit presence and the utility of the action model of interpretation. I do not imply that the correct comprehension of just these three terms is theoretically decisive. And, although I have tended to speak in terms of two-factor conflicts in my explanations and examples, I have done so only for ease of exposition and with full awareness that actions are usually a lot more complicated that that; this is especially true of the actions we analyze in our work, such as dreams, symptoms, defenses, and actings-out. The full extent of application of action concepts itself is not yet clear. But I want to go on now to discuss briefly the variety of disclaimers we encounter in clinical work and then to consider disclaimers that the analyst may introduce unconsciously or inadvertently.

DISCLAIMERS OF ACTION

Consider the following locutions, each of which disclaims action in its own way: "The impulse seized me"; "It struck me that something was wrong"; "The words poured out of my mouth"; "My conscience torments me"; "One part of me says yes while the other says no"; "This hour just rushed by"; "The future holds little in store for me"; "I am afraid to let it come out"; "Doubts creep into my mind"; "Something inside resists the idea"; "The excitement slipped away."

[7] I am not advancing a new version of the old misconception of conscious autonomy. Propositions concerning autonomy derive from, and only make sense with respect to, mechanistic drive theories. The action model is unrelated to such theories. Similarly, the issue of free will does not arise for the action model, for free will refers to action being carried out independently of some forces that a natural-science, deterministic model must presuppose; consequently, if that model is not adopted, and such forces are therefore not assumed, we are in a universe of discourse in which the idea of free will has no place. In the present context it is a universe of actions by people, actions which by definition are meaningful and goal-directed, actions which have reasons rather than determinants. The action model does not imply randomness or chaos of events. Although psychoanalysis has always been considered a purposive theory, it does not have to be one; purposiveness is only one way of defining and ordering psychological phenomena. The obvious psychological importance of representations of somatic processes does not necessitate, though it does not preclude, adoption of a theory based on bodily drives and their elaboration into psychological motives; it does necessitate a theory that in one way or another deals systematically with the decisive role in psychological development and psychopathology of representations of persistent or recurring, intensely pleasurable and unpleasurable bodily sensations, especially those connected with the psychosexual zones. In this regard, there is no "mind-body problem."

I shall only mention in passing the many disclaimers that remain unverbalized, such as self-punishment without confession of guilt and seduction without expressed desire. There are, of course, other disclaimers that are concealed behind words, such as asking, "Would you like to come along?" as a guarded way of conveying, "I want you to come along!" and observing matter-of-factly to the analyst, "You haven't said anything today," as a guarded way of demanding, "Say something already!"

Returning to the verbalized disclaimers, the first thing to note is that they seem to be drawn from a huge supply of such expressions in the language of everyday life. What I cited earlier about mind-as-place, etc., belongs here, too. One can realize at once how frequently or readily we use disclaimers. On closer inspection, one can also note how disclaimers may be classified in terms of the "mechanisms of defense," such as isolation, splitting, introjection, and projection. At the same time, one can further note that these locutions also carry traces of unconscious fantasies of fighting, being beaten, being overwhelmed, copulating, feeding, defecating, being abandoned, and so forth. Putting just this much together, one may safely conclude that everyday language is not only a record of the fundamental unconscious desires and conflicts with which people are concerned, but also a record of the many modes that people have developed to ease subjective distress. I particularly have in mind distress felt in connection with being held responsible.

We do use disclaimers to help us "get off the hook." They enable us to think and talk about difficult issues in a muted, dosed manner. We use them to protect relationships. They help us care for the other person as well as ourselves. For example, when a person says "understandingly" to a friend who has disappointed and angered him by forgetting an appointment, "It must have slipped your mind," rather than "You forgot me," or when he says about his own forgetting, "It slipped my mind," rather than "I forgot you," he is in either case protecting the relationship. He is absolving at least one of the parties of responsibility or guilt. To speak plainly of one's "forgetting" the other, unless it is a seduction to a gratifying sadomasochistic interaction, is, of course, the sort of directness that ordinarily leads to quick deterioration of relationships.

Analysands have much reason, of course, to disclaim action. They are resisting analysis all along, though not always with equal determination and vigor. On further reflection, it is in keeping with an action model of interpretation to subsume all our notions of resistance under the heading of disclaimed action, just as it is to subsume insights under the heading of claimed and reclaimed action. Defense, for example, is action. The unconscious fantasies informing defensive actions, so much stressed by Kleinian analysts, are the basis for the correct and useful designation of these actions; they are what these actions *mean*, which is to say what they *are* in psychic reality (Schafer, 1968b). Ultimately, the analyst should tell the analysand more than that he is, for instance, projecting, before going on to analyze when, why, and so forth; assuming that suitable evidence and context are available, one ought to tell the analysand who is projecting that he is soiling or bombarding someone else with his destructive substances, or setting someone else up as his penetrating, perhaps raping, persecutor, or something of that sort on some level or other.

But it is not only defense that we must be concerned with in this regard. As Fenichel indicated in the statement I quoted above, the so-called impulses or drives are actions, too. In the action model, an anal impulse is an anal action that is not being carried out. A projected anal impulse is an action or an inhibited action that, in a self-protective move, one is attributing to someone else. "I forgot you" may, in psychic reality, be a variant of the action "I killed you" or "I shit you out"; in this sense the so-called impulse is plainly a major (though nonmotoric and unconscious) action.

By disclaiming actions we limit the excitement and violence of social existence. Human beings have developed and use language to spare themselves from all manner of arousal, pain, anxiety, guilt, loss, and destructiveness. They allude to what they are passing over as they pass over it. This allusiveness is part of what we call unconscious communication. It makes up a large part of what the analyst listens for.

CLAIMING AND INTEGRATING ACTION

The analyst works on the assumption that the analysand actively brings about that from which he neurotically suffers—not, as Freud pointed out, that all misery is neurotically created and remediable, but that analysis deals with that misery that *is* neurotically created and *may be* remediable. Thus, the analyst *as analyst* sees the analysand as continuously selecting, organizing, and directing his neurotic existence. Through analysis, the nature and occasions of the analysand's activity are defined, and analysand and analyst attempt to arrive at an understanding of the reasons why the analysand arranges his life in the way he does. To this end, they examine closely the connections between his life in the past and in the present, taking into account the infantile influences to which he has, in fact, been subjected, insofar as these influences can be established with any definiteness. Always, however, these influences are understood within the framework of what I call the implicit action model. That is to say these influences come to be regarded by analysand as well as analyst as having been jointly defined by situation and person, for at all times the analysand, as he is in the analytic session and as he has been throughout his psychological existence, is to be understood as being active, purposive, choice-making, meaning-creating, and responsible. Infantile sexual theories demonstrate this interdependence, one might even say unity, of situation and person.

Passive experience—the representation of oneself as passive in relation to events—is, of course, of the utmost significance in psychological development and psychopathology. I am emphasizing that it is intrinsic to psychoanalytic understanding to regard passive experience as a mode of representation that can never tell the whole story of any psychological event or situation.

Freud demonstrated that subjectivity, the realm of "experience," is a variable human activity. People engage in subjectivity to different degrees, in different ways, at different times, and for different reasons. For Freud, preconscious and conscious representation and organization required action on the part of the subject. Freud called this action hypercathexis or attention cathexis. He showed that this action cannot be other than inconstant and incomplete. He also demonstrated that the psychoanalytic interpretation of resistances and transference repetitions expands the scope and amount of action on behalf of subjectivity. And with this change comes a change in the analysand's recognition of action itself.

With progress in his analysis, the analysand disclaims actions less flagrantly and less often. At least, he uses the kinds of locutions I just surveyed less often at critical junctures in the work. More and more, the analysand indicates a readiness to accept the responsibility of his life as action. This acceptance has nothing to do with ideas of omniscience and omnipotence, however, in that it does not imply a belief on the part of the analysand that he has caused his whole life or can cause it from now on. Nor does it preclude his having "passive" experience (passive self-representations). But more often than before he says, "I will" and "I won't," rather than "I must" and "I can't." More often than before he says, "That's the way I see it," "I decided," "I chose," "I know," and " I prefer." Leaving aside certain expansive assertions of autonomy, we recognize that these are the locutions of insight. They convey that the analytic understanding that has been achieved is not being manipulated by the analysand as something he "has"; rather, insight has become something he does or his way of doing or being. I believe this to be the import of Freud's statements that analysis strengthens and expands the ego at the expense of the id and superego: what the analysand presented before as an alien It—the aggregate of impulse, defense, conscience, problematic past and future, and external necessity—he now presents as defining aspects of himself; he *is* his impulse, defense, insights, and so forth, for they are *his* actions. His strengthened and expanded ego is his more inclusive subjectivity, and with that his more integrated and knowing claim to activity (cf. Freud, 1937).

THE ANALYST'S COMMUNICATIONS

I turn finally and all too briefly to the analyst's communications. In the light of what I have already said about the analysand's language and the way it may change, I characterize the clinical analyst's language as both attributing and denying activity to the analysand. In order to develop this proposition, I shall take as models of the analyst's language the fundamental rule of asking the analysand to say "everything that comes to mind" and some representative questions based on this rule; I shall contrast these with a representative (partial) interpretation that the analyst might make, namely,

"Because you are afraid to criticize me openly, you keep emphasizing that you couldn't like and admire me more."

First, "Say everything that comes to mind," and its variants, "What does that bring to mind?," "What comes to mind?," and "What occurs to you?" I submit that these questions involve a temporary collusion on the analyst's part with the analysand's strategy of disclaiming action. I say so on the basis of the following considerations: ideas are not entities that transport themselves to places called "mind"; nor do they transport other similar entities into places called "mind"; ideas do not "happen to" the thinker; and the mind is not something other than what the person thinks, feels, wishes, says, and carries out. I remind you of my earlier discussion of the problems of the concept *mind*.

According to the action model, the statement of the fundamental rule should convey the following ideas. "I shall expect you to talk to me each time you come. As you talk, you will notice that you inhibit your saying certain things. You may do so because you want to avoid being trivial, irrelevant, embarrassed, tactless, or otherwise disruptive. It is essential to our work that you withhold as little as possible from me. I urge you to tell me of those instances of inhibition no matter what their content may be." Similarly, rather than "What comes to mind?," the question that is conceptually and technically exact according to the action model is, "What do you think of in this connection?" or "What do you now connect with that?" or "If you think of this, what do you think of next?" Which is to say that thoughts come and go only as we think them or stop thinking them, or, in other words, that thinking is a kind of action engaged in by persons. We are responsible for all our thoughts, including, as Freud (1925) pointed out, our dreams. Yet both the fundamental rule as usually formulated and the question "What comes to mind?" imply the negation of this proposition, the very proposition on which interpretation is based. What, then, is the sense of these communications?

I think analysts generally would agree that in their customary form the fundamental rule and the questions associated with it facilitate what we call "free association." They do so by encouraging the analysand to relax his defensiveness and curtail his conscious selectivity. They invite him to be unreflective and noncritical as he thinks, to enter upon what Kris (1952) called a "regression in the service of the ego." Additionally, because they do not challenge the analysand's intent of disclaiming action, of feeling not responsible for what is "going on" in the analysis, they are less likely than a more direct approach to stimulate an immediate increase of resistiveness on his part. This approach is in keeping with the strategy of everyday speech, which, as I pointed out earlier, provides ample room for disclaiming locutions in order that people may adaptively regulate the amount of emotional strain they put themselves and others under from moment to moment. Thus, the question "What does that bring to mind?" helps the analysand approach difficult issues without feeling overwhelmed by them. From this point of view, the analyst's temporary collusion with the analysand is in the service of analytic exploration.

And yet in certain respects the rule and the questions may also be observed to be inconsistent with the aim of developing and maintaining an analytic situation. First, they are a means of circumventing resistance rather than analyzing it. Secondly, they are seductions to assume a passive position. Thirdly, rather than analyzing the regressive gratifications implied in disclaiming action, the analyst implicitly takes their side. Also, the rule and the questions often elicit defensively isolated indications of issues rather than direct involvement in the issues themselves, and so support an intellectualizing trend in the analysis. Additionally, the analyst will, in his subsequent interpretation, hold the patient responsible as a person for his response to the rule and the questions; he will do so by treating the response as an action, and by so doing he will give real support to the patient's feeling of being manipulated, if not led into ambush. These criticisms add up to a single, historically significant charge: the fundamental rule and the questions are thinly veiled carry-overs into analysis of hypnotic technique. And hypnotic technique encourages one of the purest forms of disclaimed action.

Thus, a case can be made both for and against the analytic suitability of the usual formulation of the fundamental rule and the questions associated with it, such as, "What does that bring to mind?"

Now, we all know, of course, that as an analysis moves forward, the disclaiming potential of the rule and the questions diminishes. The collusion I am describing is in no way fatal to the analysis. The reasons for this will become clear in connection with our further consideration of interpretation.

As I have said, a representative (partial) analytic interpretation might be: "Because you are afraid to criticize me openly, you keep emphasizing that you couldn't like and admire me more." Notice that the language is entirely an action language. The analyst addresses the analysand neither as a mind in which thoughts and feelings happen nor as an apparatus in which mechanisms operate, but as a person who acts knowingly and with feeling. Were the analyst to say, "You have a fear that impulses to criticize me will rise up in you, and this fear makes you act as if you have only liking and admiration for me," he would be carrying over into his interpretation the disclaiming language of his question. He would be doing the same were he to say, "Whenever you show your competence, your anxiety mounts" rather than "Whenever you perform competently, you feel more anxious"; and he would be doing so were he to say, "Your wish to suck on my penis is expressing itself" rather than "You wish to suck on my penis" or "You give signs of wishing to do so." And, certainly, in addition to everything else that would be wrong with it, to speak to the patient about specific interactions of his id, ego, and superego, *in these very terms,* would be to collude egregiously in the disclaiming of action.

As it is easy to be misunderstood in this connection, I must emphasize that I am not advocating that the analyst enter into an unverbalized contest of wills with his analysand by opposing to the analysand's disclaiming rhetoric a relentlessly circumspect mode of activistic instruction, questioning, and interpreting. Rather, I am trying to specify the reference point or base line of the analytic attitude. The analytic attitude is a way of perceiving, reacting, understanding, and communicating developed between the analyst and the analysand as they continue to work together. In the process, the patient identifies more and more with his analyst as *analyst*, which means that ever more consistently he looks at his life as largely made up of his own actions, including his interpretations of situations; or, as Freud (1920, p. 20) put it, as a life he has largely "arranged." By virtue of this development, the analysand begins to be able both to view the analysis as a collaborative effort between him and his analyst and to claim the analysis as his own. He is less inclined to regard the analysis as another "It" that he must passively suffer or desperately manipulate. This change is, of course, always a matter of degree and always subject to some regressive repudiation.

Probably, the limits of human tolerance and the problems of verbalization being what they are, the analyst can at best only approximate a consistent rhetoric of action. And, as an ideal, absolute consistency in this regard would not be truly analytic. In addition to reasons I have already given for this, I mention that by adhering to this ideal the analyst would certainly not help himself as well as the analysand to be relaxed and "free-floating." But I do want to call attention to the fact that the possibilities of the action model have not been explored systematically or technically. We are not very used to—because we are not very tolerant of—sustained action language. Not having assayed the resources of action language, we cannot know at this point what difference its consistent utilization would make in the analytic process. Would it in the long run clarify and more deeply modify resistance, or would it obscure and harden it? Would it, by frustrating them, throw into relief the unconscious gratifications obtained through extensive use of disclaimers, or would such language merely promote even more careful disguises by the analysand, as, for example, through his being compliantly action-oriented in his language? Would it expose and resolve projections, denials, intellectualizations, and other defensive strategies, or would it stimulate the analysand to contrive new modes of applying them?

Surely, the analyst's choice of words does not by itself determine everything that will happen during the attempt at analysis, but, just as surely, analytic progress depends on words, for understanding cannot be divorced from words, and some words are better manifestations than others of specifically psychoanalytic understanding. It is wrong to think of the choice of words as a part of the interpretive technique that follows understanding. In psychoanalysis the words *are* the understanding.

In this second section of my paper, I have not been driving toward a Draconian judgment and prescription concerning the clinical analyst's language. I have attempted to show the place in his interventions of locutions which claim and disclaim action, and to indicate the hazards and opportunities implied in his choice of language, which is to say, implied in the way he thinks about analysis and his analysand.

AN APPLICATION

Before coming to my conclusion, I shall venture an application of my action-model analysis of interpretation. In today's therapeutic world, it is increasingly fashionable to be contemptuous of psychoanalysis as a passive and intellectual process, a sluggish if not cowardly and unethical approach to the real issues. Quick and intense aggressive and sexual confrontation or regression, or else thoughtless reconditioning, is becoming the order of the day. We analysts know that these therapies of consciousness, transference manipulations, counterphobic gestures, expulsive fantasies, and manic dreams of self-transcendence must be superficial. I suggest that we can also say of these therapies that they disclaim the personal activity inherent in defense, inhibition, and avoidance, and in anxiety and guilt as well, for they treat these phenomena as hang-ups, anti-actions rather than actions, something like sludge or misinformation or faintheartedness—definitely not the real you or the real self.

It follows from the arguments I have presented that these are therapies that foster the disclaiming of action. They disclaim defensive action rather than impulse. Or, to put it in terms of psychoanalytic interpretation: psychoanalytic interpretation defines conflicts, symptoms, inhibitions, and anxieties as actions engaged in by people who have a stake in them, however much they may deny that consciously; it characterizes them as actions we do rather than things we have or simply have had implanted in us; it is based on the proposition that there is no wish which is not an "I wish" or a "you wish," no guilt feeling which is not an "I condemn" or a "you condemn," and no defense which is not an "I repudiate" or an "I contradict." From this vantage point, which is the vantage point of the action model, we can say affirmatively of psychoanalytic interpretation that it confronts and works through the most potentially explosive or nihilistic actions unconsciously undertaken by patients against the work of therapy itself.

III. Conclusion

I should like in conclusion to contrast the viewpoint I have been using with the traditional Freudian one. For this puspose I shall comment briefly on a well-known statement by Freud (1917); it is one to which I alluded before in a different connection. Freud said:

. . . these two discoveries—that the life of our sexual instincts cannot be wholly tamed, and that mental processes are themselves unconscious and only reach the ego and come under its control through incomplete and untrustworthy perceptions—these two discoveries amount to a statement that *the ego is not master in its own house*. Together they represent the third blow to man's self love, what I call the *psychological* one. No wonder, then, that the ego does not look favorably upon psycho-analysis and obstinately refuses to believe in it [p. 143; Freud's italics].

The two earlier blows to man's narcissism that Freud refers to are, of course, the "cosmological" blow delivered by Copernicus and the "biological" blow delivered by Darwin.

Although much remains to be worked out about it, the action model of psychoanalytic conceptualization makes possible a different and complementary view of the widespread refusal to believe in psychoanalysis. In this view, the problem is not only a disagreeable *reduction* of man's conception of his scope and influence; it is also a threatening *expansion* of this conception. In a deep sense, Freud extended man's narcissistic sense of himself. He showed that each man makes his life by what he does, and, for psychoanalysis, what he "does" includes all his mental operations and thereby all the circumstances he contrives and all the meanings he ascribes to his circumstances, whether contrived or imposed on him. Man, thus, is far more a creator and stands much closer to his gods than he can bear to recognize. That this issue usually remains unconscious does not, of course, diminish its influence.

It is Freud's commitment to mechanistic natural-science theorizing and our continuing allegiance to him in this regard that have delayed our discovering these truths about psychoanalysis. We have continued to think, with Freud, of energies, forces, structures and so forth as *acting on the person* rather than as metaphoric approaches to *actions of a person*. It has been left to such searching thinkers as Binswanger and Sartre, working within the framework of existential analysis, to begin to formulate these truths. And yet the essential ideas have been at the center of Freudian psychoanalytic interpretation from its very beginning. What, after all, did Freud show in the *Studies on Hysteria* (Breuer and Freud, 1895) but that a neurotic symptom is something a person does, not something he has or has inflicted on him? It is a frightening truth that man makes his own mental symptoms. It is an unwelcome insight that if neurosis is a disease at all, it is not like any other disease. It is an arrangement or a creation, an expression of many of an individual's most vital interests. Freud was to argue later, in his writings on society, that according to psychoanalytic findings neurosis now had to be seen as an aspect of living in relation to other people; this means, of course, that neurosis must be understood as an aspect of being human. Admittedly, the circumstances of life are often difficult, but it is not circumstances that create symptoms; it is mental activity in the face of circumstances. And just as Freud showed man making his own neurotic symptoms, he showed him, to mention only a few points, making his own fantastic sexual theories, his own sexual prowess and pleasure or lack thereof, and, far more often than he dares to admit, his own unsatisfactory "destiny."

Consequently, the widespread rejection of psychoanalysis may be understood as a species of disclaimed action. It is a way of asserting: "Do not tell us how much we do and how much more we could do. Leave us our illusions of ignorance, passivity, and helplessness. We dare not acknowledge that we are masters in our own house." In the words of T. S. Eliot, people want to feel that they are "living and only partly living." This is the frightened, resistant, action-disclaiming stance with which, in part, each of our analysands greets us.

On our part, we analysts must dare to believe that being true to Freud's discoveries need not involve adhering to his metapsychology or to any psychobiological metatheory. We must be open to the idea that other models of mind are not only possible, but also might even facilitate the achievement of a better understanding of the role of unconscious infantile sexuality and aggression in human existence. I have presented the action model as one such model. It is, for psychoanalysis, an entirely new way of thinking systematically, though, as I have said, all along it has been implicit and unsystematized in psychoanalytic thinking. As a theoretical model, as an avowed strategy of systematizing, it is not yet finished, and there are, no doubt, other models to come. Be that as it may, and contrary to what I think is a widespread feeling in the world of analysts, there does seem to be a future after all in Freudian theory.

BIBLIOGRAPHY

Anscombe, G. E. M. (1956), Intention. In: *Essays in Philosophical Psychology,* ed. D. F. Gustafson. Garden City, N.Y.: Anchor Books, 1964, pp. 30–40.

Apfelbaum, B. (1966), On Ego Psychology: A Critique of the Structural Approach to Psycho-Analytic Theory. *Internat. J. Psycho-Anal,* 47:451–475.

Applegarth, A. (1971), Comments on Aspects of the Theory of Psychic Energy. *J. Amer. Psychoanal. Assn.,* 19:379–418.

Aristotle. *Ethics,* trans. J. A. K. Thomson. Baltimore, Md.: Penguin Books, 1953.

Austin, J. L. (1956), A Plea for Excuses. In: *Essays in Philosophical Psychology,* ed. D. F. Gustafson. Garden City, N.Y.: Anchor Books, 1964, pp. 1–29.

Binswanger, L. (1936), Freud's Conception of Man in the Light of Anthropology. In: L. Binswanger, *Being-in-the-World* (trans. J. Needleman). New York: Harper Torchbooks, 1968, pp. 149–181.

——— (1946), The Existential Analysis School of Thought. In: *Existence: A New Dimension in Psychiatry and Psychology,* eds. R. May, E. Angel, & H. F. Ellenberger. New York: Basic Books, 1958.

Breuer, J., & Freud, S. (1895), Studies on Hysteria. *Standard Edition,* 2. London: Hogarth, 1955.

Buber, M. (1923), *I and Thou,* 2d. ed. (trans. R. G. Smith). New York: The Scribner Library, 1958.

Erikson, E. (1950), *Childhood and Society.* New York: Norton.

——— (1956), The Problem of Ego Identity. *J. Amer. Psychoanal. Assn.,* 4:56–121.

Fairbairn, W. R. D. (1952). *An Object-Relations Theory of the Personality.* New York: Basic Books, 1954.

Fenichel, O. (1941), *Problems of Psychoanalytic Technique,* Albany, N.Y.: The Psychoanalytic Quarterly Press.

Francis, J. J. (1970), Panel on "Protest and Revolution." *Internat. J. Psycho-Anal.*, 51:211–218.

Freud, S. (1912), The Dynamics of Transference. *Standard Edition*, 12:99–108. London: Hogarth, 1958.

——— (1915), Observations on Transference Love. *Standard Edition*, 12:159–171. London: Hogarth Press, 1958.

——— (1917), A Difficulty in the Path of Psycho-Analysis. *Standard Edition*, 17:137–144. London: Hogarth Press, 1955.

——— (1920), Beyond the Pleasure Principle, *Standard Edition*, 8:7–64. London: Hogarth Press, 1955.

——— (1925), Some Additional Notes on Dream-Interpretation as a Whole. *Standard Edition*, 19:127–138. London: Hogarth Press, 1961.

——— (1928), Dostoevsky and Parricide. *Standard Edition*, 21:177–194. London: Hogarth Press, 1961.

——— (1937), Analysis Terminable and Interminable. *Standard Edition*, 23:216–253. London: Hogarth Press, 1964.

Gill, M. M. (1963), Topography and Systems in Psychoanalytic Theory. *Psychol. Issues*, Monograph 16.

Grossman, W. I., & Simon, B. (1969), Anthropomorphism: Motive, Meaning, and Causality in Psychoanalytic Theory. *Psychoanalytic Study of the Child*, 24:78–114.

Guntrip, H. (1967), The Concept of Psychodynamic Science. *Internat. J. Psycho-Anal.*, 48:32–43.

——— (1968), *Schizoid Phenomena, Object-Relations and the Self*. London: Hogarth.

Hampshire, S. (1959), *Thought and Action*. New York: Viking Press.

——— (1962), Disposition and Memory. *Internat. J. Psycho-Anal.*, 43:59–68.

Hartmann, H. (1927), Understanding and Explanation. In: Heinz Hartmann, *Essays on Ego Psychology*. New York: International Universities Press, 1964, pp. 369–403.

——— (1939), Ego Psychology and the Problem of Adaptation. (trans. D. Rapaport). New York: International Universities Press, 1958.

——— (1947), On Rational and Irrational Action. In: Heinz Hartmann, *Essays on Ego Psychology*. New York: International Universities Press, 1964, pp. 37–68.

——— (1950), Comments on the Psychoanalytic Theory of the Ego. In: Heinz Hartmann, *Essays on Ego Psychology*. New York: International Universities Press, 1964, pp. 113–141.

——— (1952), The Mutual Influences in the Development of Ego and Id. In: Heinz Hartmann, *Essays on Ego Psychology*. New York: International Universities Press, 1964, pp. 155–181.

——— (1955), On the Theory of Sublimation. In: Heinz Hartmann, *Essays on Ego Psychology*. New York: International Universities Press, 1964, pp. 215–240.

——— (1959), Psychoanalysis as a Scientific Theory. In: Heinz Hartmann, *Essays on Ego Psychology*. New York: International Universities Press, 1964, pp. 318–350.

——— (1964), *Essays on Ego Psychology*. New York: International Universities Press.

——— & Loewenstein, R. M. (1962), Notes on the Superego. *Psychoanalytic Study of the Child*, 17:42–81.

Hayman, A. (1969), What Do We Mean by "Id"? *J. Amer. Psychoanal. Assn.*, 17:333–352.

Holt, R. R. (1967), Beyond Vitalism and Mechanism: Freud's Concept of Psychic Energy. *Science and Psychoanalysis*, 11:1–41. New York: Grune and Stratton.

Home, H. J. (1966), The Concept of Mind. *Internat. J. Psycho-Anal.*, 47:43–49.

Jacobson, E. (1964), *The Self and the Object World*. New York: International Universities Press.

Klein, G. S. (1967), Peremptory Ideation: Structure and Force in Motivated Ideas. In: Motives and Thought: Psychoanalytic Essays in Honor of David Rapaport, ed. R. R. Holt. *Psychol. Issues*, Mono. 18/19:80–128.

——— (1969), Freud's Two Theories of Sexuality: Perspectives to Change in Psychoanalytic Theory. In: *Clinical-Cognitive Psychology: Models and Interpretation*, ed. L. Breger. New York: Prentice Hall.

Kohut, H. (1966), Forms and Transformations of Narcissism. *J. Amer. Psychoanal. Assn.*, 14:243–272.

———— (1971), *The Analysis of the Self.* New York: International Universities Press.

Kris, E. (1952), *Psychoanalytic Explorations in Art.* New York: International Universities Press.

Laing, R. D. (1969a), *The Divided Self,* 2d ed. New York: Pantheon Books.

———— (1969b), *Self and Other,* 2d ed. New York: Pantheon Books.

Levin, D. C. (1969), The Self: A Contribution to Its Place in Theory and Technique. *Internat. J. Psycho-Anal.,* 50:41–52.

Lewin, B. D. (1971), Metaphor, Mind, and Manikin. *Psychoanal. Quart.,* 50:6–39.

Prelinger, E. (1972), Does Psychoanalysis Have a Future in American Psychology? *Psychoanal. Quart.,* 51: 90–103.

Rangell, L. (1969), The Intrapsychic Process and its Analysis—A Recent Line of Thought and its Current Implications. *Internat. J. Psycho-Anal.,* 50:65–77.

Rapaport, D., & Gill, M. M. (1959), The Points of View and Assumptions of Metapsychology. *Internat. J. Psycho-Anal.,* 40:153–162.

Ricoeur, P. (1970), *Freud and Philosophy: An Essay on Interpretation,* trans. D. Savage. New Haven: Yale University Press.

Rycroft, C. (1966), Introduction: Causes and Meaning. In: *Psychoanalysis Observed.* London: Constable, pp. 7–22.

———— (1968), *A Critical Dictionary of Psychoanalysis.* New York: Basic Books.

Ryle, G. (1949), *The Concept of Mind.* New York: Barnes & Noble, 1965.

Sandler, J., & Joffe, W. G. (1969), Towards a Basic Psycho-Analytic Model. *Internat. J. Psycho-Anal.* 50:79–90.

Sartre, J.-P. (1943), *Existential Psychoanalysis,* trans. H. Barnes. New York: Philosophical Library, 1953.

Schafer, R. (1964), The Clinical Analysis of Affects, *J. Amer. Psychoanal. Assn.,* 12:275–299.

———— (1967a), Ego Autonomy and the Return of Repression. *Internat. J. Psychiat.* 3:515–518.

———— (1967b), Ideals, the Ego Ideal, and the Ideal Self. In: Motives and Thought: Psychoanalytic Essays in Honor of David Rapaport, ed. R. R. Holt. *Psychol. Issues,* Mono. 18/19:129–174.

———— (1968a), *Aspects of Internalization.* New York: International Universities Press.

———— (1968b), The Mechanisms of Defence. *Internat. J. Psycho-Anal.* 49:49–62.

———— (1968c), On the Theoretical and Technical Conceptualization of Activity and Passivity. *Psychoanal. Quart.,* 37:173–198.

———— (1970a), The Psychoanalytic Vision of Reality. *Internat. J. Psycho-Anal.,* 51:279–297.

———— (1970b), An Overview of Heinz Hartmann's Contributions to Psycho-Analysis. *Internat. J. Psycho-Anal.,* 51:425–446.

———— (1970c), Requirements for a Critique of the Theory of Catharsis. *J. Consult. Clin. Psychol.,* 35:13–17.

Waelder, R. (1930), The Principle of Multiple Function. *Psychoanal. Quart.* 5:45–62, 1936.

Williams, B. A. O. (1956), Personal Identity and Individuation. In: *Essays in Philosophical Psychology,* ed. D. F. Gustafson. Garden City, N.Y.: Anchor Books, 1964, pp. 324–345.

III

INTERDISCIPLINARY STUDIES

PSYCHOLOGY

Psychoanalytic Research in Attention and Learning: Some Findings and the Question of Clinical Relevance

FRED SCHWARTZ, PH.D. (*New York*)

Some years ago, David Rapaport asked a group of us to carry out experiments aimed at testing his theory of the relationship between perception, short-term memory, and learning. The approach taken was to link the general theory of psychoanalysis to laboratory observation through a number of lower-order experimental hypotheses, just as the general theory is linked to clinical observation by lower-order clinical hypotheses. This program generated a series of experiments, most of which have been reported elsewhere (Schwartz and Schiller, 1970). In this earlier report we evaluated the findings and their theoretical implications. We then asked: are these findings of clinical relevance? In the past, proponents of learning theory have attempted to generalize from the laboratory to the clinical situation (e.g., Dollard and Miller, 1950; French, 1933; Kubie, 1934). Such attempts have not had much impact on the theory or practice of psychoanalysis—in part, because the terms of the two theories are so very different, making

Department of Psychiatry, Albert Einstein College of Medicine at Montefiore Hospital and Medical Center, Bronx, New York.

Presented at the meeting of the American Psychoanalytic Association on December 17, 1971, in New York. The author wishes to thank those who commented on earlier versions of this paper: specifically, Helen Gediman, Merton Gill, William I. Grossman, Robert Holt, Lester Luborsky, and Herbert Weiner. Constructive criticism is somewhat of a lost art, and so the author wishes to especially thank William I. Grossman for his many comments, questions, and helpful suggestions.

it difficult to distinguish between mere translation and true explanation. It seemed, then, that a program of research embedded in psychoanalytic theory might be more relevant to the clinical situation.

Nevertheless, a number of methodological objections can be raised against such an attempt. One is that behavior is overdetermined; hence, the experimental isolation of variables may distort the fabric of everyday behavior. Another is that behavior is situationally determined; hence, laboratory findings may be an artifact of the experimental situation, just as Freud's view of man can be said to be an artifact of the psychoanalytic situation (Rapaport, 1960b). A third objection is that behavior is hierarchically organized; hence, the laws operating at one level of analysis may not apply to another level, or may have only limited significance. The common denominator to such objections is the need to specify rules of inference that govern the generalization of findings from one realm or level of observation to another. Such rules unfortunately do not exist. The clinical relevance of laboratory findings thus becomes a matter of informed judgment, and depends upon one's sense of the laboratory and the consulting office as total situations. The context of observation partially determines not only what is observed but its significance as well.

The aim of this paper is to share with the reader our thinking in trying to generalize from our experimental program to the clinical situation. Part I reviews Rapaport's theory and the basic findings of our research project. The more clinically oriented reader may wish to go directly to Part II, in which we restate our basic theoretical principles and then consider the question of clinical relevance.

I. Psychoanalytic Research in Attention and Learning

As a first approximation, learning refers to changes in behavior wrought by experience. A more precise definition would have to exclude change due to such factors as maturation and the state of the organism. One can distinguish between types of learning and speculate about the mechanisms underlying this process. And one can focus on broad consequences of learning: its adaptive significance, its effect on subjective experience, and its role as a causal determinant in behavior.

Somewhat less attention has been paid to another general consequence of learning: that the internalization of past experience reduces the need to process information in the present. In driving a car, I don't have to think through the steps involved in braking, depressing the clutch, or turning the wheel. Nor do I have to analyze words into phonemes, or perceived objects into angles, lines, and sub-gestalten, in order to grasp their meaning. Much of one's everyday behavior rests on knowledge that is implicit or preconscious, freeing one to attend to a greater range of events. Learning thus appears to extend mental capacity, just as a lever can be said to extend physical capacity. This is essentially an economic or quantitative consideration.

Rapaport (1960a) hypothesized that the economics of structure formation had theoretical significance. He began with the following broad empirical generalizations: that conscious experience is finite and transitory; that the content of conscious experience is selectively determined by strategies of attention; that learning is facilitated by selective attention and repetition; and that learning, once completed, allows one to carry out a practiced task with little conscious effort. He next proposed a unified theory to account for these empirical generalizations (1959; 1960a). He postulated: that conscious experience is governed by a limited quantity of attentional energy; that selective attention redistributes this quantity, creating a region of high-energy potential; that this high-energy potential is subject to entropy or equalization; that repetition binds some of this quantity in a structure; and that learning, once completed, frees energy for other mental activity. He thus postulated a closed-system model, based on Freud's (1900) early speculations about energy and binding. The model, in essence, states that there is a limit on conscious experience, and that learning extends this limit.

The energy construct has been vigorously criticized in recent years as a holdover from a discarded scientific world-view (Holt, 1967). Psychic energy is said to be unmeasurable and without existential meaning. Lurking in the shadows are the mind-body problem and the biological fact that living organisms are open, not closed systems. I will briefly return to these points later. Here, I simply want to note that theoretical constructs, like paranoid delusions, often contain a kernel of truth, because of their, however tenuous, link to reality. The core meaning of the energy construct is that the transition from process to structure brings about a quantitative change, whether this change be conceptualized in terms of psychic energy, or information redundancy, or the establishment of phase sequences, to mention a few examples from other theoretical frameworks. Rapaport might have been on safer ground if he had postulated that perception and short-term memory are dynamic states of equilibria that are unsteady, and that learning establishes a steady state that is relatively enduring over time. The real difficulty with his model, however, is that he ascribed causal significance to a consequence of learning, assuming, in other words, that the quantitative gain from learning is the essence of the learning process. But that comment gets me ahead of my story.

The notion that consciousness is governed by a limited quantity is based on the clinical observation that states of preoccupation, acute conflict, and strong affect interfere with cognition. Quantitative examples of a central limit are well known from academic psychology, as when it is demonstrated that attention to the details of a meaningful passage interferes with reading comprehension (Postman and Senders, 1946), or when the investigator demonstrates interference between perception and retention, or between retention and recall (e.g., Brown, 1954; Harris and Haber, 1963; Sperling, 1960).

A major breakthrough was reported by Broadbent in 1958. Summarizing the work of communication engineers, he concluded that the ability to comprehend language is limited by the capacity of the human brain, as defined operationally in the terms of information theory. So as to avoid misunderstanding, it should be kept in mind that information, in this context, refers to the number of possible messages one might send or receive. The meaning of the message is irrelevant; all that matters is the number of alternatives. It was soon discovered that the informational measure did not apply if the message had to be stored or remembered before it was transmitted. For example, my ability to hear a word against a noisy background—whether the background be white noise or the chatter of friends—depends upon the number of possible words I might receive. It helps if I know beforehand that only one of five words will be transmitted against white noise, just as it helps to know the topic being discussed by my friends. But my ability to remember what was said does not depend upon the number of alternatives. The ability to hold items in short-term memory is nevertheless limited. It thus seemed that the concept of a limited central capacity might apply to memory phenomena, although the informational measure does not. Why not? Information theory deals with some future event that is more or less unpredictable. If the task is to identify one of ten lights, then what matters is the number of lights. Each light shares the same property, namely, its uncertainty. Memory refers to an experience that has occurred in the past. The event has meaning and is defined by when it occurred and where. Uncertainty is minimal. The capacity to remember is thus influenced more by the number of items to be remembered than by the alternatives one might have experienced but didn't. The exact relationship between these two limits, one on processing information in the present, the other on remembering the past, is still to be determined, although the problem was first highlighted some years ago (G. A. Miller, 1956). Parenthetically, it should be noted that limiting factors are discussed by communication theorists (e.g., Wiener, 1948, p. 174 ff.). The limiting factor may be the size of a structure, the number of component parts, their speed of operation, or the energy available to the system. Furthermore, calculations exist as to the amount of energy needed to transmit one bit of information, and J. G. Miller (1965) has suggested that a constant relationship may well exist "among measures of energy, entropy, and information." Some psychoanalytic authors have assumed that information theory and the economic point of view are mutually exclusive, although this is not necessarily true, as suggested by the above quotation.

In an initial series of experiments, we studied the remembering of materials presented only once—these are therefore experiments in short-term memory. Such memory has two significant characteristics: it is limited in amount and duration. Thus, the number of unrelated words or one-digit numbers one can remember without error is approximately seven, whereas the duration of such remembering is generally a matter of seconds. Short-term memory was made the focal point of our research because it appears to represent a transitional point between perception and learning. The object of these studies was to show that the restrictions on short-term memory are, in part, due to limits on central capacity. Two other explanations of these restrictions exist and so had to be excluded by the experimental design. One is that the mental representation of each item decays rapidly in time (trace-decay theory). The other is that presenting similar items creates an "inner confusion" which increases as the number of items is increased (interference theory). Without trying to substantiate the point in this brief summary, let me state that negative evidence exists in the case of both these theories (see Norman, 1966; Schwartz, 1969). It should also be kept in mind that Rapaport identified the capacity factor in terms of psychic energy. In what follows, however, we can only provide evidence for a capacity factor; it is only by considering the overall research project that we can say something about the energy hypothesis, per se.

Our basic design was to have subjects work on two tasks "at the same time." One task was used to place a hypothetical demand on central capacity; the other task was used to measure residual performance. The two tasks were dissimilar and, where possible, were presented to different sense modalities so as to exclude an explanation in terms of interference. The time parameter was controlled so as to exclude an explanation in terms of trace decay. We thus tried to partition central capacity into two components, by having subjects work on two tasks, one of which varied in difficulty. The findings can be summarized in the form of an analogy. Assume that a computer can receive messages from two sources and that it can print out what is received. Perception is defined as printing out the message as it is received. Short-term memory is defined as a delayed print-out; during the delay period, the computer remains active, recirculating the message (rehearsal) and organizing it in different ways (coding). Learning is defined as altering the structure of the computer—for example, placing the message on tape. The computer is limited in terms of what it can process within a given interval of time; this is the limited capacity of information theory. There is also a limit on the amount of material the computer can recirculate and organize prior to print-out; this is the short-term memory capacity of the system. If the computer receives two messages at the same time, the amount of processing required by one source limits the ability of the computer to receive and process messages from a second source, as summarized by Broadbent (1958).

What happens if one of the two messages can be recirculated before print-out? The ability of the computer to do this depends on the amount of processing required by the other source. For example, we asked subjects to do easy and difficult additions while "storing" geometric designs. Their ability to recognize the designs after a delay period varied with the difficulty of the addition task. Similarly, subjects were asked to follow a moving line with a metal stylus while "storing" words. Their ability to recall or recognize the words on a subsequent test varied with how difficult it was to follow the moving line. But clearly, difficult perceptual tasks require more time for processing. What if time is adjusted so that there is just enough time to process each message? In a subsequent experiment, subjects were given just enough time to do the easy and difficult additions, meaning that they had less time for the easy additions than for the difficult ones. Under these conditions, difficulty ceased to influence remembering. The crucial factor is thus the time needed by the computer to receive and process a message from one source while recirculating a message from another source. What happens if both messages are presented at the same time for delayed print-out? Sperling's findings (1960) suggest that having two messages in storage at the same time takes more capacity than having just one message in storage. What happens if the two messages are presented in sequence, one after the other, for delayed print-out? We tested the effects of storing the first message on recall of the second. The fact that the first message was in storage mattered; its length did not. From these and other findings, we concluded that a central mechanism needs time to receive and process messages from one or more sources, and additional time to recirculate and organize messages for delayed print-out. From a psychological point of view, short-term memory is an active process—a thought process, basically—and as such it places a definite demand on central capacity. Similar conclusions about a limited central capacity for stored events have been reached by other investigators, working within different theoretical frameworks (e.g., Murdock, 1965; Posner and Rossman, 1965).

The active nature of short-term memory itself became the object of study in some experiments. In our basic design, we instructed subjects to work on two tasks at the same time, with equal emphasis on both. In actuality, we had to go to extreme lengths to counter the tendency of subjects to focus attention on what they thought to be relevant, even if this conflicted with our experimental objectives. Our subjects were apparently motivated to use their limited capacity in a manner they thought would yield the best results. We did succeed in preventing subjects from ignoring parts of the task, meaning that it is possible to separate motive and capacity as causal determinants of behavior. Nevertheless, one could argue that the limited-capacity hypothesis should be replaced with the hypothesis that attention is selectively steered by motives. The fact that the subject is asked to do both tasks, and hence motivated to do both, would seem to preclude this alternative; but the subject may nevertheless set his own priorities, as noted above. The question remains, however: why does the subject have to set priorities if he is capable of dealing with both tasks at the same time? The answer is that he cannot, because of limits on capacity. It is nevertheless plausible that limited capacity, although a structural given, is further restricted through experience, as one learns that it is more economical to restrict awareness to relevant features of the environment. The ability to restrict awareness can wax and wane, as is known from psychopathology, and the failure to restrict awareness is an important component of thought disorder in schizophrenia.

The above findings apply to short-term memory—that is, to tasks in which remembering is tested after but a single trial. Most laboratory learning requires repeated presentations of the same material. The limited-capacity hypothesis also appears to apply to the mental strategies employed during learning. Concretely, this means that one rehearses, thinks about, organizes, or otherwise works over the presented material while attempting to learn. Operationally, this is what learning is all about, at least in the case of normal adult subjects presented with meaningful materials which they intentionally try to master. Once such learning is completed, all the complicated activities of thought that help support the process tend to drop out, with recitation becoming more or less automatic. The same logic applies to coding operations and class concepts, which, once learned, or grasped by insight, serve as tools of cognition, allowing the perceiver to overcome limits on capacity. Such structures can even be created de novo—which is itself of interest. Extended practice (i.e., overlearning), however, makes for the most efficient behavior.

We obtained evidence not that learning binds energy, but only that learning is supported by certain mental strategies. The crucial experiment in this series is too complex to summarize at this time (see Schwartz & Schiller, 1970). Essentially, we could not separate out the work involved in paying attention from the hypothetical energy bound in forming a structure. Considering all the data, the most parsimonious explanation is that learning, once completed, frees capacity, rather than binds energy. We were forced to conclude that binding refers to one of the consequences of learning, not to the mechanism underlying this process. A similar shift in interpretation can be found in psychoanalytic theory, according to Apfelbaum (1965). In the topographic model, binding was mostly a mechanism, and in this guise accounted for such end results as delay of response and drive restraint. In the structural model, the emphasis shifts to acquired meaning: learning establishes meaning, and meaning is a causal determinant in behavior. Restraint is now cognitive rather than energic in character.

Nor did we find evidence in support of the hypothesis that the energy invested in a trace is subject to entropy or equalization. Concretely, this postulate in Rapaport's model leads to the prediction that forgetting occurs in time (analogous to trace-decay theories of short-term memory). However, it is possible to so arrange conditions as to show that forgetting is not always a function of time, even though this is generally the case. The experimental findings leading to this conclusion can be found in our monograph (Schwartz and Schiller, 1970).

In taking stock, we concluded that Rapaport's model was not substantiated, especially with respect to the energy construct. On the other hand, we were led by this model to three related conclusions of general significance. These are that memory and perception are governed by a central mechanism of limited capacity, that learning extends capacity, and that overlearning automatizes response, so that one can engage in complex acts without the nagging intrusion of consciousness or meaning.

Before proceeding, a caution is in order. In the above discussion, capacity is a hypothetical construct. It is assumed that capacity is an inborn structural given, which, however, is modified by experience. The role of experience is exemplified by asking subjects to remember words embedded in meaningful sentences. This procedure greatly improves performance, because the subject can group words into larger units, based on his past experience with the language (Schwartz and Lippmann, 1962). There is thus no absolute estimate of the capacity factor in performance; there are only relative estimates, based on the kinds of subjects and materials employed. All we can really show is a reciprocity between doing two things at the same time, where what is being done is either processing a message or storing it for delayed report. Furthermore, even relative capacity cannot be measured directly; we can only measure performance, under certain experimental arrangements from which we conclude that a limit exists. The problem of quantification is, in this sense, no different than that encountered in measuring intelligence, which is also a relativistic concept.

Finally, we would like to consider briefly the existential status of psychic energy, before turning to the question of clinical relevance. The economic point of view, which includes Rapaport's theory of attentional energy, has been sharply criticized in recent years on grounds noted at the beginning of this paper: namely, that it is unmeasurable, and that it implies a mind-body dualism and a closed-system model of mind (see Apfelbaum, 1965; Holt, 1967; Kubie, 1947; Rosenblatt and Thickstun, 1970; Rubinstein, 1965, 1967). We too have questioned the value of the concept, but on very different grounds. In essence, psychic energy is a hypothetical construct, and as such, stands or falls on the basis of its usefulness in organizing data. Unfortunately, the construct has been reified in many psychoanalytic writings, leading to justifiable criticism. But such criticism should be directed at how the concept is employed, not at the concept itself. The value of a construct is an empirical matter and can be determined only on such grounds. Some of the criticism, unfortunately, also makes the error of reification, if only by implication. To argue, for example, that psychic energy is a quantitative construct, and hence should be measurable, is to assume, by implication, that it is real—that it exists. But it is not real; it is a hypothetical construct—and all that is required of such a construct is to show that it leads to predictions about behavior that are subject to quantification, or that it belongs to a network of logically related concepts (the nomological net), some of which lead to measurement. Similarly, to argue that the concept of psychic energy implies a mind-body dualism is to acknowledge that the concept has been used incorrectly. If psychic energy is real, and if it is "mental," then a problem exists when one tries to cross the gap from the mental to the physical—but no such gap exists at the level of conceptual analysis (Bertalanffy, 1964). As a construct, it is neither mental nor physical, although it is used to order data that we designate as mental. Admittedly, the concept of psychic energy has unfortunate surplus meaning, and this has led to some conceptual confusion. Other more theoretically neutral constructs can be substituted, however, suggesting that it captures something of value.

A somewhat different argument applies to the criticism that psychic energy implies a closed-system model, whereas biological systems are open. The difficulty, here, is that open and closed systems are high-order abstractions, applicable to such domains as classical mechanics and living organisms. The meaning of these abstractions change when they are applied to more restricted areas of discourse. Thus, Fairbairn's (1958) assertion that the paranoid patient maintains his inner world as a closed system is a particular way of describing behavior and has no relation to the broader conception. Similarly, the notion of a limited central capacity is a construct about data and, as such, has meaning, whether we agree that the organism, as a biological system, is open or closed.

II. The Question of Clinical Relevance

We have reviewed Rapaport's theory of attention and learning and some of the findings of our research project. On the basis of this review, we rejected the basic structure of the model, although supporting some of the constructs engendered by it. These constructs are as follows: (1) man's capacity for conscious experience is limited by inborn structural givens; (2) learning extends this limit by internalizing past experience, such that much that we experience at the moment is really implicit or preconscious; and (3) with extended practice, behavior becomes automatized, meaning that much of our everyday activity circumvents consciousness. In this revised system, consciousness is a luxury, to be indulged in when one meets situations that are novel, threatening, or especially interesting. What is missing in this revision is a mechanism, provided originally by the hypothesis that energy displacements and transformations underlie the transition from process to structure. The revised model, nevertheless, retains much of Freud's original view (1900), to wit, that consciousness is a superordinate sense organ, that its operation raises mental processes to a higher level, and that one can perceive and react without necessarily being conscious that this is happening.

The present section is concerned with the clinical relevance of this revised model. We alluded earlier to the difficulties involved in generalizing from the laboratory to the clinical situation. Before considering such objections, however, let us see if the concepts developed do indeed help us understand aspects of the clinical theory or actual clinical data. An affirmative answer to this attempt would still leave open the question whether it is justified or even helpful.

To begin with, let us assume that the limited central capacity can be used in the service of defense. Freud's (1915) model of repression proper was essentially conceived in such terms. His two-stage model—the withdrawal of hypercathexis and the establishment of countercathectic barriers—is an abstract way of saying that we initially shift attention away from something forbidden to something neutral, and subsequently learn something that excludes thinking about the forbidden. The first stage requires a constant expenditure of energy—that is, it places a strain on central capacity. Learning frees capacity by structuralizing the process, as in the classic example of reaction formation. Operationally, hypercathexis is withdrawn by thinking of something else, by maintaining a constant but irrelevant flow of speech, or by flight into activity. Such operations are effective because of limits on capacity; one cannot attend to the forbidden and to something else at the same time. The production of material in psychotherapy may thus be employed for defensive aims—a subtle strategy, since one is ostensibly following the basic rule. In general, speech can interfere with thoughtfulness, just as acting out and strong affect tend to preclude reflective thought.

Thoughtfulness, in the form of reflexive self-awareness, may in turn interfere with action, as seen in some schizoid and borderline patients. These patients are acutely self-conscious, and in addition, feel awkward, do not function as well as they might, and experience a sense of unreality. A suggestive parallel is what happens when one attends to the details of a skilled act, rather than to the object of the activity. The pianist trying to correct some mechanical flaw attends to how he strikes the keys, not to the meaning of the music. His playing momentarily suffers, but he is able to shift back to the music, once the flaw is corrected. The schizoid patient initially can also shift back from the self to the object, but reflexive self-observation eventually becomes automatized, and hence a constant source of interference. This is not to say that we are dealing only with limits on capacity in this example. Self-observation has a defensive function. But the difficulty of observing oneself while engaged in some task may enter as an independent variable, contributing to one's overall poor performance and discomfort. The sense of unreality may well come about when self-observation becomes relatively irreversible; it is at this point that the unity of experience is split.

The most obvious clinical referent of the capacity model is Fenichel's (1945, p. 168) discussion of the nonspecific symptoms of neurotic conflict (actual neurotic symptoms). According to this discussion, conflict places a demand on central capacity. Rapaport, Gill, and Schafer (1945) made this argument a central tenet of diagnostic psychological testing. Cognitive deficits associated with psychopathology are even more pronounced in borderline patients, acute schizophrenic episodes, and severe depressions. The clinical data in such cases supports a nondynamic conception, in which lowered efficiency is related to the degree to which central capacity is taken up by other demands. Most striking, however, is the lowering of cognitive functioning associated with the organic mental syndrome. Such patients, however, can be encouraged to perform at a higher level and momentarily perform adequately by deliberately exerting effort, only to then become fatigued. Mild deficits are uncovered by "loading capacity," that is, by repeating the same problem, increasing the length of the task, or introducing a memory factor. These observations readily fit a capacity model, where capacity is dependent upon the structural integrity of the brain.

Automatization is the other major construct in the model with potential clinical significance. Hartmann (1958a) devoted a chapter (pp. 86–99) to the economic gain achieved by forming preconscious automatisms, and mentioned, in passing, that "normal automatisms are frequently the predecessors of compulsion symptoms" (p. 90). Automatization precludes awareness of details, and this may explain why some defensive operations occur outside of awareness.

Words, themselves, are automatized structures, and their use tends to exclude from awareness a host of associated feelings, impulses, and fantasies. We see this in extreme form in the obsessional neuroses. Kubie's (1953) distinction between symbolic thought and "gut" memory can be understood in these terms.

The model which has been developed in this paper also has implications for the learning process, as it occurs in the psychotherapeutic situation. An essential job of the patient in treatment is to make sense of his experience. This requires the sifting and synthesis of large amounts of data. Such effort places a considerable demand on central capacity, requires the availability of appropriate conceptual structures and the ability to go behind attitudes and categories of thought that are relatively automatized. The problem is compounded by strong affects, defensive operations, and inner preoccupation, all of which place an additional burden on central capacity. The task of psychotherapy is therefore a difficult one, strictly from a cognitive point of view. Within this framework, interpretations are efforts at coding experience. To the extent that the code is appropriate, it is internalized and becomes a tool of cognition. But learning is a slow process, especially when the task is difficult, ambiguous, and occurs under conditions of high emotionality.

During the panel discussion that followed the initial presentation of this paper, Dr. Gerald Aronson suggested that neurosis could be conceptualized as a code that represents past experience in an economical fashion. Attempts to change such a code would meet with resistance from a cognitive point of view, much as earlier scientific discoveries were opposed because they demanded a restructuring of experience. The reason for such resistance is that we need conceptual codes to make sense of experience. Codes are conceptual tools that favor adaptation. The establishment of new codes requires considerable effort and leaves one temporarily vulnerable in situations that were previously dealt with more or less automatically. The freedom to choose is a virtue, as long as it remains hypothetical, but free choice tends to be avoided in everyday living, especially in the presence of anxiety.

The above formulations involve the assumption that concepts developed in the laboratory can be applied to the clinical situation. The objections to such an attempt were discussed above. As we have seen, the two situations are different: one cannot isolate one variable as explanatory (the principle of overdetermination or multiple function); and behavior exists on different hierarchical levels. Central to such objections is the dynamic point of view of psychoanalysis. This issue was clarified for me in a conversation with William I. Grossman. Let us take the example of acting out. By clinical consensus, this refers to behavior governed by a thought process that is mostly outside of awareness—I refer, of course, to unconscious fantasy. It was suggested previously that the reciprocity between thought and acting out is an example of limited capacity. We can, instead, say that the choice of the motor route is motivated. The action gratifies, while the absence of reflective thought is in the service of defense. Acting out is thus a compromise between impulse and defense, and hence fits the model of symptom formation. In more general terms, a dynamic formulation can be substituted for an economic-structural one, as suggested by Apflebaum (1965). In the examples given above defense is therefore an alternative explanation to limits on capacity.

The counterargument is that motives and defense are able to organize experience into figure and ground precisely because capacity is limited. Otherwise, one could be aware of one's behavior and its meaning at the same time. It is true that one can stop and think about the meaning of one's behavior, so that action and thought no longer compete. But one must stop and think; otherwise, the capacity hypothesis still applies. On the other hand, learning changes the meaning of behavior, and defensive strategies are learned. Because of learning, certain ideas cease to be relevant, from a cognitive point of view. Defensive strategies are codes that give meaning to experience: the absence of alternate codes precludes alternative ways of viewing reality. For example, one cannot think of oneself as both kind and sadistic, except as an intellectual exercise. Limited capacity is not at issue here, because one can carry out these mental operations in sequence. One can first consider evidence of his kindness, and then shift to evidence of his sadism. The phenomenon of reaction formation suggests that one's failure to carry out both operations in sequence is motivated, not limited.

One can continue to obsess about the primacy of dynamic versus economic-structural formulations in the clinical situation, falling back, if pressed, on the principle of multiple function (Waelder, 1936). Instead, I am going to leave this dilemma for the moment. As noted previously, a number of attempts have been made to apply learning theory to psychoanalysis. Schilder (1937), possibly with tongue in cheek, countered by psychologizing Pavlov's dog. More recently, Chomsky (1958) sharply criticized Skinner for stepping out of his laboratory into the world of language acquisition. Behind these controversies lie a family of dichotomies; molar versus molecular, organismic versus reductionistic, cognitive versus stimulus-response, etc. The point of contention here is the general hypothesis that behavior is hierarchically organized into levels, each level dependent on the next, but governed by its own laws. This hypothesis is very much a matter of contention in current psychoanalytic theory. Rubinstein (1965, 1967) and Holt (1967), while accepting the concept of levels, have criticized psychoanalytic theory for being mentalistic and anthropomorphic, and call for at least protoneurophysiological propositions, whereas Apfelbaum (1965), Klein (1966), and Grossman (1967; Grossman and Simon, 1969) argue that the theory is necessarily anthropomorphic because it is concerned with meanings and intentions—that is, with aspects of inner experience which are, by definition, subjective. The argument for levels is eloquently stated by Polanyi (1968), who points out that the design of a machine imposes boundary conditions that restrict the laws of physics and chemistry. Destroy the structure of a machine, and its constituents are still governed by the laws of nature, though the parts are released from the restrictions imposed by the machine's design. In an analogous fashion, Max Planck (1949) notes that quantum theory and the theory of relativity do not negate classical mechanics, but rather place that theory in a more comprehensive framework. The empirical data is, in some ways, even more convincing, since it is too easy to be misled by abstractions. Lashley (1951), in his classic paper on the problem of serial order, noted some twenty years ago that skilled behavior occurs at speeds that cannot be accounted for in terms of external stimulus control. This conclusion still holds, to the best of my knowledge. Held (1965), in reviewing the history of how man has explained the correspondence between an external object and its inner representation, notes the repeated failure of theories of correspondence which assume that object and image are somehow identical. Held asks how this can be, given distortion in the lens, inversion of the visual image, and changing patterns of stimulation which alter size, shape, and position. Held's own work on adaptation to disarrangement, and the experiments by Ivo Kohler (1964), lead him to suggest that correspondence is achieved by constructive powers in the system. This view is echoed by Chomsky (1958) for language acquisition, and by Lashley (1951) for serial behavior. Weiner (1969), in a review of recent neurophysiological studies of brain and behavior, notes the lack of correspondence between input and neuronal activity, the lack of correspondence between neuronal activity and observed response, and the variation in response with the state of the organism and its prior history. From a number of areas of investigation, we are led to at least consider that behavior is organized in levels of ascending complexity and control.

The concept of hierarchical levels has a number of implications for the problem at hand. Concepts such as automatization and capacity deal with man as a machine, in Polanyi's (1968) sense—that is, with the design of a mechanism. Motives and meaning may impose boundary conditions on this mechanism, according to their own laws. An example is the hypothesis that limited capacity is used in the service of defense. One answer to the dilemma posed earlier is thus that both economic-structural and dynamic considerations apply to the same behavior, but at different levels of organization. This argument combines the principle of multiple function (Waelder, 1936) with the principle of hierarchical levels. The conclusion that many variables therefore operate simultaneously does not mean that they are all equally potent as determiners of behavior—a point that is obvious, once stated. The problem, nevertheless, is to identify which variables are relevant in a particular situation.

A similar conclusion can be reached by considering the methodological principle of operationism. According to this principle, an event is defined by the operations employed. Force, for example, is defined, in part, by the displacement of a spring balance. The temperature of the room containing the spring balance is also relevant, although of little practical significance. Situational variables, however, play a highly significant role in psychology. By implication, one cannot generalize across situations without demonstrating that the same operations apply. Polanyi (1968) stated this principle when he suggested that the design of an experiment imposes boundary conditions on the behavior under consideration. Returning to our problem, this means that relationships observed under laboratory conditions may or may not apply to the clinical situation, in part because the methods of observation—the operations employed—are different. Hartmann (1958b) intuitively grasped this point when he asserted that the reformulation of analytic theory in other terms "ignores the special conditions in our field." Granting that this is a problem, how do we move across situations, if not across levels? The only answer I can give is that this is an empirical question. Whether the limited-capacity model is used in the service of defense, or the laws of learning apply to symptom formation, can only be determined by applying these principles to the psychoanalytic situation. According to this view, the psychoanalytic situation can be used to study clinical phenomena directly, and to test out hypotheses derived from experiment. Pribram (1962) has developed these maxims into a formal research methodology. It is noteworthy that the laws of learning are being applied to symptoms by behavior therapists; this development can only add to our knowledge, although their narrow definition of psychopathology omits much that is of interest from a scientific point of view.

The conclusion reached above is that the explanatory value of the capacity model needs to be evaluated clinically. This means that a number of investigators would have to look at clinical data with these constructs in mind. Perhaps more important is whether or not such an approach makes a difference, in terms of technique. A positive answer to this question would serve as a partial test of the theory. A number of technical maxims are consistent with the approach presented above, but this involves hindsight. It is nevertheless worth noting that attempts at synthesis through interpretation are not recommended during acute episodes—we would add, because of limits of capacity—and that interpretation is largely cognitive, supporting the role of concepts in coding experience. The use of speech and action to suppress objectionable material is also consistent with the model.

III. Summary

The first part of this paper reviewed Rapaport's theory of attention and learning and some findings from a research project initiated at his behest. The model explained the transition from process to structure in terms of a hypothetical energic mechanism. On the basis of our findings, we rejected the energic mechanism for lack of evidence. Nevertheless, we obtained evidence in support of three propositions: conscious experience is governed by limited capacity; learning extends capacity by internalizing experience; and overlearning automatizes response, freeing capacity.

The second part of this paper dealt with the clinical relevance of Rapaport's model. We applied the model to Freud's two-stage theory of repression and to certain clinical phenomena, including nonspecific deficits in borderline, schizophrenic, severely depressed, and organically impaired patients, and the nature of learning in psychotherapy. We then considered methodological objections to such an attempt and emphasized the need for clinical validation. A hypothesis was put forth for consideration, namely, that motives and intentions impose boundary conditions on the operation of an underlying mechanism. This conception combines the principle of multiple function with the principle of hierarchical levels. In the context of this presentation, it asserts that dynamic factors influence the role of capacity limits and preconscious automatisms in determining behavior.

BIBLIOGRAPHY

Apfelbaum, B. (1965), Ego Psychology, Psychic Energy, and the Hazards of Quantitative Explanation in Psycho-Analytic Theory. *Internat. J. Psycho-Anal.*, 46:168–181,
Bertalanffy, L. von (1964), The Mind-Body Problem: A New View. *Psychosom. Med.*, 26:29–45.

Broadbent, D. E. (1958), *Perception and Communication*. New York: Pergamon Press.

Brown, J. (1954), The Nature of Set-to-Learn and of Intra-Material Interference in Immediate Memory. *Quart. J. Exp. Psychol.*, 6:141–148.

Chomsky, N. (1958), Review of Verbal Behavior, by B. F. Skinner. *Language*, 35:26–58.

Dollard, J., and Miller, N. E. (1950), *Personality and Psychotherapy: An Analysis in Terms of Learning, Thinking, and Culture*. New York: McGraw-Hill.

Fairbairn, W. R. D. (1958), On the Nature and Aims of Psycho-Analytical Treatment. *Internat. J. Psycho-Anal.*, 39:374–385.

Fenichel, O. (1945), *The Psychoanalytic Theory of Neurosis*. New York: W. W. Norton & Co., Inc.

French, T. M. (1933), Interrelations Between Psycho-Analysis and the Experimental Work of Pavlov. *Amer. J. Psychiatry*, 89:1165–1203.

Freud, S. (1900), The Interpretation of Dreams. *Standard Edition*, 4. London: Hogarth, 1953.

———— (1915), The Unconscious. *Standard Edition*, 14. London: Hogarth, 1957.

Grossman, W. I. (1967), Reflections on the Relationships of Introspection and Psychoanalysis. *Internat. J. Psycho-Anal.*, 48:16–31.

————, and Simon, B. (1969), Anthropomorphism: Motive, Meaning and Causality in Psychoanalytic Theory. *Psychoanalytic Study of the Child*, 24:78–111.

Harris, C. S. and Haber, R. N. (1963), Selective Attention and Coding in Visual Perception. *J. Exp. Psychol.*, 65:328–333.

Hartmann, H. (1958a). *Ego Psychology and the Problem of Adaptation*. New York: International Universities Press.

———— (1958b), Comments on the Scientific Aspects of Psychoanalysis. *Psychoanalytic Study of the Child*, 13:127–146.

Held, R. (1965), *Vision and Value, Structure in Art and Science*, Vol. II. Ed. Gyorgy Kepes. New York: George Braziller.

Holt, R. R. (1967), Beyond Vitalism and Mechanism: Freud's Concept of Psychic Energy. In: *Science and Psychoanalysis*, 2, ed. J. H. Masserman. New York: Grune & Stratton.

Klein, G. S. (1966), Perspectives to Change in Psychoanalytic Theory; A Presentation at Conference of Psychoanalysts of the Southwest. Galveston, Texas, unpublished ms.

Kohler, I .(1964), The Formation and Transformation of the Perceptual World. *Psychol. Issues*, Mono. 12. New York: International Universities Press.

Kubie, L. S. (1934), Relation of the Conditioned Reflex to Psychoanalytic Technique. *Arch. Neurol. and Psychiat.*, 32:1138–1142.

———— (1947), The Fallacious Use of Quantitative Concepts in Dynamic Psychology. *Psychoanal. Quart.*, 16:507–518.

———— (1953), Some Implications for Psychoanalysis of Modern Concepts of the Organization of the Brain. *Psychoanal. Quartz.*, 22:21–52.

Lashley, K. S. (1951), The Problem of Serial Order in Behavior. In: *Cerebral Mechanisms in Behavior*, Ed. L. A. Jeffress. New York: Wiley.

Miller, G. A. (1956), The Magical Number 7, Plus or Minus Two: Some Limits on Our Capacity for Processing Information. *Psychol. Rev.*, 63:81–97.

Miller, J. G. (1965), Living Systems: Basic Concepts. *Behav. Sci.*, 10:193–237.

Murdock, B. B., Jr. (1965), A Test of the "Limited Capacity" Hypothesis. *J. Exp. Psychol.*, 69:237–40.

Norman, D. A. (1966), Acquisition and Retention in Short-Term Memory. *J. Exp. Psychol.*, 72:369–81.

Planck, M. (1949), The Meaning and Limits of Exact Science. *Science*, 110:319–27.

Polanyi, M. (1968), Life's Irreducible Structure. *Science*, 160:1308–1312.

Posner, M., and Rossman, E. (1965), Effect of Size and Location of Informational Transforms Upon Short-Term Retention. *J. Exp. Psychol.*, 70:496–505.

Postman, L. and Senders, V. (1946), Incidental Learning and Generality of Set. *J. Exp. Psychol.*, 36:153–165.

Pribram, K. (1962), Interrelations of Psychology and the Neurological Disciplines. In: *Psychology: A Study of Science*, Ed. S. Koch. New York: McGraw-Hill.

Rapaport, D. (1959), The Theory of Attention Cathexis: An Economic and Structural

Attempt at the Explanation of Cognitive Processes. In: *The Collected Papers of David Rapaport*, Ed. M. M. Gill. New York: Basic Books, 1967.

—— (1960a), On the Psychoanalytic Theory of Motivation. *The Nebraska Symposium on Motivation*, Lincoln: University of Nebraska Press.

—— (1960b), The Structure of Psychoanalytic Theory. *Psychol. Issues*, Mono. 6. New York: International Universities Press.

——, Gill, M., and Schafer, R. (1945), Diagnostic Psychological Testing. *The Menninger Clinic Monograph Series No. 3*. Chicago: The Year Book Publishers, Inc.

Rosenblatt, A. D. and Thickstun, J. T. (1970), A Study of the Concept of Psychic Energy. *Internat. J. Psycho-Anal.*, 51:265–278.

Rubinstein, B. B. (1965), Psychoanalytic Theory and the Mind-Body Problem. In: *Psychoanalysis and Current Biological Thought*, Ed. H. S. Greenfield and W. C. Lewis. Madison: University of Wisconsin Press.

—— (1967), Explanation and Mere Description: A Metascientific Examination of Certain Aspects of the Psychoanalytic Theory of Motivation. In: *Motives and Thought*, Ed. R. R. Holt. New York: International Universities Press.

Schilder, P. (1937), Psychoanalysis and Conditioned Reflexes. *Psychoanal. Rev.*, 24:1–17.

Schwartz, F. (1969), Some Problems and Notes About Short-Term Memory. *Psychol. Rep.*, 24:71–80.

——, and Lippmann, F. (1962), Cognitive and Associative Structures in Recall. *Psychol. Rep.*, 11:91–101.

——, and Schiller, P. (1970). A Psychoanalytic Model of Attention and Learning. *Psychol. Issues*, Mono. 23. New York: International Universities Press.

Sperling, G. (1960), The Information Available in Brief Visual Presentation. *Psychol. Mono*. 74:11 (Whole No. 498).

Waelder, R. (1936), The Principle of Multiple Function: Observations on Overdetermination. *Psychoanal. Quart.*, 5:45–62.

Weiner, H. (1969), Some Recent Neurophysiological Contributions to the Problem of Brain and Behavior. *Psychosom. Med.*, 31:457–478.

Wiener, N. (1948), *Cybernetics*. New York: Wiley.

PHILOSOPHY

Commentary on Freud and Philosophy

FAY HORTON SAWYIER, PH.D. (*Chicago*)

The attempt by philosophers to explain and evaluate Freud may seem both puzzling and inappropriate. Indeed, such was the underlying theme of an extended review of Ricoeur's book, *De L'interpretation: Essai sur Freud* (1965) by Michel Tort (1966) which appeared in *Les Temps modernes*. I shall not propose a *general* defense of philosophical exegesis, but offer instead four comments I feel are relevant to this issue:

(1) Any serious attempt to come to terms with a major new theory and to try to fit oneself and one's culture around it is appropriate.

(2) In the absence of *external* feedback, the language and conceptualization of a discipline grow increasingly arcane and splintered. This point applies to analysts too, for whom the temptations to a posture of omniscience and insularity are powerful.

(3) Ricoeur's own philosophy is worked out in his long dialogue with Freud, and this hermeneutic approach to some disciplines is worthy of consideration on its own merits.

(4) Ricoeur "worked through" some perturbations of his own feelings in the course of preparing and writing this book. Indeed, it has often crossed my mind that his "meeting" with Freud came to have the quality of a pseudotransference.

In this paper I shall try to isolate, to analyze, and then to bring back together several strands in the meeting of the philosopher and the doctor. My premise is that the explanation of Freud in the language of epistemology can be helpful and illuminating. To this end I shall draw attention to the use Ricoeur makes of Immanuel Kant and shall try to show in some detail how Kantian some of Freud's thought was. Ultimately, though, the encounter between philosopher and doctor was marred, because Ricoeur has been able to meet Freud only conditionally. The condition is that Freud not damage or destroy a world which Ricoeur thinks of as deeper, more meaningful. This is the world of mysticism, spirituality, art, and religion. Such a limitation on his encounter with Freud has distorted several of Ricoeur's interpretations. One result has been to dim his perception so that he failed to see that Freud was not a consistent pessimist. In the last part of this paper, I shall try to put Freud's seeming pessimism into perspective by calling attention to the logic of Freud's concept of therapy.

Each of the three aspects of Ricoeur's book which I shall discuss involves judgments about techniques or methods of discovery. Ricoeur is himself committed to the method he calls "hermeneutical" (interpretive). He not only claims that this method was also that of Freud, but he *uses* the hermeneutical method to "discover" Freud. The three foci of my attention can be characterized as follows:

(1) In a certain class of cases, learning or *dis-cover*-ing can be accomplished by decipherment instead of by observation and experimental manipulation. Clearly one must specify the class, however, and this leads into the discussion of grids and codes.

(2) Interpretation as a method of discovery reveals the social character of two texts: the pre-analytic or developmental text and that of the analysand. This second point will be considered under the section on solipsism.

(3) The manner in which a technique of interpretation or decipherment is used can be suspicious and reductive or illuminating and progressive. I shall discuss the attitudinal or emotional aspects of the interpretive technique in the final section of this paper, under the label of archaism.

Now I turn to point (1), the thesis that to interpret can be to learn. Consequently, I begin by speaking of epistemology.

Epistemology is the critical evaluation of the grounds for knowledge claims; we examine and analyze the structure of our beliefs. The examination of our convictions and beliefs and of how they interact "inside" our minds has occupied philosophers and psychologists at least since the seventeenth century. A significant part of the work of epistemologists is to bring out and to clarify some of the things which we do believe but do not know that we do, i.e., to elucidate some of the implicit presuppositions upon which much of our ordinary stock-in-trade of conviction rests. But Freud showed that there are many inner convictions and attitudes which *no* amount of logical or conceptual analysis will bring out. His clinical work convinced him that these uniquely hidden attitudes affect our lives, animate our beliefs, and are in some curious and pseudo-Aristotelian way, truly basic *personal* principles. These two aspects—the something hidden and its power—constitute respectively the topographical and the energetic aspects of the various psychic models Freud develops, and concerning which Paul Ricoeur has much to say. The language in which he says it is Kantian.

The formal surface structure of Ricoeur's book—its divisions into Problematic, Analytic, and Dialectic—is borrowed directly from that of Kant's three Critiques. To penetrate one layer below this surface analogy is to discover the fact that often the meanings of the very terms Ricoeur uses are Kantian. "Problematic" means the specification of difficulties (e.g., as Kant presents them in the introductory passages of his Critiques). "Analytic" means excavation of what underlies and is presupposed by these presenting problems. "Dialectic" means the investigation into whether or not within a given, apparently unified system there yet remain inherent contradictions, the resolution of which may require moving to another plane of interpretation. For Kant a "transcendental analysis" is one which first establishes the reality of some phenomenon and then inquires into the logical grounds of its possibility. An illustration could be: let us accept certain observances and forms of behavior as "religious," for example, the painting of the caves of Lascaux. According to what assumptions about the structure of human psychic and social life is behavior of this sort not predictable but just possible? Freud himself uses this type of transcendental analysis or retrogressive reasoning repeatedly, opening with the problematic of dreams, or of "totemism," or of slips of the tongue, etc., and reasoning backward to the grounds of their possibility, that is, toward the feelings and attitudes that underlie them. But what Kant did and what Ricoeur attempts are more general: Kant asks, in the first Critique, "on what grounds is 'real' physical science possible?" Ricoeur asks, "to what principles and assumptions must we move if Freudian science is real?"

In addition to the above Kantian terms and methods, there are several principles basic to Kant's thought which are important here. The three I find most useful are: (a) the "Copernican Revolution," with its associated hypothesis of the screen or grid; (b) the emphasis in the First and the Second Critique on the work of attaining and sustaining an ego (a self) and on gaining a fragile but nonillusory autonomy, and finally (c) the emphasis on how much of the universe-as-we-see-it is our construction, a projection of our specific needs and hopes. The "Copernican Revolution" consisted in examining the shared properties of "knowers" in order to gain insight into the interface between universal human properties and externally originated bombardment of our senses. According to Kant, the ultimate source and nature of the bombardment—the famous *ding an Sich*—must remain forever unknown to us *insofar as it is imperceptible by us*. Whatever can in no way affect you, can in no way become an object of your knowledge. "Out of sight, out of mind." Kant proposes instead something like a sensory and conceptual screen "through" which any bombardment must somehow pass in order to be registered and to count as my experience. He examines the universal contribution imposed on whatever potentially comes within our experiential field by the conditions of our sensibility and by the conditions of our "making sense." Important properties of human beings are inferred from the grid.

The second Kantian principle—the work of attaining and sustaining a self—has already been alluded to above. Fundamentally this is what was meant by "making sense" and "making ours." Kant has shown that in order to "think myself," I must sustain both my separate numerical identity, and the stability and continuity of the nonself or "other." Kant emphasized that so-called human freedom is essentially inner (e.g., to be one's own man) and that it is present only as a faint possibility, the actualizing of which is never achieved for good but must be worked toward and reaffirmed. This logically implies that there is a counterforce to autonomy. Kant, like Spinoza (to whom Ricoeur often compares Freud), has a conception of human bondage, of our enslavement to desire.

Finally, in the Third Critique, Kant tries to show that aesthetic delight is grounded in the perceptual or in the actual creation of symbolic forms congruent to our hopes, which embody our fantasies within sensory things. The making and the seeing of beauty structures our lives, as well as enhancing them.

Before drawing parallels to Freud from this condensed exposition of some Kantian principles, two comments should be made. First, Kant's retrogressive reasoning or "transcendental analysis" was generally logical rather than genetic. He sought for the logically prior and not the temporally antecedent. It was left to Piaget to attempt a genetic epistemology along Kantian lines. Second, the Kantian "object" is not primarily a libidinal object, and even the genetic studies of a Piaget do not deal mainly with prior states of feelings. I have argued elsewhere that emotional investment is implicit in both Kant and Piaget, but it is worth making clear that, in what follows, I do move rather casually between affective and cognitive realms, my only defense being that I believe the distinction is ultimately artificial and confused.

Ricoeur emphasizes three characteristics of Freud's thought which are analogous to the above three Kantian principles. These are its hermeneutic quality, its nonsolipsistic orientation, and its uncovering and underscoring of archaism. My primary job is to discuss these three categories, but in a preliminary way I offer working definitions of them in order to show the parallelism with Kant. First, by "hermeneutic" Ricoeur means, roughly, "deciphering" or "interpreting." He argues that the basic Freudian schematism is the connection of symbol to signified, and that the psychoanayltic questions are always about meanings and not about observable behavior and/or stimuli as such. Second, by "nonsolipsistic" Ricoeur means that the psychoanalytic model of human development is at least dyadic and involves other nonhallucinated persons.

Third, by "archaic" many things are meant, but the echo of archaeology is probably the most condensed image for the lot. Consider an archaeological site: its understanding is complete when the scientists have mentally reconstructed what was there before and what was responsible for leaving these and only these ruins. The ruins have no future; that is, they are not in the particular shape and disposition we find because there is anything from the future which is shaping them. Their properties are wholly functions of the past. In Ricoeur's sense, to consider persons archaeologically is similarly to reduce their personality to a vectorial product of their pasts. For example, my thought of going swimming, or my postponement of work on another paper, or my ruminations about what to cook for dinner are neither autonomous nor future-shaped (or shaping); they are "really" just so many cryptic messages about where I came from. I am, as it were, fated to say and to do the same things over and over and over: I somehow *am* these same things, these illusory projects.

If we now line up the three aspects of Kant's thought discussed above beside the three characteristics of Freud's thought which Ricoeur emphasizes, a parallelism emerges.

Kant	*Ricoeur on Freud*
Analysis of the grid and its structure and dynamics yields reliable knowledge about ourselves and our perspectives.	The basic model of psychoanalysis is hermeneutic; something inaccessible is understood in its transformations.
Our lives are ordered around an endless need to define and redefine our "self"; this presupposes a clear, stable sense of the nonself.	Psychoanalysis is fundamentally nonsolipsistic; the self is never isolated, for another is always presupposed.
Our delight in making and in noting beauty, our exaltation in the presence of the sublime, comes from a universal wish that the real world were more like our lost objects and our dearest fantasies. This regulates our hopes and interacts with ourselves and our actions.	Although explanation is primarily archaeological, the possibility that something can be made, done, learned, changed is inherent in the concept of therapy and in the works of artists.

The tool Ricoeur uses in his epistemological critique of Freud is hermeneutics, the decipherment of symbols. It is helpful here to note some prerequisites of an "interpretive" science. For example, Charles Taylor (1971) in a recent paper "Interpretation and the Sciences of Man," has said:

> Interpretation, in the sense relevant to hermeneutics, is an attempt to make clear, to make sense of an object of study. This object must, therefore, be a text, or a text-analogue, which in some way is confused, incomplete, cloudy, seemingly contradictory—in one way or another, unclear. The interpretation aims to bring to light an underlying coherence or sense [p. 3].

And Ricoeur (1965) in setting out part of his program says:

> By making dreams not only the first object of his investigation but a model (in what sense we will discuss below) of all the disguised, substitutive, and

fictive expressions of human wishing or desire, Freud invites us to look to dreams themselves for the various relations between desire and language. First, it is not the dream as dreamed that can be interpreted, but rather the text of the dream account; analysis attempts to substitute for this text another text that could be called the primitive speech of desire. Thus analysis moves from one meaning to another meaning; it is not desires as such that are placed at the center of the analysis, but rather their language. Later we will discuss how this semantics of desire relates to the dynamics expressed in the notions of discharge, repression, cathexis, etc. But it is important to stress from the start that this dynamics—or energetics, or even hydraulics—is articulated only in a semantics: the "vicissitudes of instincts," to use one of Freud's expressions, can be attained only in the vicissitudes of meaning. Therein lies the deep reason for all the analogies between dreams and wit, dreams and myth, dreams and works of art, dreams and religious "illusion," etc. All these "psychical productions" belong to the area of meaning and come under a unified question: How do desires achieve speech? How do desires make speech fail, and why do they themselves fail to speak? This new approach to the whole of human speech, to the meaning of human desire, is what entitles psychoanalysis to its place in the general debate on language [pp. 5–6].[1]

The entities deciphered at the first level are words and other behavior expressing feelings. Certain key elements in these presentations hint at a level of unintended meaning: the observable becomes symbolic of the general state-of-being of the person at the time. This symbolism is not a private language, and insofar as it is expressive it is *for* the other with whom the first person finds himself. Freud's phrase about every move being a gesture needs spelling out; gestures are for someone even when the message is covert and out-of-awareness. The careful, attentive psychoanalyst is in a way like a good cryptanalyst; he learns to read what his patient is really telling him. Why is this real message not conveyed directly? Why is it, as it were, encoded? Because the speaker is now, in effect, only a medium for transmission (cf. Blake's automatic writing). Why does the speaker not know what he is feeling, and why doesn't he express it intentionally? The classic answer here is that repression prevents certain notions and feelings from entering consciousness.

The cryptographic (or hermeneutic) analogy remains helpful; repression can be construed as secrecy. Something is there and is presented only on condition that it not be known (or read). The painstaking work of decoding means that one has discovered the chief scrambling techniques in the repertory of a particular encoding machine. For example, some of the Freudian counterparts to "scrambling" are displacement, substitution, and condensation. The explicit set of Freudian mechanisms (in essence devices for disguising) show up effectively in the light of Ricoeur's label "hermeneutics," which I have retranslated as "cryptography." It is important to notice that to the extent that a person is bound to the automatic use of one or another of these mechanisms, he is not free.

[1] Quotations from Ricoeur's *Freud and Philosophy*, trans. Denis Savage (New Haven, Conn.: Yale University Press, 1970), are reprinted with the permission of the publisher.

There are at least two more layers of meaning which may be reached by using the concept of hermeneutics or its adjunct, the Kantian screen. By doing what phenomenologists call "bracketing" consciousness, Freud has been able to offer us a cryptographic model for unconscious communication as well as a key to its decipherment. Significant knowledge has been gained about human feelings and characteristics from the general properties of the screen. What Freud has called "instincts and their vicissitudes" may be reread as "how we consciously experience what happens within us" (Ricoeur's "semantics of desire"). We have learned that to have access to conscious perception (or apperception) these inner events must undergo subtle and sometimes drastic transformations, which the analyst can often predict.

But what are the original forces working in and through us? *What* is re-presented? *What* re-pressed? These are kin to the ancient Milesian questions, and here—for instance at the start of Chapter IV of *Beyond the Pleasure Principle*—Freud was consciously speculative. The mythical and speculative cast can be explained by recalling Kant's caveats against inferences to the thing-in-itself. The parallel is clear. Kant denied that we could have scientific knowledge of those things which could not enter into our experience. Freud said that instinct—the language of the body—is never felt directly but only as varying forms of desire. Kant's system requires bombardment from without; Freud's requires an internal activity. In Chapter IV of *Beyond the Pleasure Principle* Freud all but draws us this neo-Kantian picture:

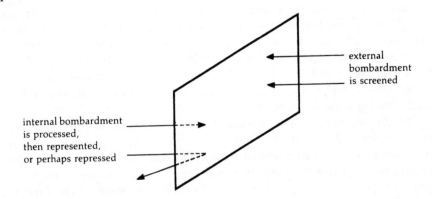

external bombardment is screened

internal bombardment is processed, then represented, or perhaps repressed

But what is "bombarding" us (from within)? Would an answer to this "what" involve just one basic force or more than one? An intelligent child can follow the progress of inquiry from describing the phenomena as screened to asking about the number and type of forces impinging on the screen. I suggest that the model of the grid leads naturally to the metapsychological inquiries concerning instincts-in-themselves. Ricoeur examines at length the transition in Freud from an undifferentiated libidinal model for speculation (with hydrodynamics as the machinery) through the first topography (Cs., Pcs., Ucs.), on to the second topographic model (ego, superego, id), and finally to the dichotomizing of instincts into Eros and Thanatos. He argues convincingly that at each step it was a characteristic combination of increased clinical experience with persistent philosophical restlessness that moved Freud on to the next model and to the next speculative meta-physics. (For a Kantian or a Freudian metapsychology is metaphysics.) For example, Freud found the phenomenon of compulsive repetition puzzling, a "problematic," however convenient as a tool for discovery in the transference this might be. And so, if we extrapolate from this, we too might ask why people go on and on doing the same old hurting thing and never bringing off anything new, any advance? And then we might postulate a second suprapsychological force, namely, Thanatos, the death instinct. I shall return to the question of repetition and its relation to Thanatos later, in considering archaism. I have spoken of it here mainly to illustrate again that the Kantian grid formula helps us to keep clear about why *Beyond the Pleasure Principle* is speculative. Since instincts speak only through the screen or grid, any inquiry as to their original and unscreened properties must, therefore, be at most only sensitive rational conjecture.

The second theme I want to play is Ricoeur's transcendental analysis of the nonsolipsistic basis for Freud's view of man. In order to bring this into focus it may help to recall the historical background of the term "solipsist." Traditional psychologists and seventeenth-century philosophers of mind have tried to conceptualize man in such a way that the entire adventure of his life is internal. Many plausible ways of considering Freud are congruent with this. The philosophical background of solipsism is primarily the creation of Descartes: man in the Cartesian image is a being alone in a closet with his wax—or with his idea of wax—engaged in a profoundly detailed and critical examination of his "ideas." The primary datum is consciousness, and the analysis of consciousness was invariably solitary. Descartes' problem, therefore, was to reconstitute an outside world from a seed which seemed to contain nothing but the ego and its ideas. In his famous enterprise of methodical, retrogressive doubt, Descartes reaches one lonely but indubitable proposition, *cogito ergo sum.* In the language of orthodox psychology this solipsistic world of ego and ideas becomes ego and drives; in the language of Freudian metapsychology the same isolated self becomes ego and internal imagery and objects. Among those who sometimes construe Freud as solipsistic are the existential, family, group, and social psychologists, all of whom suggest that Freud ignored the reality and the activity of others. By painstaking attention to the realities of the transference and to the transcendental significance of gestures, symbols, negativity, art, and religion, one can dispel this solipsistic interpretation.

Ricoeur first discusses the early Freudian metapsychology, which perhaps is solipsistically oriented. Freud may have wanted to systematize the psyche so that it, like an ideal gas, could be comprehended alone. One plausible explanation for this may have been the seduction of "hard" science and of predictive power. For, as Taylor (1971) says:

> The success of prediction in the natural sciences is bound up with the fact that all states of the system, past and future, can be described in the same range of concepts, as values, say, of the same variables. Hence all future states of the solar system can be characterized, as past ones are, in the language of Newtonian mechanics. This is far from being a sufficient condition of exact prediction, but it is a necessary one in this sense, that only if past and future are brought under the same conceptual net can one understand the states of the latter as some function of the states of the former, and hence predict. . . .
> This conceptual unity is vitiated in the sciences of man by the fact of conceptual innovation which in turn alters human reality [p. 49].

I am inclined to think that the isolated, all-but-solipsistic aspect of early Freudian models of the psyche is based on a powerful but misguided concept of human individuality. What was misguided was the concept of a desert islander as a real person. Such a concept implies that all human development is internally caused. Some ethologists are still tempted by this paradigm. Why Freud succumbed to such a notion may be ascribable partly to the physical science of his boyhood which was one-body-atomistic. Echoes of this cult of the solitary pervade political theorizing just prior to Freud too. For example the Lockean social contract presupposes autonomous human beings outside of society. But in addition Freud may have felt—and wanted to feel—both isolated and "inner-directed" as a person.

We, that is, Ricoeur and I, shall confront this charge of theoretic solipsism with a discussion of five features of Freud's work. The first and third points are mine, the second and fifth are Ricoeur's, and on the fourth we converge. First, then, coded or unconscious communication is nonetheless communication and therefore presupposes another person. Presumably, concealment implies communicability. Here we might reflect on the language of schizophrenics. Second, Ricoeur claims that human desire is always of or for another desire. For example:

> . . . it seems that desire, as a mode of being in close contact with beings, is human desire only if the intending is not merely a desire of the other but a desire of other desires, that is, a demand [p. 387].

Consequently, human emotions presuppose other persons and are nonsolipsistic. Third, there is something queer and paradoxical in trying to conceptualize the Oedipal crisis and the growth of the superego as autonomous developmental phenomena which, like puberty, for example, just happen. Fourth, the core of psychoanalytic therapy—the transference and its working-through—is obviously at least dyadic. Not only is this interaction a duality, but it is the surrogate for a set of other, earlier, powerful, two-person situations and representations. Lastly, Ricoeur draws attention to the "otherness" of man's religious constructs. The point here is not to deny the significance of the two forces spelled out by Freud and jointly "meaning" God, but to draw our attention to the fact that these two strands in God-making are reified into a super Being. The relevance of this to the present point concerning solipsism is that men individualize an entity as other than themselves when they make their gods. If "I" were in any full sense all I needed, then, as Ricoeur suggests but does not adequately develop, my projective world and god would not themselves have proper names and properties and personalities distinct from my own. Once again, at this far-out limit of "interaction," Ricoeur is calling attention to the requirement of other persons intrinsic to Freud's own systematization.

Ricoeur has shown that the basic unit in Freud's metapsychology is the dyadic unit and not the monad. This means, of course, that persons interact with and are affected by other persons. The ultimacy of the dyad implies that psychoanalysis is not committed to the old, atomistic concept of the individual. "No man is an island . . . ," even though many theorists have always found it simpler to conceptualize him in such isolation.

I have commented earlier on the meaning of the term "archaic" as Ricoeur uses it. It is around this concept that his serious criticism of Sigmund Freud revolves. Ricoeur uses the technique of dialectical self-confrontation—he confronts Freud with Freud, so to speak—discovering inconsistencies and open-endings where Freud had apparently failed to heed them. This dialectical enterprise is described by Ricoeur in a passage which illustrates, as well, his own personal investment in the encounter with Freud to which I referred at the beginning of this paper.

I said previously that the only way I can arrive at self-understanding in my reading of Freud is to form the notion of an archeology of the subject. I say now that the only way to understand the notion of archeology is in its dialectical relationship to a teleology. And so I search in Freud's work—in analysis as analysis—for the reference to its dialectical contrary. I hope to show that such a reference actually does exist there and that analysis is inherently dialectical. Thus, I do not pretend to complete Freud, but to understand him through understanding myself. I venture to think that I advance in this understanding of Freud and myself by revealing the dialectical aspects of both reflection and Freudianism.
What I wish to demonstrate, then, is that if Freudianism is an explicit and thematized archeology, it relates of itself, by the dialectical nature of its concepts, to an implicit and unthematized teleology [pp. 460–461].

Working with this, Ricoeur draws toward a religious and melioristic conclusion. I dissociate myself from his conclusion, although I concede that he has indeed drawn attention to some unexamined paradoxes in Freud's thought. What I propose to do in this final section is briefly to sketch the form of Ricoeur's criticism and then to confront it with a different argument of my own against the authority of despair. Ricoeur reaches for a mystical Eros as both a name for God and an undercurrent in Freud's thinking (do Frenchmen always believe that Germans and Austrians are at heart Wagnerians?). I suggest that here he is overinterpreting Freud's rather poignant references to the speech of Aristophanes in Plato's *Sym*-

posium, and stretching the *Leonardo* study. Concerning art in general and the *Leonardo* study in particular, Ricoeur has this to say:

> Dreams look backward, toward infancy, the past; the work of art goes ahead of the artist; it is a prospective symbol of his personal synthesis and of man's future, rather than a regressive symbol of his unresolved conflicts [p. 175].

But Ricoeur's objective is a critique of Freud on a religio-cosmic scale. For my more modest purpose no such stretching is needed.

Ricoeur says that Freud has called attention to the repetitiveness of our lives and thought, our rootedness in infancy, and our submission to a force leading us into regression and death and dissolution. He applauds (rather briefly) Freud's disclosure of the infantile and irrational content of religious myths and rituals, but he associates Freud with Nietzsche and with Marx, as members of the "school of suspicion." He claims that Freud has made possible a religion "purified" of idols, but that he failed to perceive this himself. Ricoeur repeatedly cites the creative and constructive aspect of human language, art, and religion, and suggests rather than argues that there is something in the essence of these "intentional" or symbolic forms of behavior that implies a beyond which is not just a reiterated behind.

Ricoeur comments on the ethical standards one can detect in Freud: "This prudence principle, which I would like to regard as the culmination of the reality principle, is in sum the ethics of psychoanalysis" (p. 279). Ricoeur proposes that love and art and religion and culture contain factors not reducible to elements from the past and that they are all higher values than prudence. He hints that Freud's world-view was flawed or soured, and that this led him ultimately on harsh, supposedly realistic grounds (Ananke) to collapse passion (Eros) into a merging which is regressive loss of self (Thanatos). The confluence of rationalism with Ananke is repeated in Ricoeur's study of the history of the relations in Freud's systems between consciousness (ego) and reality.

A closer look reveals, however, that Ricoeur has given us an image of Freud that recalls the "Descartes" reconstructed by Lewin (1958). This image is of an ideal human being who does nothing but notice, register, absorb, and rationalize reality. What is really real here is presumably death, destruction, running downhill, and the universal dominance of Second Law. But note that in this picture the "head" of the ideal-observer is not only incorporeal but is somehow detached from that supposed reality. How else could we speak of honest and true observation? How might universal "regression" be detected except by a substance that was separated and non-regressing? We have here in fact, the mind/body split, and Ricoeur has restored Cartesian dualism to us in the highly improbable person of Sigmund Freud.

Ricoeur's analysis of archaism is one of the few areas in which the fact of his not having been analyzed seems to me to impede his understanding of Freud. There is no doubt whatever that Freud's later writings had a pessimistic cast. I propose alternatives, however, to Ricoeur's rationalistic explanation of Freud's pessimism and archaism, and suggest that this attitude was emotionally understandable but theoretically not fully grounded.

First of all, presumably Freud himself was not immune to ordinary human feelings. If one is aging and ill, and one's disciples are falling away, and one's European heritage is being torn apart and exhibiting its ugliness and violence, what could be more natural than to become increasingly pessimistic? Here we may recall the dark views held by Hobbes and the aged Plato. As Freud himself had taught, what is more commonplace than to project one's pessimism and depression onto the world, "finding" scientific and psychoanalytic proof of it? (David Hume commented long ago that "the mind always tends to spread itself upon nature . . .")

To confront this reified despair we may with profit examine carefully some of the procedures and implications of psychoanalytic therapy itself. First of all, we do not find in Freud's clinical or theoretic writing any suggestion that therapy is a fraud. Consequently, since it is proposed as genuine, it is incompatible with a thesis of universal regression. Secondly, except for a very brief time at the start of his career, Freud never conceptualized therapy as only a means to becoming more intelligent, a better self-historian. Rather, the thesis is that one changes, one is helped. Thirdly, even were therapy simply learning, two positive propositions would follow: learning is never a purely intellectual process although it is always a positive one, and learning about oneself presupposes a prior preparatory change and implies facilitation of future progress.

Admittedly, Freud called attention to the infantilisms and the regressive qualities in our lives, but surely he does not claim that such relations with others are all we are ever capable of. It is characteristic of a certain style of response to demonstrations of human inadequacy to accuse the "demonstrator" of pessimism, evil thoughts, etc. Wounded self-esteem fights back, and the professional world is surely no less narcissistic than any other. The philosophical and scientific worlds have been made increasingly aware during the past fifty years of how vulnerable research is to distortion and of the powerful temptation to see only supporting cases and to overlook—indeed, according to Kuhn (1970) and Feyerabend (1965) to be blinded to—countercases. One style of response to this uncovering of the multiple flaws in our powers of honest thought and observation is to interpret this unmasking as a denial of any possibility of learning or of human development. This is the style of Ricoeur's argument: e.g., when Freud shows us how dismal and regressive are the ways in which we invent our gods and deal with each other, then what he is "really" doing is denying the possibility of better myth and better human relations.

On the contrary, one fundamentally optimistic note inescapable in Freud is exactly oriented around the phenomenon of therapy and is uniquely associated with the transference. Consider the proposition that "something therapeutic occurs through the transference." Match it with the palpable fact that during the transference most of the emotional and cognitive discoveries reinforce the pessimistic thesis of endless, mindless repetitiveness. For what is the transference? A complex re-enactment, but what is the looked-for result of this re-enactment and its self-disclosure? Change. Even the idea that responding to the therapist in archaic ways is "Freudian" carries within it the suggestion that there are other ways and that the patient (and therefore in principle, the human being) can move toward them. Accordingly, I infer that to have drawn attention to so many of the flawed and damaging and repetitive qualities in human relationships presupposes a sense of alternative and better ones. I assume also that the theory of the transference implies not only that better human relations and selfhood are logically possible but that they are attainable. After all, that is what the very concept of therapy ultimately implies.

In this paper I have elaborated three aspects of the epistemological approach to interpretation which seem to me helpful in examining Ricoeur's *Freud and Philosophy*. These are:

(1) Interpretation as a method of learning presupposes a particular type of material, one which is in some way "scrambled" through transformations. The concept of a transformer was discussed in the symbol of a grid.

(2) Interpretation as a method of learning is applied to something like a coded message, but codes are both made and broken with respect to other people. The Freudian concept of development was shown to be non-solipsistic.

(3) Like any other human activity, code-breaking is emotionally weighted. The feelings with which decipherment is carried on may reveal fundamental attitudes toward human life, and the therapeutic attitude implies a kernel of hope.

BIBLIOGRAPHY

Feyerabend, P. (1965), Problems of Empiricism. In: *Beyond the Edge of Certainty*, ed. R. G. Colodny. Englewood Cliffs, N.J.: Prentice-Hall.

Kuhn, T. S. (1970), *The Structure of Scientific Revolution*. 2d enl. ed. Chicago: University of Chicago Press.

Lewin, B. D. (1958), *Dreams and the Uses of Regression*. New York: International Universities Press.

Ricoeur, P. (1965), *Freud and Philosophy*, trans. D. Savage. New Haven and London: Yale University Press, 1970.

Taylor, C. (1971), Interpretation and the Sciences of Man. In: *The Review of Metaphysics*, 25:3–51 (Sept.).

Tort, M. (1966), La Machine herméneutique. In: *Les Temps modernes*, 27:1461–93 (Feb.); 28:1629–52 (March).

IV

CLINICAL STUDIES

The Role of Illusion in the Analytic Space and Process

M. MASUD R. KHAN (*London*)

. . . distance, after all, was invented by man and has no meaning outside the context of human space; it separated Hero from Leander and Marathon from Athens, but does not separate one pebble from another.

J.-P. SARTRE

Clinically, the unique achievement of Freud is that he invented and established a therapeutic space and distance for the patient and the analyst. In this space and distance the relating becomes feasible only through the capacity in each to sustain illusion and to work with it. The vehicle of this working with illusion is symbolic discourse, commonly referred to as free association by the patient and interpretation by the analyst. The relational process through which the illusion operates is the transference.

I am fully aware the "illusion" is a treacherous concept to introduce in this context because, both in the English and French languages, it has an almost exclusively prejudicial usage in terms of active or passive deception or distortion of sensory or ideational data. Only *Webster's Third New International Dictionary* gives a definition that comes somewhat close to the meaning I wish to utilize for the word "illusion." It defines one of its connotations as:

Perception of something objectively existing in such a way as to cause or permit misinterpretation of its actual nature either because of the ambiguous qualities of the thing perceived or because of the personal characteristics of the one perceiving, or because of both factors.

In spite of the prejudicial connotations of the word "illusion," it is an ironic fact that few persons will deny that human life would be impossible without the ubiquitous role of illusion in it (cf. André Maurois, 1968).

It is my contention here that Freud created a space, time, and process which potentialize that area of *illusion* where symbolic discourse can actualize. Thus Freud put maximum responsibility on language for the cure of emotional and personality disorders (Khan, 1970).

Ernst Cassirer (1946) has astutely defined the evolution of the function of the Word in human experience:

It was a long evolutionary course which the human mind has to traverse, to pass from the belief in a physico-magical power. Indeed, it is the Word, it is language, that really reveals to man that world which is closer to him than any world of natural objects and touches his weal and woe more directly than physical nature. For it is language that makes his existence in a *community* possible; and only on society, in relation to a "Thee," can his subjectivity assert itself as a "Me."

For this usage of the *Word* Freud provided a new human laboratory and a new function: namely, that of cure. This use of the Word is dependent on the capacity of the analytic situation and process to sustain illusion. When the latter breaks down, then the usage of the Word has to yield to other forms and styles of relating and experiencing.

The Area of Illusion: Taboo and Transgression in the Analytic Situation

Freud's correspondence with Fliess (1954) gives us a dramatic account of how Freud had conducted his self-analysis through analyzing his dreams. And it was this self-analysis that had helped him to transcend the hypnotic and cathartic methods of psychotherapy and invent his analytic method. In my paper, "Dream Psychology and the Evolution of the Psycho-Analytic Situation" (1962), I have discussed some aspects of this whole adventure in Freud's inner and professional life.

We know that Freud's self-analysis had revealed to him the nature of infantile sexuality and its two basic wish-systems: incest and parricide (cf. Kris, 1954). Some fifteen years later, Freud (1913) had tried to conjecture a historical event in the evolution of the species where parricide had actually taken place in the primal horde. This flight of imagination on Freud's part evoked easy ridicule among anthropologists and others. It was not till some three decades later that Claude Lévi-Strauss (1949) was able to evaluate the true worth of the hypotheses offered in *Totem and Taboo:*

> The failure of *Totem and Taboo*, far from being inherent in the author's proposed design, results rather from his hesitation to avail himself of the ultimate consequences implied in his premises . . . Freud successfully accounts, not for the beginning of civilization but for its present state; and setting out to explain the origin of a prohibition, he succeeds in explaining, certainly not why incest is consciously condemned, but how it happens to be unconsciously desired . . . However, like all myths, the one presented in *Totem and Taboo* with such great dramatic force admits of two interpretations. The desire for the mother or the sister, the murder of the father and the sons' repentance, undoubtedly do not correspond to any fact or group of facts occupying a given place in history. But perhaps they symbolically express an ancient and lasting dream. The magic of this dream, its power to mould men's thoughts

unbeknown to them, arises precisely from the fact that the acts it evokes have never been committed, because culture has opposed them at all times and in all places. Symbolic gratifications in which the incest urge finds its expression, according to Freud, do not therefore commemorate an actual event. They are something else, and more, the permanent expression of a desire for disorder, or rather counter-order. Festivals turn social life topsy-turvy, not because it was once like this but because it has never been, and can never be, any different. Past characteristics have explanatory value only in so far as they coincide with present and future characteristics.

It was this statement of Lévi-Strauss's that compelled me to reexamine the *constitution* of the analytic space, process, and relationship. I was surprised to discover how ingeniously Freud had ritualistically established taboos that made incest or parricide in this very exclusive human community of two persons impossible. The basic taboos are: of motility (lying down on the couch), and of sight and touch (the ego functions that normally intensify excitement most readily). To these taboos Freud had adjoined a revolutionary transgression: he invited and facilitated the patient to express his incestuous and parricidal wishes through the *Word*. Thus the taboos create that area of illusion where language explores and expresses the wish-systems. Without this illusion language would yield merely humiliation and remorse. Ricoeur (1965) is right when he states: ". . . it is not desires as such that are placed at the center of the analysis, but rather their language." But this language would be arid without that increment of affect which the area of illusion provides through the transference. Freud (1914) had underlined this affective valency of language in the analytic process when he postulated: ". . . the patient does not *remember* anything of what he has forgotten and repressed, but he *acts* it out. He reproduces it not as a memory but as an action; he *repeats* it." The *action* Freud is referring to here is essentially *action* into language and/or affective expressions in the session and not *action* that involves muscular and behavioral expression. With muscular action the area of illusion is transgressed and a new psychic reality actualizes.

Freud was fully aware that the analytic situation and process made very heavy demands on both the parties concerned, and it took certain maturity of growth and stability of personality organization in both parties for them to be able to work in this area of illusion through symbolic discourse. Freud had settled the issue somewhat arbitrarily by defining the suitability of cases in terms of those who could establish and sustain transference. The others he had defined as patients with narcissistic disorders that were not suitable for the analytic technique (cf. Freud, 1937). In the tradition of the so-called classical analysis this bias of appraisal holds to this day. When the behavior of patients transgresses the symbolic discourse and seeks concrete expression and/or need-fulfillment, it is defined as "acting out," and it disrupts the therapeutic alliance (cf. Anna Freud, 1969).

On the Incapacity to Sustain Illusion in the Clinical Situation: Clinical Examples

I shall give two examples from my clinical encounter with two cases where the area of illusion was extremely precariously held. In the first example it broke down completely and the treatment ended abruptly, and in the second I was able to hold it and the patient has done very well. My emphasis will be on the phenomenological description of behavior in the clinical situation. I shall not attempt to define the aetiology or the deeper psycho-dynamics of the processes involved.

The first case, Miss X, was a young girl of thirty, highly educated and extremely intelligent. She had come from a foreign country to have a con-sultation with Dr. Winnicott, who unfortunately had died by the time she had reached England. However, he had previously indicated to her that if she was not able to see him, she should get in touch with me. The patient who arrived was a very volatile and intense person. She had had analysis abroad for some six years, with three analysts. To start with, she gave a highly impassioned, vehement, and articulate account of a most traumatic childhood with brutal, possessive parents. It was quite obvious that she had specialized in presenting herself to psychiatrists. She had evi-dently lived through a sustained autistic, near-psychotic state in child-hood, had recovered from it, and had managed her university degrees very well.

What impressed me about the very first session was how she took posses-sion of the clinical situation and hurtled herself upon it. She made absolutely no allowance for the fact that I may be a different sort of person from her previous analysts. In the second session she told me that she had had three analysts before, and then gave a most viciously "objective" appraisal of each one of them, lamenting how they had failed her. She cried violently throughout her narrative, and at one point she remarked: "I cry like people drink." She told me how with her first analyst things had gone wrong because eventually her psychic pain had been so acute and unassuageable in the sessions that he had felt compelled to hold her hand. This very nearly degenerated into physical intimacy between them. But what had finally broken down the treatment there was that she took an overdose of sleeping pills and was very critically near to death, but was saved. After this, the analyst referred her to a colleague. With her second analyst she had a belligerent, negativistic confrontation throughout. The analysis never got going, and she was referred to a third analyst. He was a very sympa-thetic person and got equally emotionally enmeshed with her. From her account, it was obvious that she had a very compelling knack of making others witness her frenzied state, which she expressed with a phenomenal verbal articulateness and gestural mimetic flair. This second analysis ended after two years, with the analyst advising her to go abroad and seek analysis with someone who was more experienced. She had come to London for a visit a year earlier and consulted Dr. Winnicott for two days. When she had returned this time, as I said earlier, he had died.

By the end of the first week it was quite clear that she had eliminated me from the analytic space. I was just a passive witness whom she victimized with her excruciating pain and inexhaustible demands. Her basic need, she said, was that she wanted to live and love. She also had an extraordinary capacity to write poetry and prose. Some of her poems and stories are of a distinctly high quality and state her predicament with a pungent and incisive clarity. The extraordinary thing was that this young woman knew herself so well but could not relate to her knowledge or make any use of it. One day, in the second week of her analysis, she stated that she had already got herself into acute distress and was ringing doctors at night to come to her aid, feeling that it was quite on the cards that she would have a psychotic breakdown. She expressed this fear overtly. My interpretation to her, however, was that her real predicament is that she cannot have a breakdown. Hence she has become a perverted specialist in all types of maneuvers of psychopathy and psychopathology. She hated her parents with a violent deliberateness, complaining that they had become internalized in her as devils, and she commented: "The devils are indestructible: they cannot be exorcised; they can only change houses." I had pointed out to her in this context that she struck me not as an ill person but as a person possessed by an illness of which she herself is now largely the maker. To which she had replied: "If I could believe there can be a cure better than mine, I could surrender. But I have to compete against the offered cure with my own. For one hour of your cure there are twenty-three hours of my self-cure." I was often really astonished by the perspicacity and "insightfulness" of this person into herself. She demanded from analysis what she called "a transfusion of life," which no one had yet succeeded in giving to her.

At this point she recounted a dream which she had had a long time ago, but which to her somewhere contains the essence of her predicament. Roughly the dream is as follows:

She is sitting in a cathedral, looking up at the ceiling, and there is a most beautiful stained-glass pattern of all colors through which the light is gently seeping in. She is very happy. Then suddenly the whole roof begins to crumble and the pattern begins to disintegrate. She wakes up in terror.

Listening to her dream, I had an uncanny sensation that she was not telling me her dream but giving me a warning of what she was going to do to the illusional space of the analytic situation. To me, what was important about this dream was the fact that in her own fantasy when everything is beautiful and beatific she has a compulsion to disrupt and destroy the illusion and the structure. I indicated as much to her and she agreed with me. From this I personally felt quite certain that the treatment of this girl was going to break down, and it did.

A week later, while she was going on in this frenzied way, she came and told me about something which had been happening for two weeks that she had withheld. Her third analyst was in town on vacation, and she had managed to seduce him sexually, feeling after that, that she was completely bereft and that she was going to disintegrate mentally. At this point, it became obvious that this person could not be handled and managed in the clinical situation, and I stopped the treatment. She was perpetually either *acting into* language, which is then not symbolic discourse, or *acting upon* life, which is the total negation of any positive experience of relating that she may have in analysis.

Her language did not assimilate her experience, intrapsychic or interpersonal, any more than her body personalized her instincts or her affects. I realized that I had made a grave mistake in letting her take hold of the clinical space and process on her terms and run amok with it. I should have dosed the clinical process from the very beginning through infrequent consultations in the measure that she could tolerate them. I communicated this to her and informed her that I did not think I would now be able to correct my error and advised her to go to another analyst. After some vociferous protestations, she did go to another colleague.

It is not possible to put down in *écriture* the quality of the experience that I was confronted with through this patient. What I do want to highlight from my experience with her are three factors:

1. Her total negation of my presence.
2. Her equally militant negation of her own self as a person.
3. Her invention, out of her psyche, of an almost fetishistic, sick object which she continuously elaborated mentally, and with which she tantalized, challenged, and provoked one, driving herself to self-destruction rather than cure.

These factors did not let the space of illusion in the analytic situation crystallize. On the contrary, one found oneself pitted against her omnipotence, to which the only alternatives were capitulation or annihilation, and in this patient there was a conscious—almost willful—demand that she be annihilated in order to find her own peace and be reborn. These are literally her own words which I have put together into a precise statement. I think that many suicides do actualize from a person's militant need to destroy himself in order to start from scratch. With these persons, the area of illusion never operates, because they live in a delusional reality which they want to shed. Searles's (1965) researches give us some of the most acute examples of such predicaments.

The next case I want to present is one in which the analytic process and situation had completely broken down with the previous analyst, who referred the patient to me for her unmanageable violence and uncontainable distress in the analytic situation. I have reported aspects of the treatment in two other papers (1969 and 1971). What I want to describe here is a way of establishing a rapport with this patient that gradually had enabled us to arrive at that minimum space of illusion where symbolic discourse can begin to be an idiom of relating to the other as well as knowing the self. From my first consultation with the patient and her analyst together, I had been absolutely convinced that this young girl of twenty-four could not use language at all to relate to one, or operate in the clinical situation. It was precisely the demand of her analyst that she should *verbalize* her feelings and her unconscious fantasies, as well as her overt militant needs, that had led the patient into traumatizing her analyst, pulling her hair, and breaking up the furniture in her consultation room at various critical phases of the treatment.

When she came for the first session with me, she refused to lie down, saying that she had never lain down; she also refused to talk. I accepted that, explicitly pointing out to her that I could really sympathize with her total incapacity to use language as an idiom of either expressing herself or relating to me. She stood leaning heavily against the wall with her hands behind her back. She stared vacantly and ferociously at the room and all the objects in it. I remained seated in my chair with the distance between us. All she could shout at me from time to time was: "Say something. You know it all." Of course, I knew nothing. I had deliberately refused to take the history of her life during the first consultation, because I knew that such information only compels one to be clever with one's patients, when what they really demand of one is a rapport born of ignorance.

I could sense that she was reaching a point where she would boil over and have to act at the space or transgress its neutrality by doing something violent. I let her move around and touch the books, but not my things. Minimum motility and touch, and maximum sight were allowed to her. Only touching personalized the space and time for her and made it bearable to be in the analytic situation. This impasse went on for months. In fact, there is a whole impression of her body with the clean smudge of her hands on the wall where she used to stand. It was my capacity to hold her in the analytic space in this way that gradually led to her toleration of me as a separate person, distant but related. I must add that if I found her boiling over, or myself getting exhausted, I would terminate the session after only ten minutes. She could accept that, grudgingly, but she had to be *facilitated* to leave, because separating at the end of the session was acutely traumatic to her.

It would be wrong to say that the whole encounter was always mute. She spoke a little bit here and there, and I would verbalize the fluctuation of her mood or feelings as I could sense them in her body presence. From this we gradually built up a trust in each other, because she could now really believe that not only could I tolerate her incapacity to use language, but also I could work with her at least minimally in spite of it. From these little details an illusional space began to establish itself between us, and a distance was created which related us, and in this illusional space and distance she could begin to explore language as playing.

It is not my intention to go into the psychodynamics or the etiology of the illness of this person. After about a year she was able to use the couch, though even then for a long time she was able to say nothing, and when she started to use the couch we had to tolerate the fact that she might leave the session after only five minutes.

Now, some three years later, language is beginning to be both a creative and an effective way of sustaining the illusion and using the distance between us for her to talk about herself to me. In life, this girl, who had been totally incapacitated for ten years, is doing very well as a university student, and is married.

Before I stop the clinical narrative, I do want to stress something which this patient herself now evaluates as the most important thing I contributed toward making analysis a feasible experience for her. She felt that her incapacity and rage were both valid to me as existential facts, and that I had not tried to intrude upon these two areas of her experience with interpretations. It is important to remember about this case that the overt picture of her childhood gave no indications that she was going to be so ill at puberty. She was a happy, social, and gay child, who had done fairly well at school, particularly in sports. It was at puberty and the onset of menstruation that she had broken down completely into a bizarre illness, marked by extreme phobic attitudes, anorexia, and violent outbursts of panic and rage. While she could not talk in the clinical situation, in life she was a voracious listener. Her listening was a way of shedding herself instead of knowing herself, and what made the analytic process excruciatingly humiliating for her was that it reversed the process of shedding herself through the other's language into knowing herself through the other's interpretations. She had used the other's language almost concretely as an "organ" to cling to the other with and destroy the distance between her and the other. All her previous analyst's attempts to interpret to her were experienced by her as malicious and deliberate attempts to distance and reject her. By letting her be in the clinical space, by establishing a physical distance between her and me, and facilitating her to tolerate it experientially, I was gradually able to create that *espace humaine* of Sartre's idiom, in which distance potentiates illusion and language both captures its realities as well as relates because of the distance.

"The Period of Hesitation": Playing and Transitional Phenomena

The clinical material that I have presented can be most creatively discussed through the concept of illusion which was introduced to psychoanalysis by Winnicott, and his definitive statement of it is in his paper, "Transitional

Objects and Transitional Phenomena" (1951). But in the evolution of Winnicott's clinical and conceptual work there is a pre-history to it which I wish to spell out here because of its crucial importance for my use of this concept. In his paper, "The Observation of Infants in a Set Situation" (1941), Winnicott reported on the specific rhythm in a baby's way of handling a spatula that he had observed in the clinical situation of his interview with the infant and the mother together. Winnicott postulated three stages of an infant's relating to and use of the spatula, which he considered normal for an infant between the ages of five months and thirteen months. This is such an important description that I would like to give it in Winnicott's own words:

Stage 1. The baby puts his hand to the spatula, but at this moment discovers unexpectedly that the situation must be given thought. He is in a fix. Either with his hand resting on the spatula and his body quite still he looks at me and his mother with big eyes, and watches and waits, or, in certain cases, he withdraws interest completely and buries his face in the front of his mother's blouse. It is usually possible to manage the situation so that active reassurance is not given, and it is very interesting to watch the gradual and spontaneous return of the child's interest in the spatula.

Stage 2. All the time, in "the period of hesitation" (as I call it), the baby holds his body still (but not rigid). Gradually he becomes brave enough to let his feelings develop, and then the picture changes quite quickly. The moment at which this first phase changes into the second is evident, for the child's acceptance of the reality of desire for the spatula is heralded by a change in the inside of the mouth, which becomes flabby, while the tongue looks thick and soft, and saliva flows copiously. Before long he puts the spatula into his mouth and is chewing it with his gums, or seems to be copying father smoking a pipe. The change in the baby's behaviour is a striking feature. Instead of expectancy and stillness there now develops self-confidence, and there is free bodily movement, the latter related to manipulation of the spatula.

I have frequently made the experiment of trying to get the spatula to the infant's mouth during the stage of hesitation. Whether the hesitation corresponds to my normal or differs from it in degree or quality, I find that it is impossible during this stage to get the spatula to the child's mouth apart from the exercise of brutal strength. In certain cases where the inhibition is acute any effort on my part that results in the spatula being moved towards the child produces screaming, mental distress, or actual colic. The baby now seems to feel that the spatula is in his possession, perhaps in his power, certainly available for the purposes of self-expression. He bangs with it on the table or on a metal bowl which is nearby on the table, making as much noise as he can; or else he holds it to my mouth and to his mother's mouth, very pleased if we *pretend* to be fed by it. He definitely wishes us to *play* at being fed, and is upset if we should be so stupid as to take the thing into our mouths and spoil the game as a game. At this point, I might mention that I have never seen any evidence of a baby being disappointed that the spatula is, in fact, neither food nor a container of food.

Stage 3. There is a third stage. In the third stage the baby first of all drops the spatula as if by mistake. If it is restored he is pleased, plays with it again, and drops it once more, but this time less by mistake. On its being restored again, he drops it on purpose, and thoroughly enjoys aggressively getting rid of it, and is especially pleased when it makes a ringing sound on contact with the floor. The end of this third phase comes when the baby either wishes to get down on the floor with the spatula, where he starts mouthing it and playing with it again, or else when he is bored with it and reaches out to any other objects that lie at hand.

What I want to stress in this description of the child's play with the spatula is what Winnicott calls "the period of hesitation," because in my clinical experience this observation and concept have very important implications for understanding certain types of resistances that we encounter in cases like the two which I have reported. The "period of hesitation" is in fact the matrix for the emergence of the area of illusion. The concept of resistance in classical psychoanalysis takes for granted the capacity to operate in the area of illusion, and implies only a conflictual interference in the person's ability to use it. Whereas the concept of "the period of hesitation" connotes the emergence of a capacity which is as yet far from established as an ego function.

To return to Winnicott's argument. In his paper, "Primitive Emotional Development" (1945), Winnicott gave his first schema of early psychic development in the infant and the importance of the maternal holding environment for the fruition of ego functions and processes in the psyche of the infant. Three processes, he postulated, start very early: integration, personalization, and realization. He also argued that: " . . . at the theoretical start the personality is unintegrated, and that in regressive disintegration there is a primary state to which regression leads. We postulate a primary unintegration." He related this state of unintegration to the whole issue of dissociation. Later I shall discuss my given case material in these terms. Winnicott's view of the earliest interaction between infant and mother in the feeding situation is that to the infant's hunger to suck at the breast the mother provides the complementary wish "to be attached by a hungry baby." And he infers that "these two phenomena do not come into relation with each other till the mother and child *live an experience together*." Winnicott conceptualizes further:

> I think of the process as if two lives came from opposite directions, liable to come near each other. If they overlap there is a moment of *illusion*—a bit of experience which the infant can take as *either* his hallucination *or* a thing belonging to external reality.

We all know, or at least we pretend to, Winnicott's concept of the transitional object. I shall state only the essentials of his complex hypothesis, namely:

> The mother, at the beginning, by an almost 100 per cent adaptation affords the infant the opportunity for the *illusion* that her breast is part of the infant. It is, as it were, under magical controls. . . . *The intermediate area to which I am referring is the area that is allowed to the infant between primary creativity and objective perception based on reality-testing.* The transitional phenomena represent the early stages of the use of illusion, without which there is no

meaning for the human being in the idea of a relationship with an object that is perceived by others as external to that being . . . [italics mine].

The infant cannot be said to know at first what is to be created. At this point in time the mother presents herself. In the ordinary way she gives her breast and her potential feeding urge. The mother's adaptation to the infant's needs, when good enough, gives the infant the *illusion* that there is an external reality that corresponds to the infant's own capacity to create. In other words, there is an overlap between what the mother supplies and what the child might conceive of. . . . *Of the transitional object it can be said that it is a matter of agreement between us and the baby that we will never ask the question "Did you conceive of this or was it presented to you from without?" The important point is that no decision on this point is expected. The question is not to be formulated.*

To these basic hypotheses Winnicott was to add only one more element that is important for us to note here: namely, his differentiation between magical control and omnipotence and *the experience of omnipotence.* In his paper "Communicating and Not Communicating Leading to a Study of Certain Opposites" (1963), he postulated:

At this early stage the facilitating environment is giving the infant the *experience of omnipotence;* by this I mean more than magical control, I mean the term to include the creative aspect of experience. Adaptation to the reality principle arisen naturally out of the experience of omnipotence, within the area, that is, of a relationship to subjective objects.

I shall now explore the implications of Winnicott's hypotheses for a reevaluation of the therapeutic space created and established by Freud. Though there has been a lot of research published on the extension of the classical analytic technique to meet the regressive needs and demands of borderline patients, an actual reevaluation of the analytic therapeutic space has been undertaken only by Winnicott (1954 and 1971), Balint (1968), Milner (1952 and 1969), Sechehaye (1951), Stone (1961), and Viderman (1970). In my discussion now my emphasis will be on the provision of the analytic space as illusion to the patient when the patient is incapacitated to meet it as such from within his own psychic means.

Toucher Pour Voir

In Winnicott's hypothesis of the provision of illusion by the mother for the infant, and the gradual actualization through developmental processes of the infant's ability to play with this illusion and create it for himself—time, sight, touch, smell, and movement play essential roles. Winnicott is not the only analyst who has emphasized the importance of sight and touch in the crystallization of the early ego functions. Hoffer, in his paper, "Mouth, Hand and Ego-Integration" (1949), wrote significantly about the role of those organs in the integration of early ego functions. From another angle, Spitz (1965) discussed the shift from "contact perception" to "distance perception"—that is, from tactile to visual perception—in early child development.

Perhaps the extension and enrichment of the scope of analytic therapeutic space owes more to the advent of child analysis than to any other factor. Certainly most of the analysts who have experimented with the enlargement of the therapeutic space have been child analysts. By definition, the treatment of children transgressed the basic taboos that Freud had established for the therapeutic space: namely, children could not be expected to verbalize only from a prostrate and passive position. And all Winnicott's researches certainly derive from his practice as a pediatrician. In his Squiggle Game technique, Winnicott most ingeniously provides a space and the *means* (paper, pencil, and crayons) through which a young patient can "live and experience together" with him, and in this space touch, sight, and movement become the creative components of the total therapeutic event. Winnicott gives us such poignant and vivid as well as joyous accounts of this in the case histories of his Squiggle Game technique in his book, *Therapeutic Consultations in Child Psychiatry* (1971).

The essence of the therapeutic space that Winnicott establishes with the child in the Squiggle Game is that it is a transitional space, in which both Winnicott and the child are separate and private to each other, and yet, through playing on the surface of the paper, both find a relating and a communication. Winnicott makes a very specific distinction between *relating* and *object relationship* in this context. It is because there is only relating without the sophistication of an object relationship that he can find his access with the child to the child's reverie. Each interview builds up to a critical moment which is unanticipatable and has an element of surprise in it, and only from there is it possible for Winnicott to know whether the interview will work toward a positive or a negative end.

Influenced by Winnicott's work, and guided by her own aptitude and intuition, Marion Milner (1969), in her extensive narrative of some twenty years' therapeutic care of her patient, Susan, gives a very moving and bold account of how this extremely sick girl only began to use the therapeutic space when she found the trust to draw and used drawings as an idiom of relating and being in the analytic situation. Discussing the problem of how to use the enormous number of drawings that Susan brought with her, Milner states:

> My first way of looking at this sheer amount of them was in terms of what I saw as her desperate need for a continued contact with a bit of external reality which was "other" and yet completely responsive to what came from her; the paper became as it were a substitute for the responsive ideal mother, receiving the slightest movement of her hand and giving it back into her eyes, a hand-and-eye co-ordinated interchange, a reciprocal give-and-take on a primitive non-verbal level; in fact, a relation to an ideal mother-me who would be with her whenever she needed, since there could always be a pencil and

paper handy to be held and touched. But I saw it also as a touching that was reparative, not just a way of seeking comfort in loneliness, but seeking to do reparation for all her destructive intentions or actions. Also I saw her as, through her drawings, constantly creating a bridge between me and herself, a basis for communication, since I believed her drawings did all have meaning potentially; even if I did not as yet understand more than a small part of them I had at least made the attempt to relate them to what had gone on between us during the years. Thus these so many bits of herself that she had given me had, I thought, been modified by my capacity to see her as a whole continuing person, even if she could not yet see herself or me as that. And even when the drawings were not interpreted, or not even seen, by me, they did seem to have provided some sort of substitute for the mirror that her mother had never been able to be to her; they did in a primitive way give her back to herself, as well as providing a substitute for me from one session to the next.

What strikes me as most impressive in Milner's statement above is the talent in her patient to find a space (the paper) where she could transfer the processes of the therapeutic space and utilize motility (drawing), touch, and sight to actualize experience of herself and the analyst which her language could neither encompass nor express. And Milner's emphasis on the reparative value of touching through this "hand-and-eye co-ordinated interchange" is indeed most revealing. In the classical analytic space we rely upon language to do all this. Furthermore, we create a void and an absence *from* our presence to provide that space of illusion where the patient can use symbolic discourse, which we receive symbolically and interpret in similar idiom. Hence Viderman (1970) is right when he concludes his examination of the analytic space by the formulation:

A tree trunk is not a barrier. However it can become one. To do so requires an intelligence capable of making tools, a will to create objects. In the analytical situation, the word does not equate language. The analyst does not use his ears simply to hear but to transform that which he hears. He does not so much listen to language as to the possible meanings of a word which has no meaning other than that which he will endow it with.

Language in the analytic situation is largely a making and a transforming of experiences, both for the patient and the analyst. It is more than reportage or hearing. It is more than a vehicle of memory or meaning. It is more than relating as well. It is an experiential entity that is fabricated out of illusion, fantasy, and the *vécu*. As such, it is an artifact and an achievement, the production of which entails very sophisticated ego capacities in both the parties concerned.

When these capacities are lacking, then illusion breaks down, fantasy degenerates into mentation, and language usurps the functions that are the right of other organs of experience, such as bodily behavior (motility and touch), sight, and taste.

Like illusion, *voir* is another equally treacherous word to use, since its connotations stretch from a mere perceptual physical and neural act to sagacity. One recalls immediately Rimbaud's cryptic and startling passage in his letter to Georges Izambard from Charleville on May 13 (?), 1871:

> I'm lousing myself up as much as I can these days. Why? I want to be a poet, and I am working to make myself a *seer:* you won't understand this at all, and I hardly know how to explain it to you. The point is, to arrive at the unknown by the disordering of *all the senses.* The sufferings are enormous, but one has to be strong, to be born a poet, and I have discovered I *am* a poet. It is not my fault at all. It is a mistake to say: I think. One ought to say: I am thought. Pardon the pun.

Indeed! Between the conjugations of the verb "to see" and the sagacity of the "seer," the spectrum is from illusion, through delusion, to insight! We know too little to adjudicate upon the issues involved, but we have the right to examine them.

I shall now discuss the case material presented in terms of these hypotheses. The first patient, Miss X, had made out of language and mentation a frenzied existence which had a momentum all its own. Instead of knowing herself through it or relating to the other with it, she continuously fabricated it into an almost addictive mental state. Hence the reality of the analytic space and the analyst as a person were violently negated by her language as well as by her emotionality. This usurpation of the legitimate functions of the bodily organs which constitute the totality of a person's life experience only by mentation and language, I consider to be a very pathogenic distortion of the ego (cf. Khan, 1969).

To touch with words and to see with words were in her case a perversion of the ego faculties of sight and prehensile contact. Hence she experienced herself as always floating in an uncanny unreality which had neither physical sentience to it nor psychic limits. She also concocted the most bizarre delusions about others, because in any experience of the other she could allow for neither their reality nor that illusion which permits imaginative expression of self and empathic knowing of the other. It was also very typical of her that she did not allow for what Winnicott calls "the period of hesitation." She hurtled herself upon one with language. Therefore, though one was amazed by the extraordinary phenomenological descriptions of her states, in fact they had no insight to them because they were devoid of sight and touch. She lived in an anguished search after sentient loving and being loved, without allowing her body its natural physical say in the matter. Miss X was *held* by her language and mentation, and to this nothing external could ever find access or entrance—whereas the second girl was seeking to find a space which would *hold* her.

The second patient was basically staking a claim for her need to be allowed "a period of hesitation." Through staying silent and thus unknowable, and by touching the walls with her hands and the whole of her body, and looking and exploring the space with her sight, she would gradually create that trust in relating and being related to which allowed for her privacy and yet crystallized very slowly that dimension of illusion in which symbolic discourse could begin to be created and shared by us as separate entities. All her violence and rage with the previous analyst was reactive to the analyst's legitimate demands, in terms of the professional tradition, for her to speak herself into language. This had led to extreme and macaber episodes of acting out outside analysis, and physical assault on the space of the analytic situation and the person of the analyst, reducing everything to utter chaos.

I have referred to Winnicott's concept of unintegrated states as an inherent experience of infancy development. In this girl, the demand was to enable her to be unintegrated as a person in the analytic space and relating, so that she could gradually personalize in time. In extreme contrast to this was Miss X's continuous and precipitate pseudo-integrating of herself in terms of language.

Conclusion

I have tried to explore the role of illusion as it operates in the analytic therapeutic space and relating between the analyst and the patient. It is my hypothesis, following Winnicott's concept, that one task of the analyst is to enable the patient to establish this area of illusion. By and large, with the well-chosen case, we do not have to concern ourselves with this matter because language absorbs it naturally in its symbolic functions. But—through early developmental distortions of ego functions, and/or their precocious dissociated exploitation—language can become a usurper of the space of illusion and experience. From these two case histories I have tried to show how in such cases the burden is on the analyst to curtail the hyper-mentation in the patient so as to facilitate the emergence of the area of illusion and "the period of hesitation." It cannot always succeed, but an awareness of these factors can help us to make the therapeutic space available to very disturbed patients who otherwise find themselves utterly incapacitated to function in the analytic space and process. I have further suggested that seeing when a patient is in a regressive area of primitive psychic functioning and affectivity has to be very much reinforced by touching if it is to establish its true function as an ego experience in the patient's *vécu*.

BIBLIOGRAPHY

Balint, M. (1968), *The Basic Fault*. London: Tavistock Publications.
Cassirer, E. (1946), *Language and Myth*. New York: Dover Publications.
Freud, A. (1969), *Difficulties in the Path of Psychoanalysis*. New York: International Universities Press.

Freud, S. (1913), Totem and Taboo, *Standard Edition*, 13:1–162. London: Hogarth, 1953.
—— (1914), Remembering, Repeating and Working-Through, *Standard Edition*, 12:145–156. London: Hogarth, 1958.
—— (1937), Analysis Terminable and Interminable. *Standard Edition*, 23:209–253. London: Hogarth, 1958.
—— (1954), *The Origins of Psychoanalysis*. London: Imago.
Hoffer, W. (1949), Mouth, Hand and Ego-Integration. *Psychoanalytic Study of the Child*, 3–4:49–56.
Khan, M. M. (1962), Dream Psychology and the Evolution of the Psycho-Analytic Situation. *Internat. J. Psycho-Anal.*, 43:21–31.
—— (1969), Vicissitudes of Being, Knowing and Experiencing in the Therapeutic Situation. *Brit. J. Med. Psychol.*, 42:383–393.
—— (1970), The Therapeutic Frame of Freud. *The Psychoanal. Study Society*, 5:245–261.
—— (1971), Dread of Surrender to Resourceless Dependence in the Analytic Situation, a paper read at 27th International Psychoanalytical Congress.
Kris, E. (1954), Introduction to *The Origins of Psychoanalysis*. London: Imago.
Lévi-Strauss, C. (1970), *The Elementary Structures of Kinship*. London: Social Science Paperbacks.
Maurois, A. (1968), *Les Illusions*. Paris: Hachette.
Milner, M. (1952), Aspects of Symbolism in Comprehension of the Not-self. *Internat. J. Psycho-Anal.*, 33:181–195.
—— (1969), *The Hands of the Living God*. London: Hogarth.
Ricoeur, P. (1965), *Freud and Philosophy: An Essay on Interpretation*. New Haven, Conn.: Yale University Press.
Rimbaud, A. (1871), Letter to Georges Izambard in *Rimbaud*. Middlesex, England: Penguin Poets.
Sartre, J.-P. (1954), The Paintings of Giacometti in *Situations*. London: Fawcett Crest Books.
Searles, H. (1965), *Collected Papers on Schizophrenia and Related Subjects*. London: Hogarth.
Sechehaye, M. A. (1951), *Symbolic Realization*. New York: International Universities Press.
Spitz, R. (1965), *The First Year of Life*. New York: International Universities Press.
Stone, L. (1961), *The Psychoanalytic Situation*. New York: International Universities Press.
Viderman, S. (1970), *La Construction de l'Espace Analytique*. Paris: Denoël.
Winnicott, D. W. (1941), The Observation of Infants in a Set Situation. In: *Collected Papers: Through Paediatrics to Psycho-Analysis*. London: Tavistock Publications, 1958.
—— (1945), Primitive Emotional Development, *Ibid.*
—— (1951), Transitional Objects and Transitional Phenomena, *Ibid.*
—— (1954), Metapsychological and Clinical Aspects of Regression within the Psycho-Analytical Set-up, *Ibid.*
—— (1963), Communicating and Not Communicating Leading to a Study of Certain Opposites. In: The *Maturational Processes and the Facilitating Environment*. London: Hogarth, 1965.
—— (1971), *Playing and Reality*. London: Tavistock Publications.
—— (1971), *Therapeutic Consultations in Child Psychiatry*. London: Hogarth.

Concerning Therapeutic Symbiosis

HAROLD F. SEARLES, M.D. (*Washington, D.C.*)

In 1958 I postulated that symbiotic relatedness constitutes a necessary phase in psychoanalysis or psychotherapy with either neurotic or psychotic patients, and introduced the term "therapeutic symbiosis" for this mode of patient-analyst relatedness (Searles, 1959a). In 1959 I stated that what the analyst offers the patient which is new and therapeutic, in this regard, is not an avoidance of the development of symbiotic, reciprocal dependency with the patient, but rather an acceptance of this (1959b). My several subsequent discussions of this subject have included mention of the role of symbiotic relatedness in healthy, adult living (1965, 1967).

The present paper is the third in a series of reports on what I have learned in recent years concerning autism, symbiosis, and individuation. In these papers I am concerned not only with patients suffering from schizophrenia of varying degrees of severity but also with, for example, the subtle autism that emerges in the course of the neurotic patient's analysis. The first two papers included these passages:

> The categories . . . of pathologic symbiosis, autism, therapeutic symbiosis, and individuation depict what I regard as successive phases of ego development in therapy. Whether any one patient needs to run that whole course will depend upon the level of ego development he has already attained at the beginning. He may already have achieved, for example, a strong capacity for a therapeutically symbiotic relatedness, in which case the first two phases of ego development would be relatively little in evidence in one's work with him [Searles, 1971, p. 70].
>
> I have described it as characteristic of this phase of transition between autism and therapeutic symbiosis that the analyst now begins to find it feasible effectively to make transference-interpretations. This is in contrast to the earlier, autistic phase, during which he has had to adapt to long stretches of time during which

Presented as the Sixth Annual Franz Alexander Memorial Lecture, under the auspices of the Cedars-Sinai Divisions of Psychiatry and the Southern California Psychoanalytic Society and Institute, in Los Angeles on March 21, 1972. An earlier version had been presented to the Canadian Psychoanalytic Society, Ontario, in Toronto on January 27, 1972.

he has been given to feel useless, neglectful, irrelevant, uncaring, incompetent and, more than anything else, essentially non-human, precisely for the reason that the patient has needed to regress, in his experience of the analyst, to the level of the young child's experience of the mother as being something far more than merely human as a person is seen through adult eyes. The patient has needed to come to experience the analyst as being equivalent to the early mother who comprises the whole world of which the infant is inextricably a part, and before he has achieved sufficient of an own self to be able to tolerate the feeling-experience of sensing her as separate from his own body, and the two of them as separate from the rest of the actual world. The transition phase likewise stands in contrast, as regards the timeliness of transference-interpretations, to the subsequent phase of therapeutic symbiosis, in which such interpretations are almost limitlessly in order [Searles, 1970, pp. 12–13].

I shall use the term "therapeutic symbiosis" in this paper to include both ambivalent and pre-ambivalent types of symbiosis in the patient-analyst relationship, although earlier I had reserved that term for pre-ambivalent symbiosis—that is, a symbiosis which is felt as a thoroughly adoring, contented oneness, and which is traceable genetically to experiences in the very early infant-mother relationship, before significant increments of hate had come to intrude into this oneness and transform the emotional matrix of it into one of pervasive ambivalence. Both types of symbiosis are clearly full of potential for therapeutic effect, as, indeed, is each of the other phases of ego development that are mentioned in the first quotation above. Moreover, I have come to regard it as impossible to find any clearly defined, long-sustained instance of pre-ambivalent symbiosis and am more than ever mindful of a reservation I expressed in 1961:

> There is no sure criterion by which we can know . . . whether we are involved in a genuinely preambivalent symbiosis with the patient, or rather in the predominantly paranoid symbiosis which is a defense against hatred . . . and we must remain open-minded to the ever-present possibility that . . . a basically constructive, subjectively preambivalent symbiosis will be misused unconsciously from time to time, by both participants, to keep increments of particularly intense hostility out of awareness [1961, p. 181].

The Patient as Symbiotic Therapist

An understanding of the nature of therapeutic symbiosis requires that one grasp something of the extent to which the patient is himself devoted to functioning as a therapist in relationship to his officially designated analyst, as well as in his relationships with other persons in his life. Not only is the striving for an essentially psychotherapeutic effect upon the other person a concern of those relatively few persons who select the practice of psychoanalysis or psychotherapy as their life work, but it is also a basic and pervasive concern of human beings generally. But probably it is those persons whose childhoods to a large extent were devoted to functioning as therapist to other family members, and whose therapist-functioning proved both complex and absorbing and fundamental to their sense of personal identity, as well as frustrated in clear and lasting and acknowledgedly successful results, for whom such activity becomes a naturally absorbing adult-life work.

Although one can usefully explore the ways in which a genuine individual—that is a person who possesses a whole self, a person who has a relatively whole ego—thus unofficially functions as therapist to other persons who likewise have experienced psychological individuation and are thus whole individuals, I am concerned here with the "symbiotic therapist," the person who himself has not firmly achieved individuation, and whose most deeply meaningful human relationships consist in his complementing the areas of ego-incompleteness in other persons. This mode of relatedness is founded upon a relationship with his mother in which his ego-functioning was fixated similarly at a level of relatively infantile fragmentation and nondifferentiation, partially because the precarious family-intactness required that he not become a whole person but remain instead available for complementing the ego-incompleteness of the others in the family, individually and collectively.

The patient seen in this light is not merely a victim exploited by mother and family; to leave the conceptualization at that is to take into account only the potentially hostile components of what is transpiring. In these symbiotic processes, just as self and object are not clearly demarcated, neither are hate and love clearly differentiated. It is as much as anything the patient's nascent capacity for love, and for the development of mature human responsibility, which impels him to perpetuate this mode of relatedness. From the not-yet-well-differentiated, "selfish" point of view, he strives, for his psychological and physical survival, to maintain the only mode of relatedness he knows, and hopefully to so enhance, so strengthen the mother as to enable her to mature further, to provide himself with a model for identification, for the sake of his own maturation. From the "altruistic" point of view, which is also not well differentiated, he goes on literally sacrificing his own potential self, for the sake of complementing the mother and thus ensuring her survival.

Just as the seeds of the most intense paranoid hate can be found in all this, so, too, can be found here the sources of the most genuinely selfless human love. The more ill a patient is, the more deeply indispensable does he need to become, at this pre-individuation level of ego-functioning, to his transference-mother, the analyst. This necessary transference evolution is made all but impossible by the traditional view of the analyst as the healthy one, the one with the intact ego, who is endeavoring to give help to the ill one, the patient, seen as afflicted with an "ego defect" or "ego deficit." The latter is thus "afflicted," indeed, but to some real degree, so (like everyone else) is the analyst. Without this "affliction," in fact, he could not hope to function effectively as the analyst in the therapeutically symbiotic phase of the patient's treatment.

No one becomes so fully an individual, so fully "mature," as to have lost his previously achieved capacity for symbiotic relatedness. The so-called "ego defect" of the schizophrenic patient, seen in its dynamic function rather than as static crippledness, is really the area of his most intense, though fixedly symbiotic aliveness, and is of the same nature as the symbiotic basis of healthy adult ego-functioning—that basis which enables a healthy adult to come to feel, creatively and restoratively, at one with (or, one might say, part of) another individual, a group of his fellow human beings, mankind generally, the whole external world, a creative idea, or whatever.

In psychoanalytic treatment what is needed, more than anything else, to resolve the fixation in the patient's ego development—his having achieved, that is, only a fragment, or fragments, of an ego—is his discovery that a fellow human being, the analyst, can come to know, and to work with him in implicit acknowledgment of his indispensably important role in the analyst's own ego-functioning. Only through such a process can the patient become a more whole individual. Further, the individuation which he undergoes more successfully this time, in the context of the transference relationship, is in a real sense mutual, in that the analyst too, having participated with the patient in the therapeutic symbiosis, emerges with a renewed individuality which has been enriched and deepened by this experience. Just as we need to realize that, in healthy human living, symbiotic relatedness is not confined to infancy and early childhood but forms, at largely though not entirely unconscious levels, the dynamic substrate of adult living, so, too, individuation is not a once-and-for-all, irreversible process. It is not only a deeply ill patient who can achieve, in psychoanalytic treatment, a fuller individuation than the relatively fragmentary and superficial individuation he had achieved in childhood. A healthy adult, too, by definition, lives a daily and yearly life which involves, in its most essential ingredients, experiences—whether measured in moments or phases of his life—of symbiotic relatedness and re-individuation.

It is currently one of our great human tragedies that hundreds of thousands of persons are living out their lives in gigantic mental hospitals, existing largely in chemical cocoons, because behind our scornful shunning of them is our unformulated sensing that any one of them, if we were to permit him or her to do so, would become personally more a part of us than we dare to allow.

In recent years I have learned that one of the most heavily defended emotions in the schizophrenic patient is his sense of guilt at having failed to enable his fragmented mother to become a whole and successful mother to him. This sense of guilt is based partially upon subjective omnipotence and is therefore to a degree irrational; in this regard it is analogous to the guilt we would have the supposedly omnipotent "schizophrenigenic mother" bear, single-handedly, for the fact of the patient's schizophrenic illness. But it is essential for us to perceive that the patient's sense of guilt at having thus failed his mother has also a realistic aspect, for it is this realistic component which provides the key to his capacity for developing a sense of more mature responsibility in his interpersonal relationships in general. It is only as he comes to enable his analyst to function as analyst—analogous to mother—in relation to him (despite whatever intense hatred and other "negative" feelings) that the crippling effect of this heretofore unconscious guilt can be undone. We can now see, in retrospect, that the pathogenic introjects which have comprised the core of his schizophrenia have represented not only his unconscious means of coping with an otherwise intolerable outer reality, but also his unconscious, primitive way of trying to heal that "outer reality"—that is, those most deeply ill components of mother and subsequent mother-transference figures—by taking those components into himself and trying thus to free her (and her successors) from the burden of them.

The Phase of Ambivalent Symbiosis

As regression deepens in the analytic relationship—regression not only on the part of the heretofore autistic patient but also on the part of the analyst, who, as I described in an earlier paper (1970), has become considerably caught up, himself, in autistic processes—there are now encountered sudden and increasingly frequent bits of the ego-splitting, intense ambivalence against which, in the history of each participant, autistic processes had developed as a defense. In this stage of ambivalent symbiosis, in which ego boundaries are by definition unreliable in either participant, there is much of both projecting and introjecting, with each person feeling threatened by the other by reason of the other's personifying one's own as-yet-unintegratable inner contents. For example, each projects upon the other his own murderous feelings, and feels correspondingly in fear for his life. The loss, for each, of what he has felt to be entirely his own (autistic) world—its disruption by, for example, one's patient who now feels to be chaotically permeating one's whole life—is accompanied by intense rage, fear, and the most primitive kinds of loss reactions. One's subjective experience is that one no longer has either a world, or a self, of one's own.

It is to be noted that ambivalence which is largely unconscious, rather than conscious and therefore integratable by the ego, requires symbiotic relatedness with the other person, relatedness in which the other personifies those components of the ambivalent feelings which one is having to repress at the moment. Contrariwise, when one can face and accept his own ambivalent feelings, one can be a separate person and can react to the other as being, also, a separate person. I shall never forget the sense of achieved inner freedom which enabled me to tell a hebephrenic woman, in relation to whom I had been enmeshed in anguished symbiotic relatedness for years, that I would never allow her to visit my home—as she long had yearned to do—even if my refusal meant that she would stay in a mental hospital all her life. Where one draws the line, in such matters, is an expression of the analyst's individual self; this is where *I* draw the line. Theoretically, it is not essential, and it may be unwise, although in my experience rarely if ever disastrous, to say these things to the patient; the important thing is that one become able to feel them—to feel, in this instance, a degree of intense rejectingness which I had projected for years, heretofore, upon this, in truth, remarkably rejecting woman. The degree of ambivalence of which I am writing is so intense that it can be met, as I hope to show further in this paper, only if the two participants function to a high degree as one in the experiencing and acknowledging of it.

Some years ago, at a time when I had not experienced enough *pre-*ambivalently symbiotic relatedness with my patients to be able to conceptualize it, and when I assumed all symbiotic relatedness to be highly ambivalent, I wrote in my notes, following a session with this same woman:

I have referred to symbiotic relationships in two recent papers and have been wanting lately to try to describe in detail what are the characteristics of such a relationship. I have just come from an hour with Carol Fleming[1] which has been like hundreds of similar hours with her and which is, I think, a typical one to represent the [ambivalently] symbiotic relationship.
When I went up to see her she was lying in bed, silently, in her bare-walled room—lying in her steel bed—and the only other items of furniture were the two chairs. I felt a sense of deep discouragement when I went in there, and aversion to going ahead with the work. As the hour progressed, an hour in which she said little and this only in a fragmentary fashion, while looking antagonistically toward me most of the time, I noticed that what I felt was perhaps most of all a sense of helplessness in the face of my own feelings, and a non-acceptance of them, whether these were feelings of antagonism, or sympathy, or tenderness, or what-not. I felt strong urges to simply abandon the work with her and abandon her, but felt again a sense of conflict and helplessness at doing this.
I felt a sense of what one might call being at the mercy of her own playing upon my feelings, whether by making me antagonistic through hateful behavior, or by evoking tenderness and sympathy from me when she would suddenly have a friendly look on her face and make a kind of beseeching gesture. Another thing to be stressed is that my feelings were in quite a welter and were rapidly changing. At one period in the hour I got to feeling as though we were two rattlesnakes with our fangs in one another's necks, each refusing to let go because by staying in the relationship we were best expressing the boundless hatefulness we felt toward one another. Throughout the hour there was an element of dissatisfaction on my part with my own feelings.

A few months earlier I had written:

The entire time of the small group [one of several groups into which the overall therapist-staff were divided, which met regularly to discuss, informally

---

[1] A pseudonym.

and as candidly as we could, whatever were the most pressing problem situations at the moment] today was taken up with my presenting my work with Carol Fleming. I brought it up because I was feeling under a good deal of pressure about the forthcoming visit of the mother and father. As I was telling the others about the way it was going with Carol, I began to see more and more indications in myself of a massive submerged rage at her because of my feelings of failure in the work. I felt as though there were a large, heavy stone in me . . . it felt unmistakably like depression with a good deal of rage associated with it. The thing that came to me in the course of presenting this was that even my "positive," tender feelings toward her were a burden to me, as well as my formerly strong feelings of cruelty and sadism. These "positive" feelings were a burden, I felt, because I did not feel free to express them to her—as by, for instance, touching her head when I felt like it. I have felt all along that such expressions of tenderness were a kind of misuse of my therapist position, something which would frighten her and would simply be a kind of gratifying of my own dependency feelings, using her as a mother-figure. In the course of the rest of the day it came to me that the *most important thing in my life at Chestnut Lodge*[2] at present is my anger at Carol Fleming. It was a quite startling thing, indeed, to come to this realization; it occurred to me later that this may be some measure, too, of the importance of the relationship to the patient herself.

No one or two vignettes can be fully typical of the varied clinical phenomena which I am conceptualizing. This patient, for instance, was still more invested in her years'-long autism, still relatively little invested in explicitly discernible, ambivalently symbiotic relatedness, than have been most of the patients I have in mind as I write.

With these latter patients, most of whom in my experience have been borderline schizophrenic or ambulatorily schizophrenic—considerably more readily accessible, that is, than the woman I have just mentioned—there is the additional circumstance that both participants almost constantly react to one another, whether in a verbal, or in a tangibly nonverbal, fashion and with feelings that shift rapidly about over the whole spectrum, from fury to tenderness to scorn, and so on, often in extraordinary mixtures of emotions.

Much of my own experience with ambivalently symbiotic relatedness has occurred during the final several months of my eleven years of work with a hebephrenic man who had achieved by now this way of functioning, at a time when both of us knew that before long I would be leaving the hospital where he dwelt; and during my work with some hundreds of borderline or ambulatorily schizophrenic patients with whom I have had one-time interviews for consultative and/or teaching purposes. I have wondered about the role of mutual separation anxiety in this so-active responding, under these special circumstances of approaching termination or

[2] I am chagrined to see that I had to write, and to feel, this qualification: "at Chestnut Lodge"; I could not experience this simply as the most important thing in my life. This I regard as evidence of my then-unconscious resistance to acknowledging the patient's full importance to me—my own resistance, that is, to the development of a fully felt, pre-ambivalently symbiotic relatedness with her.

one-time interviews. But my experiences with various other long-range treatment cases have confirmed my belief that the separation anxiety involved has less to do with the imminence of physical separation than with the imminent threat to both participants lest their lively symbiotic relatedness give way at any moment, unpredictably and uncontrollably, to autism or individuation (outcomes which do not seem differentiated in the patient's grasp of the situation, nor at all well differentiated in my own understanding in that context). Thus the imminence of either outcome poses the same subjective threat of one's being torn asunder at any moment.

The symbiotic instability of ego boundaries makes it impossible to know whether the anger or depression, for instance, which one suddenly experiences is one's "own," or whether one is empathically sensing a feeling of the patient's "own" against which *he* is successfully defended unconsciously (as by projection). Also, as regards the patient's verbal communications, it is often impossible to know, and it feels urgently important to ascertain, whence and to whom these communications are coming.

For example, one such patient who at a nonverbal level was well established in ambivalently symbiotic relatedness with me, but who had not yet achieved a comparable level of verbal articulateness, confined his verbal communications over many months to certain stereotyped comments. In one session, he expressed each of the following stereotyped comments at least once: "Take your time." "Abide with what ya have." "Remain happy." "Time and place f'r everything." "No need to say." For me it was something like listening to one side of a telephone conversation. I told him that I had no way of knowing whether each of these comments was—and here I utilize numbers, which I did not use in communicating to him—(1) his response to thoughts he was having, (2) his response to voices he was hearing, (3) his conjecture as to what I was thinking, (4) his accurate report to me of what he was hearing the voices say, or (5) some mixture of all these. Not surprisingly, in response to so complex a comment from me, he offered no illuminating reply. I assume that he was quite unable to differentiate among these various possibilities, to which I now added another: (6) were his stereotyped comments giving behavioral expression, by processes of introjection, to what he tended unconsciously to perceive as being my own silently hallucinated state? I was not in fact subject to hallucinations, stressful though these sessions often were; but one of his most discernible transference reactions was in terms of my being his "shell-shocked" father (who had died long ago), a man so ego-fragmented as to have been incapacitated from useful career activity throughout the patient's childhood, and a man who may well have suffered, therefore, from hallucinations.

Considerably earlier in the work I had become aware, more simply, that things he said could be expressive of *my* presumed feelings or attitudes, from his point of view, as well as of his own feelings and attitudes. When, for example, in the middle of a prolonged silence he would say reproachfully, "You don't ever intend to say," this seemingly could refer variously to how he viewed me, or how he viewed himself, or how he assumed I viewed him. On another occasion, when I went into the building where he lived to have the hour with him, I found him standing outside the nearby nurses' office, and he made no move to follow me down the corridor to his room. After a few minutes of my sitting in his room with the door open, waiting for him, I went out and got a newspaper near that office and brought it back to the room, ignoring him as I went by. After a relatively brief time he came into the room, saying, "Who the hell needs *you*, you slimy son-of-a-bitch?," which could express equally well his attitude or the one I had manifested in getting the newspaper. What makes it feel so important to the analyst, at this stage of things, to try to locate the ego boundaries is that there is so much unintegrated, and therefore uncontrollable, hostility in the relationship. For example, the memory was still fresh in my mind of a time when he evidently had suddenly heard a hallucinatory voice, coming from me, saying deeply insulting things to him, and had reacted with such barely-contained, explosive fury that I felt physically frightened of him and thoroughly helpless to affect what was going on in him.

The Role of Jealousy in the Fragmented Ego[3]

In my work with the above-mentioned man, as well as with another patient earlier and many subsequently, I have seen that ambivalently symbiotic relatedness often comes to have, at first weirdly, a quality of *group* relatedness, with jealousy a most important and difficult complicating factor. It is commonly assumed that jealousy is an emotion that occurs in a context of three actual persons (Farber, 1961). But in these patients—and, again, I refer not merely to grossly ego-fragmented hebephrenic patients, but to any patients in whom schizoid components come to light in the course of analysis, which in my opinion then includes patients generally—the pathogenic introjects have the subjective personal identity value, and interpersonal impact, of persons. It is when the analyst comes to be invested, by the patient, with a personal significance approximately equivalent to that with which the introject in question is invested—when, in simpler words, the analyst comes to be as important to the patient as the latter's own "self" is to him—that the analyst now feels, and the remainder of the patient's identity (i.e., the area not comprised of the introject) now feels, pitted in an intense three-(or more) way jealous competition.

[3] An excellent paper by Pao (1969), "Pathological Jealousy," while not containing the concepts I am putting forward here, provides a useful psychodynamic background for them, as well as a valuable survey of the literature concerning jealousy.

For example, the hebephrenic man I have been mentioning used to relate during the sessions to hallucinatory voices which made me feel, by contrast, totally insignificant to him. When I would try to interrupt his dialogue with a hallucinatory figure, he would snap in vitriolic fury, "Shut up! I got company!" But it was only as my feeling-significance to him increased that I began to feel jealous when he would turn from relating to me, to relating to an hallucinatory voice. At such times I had a distinct sense that a group relationship was going on in the room, and I have often had this feeling with a similarly ego-fragmented woman with whom I have worked for many years. Still later, in my treatment of the hebephrenic man, I became so sure of my importance to him that I could know that the hallucinatory phenomena he manifested were secondary to the events transpiring between us, and I no longer felt vulnerable to such jealousy.

The patient's own jealousy of himself, springing from a part of him which feels left out from another part to "whom" the analyst is responding, constitutes an enormous resistance in the treatment. That is, when one island among those comprising the patient's collective "self" is able to work with the analyst in making a step forward in the work, another such island "who" feels left behind and intensely jealous, reacts with savage vindictiveness against what the two coworkers have accomplished together, and against the collaborative relationship between them. Such a patient's "self" is largely comprised of a collection of poorly integrated introjects. I surmise that the jealousy is traceable in part to early life experiences of unmasterable jealousy at the closeness between two other actual persons—the parents, for example, or the mother and a sibling adored by her—jealousy which was not resolved in the patient but was unconsciously defended against by his introjection of the two, emotionally close, other persons. But I surmise that, more importantly, the jealousy had a counterpart *within the mother* (or other mothering ones) *herself*, such that the child had to cope with, and to try introjectively—by taking into himself, that is—to make whole a mother whose ego was fragmented and ridden with just such "intrapsychic" jealousy.

In the course of treatment, this jealousy can best be dealt with as an unconscious defense against the therapeutically necessary, but at first frightening to both patient and analyst, fusion involved in pre-ambivalent symbiosis. It seems to me that the instances of the acting out of such jealousy that are most disruptive of the treatment occur before there has developed any strong pre-ambivalent relatedness in the transference. Any jealousy phenomena which occur later, after individuation has occurred, while perhaps not inconsiderable, can be dealt with by the now whole patient and the now whole analyst, as they explore the meaning to their relationship of some third whole person outside the office.

Finally, I shall give an example from my work with a schizoid patient—a patient whose degree of illness is common in an office practice. For several years I found this man infuriatingly smug. But the time came when, to my astonishment, I realized that what I was feeling now was jealousy; *he* so clearly favored his *self* over *me* that I felt deeply jealous, bitterly left out of this mutually cherishing and cozy relationship between the two "persons" who comprised him. I emphasize that this did not happen until after several years of my work with him. In retrospect, I saw that I previously had not developed sufficient personal significance to him (in classically psychoanalytic terms, had not been sufficiently cathected as a separate object in his experience of me), to sense these two now relatively well-differentiated "persons" in him and to feel myself capable of and desirous of participating in the "three"-way, intensely jealousy-laden competition. It is my impression that such schizoid patients usually prove so discouragingly inaccessible to psychoanalysis that the analyst and the patient give up the attempt at psychoanalysis before they have reached this lively but disturbing (to analyst as well as patient) stratum, this stratum in which the patient's ego fragmentation becomes revealed and the nature of the transference becomes one of a murderously jealous "three"-way competitiveness.

Technique During the Phase of Transition from Autism to Therapeutic Symbiosis

The oftentimes long, seemingly static phase of autism proves in retrospect not to have been a mere marking of time before the onset of the discernibly active therapeutic processes of the symbiotic phase, but rather to have comprised the necessary establishing of the reliably strong context within which these latter changes can be allowed to occur. For me, this finding substantiates the positive emphasis which Milner (1969) places upon what I am calling autism. She writes of "the theme of premature ego-development and the necessity, for healthy mental growth, for recurrent times when retreat into absent-mindedness [i.e., autism] is possible," and suggests that "behind the states that are talked about by analysts as auto-erotic and narcissistic [i.e., autistic] there can be an attempt to reach a beneficent kind of narcissism, a primary self-enjoyment . . . which, if properly understood, is not a rejection of the outer world but a step towards a renewed and revitalized investment in it" (Milner, 1969). She also cites Heimann's (1962) paper which concerns narcissistic withdrawal for creative work and the need for research into the changes that narcissism undergoes from its primitive manifestations, so that it becomes compatible with ego creativity and object relations.

The autistic phase involves the formation, in my view, of what Hartmann (1939) has termed "the average expectable environment," what Winnicott (1941) has called "the good-enough holding environment," and what Khan (1963, 1964) describes in terms of the mother's role as protective shield.

A high degree of reliability develops during the autistic phase. This reliability, whether expressed in terms of punctuality, regularity of seating arrangements, or whatever constellation of outward trappings in the treatment situation, must have to do with both participants' developing sureness as to what the situation will, and will not, permit. Sometimes extraordinary patience and what might seem to be inexcusable leniency are necessary on the analyst's part; other times demand murderously impatient firmness—whatever gives truest expression to the analyst's individual self in meeting the needs of the immediate treatment situation.

In my work with one chronically schizophrenic woman, I developed a technique which I described with some embarrassment to my Chestnut Lodge colleagues as the Chinese water-torture method, for the reason that it appeared on the surface to be so highly sadistic. In fact, this technique developed out of absolute necessity and proved to be immensely useful. It consisted simply in a maddeningly rigorous application of a technique emphasized many years ago by Rogers (1942): repeating what the patient said and simultaneously indicating a readiness to hear more, but without going a single step beyond her. The woman had an extremely tenuous sense of identity and was terribly afraid, therefore, of venturing forward on her own; individuality was equivalent, for her, to hopeless insanity. On the hundreds of occasions in the past when I had ventured encouragingly a bit beyond her, she had immediately reacted to me in totally alienated horror and condemnation, typically cutting me off from her with a shocked, awed, "You're crazy, Dr. Searles!" I had learned the hard way that I must be *with* her at each of her most tentative steps, repeating each of her tentative comments—often only the first part of an intendedly full sentence, which unaided she could not complete—but that I must not get at all *ahead* of her.

I was amused when, in a staff presentation, one of my colleagues, who had found my presentation of one of my typical interviews with her quite disturbing, said in angry protest:

. . . in that interview, every word practically that she said, you seized on it, you repeated it back to her and then you asked her some further data on it, as if you had to control each and every thing that she did. I wonder, God, this would be an awful rigidly structured business, and I wonder what she might think of the meaning of that in terms of her own aggressive feelings—why this has to be done. Surely when she said something was driving her crazy, I think I would have had the same feeling, that if somebody was doing this to me, I'd really feel that I was going nuts and would feel like tearing out my hair or something.

I was amused at his reaction both because of what I felt to be the accuracy of his description of what I was doing with her, and because the nature of his emotional reaction to it was so akin to the emotional reaction which was developing within the patient herself—a therapeutically most welcome development. My relationship with her progressed through a subsequent phase of ambivalently symbiotic relatedness, during which there were a great many stormy sessions in which we both participated most actively; and a later, clearly identifiable and prolonged, phase of pre-ambivalently therapeutic symbiosis which was of enormous growth-value for both of us, and which enabled her to achieve a stronger degree of subsequent individuation than any others among my chronically schizophrenic patients have, so far, ever achieved. These later developments could not have occurred, I am convinced, without my having functioned during that autistic phase as a kind of exoskeleton for her.

In my paper concerning neutral therapist responses (1963), I detailed something of the clinical events which indicated that, in my work with one chronically schizophrenic patient who lay mute and motionless throughout the analytic sessions for months—months during which he evidently was hovering on the brink of death—it was my functioning meanwhile as a progressively mute and motionless inanimate object which served eventually, where more "active" measures had all failed, to help him to become genuinely alive and increasingly functional.

One way of construing all this is to see that the analyst must come to personify the patient's own autistic rigidity, in order for that rigidity to become translated into increasingly well-differentiated and consciously utilizable ego strength. This is achieved partially through the patient's identification with the analyst's timely and skillful "becoming alive" and his readiness to venture forth in various constructive ways from so rigid and "inanimate," but for all patients at times so necessary, a transference position. In everyday office analytic practice, the patients—and these include not only ambulatorily schizophrenic and borderline patients, but also neurotic ones—who complain most of the analyst's remoteness and changelessness are the very persons who need most, for the sake of the resolution and integration of erstwhile autistic components within themselves, to have him function thus in relation to them.

In my experience, for the resolution of the patient's autism to occur, the analyst must do more than function as a more reliable maternally protective shield for the patient than the latter's biological mother had been during his infancy and early childhood, in the manner that Khan has described. First the analyst must have become increasingly free in his acceptance of the *patient's* functioning as *his*—the analyst's—maternally protective shield. In my own way of conceptualizing it: to the extent that the analyst can become able comfortably and freely to immerse himself in the autistic patient as comprising his (the analyst's) world, the patient can then utilize him as a model for identification as regards the acceptance of such very primitive dependency needs, and can come increasingly to exchange his erstwhile autistic world for the world comprised of, and personified by, the analyst. This progression of events is in actuality comprised not of discrete, once-and-for-all shifts forward, but rather of blended and ever-oscillating processes, so that at one moment the exoskeleton is being provided by the analyst, at the next moment by the patient, and, increasingly, by both at once and at one.

What I am describing here requires, again, an appreciation of the patient's therapist-orientation. Through the evolution of the transference the analyst, in finding the patient's autistic functioning to be serving as an increasingly important maternal-shield in his own ego-functioning, is reacting like the ego-fragmented mother whose own functioning has required that the patient remain fixated at the level of autism, as the foundation stone of her own precarious existence. What the analyst brings into the patient's life that is new is that he, unlike the mother earlier, has a sufficiently well-integrated ego to dare to *know* how indispensably important to him is this patient, this autistic patient who is able meaningfully to relate to him, at first, only as the maternal shield for those least well-integrated components of the analyst upon·which the patient's transference to him as an ego-fragmented mother is based.

In other words, the analyst must dare to know that, at this very primitive level, the patient is functioning, and has been functioning, as his mother-therapist. To the extent that he is conscious of this, he need not acknowledge it explicitly to the patient. It becomes mutually and implicitly understood that the patient has been helping him to confront areas of himself with which he had been previously largely unacquainted. As these areas become integrated into the analyst's conscious ego-functioning, he becomes more and more the strong mother the patient has been needing. Since the patient has been mothering him successfully, as the patient's infant or fetus, there is now no humiliation for the patient in becoming increasingly aware of his own infant-need, now, for the analyst as mother.

In a recent paper (1972) concerning my work, extending over many years and still continuing, with a deeply ego-fragmented and delusional woman, I described my gradual discovery of the awesome extent to which her highly delusional world was in actuality flowing from, and thus was based upon, her responding to various real but predominantly unconscious components of my personality—that is, heretofore largely unconscious ways of my functioning with her during the sessions. Notable for me in this increasingly clear realization of the extent to which I have been personifying a God-the-creator, early mother to the patient, is the extent to which I previously had shied away from experiencing myself as possessing this degree of importance to her. For me personally, it has been easier to adore the patient as God-like, than to feel so adored by her.

In my recent papers (1970, 1971) concerning autism I have described how the analyst is thrown, in response to the autistic patient, back upon his own autistic processes. A development which comes eventually to contribute to the resolution of this autistic mode of relatedness is the analyst's surprised, recurrent, and deepening realization and acceptance of the fact that these two seemingly so separate worlds, his world and that of the patient, are but separate outcroppings of the unconscious ground joining the two of them. This principle is commonly manifested in the analyst's finding, during, for example, one of the frequent periods of silence with a boringly schizoid patient, that his self-examination of his preoccupying and supposedly quite free associations, as he is managing to get through this workaday time by dint of such inner "freedom," yields, as he begins to examine these associations, new and highly informative cues to what is going on between himself and the patient, and within the patient. The analyst's own "private" or "autistic" inner world is not nearly so far apart from the patient as he, the analyst, assumed it to be.

Summary

In this paper I have discussed various processes which are relevant to therapeutic symbiosis, including the patient's functioning as symbiotic therapist to the analyst, the phase of ambivalent symbiosis and various matters of analytic technique during that phase, and the realm of "intrapsychic" jealousy—jealousy, that is, based upon the fragmented state of the ego. Throughout the paper, I have attempted to highlight the therapeutic role of reciprocal identification processes between patient and analyst.

BIBLIOGRAPHY

Farber, L. H. (1961), Faces of Envy. Rev. Existential Psychol. and Psychiat., I (Spring 1961), No. 2. Reprinted on pp. 118–130 of his book, The Ways of the Will—Essays toward a Psychology and Psychopathology of Will. New York and London: Basic Books, 1966.

Hartmann, H. (1939), Ego Psychology and the Problem of Adaptation. London & New York: Imago; New York: International Universities Press, 1958.

Heimann, P. (1962), Notes on the Anal Stage, Internat. J. Psycho-Anal., 43:406–414.

Khan, M. M. R. (1963), The Concept of Cumulative Trauma. The Psychoanalytic Study of the Child, 18:286–306.

—— (1964), Ego Distortion, Cumulative Trauma, and the Role of Restruction in the Analytic Stituation. Internat. J. Psycho-Anal., 45:272–278.

Milner, M. (1969), The Hands of the Living God: An Account of a Psychoanalytic Treatment. New York: International Universities Press. Pp. 155, 383.

Pao, P-N. (1969), Pathological Jealousy. Psychoanal. Quart., 38:616–638.

Rogers, C. (1942), Counseling and Psychotherapy. Cambridge: The Riverside Press.

Searles, H. F. (1959a), Integration and Differentiation in Schizophrenia. J. Nerv. and Ment. Dis., 129:542–550.

—— (1959b), The Effort to Drive the Other Person Crazy: An Element in the Aetiology and Psychotherapy of Schizophrenia. Brit. J. Med. Psychol., 32:1–18.

—— (1961), Phases of Patient-Therapist Interaction in the Psychotherapy of Chronic Schizophrenia. Brit. J. Med. Psychol., 34:169–193.

—— (1963), The Place of Neutral Therapist Responses in Psychotherapy with the Schizophrenic Patient. Internat. J. Psycho-Anal., 44:42–56.

—— (1965), Collected Papers on Schizophrenia and Related Subjects. London & New York: Hogarth; New York: International Universities Press.

—— (1967), Concerning the Development of an Identity. *Psychoanal. Rev.*, 53:507–530.
—— (1970), Autism and the Phase of Transition to Therapeutic Symbiosis. *Contemporary Psychoanalysis*, 7:1–20.
—— (1971), Pathologic Symbiosis and Autism. In: *In the Name of Life—Essays in Honor of Erich Fromm*, ed. B. Landis and E. S. Tauber. New York: Holt, Rinehart and Winston. pp. 69–83. (This paper is actually the first in my current series, but appeared second because of a one-year delay in publication.)
—— (1972), The Function of the Patient's Realistic Perceptions of the Analyst in Delusional Transference. *Brit. J. Med. Psychol.*, 45:1–18.
Winnicott, D. W. (1941), The Observation of Infants in a Set Situation. In: *Collected Papers*. London & New York: Tavistock; New York: Basic Books, 1958.

V

PSYCHOANALYTIC EDUCATION

The Clinical Conference in Teaching and Learning the Psychoanalytic Process

PAUL A. DEWALD, M.D. (*St. Louis*)

An important body of psychoanalytic understanding which must be acquired by a candidate during his training is an integrated and workable clinical and theoretical conceptualization of the psychoanalytic process and of his role in it. Although this subject is touched upon in fragmentary fashion in a number of different educational experiences in the usual psychoanalytic curriculum, insufficient attention has at times been given to the problem of helping the candidate synthesize these fragmentary experiences.

The personal analysis is indispensable in helping the candidate develop himself as a psychoanalytic instrument and in preparing him for his role in the psychoanalytic process, but it should not be considered as a means of acquiring a conceptual awareness of the analytic process itself. Although the candidate in a successful personal analysis acquires an emotional awareness of the progressive process from the analysand's point of view, and although this form of learning equips him to empathically understand the role of the patient in later clinical work, an emphasis on the cognitive and conceptual elements of his own analysis frequently serves the function of resistance.

Seminars on psychoanalytic technique frequently offer general principles or theoretical ideas, but application to the clinical situation and to the sequential unfolding and development of an analytic process usually cannot be documented in this type of course. Theoretical seminars on metapsychology likewise may touch on this subject, but usually from an abstract and highly conceptualized point of view, which is frequently at some distance from the clinical phenomenology and data from which the conceptualizations are extrapolated.

Presented at the Geographic Training Analysts Meeting, Institute for Psychoanalysis, Chicago, on October 16, 1971; and at the annual meeting, American Psychoanalytic Association, Dallas, Texas, on April 28, 1972.

Individual supervision of the candidate's analytic work offers a format in which to observe the unfolding and development of the analytic process in the case in question. But the pressures of day-to-day clinical responsibility, therapeutic intervention and technique, and the necessary focus on the candidate's countertransference problems, as well as the transference vicissitudes of the student-teacher relationship, may make this a less than ideal situation in which to develop general conceptualizations regarding the overall process. The usual length of a completed case means that it may take several years or more for the candidate to be able to observe and assess the final effects of some of the interactions from the early or middle phases of his work with the patient. In addition, many supervisors, while effective clinicians, may be uneven in their capacity for presenting conceptual material for the candidate's understanding. And reliance on this educational experience alone gives the candidate an exposure to only a relatively small number of cases, all analyzed by one person (himself).

Exposing the candidate to a variety of clinical conferences may offer the type of conceptual understanding which we are seeking and may broaden his clinical experience by allowing him to become familiar with larger numbers of cases that do not require his immediate therapeutic responsibilities. This setting offers an opportunity to view the psychoanalytic process from a vantage point somewhat "outside" the immediate situation, thus fostering more cognitive elements of the learning process. Hopefully, the candidate can then extract from these various experiences (including his own cases) those elements which are common to the psychoanalytic process, as contrasted to the individual vicissitudes of any one case. But often these conferences are focused on one or another aspect of the total problem, and the full sweep of the analytic process from beginning to end is seldom undertaken.

As a result, the integration and synthesis of the various educational fragments regarding this important subject are left to the initiative and individual skills of the student. Periodic reports or final termination summaries are often used as stimuli to encourage this type of integrative work. The application for membership in the American Psychoanalytic Association, for example, is largely devoted to this type of summary and demonstration of the analytic process. But my experience on the membership committee convinces me that generally this phase of the application is poorly executed. Those case reports which indicate a good working concept of the process of psychoanalysis are indeed a rarity.

Lustman (1967) has pointed to a number of these issues: "We want to encourage the development of modes of thinking, of conceptualizing, of communicating" (p. 869). And he raises the important question, "How does one correlate and integrate theory and clinical material?" (p. 873). He suggests that an important function of the curriculum "is to bridge and help synthesize certain aspects of the experience of the personal analysis and supervision" (p. 874).

Fleming and Benedek (1966) show the frequent limitations of the supervisory situation:

The immediacy of the clinical process has been too pressing for both analyst and teacher. This fact has tended to limit any study of the process to the individual case . . . and to prevent formulation of general principles (p. 6). . . . Teaching as a process is the most important and probably the most difficult of the supervisory tasks (p. 53). . . . the abstract concept of process, even vaguely perceived by a student, serves as a background on which the clinical phenomena and the mutually facilitating relationship between the specific elements and the total process take shape and position, moving along a visible course (p. 54).

Ekstein (1969) indicates many of the problems in psychoanalytic education, particularly emphasizing the various emotional factors that may impinge on the teacher as well as the candidate. In his consideration he points to the curriculum as "that point of gravity which gives their cooperation purpose and goal direction" (p. 322).

I would therefore suggest that it is necessary for us as educators to devise a more effective methodology for teaching and learning about the analytic process. But before this can be effectively undertaken, it is necessary to develop our own ideas concerning those common elements in the psychoanalytic process which can be said to be significant in most or all cases, while still taking account of the variations in the process from patient to patient, as well as the variability in style and technique from analyst to analyst.

As a starting point for these discussions, I will therefore attempt to present some schematic ideas regarding the nature and unfolding of the psychoanalytic process.

Therapeutic psychoanalysis can be conceptualized as a continuous process of interaction occurring between analysand and analyst, in a specifically structured situation and relationship in which each participant is acutely sensitive and responsive to the total behavior and reactions of the other. This can be seen as a collaborative venture in which each participant has a complementary role vis-à-vis the other, and neither one can bring the process to a successful conclusion without the continuing work and participation of the other. The goal of these interactions is to set in motion within the patient a progressive and lasting intrapsychic change in his mental and emotional life, the aim of which is the reduction or elimination of those pathogenic psychic structures that had produced and sustained his neurotic disability, or had interfered with the spontaneous process of normal psychological maturation. The expectation is that when the unconscious conflicts and psychic structures that evolve from them have been reduced, modified, eliminated, or replaced by more adaptive and effective ones, the normal processes of maturation and development will again resume within the patient.

Although the analyst may undergo change in his professional skills and understanding as a result of this process, and although at times there may also occur emotional or psychological change within him, nevertheless intrapsychic structural change in the analyst's personality is *not* a goal of the psychoanalytic process as it is for the patient. In other words, the analyst serves as a catalyst in the production of intrapsychic change in the patient. His physical presence, his personal characteristics, and the multiple activities that he undertakes during the course of an analysis are necessary to the progress and ultimate successful unfolding of the analytic process, but at the end of the experience the analyst remains *relatively* unchanged in his level of personality functioning as compared with his status at the beginning.

The psychoanalytic interaction and relationship is a unique one in human experience, and the various component elements in the structure of the analytic situation make important contributions to the development and unfolding of the psychoanalytic process. Although experienced analysts take these elements for granted, we must keep in mind that, for the candidate, it is important to demonstrate and clarify their rationale and their impact upon the total process. Such things as the role of the patient and his willingness to accept it; the role of the analyst with the professional skill and commitment which this entails; the frequency and duration of the sessions; arrangements regarding the fee; the use of the couch; the delaying of major life decisions; and the explanation to the patient of the "basic rule" are all important elements in the establishment of an analytic situation. And their significance should be demonstrated to the candidate, along with an understanding of how his activity in structuring the situation may facilitate or impede its establishment.

Upon the background of this structured situation and as a result of the way in which each of the participants moves into his respective role in the interactions between them, there then develops the unfolding analytic relationship with its two major components of the therapeutic alliance and the transference neurosis. The patient's contributions to the evolving therapeutic alliance include his conscious motivations for analysis; his ability to follow the analytic procedure; his capacity to tolerate anxiety and other unpleasurable affects in the service of the therapeutic task; his willingness to reexperience old conflicts with the ultimate goal of their resolution; his capacity to delay immediate relief in favor of long-range goals; his capacity for self-observation; his capacity for trust in order to make use of the analyst as a helping instrument; and his ability to understand and integrate the analyst's interventions.

The analyst's contributions to the unfolding and establishment of the therapeutic alliance require his recognition that the development of this aspect of the total relationship has priority and determines the nature and timing of his interventions. His role in the establishment of the therapeutic alliance demands a great deal of him: his ability to maintain a therapeutic atmosphere; his capacity to encourage the patient's participation in it; his capacity for empathy, understanding, and analytic insight; his nonjudgmental attitude; his ability to present painful material in a tactful and analytically appropriate fashion; and his ability to use himself as an analytic instrument without major contamination by countertransference forces. As a result of the analyst's model which is transmitted to the patient through his various verbal and nonverbal interventions and attitudes, one essential aspect in the development of the therapeutic alliance is the patient's gradually increasing capacity to identify himself partially with the analyzing functions of the analyst, thereby fostering a therapeutic ego split into self-observing as well as experiencing functions. While the major emphasis on the development of a therapeutic alliance usually occupies the beginning phase, its importance is continuous throughout the entire analytic process. If the vicissitudes of the analysis disrupt or interfere with this aspect of the relationship, the analyst must recognize such disruptions, and in his interactions with the patient must give priority to its reestablishment. Although the analyst's most active efforts in fostering the development of a therapeutic alliance occur in the beginning and early middle phases of the analysis, the alliance itself is maximally active and continuously operative during the latter part of the termination phase. It is here, generally with minimal help from the analyst, and as the transference components of the relationship are being resolved, that the patient best demonstrates his internalized analytic functions, his ability to observe himself and his own behavior, his capacity to renounce infantile and childhood wishes, and his ability to continue in self-analytic work.

The other major line of development in the analytic relationship involves the gradual unfolding and evolution of the transference components, resulting in the establishment, exploration, and ultimate resolution of a transference neurosis. Both participants in the process make major contributions to this development. The patient's contributions arise from his capabilities for object relatedness, for conscious experience of drives and affects, for developing the technique of free association, and for regression in the service of the ego and the therapeutic task. An important element is his capacity to perceive the transference phenomena in the context of their therapeutic necessity, and therefore to recognize the "as if" characteristics of the transference neurosis within the framework of the therapeutic alliance.

The analyst's contributions to the unfolding transference neurosis include his capacity to permit himself to be used by the patient as a readily available transference object; his maintenance of personal anonymity; his interpretations of the patient's defenses and resistances against the emergence of a transference neurosis; his interpretations of the contents of the transference elements; and his noncritical, nonjudgmental, and anxiety-free acceptance of the patient's projected transference distortions as they occur. Another important element is his capacity to maintain transference abstinence at an optimal level, thereby not only facilitating conscious recognition of the intensifying underlying drives and fantasies, but also making the situation "safe" for the patient's verbal expression of the transference conflicts. The analyst must recognize that in terms of the transference demands, abstinence evokes frustration in the patient; while in terms of the therapeutic alliance, such abstinence is necessary if the patient is to explore his transference reactions fully. The analyst's capacity to tolerate anxiety and ambiguity in the transference-countertransference relationship without undue discomfort and without the necessity for premature closure are important elements in the interaction for the patient as he experiences the conflicts evoked by the analytic process. And the analyst's suspension of moralizing judgment or advice permits the patient's superego functions also to become a part of the transference relationship, and ultimately to be analyzed.

It is not possible here to document in detail the central significance of the regressive transference neurosis as the final common pathway in the expression of core psychic functions and conflicts from the infantile and childhood periods of development. Nor is it necessary to document the alternation of transference experience and self-observation in the patient, with the progressive undoing of repression, the acquisition of insight, and its application in the working-through process, as these occur in the exploration and elaboration of the transference relationship. Nor can I dwell upon the phenomenology of the resistances and the analyst's role in helping the patient recognize and cope with them. Nor is it necessary to spell out the dynamics of the termination phase in which renunciation of the infantile and childhood drives and objects through the prototype of the transference relationship activates the characteristic and necessary processes of grief, mourning, transference resistance, and the final reworking of previously elaborated conflicts.

However, as teachers it is essential that we recognize the need to document all these various phenomena in considerable detail for the candidates, and also to demonstrate from the data of the analytic interaction how the interventions or noninterventions of the analyst tend to facilitate or to interfere with these ongoing processes within the patient.

Up to now I have conceptualized and summarized an extrapolated model of what might be considered the "classical case" process. In the actual clinical situation the various elements described (of the analytic situation, of the therapeutic alliance, and of the transference neurosis) may show considerable variation from case to case.

Some of the variability may arise from factors within the analyst, and the impact upon the process of such issues as inadequate understanding, lack of clinical experience, personal analytic style, or persistent countertransference conflicts (which, while well-known to experienced analysts, must be documented for candidates). Even assuming optimal functioning of the analyst, there will still be considerable variation in, and possible disagreement about, whatever specific interventions he makes in the analytic process; and conceptualization for the student of what is an analytic process must allow for individuality of style, technique, and understanding.

Greater degrees of variation result from the patient and the specific influences of his psychopathology upon the unfolding of the psychoanalytic process. There may be specific conflicts which interfere with his ability to assume the role of the analysand in establishing the analytic situation. In some cases intense transference expectations and behavior patterns may block the development of the therapeutic alliance (i.e., narcissistic personality structure, inability to experience basic trust, etc.), and its emergence as ·a genuine component of the analytic process may occur only late in the treatment course. In other cases the nature of the major fixations will determine which transference conflicts will predominate and will affect the rate and sequence of their development as manifest transference behaviors. The degree and intensity to which a regressive transference neurosis develops is another patient variable, and in cases where its presence is minimal, highly inferential, or emotionally remote, the question is frequently raised, "Was this a true analysis?" And it is difficult to define a level of manifest transference intensity which distinguishes a genuine analytic from a nonanalytic therapeutic process. But for the student's optimal learning, these issues must be illustrated from clinical material in such a way that general conceptualizations can be developed while still allowing for individual variation.

As described previously, the goal of the psychoanalytic process is the progressive production of intrapsychic change in the patient's derivative and core psychic functioning, in an attempt to modify those psychic structures which had produced or sustained the various neurotic adaptations which prevented spontaneous maturation. It is not possible here to develop in detail a conceptualization of structural intrapsychic change, but since one of our teaching goals is a cognitive understanding of the relationship between clinical phenomenology and metapsychological inference, and since we also hope to develop within the student a metapsychological conceptualization of the psychoanalytic process, a few words about the process of change may be appropriate.

Operation of the core psychic structures might be schematically conceptualized as follows. The infantile and early childhood drive organization is accompanied and expressed by a variety of fantasies and object choices organized in accordance with the primary process and the pleasure principle. Simultaneously, there develop a variety of primitive superego fantasies associated with the particular drive and/or object choice. There also exist multiple primitive ego fantasies of dangerous or traumatic situations associated with the drives and superego demands, resulting from the immaturity of the ego and the incomplete development of reality testing at the time of the original conflict. The ego perceptions of danger or of superego threat evoke a variety of affective responses, and as a defense against these painful affects there occurs the development of automatic defensive and/or adaptive ego responses. The entire complex is structured in the sense that stimulation of a particular drive or conflict sets in motion the relatively fixed and automatic associated sequence of psychic operations. Multiple derivative structural sequences may be built upon the basic core in an increasingly elaborate, complex, and layered fashion, and, particularly following repression of the core conflicts and the structures evolving from them, their continuing active dynamic effects are manifest in multiple aspects of derivative personality structure.

Structural change may potentially occur at any point in these sequences of psychic operations. Initially, change begins at derivative levels, but as the full-blown regressive transference neurosis unfolds, change is increasingly sought at the core level.

This potential for change arises from the fact that the regressive transference phenomena occur in an individual who simultaneously maintains adult, rational, self-observing, reality-oriented, and integrative ego functions which he can apply to the resolution of the transference conflicts and experiences in the working-through process.

The instinctual drives themselves cannot be qualitatively changed, but increasingly conscious awareness of the drives, the objects upon which they are focused, and the fantasies by which they are expressed can lead to a quantitative redistribution of their relative importance. As there occurs an exploration of the various archaic superego fantasies and expectations, and as these are subjected to secondary-process awareness and judgments, a change in the nature and intensity of these component forces becomes possible. The same process of judgment and reality testing may be applied to the various nonmoralistic ego perceptions of childhood danger situations, with resulting modification in the degree to which they are now perceived as dangerous and therefore in their impact upon the personality. This same type of change may also occur in the ego's scanning of the environment for objects upon whom drives can be discharged, with a more conscious and rational selection of age-appropriate conflict-free objects, thereby again modifying stereotyped, unconscious object choices.

Another potential for change is an increased tolerance of unpleasurable affects such as anxiety, depression, guilt, shame, etc., thereby reducing the immediate and unconsciously automatic use of defense mechanisms to eliminate these affective signals. The patient can also increase his tolerance of the frustration of ungratified instinctual drives, thereby reducing the automatically impelling and motivating power that such forces induce. And, finally, another potential point of change is in the choice of defensive and adaptive ego mechanisms used by the individual to cope with the unpleasurable affect states, replacing them by consciously selected ones more in keeping with the secondary process and the reality principle. Such a shift of defensive, integrative, and synthetic mechanisms can permit more effective and less disabling states of adaptation to irresolvable conflict.

The opportunity for the patient to achieve an increment of structural change in basic personality forces exists as a result of the modification of any one of the various elements in the automatic, previously unconscious sequence described above. In the more effective analytic situations, modification occurs in several or all elements in the structured sequence, although the degree of change may vary from one to another. The analyst's equal interest in promoting therapeutic change in all of the different component elements of these structured responses encourages the patient to try to achieve a maximal degree of modification as he applies his deepening insight in the working-through process.

During the process of therapy it is frequently necessary that one structural element be modified (i.e., a defensive function of the ego), as a prerequisite step before change in another component function in the sequence can occur (for example, the emergence into consciousness of an unconscious fantasy of a danger situation, which can then be dissolved by the process of adult reality testing). In some instances change results from the reduction in intensity or the elimination of one or more elements in the structured sequence of responses. In other instances, old structures are not only reduced or resolved, but also may be replaced by new, more mature, and more effective structured sequences and responses. Such change may be reflected in a particular or specific area of function, but in other cases the change may be more global in the total integration of characteristic behavior patterns, states of consciousness, or modes of conflict resolution.

During the analysis itself, analyst and patient are primarily occupied with attempts at modifying the specific individual microstructures which comprise the stereotyped sequential elements related to any one particular psychic conflict. As a result of the cumulative effect of work focused at the level of particular microstructures, and as a result of the potential for using one specific conflict solution as a prototype for the resolution of other similar conflicts, there occurs a corresponding modification in the organization of the various macrostructures as well.

The psychoanalytic process facilitates such progressive changes in a variety of ways. As a result of the continuing interactions between patient and analyst, there is developed the therapeutic alliance and, with the increasing regression in the service of the therapeutic task and the optimal level of transference abstinence, the unfolding of the transference neurosis. With the developing transference neurosis, the patient experiences increasingly regressive levels or layers of psychic conflict, expressed in behavior which is structured as a repetition of old conflict states in the transference wishes and distortions of the analyst and the analytic relationship. The various transference behaviors, perceptions, and conflicts are subsequently analyzed, initially by the analyst, into their individual component microstructural parts. When the analyst intervenes to block or to interpret the operation of a resistance, he tacitly encourages the patient to identify with him in the therapeutic alliance and to try to decrease the intensity or automatic nature of its use. When the analyst interprets a previously unconscious wish, fantasy, or expectation, he also tacitly encourages the patient to identify with him and to apply conscious secondary-process, reality-oriented ego judgments to the contents in question. By maintaining the analytic situation, he provides a model for the firm distinction between thought and action, and for the increased willingness to tolerate unpleasurable affects.

Simultaneously, or in various sequences of oscillation between self-observation and emotional experience, the patient in the therapeutic alliance and with the expanding insight provided by the analyst's interpretations observes the phenomenology and implications of his transference behaviors as these represent prototypically structured responses. From the viewpoint of the secondary process, the reality principle, his current life status, objects, and opportunities, his increased ego resources and potentialities for problem solving, and his increasing expansion of self-awareness, the patient applies these ego functions to the task of working through and thereby gradually modifying, eliminating, or replacing the previously pathogenic psychic structures.

The analytic candidate must develop not only a metapsychological conceptualization of the changes that he anticipates analysis will produce, but also the observational skills necessary to assess and evaluate this process of intrapsychic change and his interventions and responses to it, and he must correlate his clinical phenomenological observations with metapsychological conceptualizations.

In the literature there are frequent references to the idea that the analyst's function is to facilitate the development, elaboration, and ultimate resolution of the transference neurosis "through interpretation alone." It may therefore be important here to emphasize other aspects of the analyst's function which are not so clearly enunciated as part of the process, as the patient struggles with acquisition of insight and working through of conflict.

Inevitably, some of the analyst's personal characteristics as a real person will be discernible by the patient, and depending upon how they interlock with the patient's personality and pathology they may impinge upon the interactions between them. The analyst's physical presence in a silently listening role can offer a large measure of emotional support to the patient. Verbalization to a person who shows by his interventions that he can empathically share and understand conflictual and painful experiences tends to relieve the patient of the sense of alienation and loneliness which he felt at the time of the original conflicts. The frequency and duration of the sessions, with the anticipation of soon being with someone who will at least attempt a nonjudgmental understanding, offers an important emotional gratification and encouragement to the patient.

I have already mentioned the analyst's presentation of himself to be used by the patient as a transference object, and the behavior by which he manifests his capacity to accept and tolerate the patient's various transference distortions of him without personal need to correct them. And I have stressed the importance of his maintaining transference and countertransference abstinence, as well as his role as a model in the therapeutic alliance. Thus, throughout the entire process, the various behavioral manifestations of his professional commitment to the analysis and to the progress of his patient play an important role.

Although he seeks to avoid direct suggestion to the patient regarding behavior or thought processes, the analyst nevertheless exerts a powerful indirect force of suggestion. His entire approach to the patient's pathology imparts the suggestion that coming to grips with psychic truth will offer a more gratifying and fulfilling way of life than the previously established neurotic patterns. In a setting in which he intervenes relatively infrequently, the choice of associations which the analyst makes in timing his intervention or the content of the patient's material to which he responds, will serve as a powerful indirect suggestion to the patient regarding the analyst's interest, his evaluation of the relative importance of the patient's material and behavior, and his scale of values. This issue needs to be clearly demonstrated to candidates who otherwise may not be in a position to recognize that at times the material which they hear from the patient is the result of a previously imparted indirect suggestion by them.

The significance of catharsis and abreaction have perhaps been depreciated since Freud's reformulations of therapeutic technique, but the analyst's capacity to encourage and tolerate these phenomena is another important attitudinal force in the psychoanalytic process. Catharsis and abreaction are not of themselves productive of structural change, but they are frequently necessary precursors in a process of desensitization to unconscious conflict which then permits its access to consciousness as the first step toward structural resolution. It is against the backdrop of these other functions that the analyst's various verbal interventions, interpretations, and reconstructions can be effective.

I would now like to return to the implications of these comments for the teaching-learning situation. The analogy has frequently been drawn between the clinical conference and the scientific teaching laboratory. The teaching laboratory is used to develop methodological skills, to illustrate didactic concepts in their realistic application, to stimulate acquisition of observational skills, and to acquire the principles of using raw data to confirm or modify existing theory.

I am emphasizing this issue because I feel it essential that we develop methods of teaching and learning which emphasize the difference between data and inference, and that we teach a methodology for checking on the correctness and "analytic truth" of the analyst's observations and inferences. We must also develop principles of methodology for the analyst's observation of the impact and effects of his total behavior upon the patient. Such an educational goal can also more effectively permit us to account for differences in style and technique in analytic work and thus encourage the development in the student analyst of his own individualistic style and approach.

In this connection, although it may in some ways seem artificial, let me say that in my opinion it is necessary to distinguish the psychoanalytic process itself from the analyst's functioning in it. It is generally accepted that, as the analyst listens to the patient's associations, a large number of mental functions occur within him simultaneously. In his state of evenly hovering attention, he is observing not only the patient and the patient's associations, but also himself, his own associations and memories, his own fantasies and affective experiences, his own empathic awareness, his own countertransference reactions, etc. At the same time, he is also developing a variety of inferences regarding his conceptual understanding of the patient's material, which may occur at various levels simultaneously. All of this silent internal mental functioning within the analyst is a necessary part of his role and skill, and he cannot conduct an analysis effectively without these mental processes occurring. However, only when he shares some of this with the patient (verbally or nonverbally, intentionally or unintentionally, consciously or unconsciously) does it become a part of the analytic process itself. At that point the activity in the analyst which is perceptible to the patient becomes a contribution to the total interaction between them. The analyst must then observe the impact of his intervention (or his decision to remain silent and not intervene) upon the patient and the process. He uses the data of these observations to draw further inferences and to plan for further interventions. Thus in the actual clinical situation an analyst's intervention may occur as the result of an intuitive hunch, a reaction to his own fantasy, a response to an empathic experience toward the patient, or as the final result of a carefully reasoned series of sequential thoughts.

But unless the student is to learn merely by imitation, it is necessary to find methods by which to help him recognize the various alternative implications, meanings, and levels of interpretation which may be drawn from the data at any one particular moment, and to help him conceptualize the process by which the analyst selects the intervention he finally chooses to make. And then it is important to demonstrate from the subsequent data and interactions of the analytic situation the impact and effect (facilitating, interfering, or neutral) of the analyst's intervention.

As mentioned earlier, the clinical conference offers a format for doing this without the pressures of therapeutic responsibility and countertransference forces that the candidate experiences in his supervised work. It is not only possible but appropriate to shift the focus in such a teaching exercise from a detailed microscopic investigation of some particular element of the analytic process to a broader macroscopic view of its longitudinal evolution, or to a metapsychological consideration of the theory of the process and manifestations of structural change. Ideally, there will be a continuing shift of focus or emphasis from one set to another, so that the student can practice and develop his integrative and synthetic capacities in such a way as to be able to observe, conceptualize, and respond to the patient's material at varying levels simultaneously. The ultimate goal is for these elements in his functioning to become autonomous ego functions in the analyst, so that he continually carries a conceptual understanding of the basic issues in the psychoanalytic process and his role in it as a background and framework for his therapeutic work.

The importance of this kind of teaching situation reflects the students' need to develop skills of observation and to differentiate between data and inference in the clinical situation. Various experimental attempts to tackle the problem of consensual validation of psychoanalytic inference and inter-pretation have run into the "six blind men and the elephant" problem. Even groups of experienced analysts responding to the same clinical material frequently show wide variations in their understanding and in what they would consider to be an appropriate response. The student must become aware of this variety of possible formulations and inferences drawn from the primary data, must recognize the potential choices that he has in response to them, and must then be able to observe the impact of his final decision on the psychoanalytic process. This understanding can also be useful in helping the student differentiate between the important or essential aspects of the psychoanalytic process itself, as compared with differing styles of technique or differing personality characteristics among analysts. The sepa-ration of these issues, I feel, can help the student internalize for himself a conceptualization of the essence of the psychoanalytic process, which he can then integrate with his own particular personality and style.

Another issue which I believe needs to be studied is the implication for the learning process of the usual phenomenon in most institutes that almost all detailed case presentations of any duration or depth are presented by candidates. The effects of the student analyst as a model in treating and then presenting his case, and of the teacher as an "all knowing" critic have not been fully studied. Most senior analysts do not keep extensive process notes on their therapeutic work with patients, and hence are not in a position to present the necessary detailed material which would permit the student to conceptualize the analytic process as conducted by an experi-enced person. There is also the issue of the defensiveness of some analysts in revealing their detailed clinical work to colleagues or candidates, lest they be subject to criticism and narcissistic injury. But the question would have to be raised whether candidates might more effectively learn about the psychoanalytic process if exposed to the model of the work of a more senior and competent person well beyond themselves in his level of sophisti-cation, training, and experience.

The analytic process is frequently conceptualized as having a beginning, middle, and terminal phase, and not infrequently clinical conferences are organized and presented in keeping with this breakdown. A beginning-phase conference would probably focus on the structure of the psychoanalytic situation and the significance of the various elements within it. It would also emphasize the development of a therapeutic alliance, documenting the roles of the patient and the analyst in facilitating or in impeding this aspect of the relationship. It would also seek to document the evidences of the beginning emergence of the transference neurosis, again focusing on the interactions between patient and analyst which bring this about.

A middle-phase conference might focus primarily upon the phenomenol-ogy of the transference neurosis and of the analyst's role and use of himself as the transference object. Involved in this would be the issues of transference frustration and abstinence, and of the patient's reactions to this, as well as his progressively increasing tolerance of other affects. The focus might also include the interpretive process with its impact on the patient and his subsequent progress in terms of the phenomenology of unconscious resistances, the emergence of previously repressed psychic experience and conflict, and the broadening and deepening of insight. It might also emphasize the utilization of this insight in the working-through process, and as part of the progressively deeper exploration and elaboration of the transference neurosis with its re-creation of the infantile and childhood drives, fantasies, ego and superego states. Included also would be an elaboration of how these core conflicts are successively modified and altered in various derivative forms, and of how they are repeatedly experienced in the transference relationship and also in the patient's current life situation. In this phase there would also be a focus on the therapeutic split in the patient between experiencing and self-observing ego functions, and an emphasis on the increased capacity for unimpeded free association and for controlled therapeutic regression in the service of the ego and the therapeutic task.

A termination-phase conference might focus on the shifting dynamic significance of the termination phase, with its emphasis upon voluntary renunciation of the infantile and childhood wishes and objects through the prototype of the analyst as transference object. It should document the accompanying mobilization of grief and mourning, and with it the multiple responses and resistances to the process of renunciation. This would include the changing roles of patient and analyst in their interactions, as well as the further working through, reintegration, and resolution that accompanies this phase of the process. It should also include the assessment of the degree of structural change which has occurred as a result of the analysis, and the development in the candidate of the various criteria by which such change is recognized and evaluated.

For the most part our teaching format has remained the traditional clinical conference, and the chief variable has been the individual skills of the specific instructor. And this format in the hands of a skillful teacher has served us quite well. But we must recognize that for most of the candidates the clinical conference is a largely passive learning experience with only intermittent periods of active interaction and participation. Educational theory and experimentation clearly show that the greater the sustained activity and participation of the student, and the greater his involvement in continuous problem solving, the more effective is the learning process.

It seems to me that as psychoanalytic educators we should ask ourselves whether our current practices in teaching the psychoanalytic process are optimally designed and functional. After examining our present educational procedures and evaluating their effectiveness, are we fully satisfied with the results for most of our candidates? Are there alternate or additional educational experiences which would improve our candidates' learning responses? Does our present clinical-conference format meet the needs of all candidates, particularly those quiet and relatively passive ones? Might "role playing" both as analyst and as patient be helpful? Can we develop techniques which require the candidate more actively to make judgments and predictions about the clinical material? Could we, for example, randomly introduce material from different parts of a completed analysis and require all students to predict what the proper sequence was and to explain the reasons for their decisions? Could our senior analysts present detailed material more frequently? Have we considered whether audio or visual recordings of analysis (recognizing the alterations which the recording process itself introduces) might help our educational efforts? If we are ourselves hesitant to make such recordings, might we obtain duplicates from those centers which are already doing so? Could institutes—perhaps in cooperation with other institutes—develop a useful central index of cases illustrating and contrasting the psychoanalytic process, perhaps along lines analogous to the Hampstead Index? Would it be possible to adopt such material for use in a programmed learning situation, thereby increasing active and sustained participation by all the candidates?

These represent only a sample of the kinds of educational questions that might be raised and possibly tested. They illustrate the ever-present challenge to educators to assess and reevaluate methods and goals of the educational process. I hope that these comments and questions can serve as a departure point for a consideration of some of the many issues involved.

BIBLIOGRAPHY

Ekstein, R. (1969), Concerning the Teaching and Learning of Psychoanalysis. *J. Amer. Psychoanal. Assn.*, 17:312–332.
Fleming, J., and Benedek, T. (1966), *Psychoanalytic Supervision*. New York & London: Grune & Stratton.
Lustman, S. L. (1967), The Meaning and Purpose of Curriculum Planning. *J. Amer. Psychoanal. Assn.*, 15:862–875.

The Training Analyst
as an Educator

JOAN FLEMING, M.D. *(Denver)*

For many years there has been a certain pessimistic attitude among analysts about the education of analysts. This has been especially true with reference to the training analysis. David Kairys (1964) comments on the dearth of literature on training analysis. He attributes this partly to the feeling that "the problems of analyzing within a training program are intrinsically insoluble and no longer worth discussing" (p. 485). Many other analytic educators today, however, are more optimistic, perhaps braver, perhaps more stubborn, perhaps more ready to accept the challenge of these seemingly insoluble problems. The First Conference on Training Analysis held in Pittsburgh in 1965 (see Babcock, 1965) and the Pre-Congress Conference on Training Analysis in 1965 are evidence that efforts are being made in this direction.

The Pittsburgh Conference was a unique event; it was an experiment in trying to define the educational role of a training analyst and the complications which confront us in trying to carry it out. That conference was organized to encourage free and open discussion of clinical data in order to learn from actual experiences what the problems are. We did not know if this could be done profitably. Nevertheless, we tried and came away stimulated by new perspectives.

Over the last thirty years, the struggles within and between our institutes have been based to a large extent on the proprietary power vested in "the right to train." This kind of strife indicates some basic trouble in our educational household. It emphasizes not just the importance of these so-called insoluble problems but the necessity to keep on discussing them. In this endeavor lies the preservation of what is good from the past and the nurturing of the spirit of inquiry with which Freud began his studies. Both the old and the new are vital to the future of psychoanalysis. Our profession has seen too often the unhappy effects of attempts to take one position and discount the other. The battles over orthodoxy, over what is classical analysis, over neo-Freudian inclusion of cultural and interpersonal factors,

Read at the Second Three Institutes Conference on Training Analysis, held in Topeka, Kansas, April, 1969.

actually are manifestations of the ever-recurring anxieties that develop when security and comfort are threatened by the strange and unfamiliar. It is up to us not to be intimidated by the famous "syncretistic dilemma" (Lewin and Ross, 1960), but to continue to explore the issues in this seemingly irreconcilable situation in which education is mixed with analysis.

The dichotomy "to treat versus to teach," which raises such difficulties for analytic educators, is more apparent in the supervisory situation than in the training analysis, but it presents itself there too. The issue is often seen as jurisdictional. According to this view, treatment is the territory of the training analyst, teaching the responsibility of the supervisor—and neither should trespass on the other's ground. However, since both therapy and learning can be blocked by unconscious conflicts, it behooves us to investigate where the blocks come from and how they can be removed, rather than to argue over who should do it. Analysts should understand these things better than anyone else; yet, in spite of the advances against cultural resistances since Freud shook the tradition-bound medical profession and the Victorian world of the 1890s, the history of psychoanalysis is full of repeated turmoil over these proprietary issues. Interestingly, it is in the area of education and government, Freud's two "impossible professions" (1937, p. 248), that the worst battles have been fought. Freud called psychoanalysis the third "impossible" profession. I hesitate to remind you of that because, if it is so, then educators of psychoanalysts (whatever their proprietary jurisdiction) are confronted with educating for the impossible!

Nevertheless, undaunted by pessimism and the impossible, I want to emphasize a point of view concerning psychoanalytic education and then apply it to some special problems of the training analysis. Stated briefly, *the overall goal of psychoanalytic training should be to make self-analytic skills readily available for working as an analyst:* "each phase of the training program contributes in special ways to this overall goal, and each psychoanalytic teacher can enhance his effectiveness if he orients the content and method of his teaching in this direction" (Fleming and Benedek, 1966, p. 34). This point of view is not new. Freud described it in 1910, and others have followed him. The Pittsburgh Conference report is very explicit about self-analysis as an educational goal and the training analyst as an educator as well as a therapist of an analyst-to-be. In this paper I want to examine in greater depth some of the linkages between learning and therapy, integrating the treatment goals of the training analysis with other educational objectives.

In preparing this paper, I returned to the early history of psychoanalysis, attempting to trace the concept of the analytic experience as an essential part of learning to become an analyst. In 1910 Freud (p. 145) specifically connected the growing evidence of countertransference as the reason for his first recommendation that a prospective analyst begin with a self-analysis. In this recommendation I believe Freud was referring to his own experience in analyzing himself, which he described in his letters to Fliess (1954).

Freud recognized the necessity for analysis with an experienced analyst (1912) and in 1937 made his strongest statement about self-analytic skills and the educational role of the training analyst.

It is tempting to present the evolution of Freud's thinking as revealed in his writings over the years, but I would rather proceed to the more specific problems which a training analyst encounters in his educational role and which make a training analysis different from a non-training analysis.

In Freud's final statement (1937) about how to become an analyst, he stressed the need for a therapeutic experience and for a never-ending self-scrutiny in order to manage the inevitable countertransferences which confront an analyst. This correlation between countertransference, a training analysis, and an ongoing self-analysis may seem very clear to us today; nevertheless, although countertransference was recognized, its investigation was neglected for over thirty years (Racker, 1968, p. 3), and self-analysis was hardly a term in our vocabulary until after the publication of the letters to Fliess in 1950. Training analysis has become an institution, but its therapeutic role has been emphasized to the exclusion of anything else, and its specific educational contribution and the special problems rooted in its training function have received little scientific attention. This is in spite of the fact that the interfering effect of countertransference on both the therapeutic alliance and the transference neurosis has been generally recognized for some time.

Many of the authors who have written about training analysis have concentrated on the adverse influence of the realities of training on the therapeutic alliance and the transference neurosis (Gitelson, 1948; Kairys, 1964; Greenacre, 1954; A. Freud, 1938). These authors speak of "reality" as a contaminant which prevents the development of an analyzable transference neurosis. They stress the importance of separating education from therapy. Kairys would keep the analysis of a candidate from any involvement with educational and administrative aspects of training. Other authors, notably Bibring (1954), Benedek (1954), Weigert (1952), and Racker (1968), recognize that difficulties are presented by the training situation, but they feel that these difficulties need not prevent a good analysis. They feel the realities cannot be ignored but may actually be useful in working through to an insightful differentiation of transference from the distortions of current reality. Weigert says that "exclusion of the training analyst from official influence on the analysand's career indicates some doubts in the analyst's objectivity, i.e., his mastery of countertransference." Benedek (1954) discusses the so-called neutrality of the training analyst in terms of a conflict over being a good parent. She describes the efforts to remain "outside of the professional reality" of the candidate as important in the development of observable transferences. But she feels that these transferences often stimulate a conflict in the training analyst over the wish to be helpful and protective as against the fear of being over-protective and indulgent. It is her opinion, which Weigert also supports, that efforts to solve this counter-transference have resulted in an over-emphasis on educational neutrality and the significance of anonymity in a training analysis. In other words, neutrality and anonymity are important in facilitating the development of an analyzable transference neurosis in the usual therapeutic analysis. For a training analysis, however, these attitudes may reflect a countertransference conflict which can have a negative influence on optimal analytic results for a candidate.

I believe we can assume that sometimes such a countertransference conflict does exist. If we look at it objectively, we can see how it might influence the educational role in different ways. For many training analysts with this problem a strict avoidance of any participation in career progression decisions becomes the essential position. Others seem to feel that their knowledge of the candidate is better than that of any other person and that, therefore, they should be the sole arbiter of progression in training. These two contradictory positions have determined many of the educational procedures established by training facilities, both in America and abroad.

If we examine these attitudes as objectively as possible and in the light of actual experience, it seems clear that although neutrality and anonymity do have a favorable effect on the regressive re-experiencing of a childhood conflict so necessary for a good analysis, they may interfere with the resolution of that conflict. I believe the trouble lies not in the reality of the professional relationship or the lack of objectivity or anonymity, but in the failure to differentiate transference from reality. Reproduction of the past is not usually so difficult in a normally conducted analysis; interpretation by means of reconstruction of childhood events, including fantasies, is not so difficult either. The challenge for both candidate and training analyst is "to differentiate the realistic factors of the training situation from the crosscurrents of transferences and countertransferences" (Weigert, 1952). It is the confusion of the present with the past that distorts the perception of current reality. This is a phenomenon which must be worked through in any analysis. The difference between transference and reality must be experienced and then integrated into insight. I believe that in many respects this level of insight is more possible in a training analysis than with the usual patient. A training analysis offers sharper confrontation with the incongruity of transference reproductions, just because of the current actuality of training goals and the educational role of the training analyst in accomplishing them. This confusion and its differentiation can be better focused for interpretation. The therapeutic goals and the training goals may interfere with each other, but I believe that the actualities of the training goals need not be looked upon as "contaminants" in the sense of impurities which spoil or harm the analytic experience. I hope to demonstrate how the educational role of the training analyst can deepen and expand the therapeutic results.

If a candidate in the beginning of his training analysis possesses an aptitude for analytic work, he will be able to permit the regression in time orientation and secondary-process thinking which is necessary for a transference neurosis to develop. If good analytic work has been done on the way, the candidate-patient will tolerate this re-experiencing of a regressed ego state in the service of the analytic goal. Immediate, present-day events, such as the knowledge that he shares his analyst with a fellow candidate, can trigger sibling rivalries and other conflicts in analytically useful ways. Such reality events, in my experience, have enabled the patient to experience the warded-off affects more completely when I have not warded off the reality perception but, instead, encourage associations activated by the reality. The technical problem at this stage in any analysis seems to me to demand that the analyst recognize how the patient may be using reality as a defense against regression by emphasizing the unreasonableness of his feelings about his rival. At this stage in a training analysis, the patient may be even consciously avoiding reporting his thoughts and feelings in this area on the grounds that such reality events are irrelevant.

For example, seeing a smile on my face as the previous candidate-patient left the office stimulated a flash feeling of anger in an analysand. He reported the flash of anger when he saw me, but at first he could give no explanation and began to talk of an argument he had with his wife for letting their three-year-old son claim her attention during the night. This was a present reality event, too, but since the flash of anger was in relation to me, I interpreted his use of the event with his wife as a displacement from anger directed toward me. But I was told there was no reason for his being angry at me. For some minutes he was not to be diverted from talking about his wife and her indulgence of the three-year-old. Discharge of affect was in full swing in spite of the fact that his anger at her was not really reasonable either. I repeated my interpretation of displacement and suggested, without result, that he try to recall what might have preceded the flash of anger at me. Knowing something of his sibling-rivalry situation, I refrained from giving a genetic interpretation of the transference at home or with me. Affective discharge seemed more important at the moment, but he was resisting the immediate impact of the infantile reliving with reference to me. Consequently, I asked if he ever had any thoughts about the previous patient, B. To his surprise, he suddenly had an image of my smiling face as I opened the door to let B out and waited for him to come in. The image did not last long, but its recall permitted further recall of thoughts that I preferred B and would have liked to be with B longer, that I was not eager to see him next because he was such a difficult patient and would probably never make it at the institute, that B would get there first, etc. The anger had gone underground again and he was feeling frustrated and depressed.

I acknowledged his mood and pointed out that he was feeling things he had felt about his older brother in childhood. I let the anger at me remain repressed for the time being. As he recovered his equilibrium, he said that this morning's experience had taught him how important it was to pay attention to little flashes of feeling and to talk about them even when they made no sense. This incident occurred early in this man's analysis. I felt I could wait for further regression and transference development to occur. I did not feel that his integration of the morning's experience on an objective and intellectual level toward the end of the hour was altogether in the service of resistance. I thought of it as his learning an important fact of analytic work which would help him tolerate further regression in himself later and would be useful in his professional work as time went on. My thought was related to the educational goal of his analytic experience and my interest in his success. Perhaps this interest was a countertransference resistance, but, at that moment in his analysis, I felt his intellectual insight was not seriously interfering with his transference reliving but would strengthen his ego for further analytic work; neither did I feel any conflict over my pleasure in his intellectual achievement which would have actual value for him later. If I had been in conflict over my identification with my patient as a professional student, I might have interpreted his resistance against further transference reproduction of his sibling rivalry and depreciated his compensatory coping ability.

From this example of an incident in analysis which had both therapeutic and educational value, I would like to go on to discuss four problems which appear in a training analysis that are not present in the usual therapeutic situation. I hope to show that the exigencies of training when imbricated with educational realities have a bearing on both the therapeutic transference-countertransference interactions and on the development of self-analytic skills. These four problems are related to, first, the candidate's experience of being a patient; second, his experience in being an analyst also; third, his integration of the simultaneous experience of being a patient and a student-analyst with both a training analyst and a supervisor; and fourth, his experience in terminating his training analysis.

Probably the most important experience for an analyst-to-be is to learn what it is like to be a patient in analysis. This sounds like a simple statement, but as a therapeutic objective and an educational experience it has far-reaching professional implications. It touches on the persistent resistances of a "normal" candidate, on the special problems of a working alliance in a training analysis, on analysis of career motivations, as well as narcissistic character defenses. All of these topics bear directly on the development of an analyzable transference neurosis and, therefore, indirectly on the development of self-analytic skills.

To be a patient has different meanings, depending on many factors. Most patients are seeking help in order to achieve relief from suffering. Relief from suffering is also the most powerful motivation for cooperating in an analytic working alliance. Only a few candidates fall into this category at the beginning of the training analysis. More frequently, the ego-syntonic motivation is to accept the role of patient, admitting a need for help because they are "not living up to their potential." These candidates lack self-confidence but often resist a working alliance for a long time because the inevitable exposure of infantile conflicts threatens an already vulnerable self-esteem. Many candidates, however, fall into a third group. They do not suffer or lack self-confidence, at least on the surface. Their choice of medicine as a career is often determined by an idealization of the image of a doctor and even a defensive identification with the "aggressor" in childhood illnesses (Simmel, 1949). This group has a stronger defensive system than the second group. Their defenses are buttressed by the gratification of being the recipient of admiration and other omnipotent fantasies from patients whom they have helped. Consequently, it is easy to understand their resistance to the analytic pact. They experience it as "being put down" by the establishment which requires them to behave like patients when "this is really for training."

For them, being a patient is associated with a weak, depreciated image which, in spite of conscious ideas to the contrary, touches the deepest core of narcissistic investment in the self. Understanding the roots of this transference resistance does not make analysis of it easy. It is especially difficult because this resistance manifests itself in the early stages of analysis and interferes with the development of what Greenson wisely calls a "working" alliance (1965) rather than a "therapeutic" alliance. The goal of the alliance is the same whatever term is used, but the connotation of mutual cooperation is more accessible in the word "working." The word "therapeutic" implies passivity and manipulation and conjures up a sense of shame in being a patient. Unfortunately, this problem is more prevalent in psychiatry than in other branches of medicine, where a patient who actually hurts physically is willing to be passively manipulated if it will help. Even with these patients, however, the factor of shame and the feelings of humiliation must very often be considered and occasionally even become a livesaving matter, e.g., in the treatment of a patient with a coronary occlusion (Lewis).

So far I have talked about the phenomenon of the narcissistic resistance which complicates the initial stages of a training analysis. If this resistance is understood by the training analyst and if his own self-esteem does not need to be supported by a candidate's "submission" to a mutually projected image of a patient as being a depreciated object, then by his attitude and technique in enlisting cooperation on a partnership basis, he can gradually help the candidate overcome his resistance. When this happens, a very significant piece of analytic work will have been accomplished and a step toward restructuring a more effective work ego in the student-patient will have been taken.

For psychoanalytic educators the importance of understanding this problem cannot be overemphasized. It manifests itself in both parties to the analytic situation, and where it is not part of the training analyst's self-insight or accessible to his self-analytic work, it may interfere irreparably with development of an analyzable transference neurosis. This outcome blocks not only the therapeutic goal of a training analysis, but also the first-hand experience of regression and working through which analysis of a transference neurosis provides.

Such a derailment of an optimal experience for a student-analyst may not even be seen as such in a first round of training analysis. There are many circumstances which contribute to such a state of affairs. The evidence often does not appear until a test of empathy and self-analytic skills occurs in the supervised analysis. The supervisor may be the first to observe the blind spot or defensive reaction to the patient's regression which can be presumptive evidence of a deficit in the experiential learning to be expected from a training analysis. Such evidence is presumptive, of course, until the student's self-analytic skills are tested further by the supervisor. But if the supervisor encounters resistance against this self-examination, he can assume that a fundamental attitude toward being an analytic patient, i.e., an object of continuing self-analysis, has not been accomplished in the student's training analysis.

Partial awareness of this problem is seen in the selection criterion which puts a plus value on an applicant's insight into the fact that he has difficulties that need analytic help. This insight is assessed as a measure of his ability to become a patient, which Greenson (1967, p. 360) rates as a prime measure of analyzability. It may be a part of his conscious motivation for seeking analytic training. More often not. Other valuable information is obtained on admission by inquiry into an applicant's response to failure and experiences of shame and humiliation. Such an evaluation gives valuable clues to whether or not the task of "being a patient" will be a serious obstacle in his analysis.

Two clinical vignettes will illustrate the two sides of this problem from an analytic educator's point of view. In the first one, a countertransference in the training analyst probably contributed to a prolonged resistance against a working alliance and blinded the analyst to an early narcissistic defense transference. The analysand was just finishing his residency. A top performer in his group but with a long-standing sense of inferiority well covered up, he was given instructor's rank several months before graduation. At about the same time he applied for analytic training and was deferred. The reasons for deferment are not as important here as his reaction to rejection and the way in which his manifest attitude to analysis aroused a counterreaction in myself, his training analyst. He responded to the feeling of failure and shame with a sour-grapes attitude on the one hand and, on the other hand, a compensatory struggle with me to prove there was nothing wrong with him. In other words, he was not sure he wanted to be an analyst anyway, and, if I thought he needed to be analyzed, he would prove how wrong I was and frustrate me just as he had been frustrated by the Admissions Committee. The first thing I became aware of was a feeling of annoyance and the thought that the patient was wasting my time. I had accepted him for analysis under pressure from both outside and inside. To some extent, I was staking my *Menschenkentnis* on this case, for I had been willing to accept him at admission and here he was rejecting and defeating me. Not all of this recognition of my wounded self-esteem or my narcissistic motivations for trying to analyze this patient came into awareness at once or easily. But, by the time they did, the patient felt rejected by me, too, and was experiencing his relationship with me as being all too similar to fantasied rejection in childhood. For a long time all I could see were the defenses which he had used on many occasions when a current incident reactivated the childhood disappointment. Gradually, as I gained command of myself, it was possible to establish a working alliance and to interpret the transference neurosis which developed. I considered transferring him to another analyst, but it seemed as though that would only compound the difficulties.

The second vignette illustrates how deep-seated and unconscious the negative attitude toward being a patient can be. In this case the patient was an experienced analyst, in a second analysis, who worked hard and whom I considered an ideal analytic patient. The working alliance was good and the analysis moved along well. Imagine my surprise when one day he said, "You know, the funny thing about this analysis is I feel like a patient." With a shock I wondered to myself what else he had been feeling like and realized we both needed to do some work on "What's a patient?!"

Once the initial hurdles are overcome and the candidate accepts himself as a patient, the usual analytic work proceeds. If all goes well, the candidate experiences things that he has heard about and observed in patients during his residency training, such as resistance, regression, transference, etc. During this stage of his own analysis, however, he is usually too busy with being a patient to call his experiences by any conceptual name. It is during this phase that he learns to associate against resistance, to introspect, to tolerate himself differently, to objectify his own experiencing, and to assimilate painful truth on the road to self-discovery. These are the experiences that result in freedom from neurotic conflicts and in insight and structural change. They also provide experiential learning about the basic elements of the analytic method, learning which has a bearing on self-analytic skills but which will become more cognitive in later phases of training.

As the working alliance is established and the transference neurosis develops, the infantile roots of career motivations appear. It is in relation to the candidate's wish to progress in training that the training analyst's sensitivity to his patient's shifts in ego modification must be very keen and his countertransference responses (to use Racker's concept) must be conflict-free and reality-oriented. Such wishes from the patient may be seen as competitive resistance, as an acting out of infantile fantasies of taking father's place, or they may be more oriented to professional reality goals.

The analysis, and especially the training analyst, is put to a second crucial test when the candidate-patient becomes ready to move into a position of student-analyst. We must be able to assume that the training analyst can assess how ready his patient is to start analyzing his own patient. What belongs to infantile carry-overs and what belongs to current career goals on a realistic basis needs to be explored and differentiated. The Pittsburgh Conference report (Babcock, 1965, p. 57) describes discussion of these issues and states as a conclusion that "the best the training analyst can do is to learn how to assess the growth of the candidate's capacities for empathy and self-analysis, in order to help the candidate assess himself and come to a decision about his career." My remarks are aimed at a deeper exploration of some of the points to be considered by the training analyst in learning how to do this. For the training analyst to abdicate his responsibility for making this diagnostic differentiation and for participating in the necessary interpretive work is to abandon his candidate-patient in a crucial phase of his analysis—a phase that includes not only the re-solution of his Oedipal conflict but also the re-solution of his adolescent conflict and the development of a mature ego capable of reality-oriented self-assessment—a basic attitude and skill for the self-analytic tasks of his professional work ego.

When a candidate poses questions of career progression (matriculation, termination, supervisory conflicts, or even a return to analysis), he confronts his analyst with a problem of double vision. In an oedipal transference, one image is that of a child caught in the web of oedipal fantasies which protect him against the narcissistic injury of recognizing his real limitations at that level of development. The other image is that of a chronological adult who presents himself as a younger colleague with or without demonstrated potentials for analytic work. Both images must be looked at and perceived in the perspective of the transference neurosis and in the frame of adult reality assessments. This is the analytic task of the training analyst, keeping this third eye and ear on his own responses in each of these frames of reference.

If the training analyst backs away from taking a reality stand, the analytic situation is likely to become a replica of parental failure to help a growing child learn to assess the reality of his ambitions in the frame of his abilities and limitations. The evaluating analyst may be seen as a hostile judging parent, but let us remember that the parent who does not evaluate his child's behavior, who cannot say no, set limits, or express disapproval may very often not be helpful or understanding. Such a parent is not providing a good framework of reality, both physical and social, against which the child's knowledge of danger and limitations can grow so that he can survive physically and can develop coping mechanisms that permit behavior in tune with environmental and social expectations. The nonjudging parent may identify with his child and in his overpermissiveness actually do harm by failing to confront him with the realities of life, allowing childhood delusions of omnipotence to persist. The neutral parent may even have a destructive effect. No child believes in neutrality. Such parental behavior is felt as indifference or even, "if you are not on my side, you are against me." Many a patient repeats this childhood stance and complains, "you don't understand me," meaning, "you don't agree with me and see it my way." Experiences with an honestly evaluating parent assist a child's ego to develop a good sense of reality, tolerance for frustration, and skills for balancing pleasure and pain, frustration and gratification, and for integrating id, super-ego, and social pressures.

The candidate who is always expecting hostile frustration from his analyst, whether it be in the area of immediate gratification of an expected, even demanded, response or in the area of more distant career progression, is suffering from a transference resistance which distorts the whole meaning of analysis; he is reproducing a situation from the past which needs to be differentiated from the present or is projecting childhood fantasies which he has not outgrown or integrated into a reality-oriented ego structure. Unfortunately, there are immature, hostile parents who do envy and compete with their children, who, like Laius, are afraid of being displaced or surpassed by the baby Oedipus.

Unfortunately, there are some analysts whose narcissistic needs and other childhood conflicts have remained unintegrated and unmodified by insight. But, on the whole, analysts struggle with these conflicts and, in my experience, succeed in being fair most of the time. In assessing questions involving the candidate's career progression, the danger, as I see it, is in the analyst's not being able to say no when he recognizes interfering pathology or lack of aptitude. If the analyst stays "neutral" and "uninvolved," saying nothing either to the candidate or the Education Committee, he is shirking his educational responsibilities. Such analysts permit a candidate to progress when he should be stopped. They rationalize their silence not only with a cloak of neutrality but by a persisting countertransference hope that the candidate will "get away with it," or "get by," or change, or go back to analysis with someone else, etc. In my experience, the more an analyst's doubts, questions, and positive evaluations can be shared with an objective, like-minded group of colleagues, the better he can understand the problem, clarify the issues, and arrive at a decision with more confidence. Objectivity in these situations increases in the evaluating training analyst and in the group who listens and assesses all of the evidence as to a candidate's readiness for analyzing a patient under supervision. It is a learning experience for all concerned which, according to Grete Bibring, provides the training analyst with "helpful perspectives on his candidates" (1954, p. 171).

To my mind, a candidate's experience of how his training analyst participates in such professional moves makes a big difference in his attitude toward analysis in general and toward his future use of self-analytic skills. An honest, "I don't know if you are ready to start with a patient," or, "I don't think you are ready," or, "Yes, I think so," followed by, "And what is your reaction to what I say?" provide more productive analytic work than a dead silence or an interpretation which does not include the realistic elements of current professional ambition, or a statement such as, "You know I have nothing to do with your training."

At this point in a training analysis, the defensive countertransference of the training analyst is on the scales, since the patient will respond with elements of transference reactions regardless of what the analyst does. The technical problem is to keep the lines open for observation and to keep the training analyst's responses as conflict-free and reality-oriented as possible. Children are very sensitive to the hypocrisy that is evident when their parents ignore, or keep quiet about, or identify with something that seems to bring secondary gain. Patients are like children in this respect and can sense the hypocrisy in a training analyst who protests a pseudoneutrality on this subject. For, regardless of protest, I have yet to see a training analyst who is not interested in the professional progress of his candidate-patient. It would not be natural or human. The line should not be drawn on such a basis, but rather on the demonstration of differentiation between transference and reality for both patient and analyst. It is not important whether the training analyst writes a letter to the Education Committee. The important thing is the way he handles reality while simultaneously keeping the analytic process moving ahead. For the candidate who is not only a patient but about to become an analyst, too, the attitude of his training analyst toward the meaning of this shift in his identity can determine the candidate's own attitude toward the never-ending process of making himself the object of analytic exploration of transference distortions and reintegrating them in the light of current reality.

Let me refer you to Greenson's example of the disastrous effect of an analyst's inhuman ignoring of a reality crisis in the life of his patient (1967, p. 219). This student-analyst failed even to acknowledge his patient's absorbing concern and anxiety for her sick child. He was unable to recognize the validity of Greenson's questioning of his attitude until the third supervisory hour. In this example, not only his readiness to analyze a patient can be questioned but also the quality of his training analysis. If he had had any aptitude for analytic work, his lack of ability to assess immediate reality and to observe his own behavior in relation to the totality of the analytic process would at best suggest a poor prognosis for the development of self-analytic skills. Something in his experience as a patient had gone awry. Since, in Greenson's report, the student-analyst did not seem to accept the confrontation except with some defensive counterreaction of his own, one wonders if he would even bring it up in his training analysis. It might not occur to him in the analytic situation, or he might succeed in isolating or withholding the incident, supported by a rationalization that his experiences with patients or supervisors did not belong in analysis.

I have heard this rationalization used, after a candidate becomes a student-analyst, to explain why he seldom talks about his patients or his supervisors. These two sets of experiences are normally laden with emotion and conflict and, therefore, should appear in his associations. I consider it a serious resistance if they do not appear directly. If I cannot identify any disguised clues, I begin to wonder about something in my countertransference. On one occasion, my student-patient had begun a new case with a new supervisor. Early in the situation he talked about his patient and who the supervisor was, but he omitted anything about the supervisory relationship. When I realized this and asked him about it, he said with too naïve sincerity, "I thought you did not want me to learn anything from him." As we worked on this, he went on to say, "I knew you did not like him and would resent my talking about all he has been teaching me." Needless to say, there was plenty of analysis and self-analysis to be done here. It was true; I did not like the supervisor, which I acknowledged, but went on to point out how he was using this bit of reality to perpetuate a feeling he had had about his mother, both before and after she and his father were divorced when he was about twelve years old.

This example illustrates an important point for our discussion here: a patient's knowledge about his analyst can be used to support transference resistances, and the manifest way in which the resistance is expressed can fit so easily into the analyst's economic and dynamic state of mind that the patient's resistance is not felt as such. A countertransference blind spot can allow what in this instance was an important transference to go unanalyzed. I think the way in which a student-patient brings his supervisory experiences into his own analysis depends a great deal on his analyst's countertransference rivalries. In direct correlation, it influences the student's attitude toward the self-analysis of his countertransferences when he is on his own.

So far, I have tried to indicate the educational objectives which are inherent in the beginning phase of a training analysis. Learning to be a patient and being a patient teach a candidate the fundamentals of what he needs to know experientially about himself and the analytic method. Many training analysts think that a candidate should have experienced at least the beginning of his transference neurosis before he is considered ready to begin theoretical courses or to analyze a patient under supervision. They argue that both of these progressive steps tend to distract from an optimal concentration on his work as a patient. But equally important are the experiences of being a patient and an analyst in rapid succession, if not simultaneously. For this reason a training analysis should not stop prior to beginning a first case. On the other hand, there are educational advantages to its coming to a termination before graduation. I will elaborate further on these two points.

Being in analysis and supervision at the same time is a third major educational experience which needs analyzing. It provides situations of triadic relationships which are very helpful in activating conflicts of loyalty and competition in the student-patient that take him deeper into oedipal and adolescent transferences. The multiple triangles offered by these new situations stir up countertransferences as well as transference conflicts. Unfortunately, they are supported by the patriarchal organization of our professional relationships, especially in their educational aspects. I have already referred to several. I will mention, however, a very significant contribution which the training analyst makes to his student-patient's self-analytic skills. By way of his own attitude toward countertransference and by freeing his candidate to learn from someone else, the ground is prepared for the student to tolerate the confrontations of countertransferences necessary in supervision. Such confrontations can be accepted by a student-analyst when he has learned from his training analyst to look into himself with curiosity, to examine his own reactions, and to build not only insight for himself but understanding of the analytic process on the basis of his self-analytic efforts.

Termination of his training analysis is the fourth major experience as a patient which contributes to development of a candidate's self-analytic skills. After all, the whole training program is geared toward educating analysts who can independently treat patients by the analytic method. Therefore, it seems logical that his teachers will be interested in knowing how a student is able to analyze on his own—without the support of a training analyst and with decreasing frequency of official supervision. In this respect it can be stated that evidence of self-analytic skills is the most .significant measure of a student's qualification for graduation.

Interminable as analysis is for an analyst, the maturational value to be achieved in a termination experience cannot be provided in any other way. But working through to emancipation from childhood conflicts and renunciation of childhood ties is a phase of every good analysis. Is there something more in a training analysis? I believe there is. Specifically, this something more involves the opportunity for a continuing relationship between a candidate and his training analyst but on a different basis than in the analytic situation. Having worked so hard at being a patient, the student-analyst must now work equally hard at shifting to another level, that of colleague and friend. There are some analysts who say this cannot happen and some who say it should not. Both groups seem to me to sell analysis short. Their attitude says, "once a child, always a child, never a grown-up to a parent." If so, the reality principle is negated by both parties, and I believe the responsibility for the failure to accept the adult status of his "child" would belong to the training analyst.

The problem is a matter not simply of analyzing through to a good analytic termination but of being able to develop a new and different relationship, should circumstances permit. If the trouble lies with the candidate, the analysis has failed in some way to reach an optimal end point. If the analyst is unable to make the differentiation, but tends to perpetuate a patriarchal culture in the profession, it will be that much more difficult for his former patient to consolidate the self-analytic skills so essential for both the science and art of the profession. He will inevitably identify with the patriarchal image and all its burden of defensive countertransference.

Questions about who has the "right to train" will continue to sidetrack the more vital questions of what an analytic student needs to learn, how we can help him learn, and how we know he has learned.

In conclusion, let me say that I feel it is essential to continue an exploration of educational goals and teaching methods, as well as research into theory and technique. The two fields of investigation are more closely interrelated in psychoanalysis than in other professional fields, but, so far, the latter has absorbed most of the scientific energies of psychoanalysis. The scientific study of educational problems has only just begun. I say this in spite of the complaint heard in the late fifties and early sixties that "education" was taking too much of the time, interest, and financial resources of the members of the American Psychoanalytic Association, to the detriment of "science." It seemed to me then, as it does now, that such complaints were shortsighted and failed to realize that good psychoanalytic education for new generations of analysts is the best insurance for a steady scientific advance.

BIBLIOGRAPHY

Babcock, C. G. (1965), Training Analysis: *A Report of the First Three Institutes Conference.* Pittsburgh.

Benedek, T. F. (1945), Countertransference in the Training Analyst. *Bull. Menninger Clin.,* 18:12–16.

—— (1955), A Contribution to the Problem of Termination of Training Analysis. *J. Amer. Psychoanal. Assn.,* 3:615–629.

Bibring, G. L. (1954), The Training Analysis and its Place in Psychoanalytic Training. *Internat. J. Psycho-Anal.,* 35:169–173.

Eitingon, M. (1926), An Address to the International Training Commission. *Internat. J. Psycho-Anal.,* 7:130–134.

—— (1937), Report of General Meeting of the International Training Commission. *Internat. J. Psycho-Anal.,* 18:346–348.

Fleming, J., and Benedek, T. F. (1966), *Psychoanalytic Supervision: A Method of Clinical Teaching.* New York, Grune & Stratton.

Freud, A. (1938), The Problem of Training Analysis. In: *The Writings of Anna Freud,* 4:407–425. New York: International Universities Press, 1968.

Freud, S. (1954), *The Origins of Psychoanalysis: Letters to W. Fliess, Drafts and Notes 1887–1902.* Marie Bonaparte, Anna Freud, and Ernst Kris, Eds. New York: Basic Books.

—— (1910), The Future Prospects of Psychoanalytic Therapy. *Standard Edition,* 11:141–151. London: Hogarth, 1957.

—— (1912), Recommendations to Physicians Practicing Psychoanalysis. *Standard Edition,* 12:111–120. London: Hogarth, 1958.

—— (1914), On the History of the Psychoanalytic Movement. *Standard Edition,* 14:7–66. London: Hogarth, 1957.

—— (1937), Analysis Terminable and Interminable. *Standard Edition,* 23:210–253. London: Hogarth, 1964.

Gitelson, M. (1948), Problems of Psychoanalytic Training. *Psychoanal. Quart.,* 17:198–211.

Greenacre, P. (1954), The Role of Transference. *J. Amer. Psychoanal. Assn.,* 2:671–684.

Greenson, R. R. (1965), The Working Alliance and the Transference Neurosis. *Psychoanal. Quart.,* 34:155–181.

—— (1967), *The Technique and Practice of Psychoanalysis.* New York: International Universities Press.

Heiman, P. (1954), Problems of the Training Analysis. *Internat. J. Psycho-Anal.*, 35:163–168.

Kairys, D. (1964), The Training Analysis; A Critical Review of the Literature and a Controversial Proposal. *Psychoanal. Quart.*, 33:485–512.

Kramer, M. (1959), On the Continuation of the Analytic Process After Psychoanalysis (a Self-Observation). *Internat. J. Psycho-Anal.*, 40:17–25.

Lewis, H. (1964), Personal Communication.

Lewin, B. D., and Ross, H. (1960), *Psychoanalytic Education in the United States.* New York: W. W. Norton.

Racker, H. (1968), *Transference and Countertransference.* New York: International Universities Press, 1968.

Simmel, E. (1949), The "Doctor Game," Illness and the Profession of Medicine. In: *The Psychoanalytic Reader.* R. Fliess, Ed. New York: International Universities Press, 291–305.

Ticho, G. (1967), On Self-Analysis. *Internat. J. Psychol-Anal.*, 48:2, 308–318.

Tower, L. E. (1956), Countertransference. *J. Amer. Psychoanal. Assn.*, 4:224–255.

Weigert, E. (1952), Contribution to the Problem of Terminating Psychoanalysis. *Psychoanal. Quart.*, 21:465–480.

VI

HISTORY OF
PSYCHOANALYSIS

Freud's Novelas Ejemplares

in which are related the pica-
resque adventures of the ingeni-
ous hidalgo Don Cipion Freud
in the city of Seville: with fur-
ther comments on the Academia
Castellana and Miguel de Cer-
vantes Saavedra

JOHN E. GEDO, M.D. *and*
ERNEST S. WOLF, M.D. (*Chicago*)

I

"When I was a young student, the desire to read the immortal *Don Quixote* in the original of Cervantes led me to learn, untaught, the lovely Castilian tongue"[1] (Freud, 1923, p. 289). It was in these proud words that Freud recalled in 1923 how, more than five decades earlier, he had, "*sin maestros*," embarked on his first independent intellectual exploration. The self-proclaimed *conquistador* of the *terrae incognitae* of the mind took his maiden voyage in the wake of Miguel de Cervantes Saavedra; like his admired predecessor, Columbus, he reached safe harbor at Seville. In this essay, we shall attempt to trace the route of this journey and to make an inventory of the treasures he brought back from this New World.

The deep personal significance that *Don Quixote* had for Freud did not escape the attention of Ernest Jones (1953, pp. 174–175). It could hardly be a coincidence that Freud returned to this book as soon as the departure of his fiancée's family from Vienna separated him from his beloved Martha. Moreover, he urged his prissily reluctant bride-to-be to share his preoccupation: "But do finish *Don Quixote*," he exhorted her on September 8, 1883. He had sent her a copy while he was once more immersing himself in the adventures of the hero of his mid-adolescence: "While in the midst

---

[1] "Siendo yo un joven estudiante, el deseo der leer el immortal D. Quijote ed el original cervantino, me llevó a aprender, sin maestros, la bella lengua castellana." [Translated from the original Spanish by James Strachey.]

of the book today I nearly split my sides; I haven't laughed so much in ages. It is so beautifully done" (E. Freud, 1960, Letter 15, p. 44). His enthusiasm was by no means confined to Cervantes' humor, of course; for Martha, he specified the serious meaning behind it in this way: "Don't you find it very touching to read how a great person, himself an idealist, makes fun of his ideals? . . . [once] we were all noble knights passing through the world caught in a dream, misinterpreting the simplest things, magnifying commonplaces into something noble and rare, and thereby cutting a sad figure" (Jones, 1953, p. 175).

"A great person!" . . . Can we doubt that here is another instance of Freud's unusual capacity, which has been demonstrated in a number of contexts, to identify readily with great men?[2] It is essential to note that the identification is two-fold: not only with the wise and benign, yes, even loving smile of the author, but also with the ridiculous but noble hero. Freud felt like a fond father contemplating his offspring and seeing himself again: "we men always read with respect about what we once were and in part still remain" (p. 175). In fantasy, he was quite capable of discarding the adult vantage point altogether; in a letter of November, 1884 (E. Freud, 1960, Letter 54, p. 126), he reveals the source of his habitual address of Martha as his "Princess": "do you remember the condition the hero makes to all knights he had conquered? They have to walk to Toboso and kiss the hand of the incomparable Dulcinea. Now my six students are kissing your hand." Thus even the oedipal drama takes place on the *camino real* to Seville, rather than where three roads meet on the way to Thebes! And *this* is how dreams became the royal road to the unconscious, the dreams of noble knights passing through the world . . .

The struggles of his betrothal were not the first events which had made Freud enact one of Cervantes' dramas, and we shall have more to say about the circumstances which had impelled him to do so on a previous occasion. At this point, it may suffice to recall that we possess further evidence of the importance of Cervantes for Freud. He made several references to the novelist's insights into unconscious motivations, mostly put into the mouth of Sancho Panza, the "practical philosopher" (1901). He cited Sancho's awareness of the ambivalent significance of taboos (1912–1913), as well as his Solomonic wisdom in detecting a woman's unconscious collusion with her ravisher (1901). As late as 1920, he wrote Groddeck (E. Freud, 1960, Letter 188, p. 329) that *Don Quixote* is "the immortal prototype of every humorous novel"; earlier, he had written a superb summary of the heart of this *chef d'oeuvre:*

> The ingenious knight Don Quixote de la Mancha is . . . a figure who possesses no humour himself but who with his seriousness offers us a pleasure which could be called humorous . . . Don Quixote is originally a purely comic figure, a big child; the phantasies from his books of chivalry have gone to his head.

[2] See Jones, 1953; Lowenfeld, 1956; Schlessinger *et al.*, 1967; Schönau, 1968; Miller *et al.*, 1969; Gedo and Wolf, 1970; Wolf, 1971.

It is well known that to begin with the author intended nothing else of him and that his creation gradually grew far beyond its creator's first intentions. But after the author had equipped this ridiculous figure with the deepest wisdom and the noblest purposes and had made him into the symbolic representative of an idealism which believes in the realization of its aims and takes its duties seriously and takes promises literally, this figure ceased to have a comic effect. Just as in other cases humorous pleasure arises from the prevention of an emotion, so it does here from the interference with comic pleasure [1905, p. 232].

Perhaps all we need to add to this critique is the judgment of Leo Spitzer (1969) that Cervantes' narrative is an exaltation of the independent mind of man—a historical miracle in the Spain of the Counter-Reformation. Little wonder that the founder of psychoanalysis felt him to have been a kindred spirit!

Spitzer also reminds us of what a curious cultural phenomenon it was that in Europe *Don Quixote* became a book read in childhood. Freud's letter of 1923 to his Spanish translator does not reveal how early he had first encountered the ingenious *hidalgo*, but it does show that the novel had sufficiently impressed him before he was sixteen to move him to teach himself Spanish so that he might reread it in the original. Although extra-curricular language studies may have been routine in nineteenth-century Central Europe, self-instruction in what was minimally a seventh language for a boy in the gymnasium must have been rather unusual, to say the least. Perhaps the motive behind this strenuous effort is even more astonishing than its performance and underscores the vital significance that Cervantes had acquired for the young Freud. He had a need to absorb the untranslatable qualities of Cervantes' style and language, to take in the formal elements in their original purity. This intense interest in the aesthetics of literature was entirely characteristic for him; we can still sense his love for the *"bella lengua castellana"* half a century later.[3] Clearly, Freud's immersion into Cervantes had not been a child's excited fascination with an adventurous tale but an expression of the sensibilities which were to lead to the Goethe Prize for Literature fifty-eight years hence.

That more was involved than the study of literary style was revealed in a letter of February, 1884, to Martha Bernays (E. Freud, 1960, Letter 37), which describes the relationship to Freud's fellow student, Eduard Silberstein:

We became friends at a time when one doesn't look upon friendship as a sport or an asset, but when one needs a friend with whom to share things.

[3] In previous articles dealing with his correspondence with Emil Fluss, we have discussed the importance of the literary heritage for the adolescent Freud (Gedo and Wolf, 1970; Wolf, 1971). We stated at that time that Freud's letters of 1872 already showed evidence of his genius, both as a psychologist and as a writer. It may be appropriate to add at this time that his insistence on reading Cervantes in the original is an even earlier manifestation of that genius—one which cannot be precisely dated as yet, by the way. Eissler (1971a, 1971b) has also stated the belief that Freud's unique capacities stemmed from his supreme sensitivity to language.

We used to be together literally every hour of the day that was not spent on the school bench. We learned Spanish together, had our own mythology and secret names, which we took from some dialogue of the great Cervantes. Once in our Spanish primer we found a humorous-philosophical conversation between two dogs which lie peacefully at the door of a hospital, and appropriated their names; in writing as well as in conversation he was known as Berganza, I as Cipion. How often have I written: *Querido Berganza!* and signed myself *Tu fidel Cipion, pero en el Hospital de Sevilla!* Together we founded a strange scholarly society, the "Academia Castellana" (AC), compiled a great mass of humorous work which must still exist somewhere . . . [pp. 96–97].

Harbingers of Wilhelm Fliess and the International Psychoanalytic Association!

Mirabile dictu, some of the records of the Academia Castellana, Sigmund Freud's earliest creative efforts, are still in existence; Stanescu (1965) has summarized what has been preserved. There are seventy letters, of which thirteen are partially, and twenty-two entirely, in Spanish. Most of the letters are signed "Cipion," a number of others "D. Cipion"; in several the signature is accompanied by a code which stands for "dog in the hospital of Seville, member of the Castilian Academy," or some variant. (See also Stanescu, 1967. One letter has been published in its entirety in E. Freud, 1968, pp. 5–8.)

The fragment of the Freud-Silberstein correspondence thus far made public permits the conclusion that the two families were well acquainted. Whatever the externals of these relations may have been, they fade into insignificance in comparison to the psychic reality revealed by the dramatization of Cervantes' *Novelas Ejemplares* by the adolescent Freud. We gain unprecedented insights into the roots of psychoanalysis through Freud's chance encounter with the celebrated *Colloquy of the Dogs* and his twinship with Silberstein. Freud could still describe the psychic reality of this relationship in 1928, three years after Silberstein's death:

> Several years during my boyhood and youth were passed in intimate friendship, yes, even in brotherly fellowship with him. Together, *sin maestro,* we learned Spanish, read Cervantes—signed our letters to each other with the names of the two *perros en el Hospital de Sevilla:* Scipione and Berganza!" (Stanescu, 1965; our translation).

"Beloved Berganza!" . . . For over a decade Cipion Freud poured out a stream of friendly advice, biting aphorism, exhortation, and miraculous insight to his brother Berganza in the manner of the Cervantes of the dramatic moralities, the *Novelas Ejemplares.*

Perhaps the most fascinating aspect of Freud's captivation by Cervantes is the significance of this Academia Castellana. The light that the example of Freud can throw on the transformation of genius in adolescence may have broad applicability for a psychoanalytic theory of the formation of psychic structure; these aspects cannot be taken up in this essay. Here we shall focus on the particular psychological strivings which may have found their outlet through the formation by Freud of this secret society, i.e., the manner in which *Don Quixote* and some of the *Novelas Ejemplares* expressed and satisfied some of his individual emotional needs at that time.

II

Freud's passionate interest in *Don Quixote* and his immediate elaboration of an intricate parody of *The Colloquy of the Dogs* into an independent work of art provide us with an unprecedented avenue of insight into the deepest concerns of his adolescence. The extent of secrecy surrounding these fantasy activities, the fragmentary nature of the clues from which their meaning must be reconstructed, and the unavailability of the full text of the Silberstein correspondence would discourage interpretation were it not for one circumstance: namely, that the works of Cervantes have such overt autobiographical significance. It is widely recognized that all of his literary productions are reflections of his personal experience, especially in their evocation of the land and people, in their descriptions of everyday life, and in their faithful reproduction of contemporary manners and civilization. Through his immortal characters, Cervantes is generally believed to have created graphic and deeply revealing projections of aspects of his own self (see Starkie, 1964).

With such autobiographical art, especially when actual correlations with events in the author's life are possible, applied analysis may legitimately arrive at interpretations of unconscious meanings. These aspects of Cervantes can serve as mirrors reflecting the conflicts of the young Freud who was so gripped by them, and who, as we have seen, identified with them explicitly.[4] It might be said that the Academia Castellana was the only "symptomatic product" (see Eissler, 1971a, p. 528) Freud ever created, so that it may reveal more about his central conflicts than his mature works are likely to do (see Gedo, 1968).

We may be able to discern the meaning of the Academia Castellana for Freud through the interpretation of the hidden psychological themes in the works of Cervantes. To facilitate this exposition, we must first refresh the reader's recollection of some salient aspects of the author's biography. Cervantes was born in 1547 into an impoverished branch of a distinguished family of Castilian warriors and aristocrats. He spent a lifetime of tenacious and honorable effort to lift himself from poverty, scandal, and degradation in spite of repeated failures and disappointments. Even the literary triumphs

---

[4] A more extensive discussion of the methodological problems of this type of applied analytic interpretation can be found in Gedo (1972b).

of his old age did not prevent him from dying in 1616 in real poverty, his hopes for the patronage of some discriminating grandee unfulfilled.

Cervantes' father was a physician without diploma "whose adult life consisted of dreary wanderings from village to village in flight from his creditors" (Starkie, 1964). Scandalous stories involving his beautiful aunt were the forerunners of similarly disreputable alliances by his sister and ultimately by his daughter, women "who made their living out of rich men" (Brenan, in Nelson, 1969). At the age of sixteen, Miguel, along with his younger brother, became a pupil at the Jesuit school in Seville; there is a touching testimonial to the "loving care and industry [of these] pious fathers" in *The Colloquy of the Dogs*. He first published some verses at the age of twenty-one but soon afterward went into exile to escape the consequences of a forbidden duel. After brief service in the household of a cardinal in Italy, Cervantes enlisted as a private soldier for the great campaign of 1570 against the Turks. He fought with conspicuous heroism at the pivotal battle of Lepanto, where he sustained multiple wounds which deprived him of the use of one arm. After his recovery, he participated in the capture of Tunis. In 1575, a galley on which he and his brother were returning to Spain was captured by the Turks, and he was held as a slave in Algiers for five years. He became the leader of the prisoners there; some of them came to regard him as "their mother and their father." He organized several attempts to escape with such tenacity and courage that the viceroy made him his personal property for better surveillance. These distinctions made it much more costly to ransom him, so that his freedom was not secured until several years after that of his brother. Their frantic efforts to raise money to free their two sons completed the ruin of the Cervantes family. After his liberation, Miguel therefore had no choice but to continue in military service, although his disability made promotion hopeless. He served in the campaigns to secure the Portuguese crown for Philip II, but he also resumed his literary efforts. At the age of thirty-six he left the army, and in 1585 he married and published his *Galatea*, a pastoral romance.

Unable to earn a living as a litterateur, Cervantes obtained a government job, that of a tax collector in Andalusia. His mediocre writings for the theater could not compete with the genius of Lope de Vega. His success as an itinerant bureaucrat was no greater. He became liable for a large sum of money embezzled by one of his subordinates, and this debt hung over him for the rest of his life. He was briefly in prison and lost his position, but around the turn of the century, in Seville, he began the first of his *Novelas Ejemplares*—the supreme example of the picaresque tale, *Rinconete y Cortadillo*. The first part of *Don Quixote* followed in 1605 and took Europe by storm, but this did not bring financial relief, and Cervantes had to support himself through menial work. The full set of *Exemplary Novels* was published in 1613, and the second part of *Don Quixote* appeared only a few months before the author's death in 1616. In the theater pieces of his seventh decade, Cervantes showed that he could learn from the example of his great rival, Lope, and he was thus able to crown his oeuvre with some signal contributions to the Spanish drama of the *siglo de oro*.

III

In order to place our discussion of the works of Cervantes into the context of their significance for Freud, it may be most cogent to point out that the very idea of a mock-serious *academia* is taken from them. The profusion of pretentious successors to Plato's Academy during the Renaissance was one of the favorite targets of Cervantes' satire; it may be recalled that even Quixote's Manchegan hamlet had its Academia of Argamasilla. As Freud had taken the characters of Cipion and Berganza from Cervantes' *Colloquy*, it seems reasonable to assume that the Academia Castellana was similarly inspired by the Academy of Imitators mentioned in the *novela*; the latter actually existed in Madrid for the purpose of emulating the writers of the Italian Renaissance, imitation being the sincerest expression of admiration. The fatuity of such enterprises is brought into high relief in another of Cervantes' *novelas* through the contrasting example of the "infamous academy" of Monipodio,[5] a confraternity and "school," which prepared those who were willing to learn for the actualities of life in the city of Seville. This matter is of more than passing interest in the light of Ellenberger's recent suggestion (1970) that the unusual structure of organized psychoanalysis constitutes a covert revival of the structure of philosophical schools of antiquity. It would seem that we have all become members of the Academia Castellana!

The Colloquy of the Dogs is in its entirety a gentle parody and an extension of Erasmus' *Familiarium colloquiorum opus*, "a rich and motley collection of dialogues, each a masterpiece of literary form, well-knit, spontaneous, convincing, unsurpassed in lightness, vivacity and fluent Latin; each one a finished one-act play." (Huizinga, 1924, p. 156). Although the great humanist's excursion into satire was reproduced in a stream of editions and translations that flowed almost uninterruptedly for two centuries after the First Edition of 1519, Cervantes' return to this precedent was in itself an act of courage, as in Spain "Erasmista" was a term of opprobrium for departures from Catholic dogmatism. The *Colloquia* of Erasmus, in spite of their tone of jesting and mockery, constitute "a profoundly serious moral treatise" which puts forward a "passionately desired, purified Christian society of good morals, fervent faith, simplicity and moderation, kindliness, toleration and peace . . . " (Huizinga, 1924, p. 157). The literary tradition Freud had chosen to follow in his adolescence thus had impeccable humanist

---

[5] The name "Monipodio," the literal meaning of which is "a gang," suggests the merging of the many into one.

antecedents. In a letter of 1511 to Sir Thomas More, Erasmus had defended the "sportiveness" of his theme by referring to the fact "that the same was practised by great writers in former times"; specifically, he mentioned Plutarch's dialogue of Gryllus and Ulysses as one of his sources (Erasmus, in Huizinga, 1924, pp. 209–210).[6]

Cervantes *Colloquy* takes the form of a dialogue between Cipion and Berganza, who have suddenly and miraculously acquired the gift not only of speech but also of reason, "whereas the difference between brutes and men lies in the fact that man is a rational animal and the brute an irrational one." Subsequently we learn that we may actually be in the presence of twin brothers changed into beasts through witchcraft—but more of that later. At any rate, there is plentiful internal evidence that the life story of Berganza, which takes up most of the dialogue, recapitulates that of the author. On the other hand, it is plain that Cipion, the Spanish form of "Scipio,"[7] also represents Miguel de Cervantes. He is clearly asserting his identification with the great Roman commander, Scipio Africanus the Elder, conqueror of Carthage.[8] It is a subtle reproach to the fatherland by the forgotten hero of Lepanto and the assailant of *Carthago rediviva*, Ottoman North Africa. It must be recalled that twelve years after his crushing victory over Hannibal[9] at Zama, Scipio and his brother were brought to trial in front of the Roman Senate for alleged misappropriation of funds. How Cervantes must have longed to have been able to respond to *his* accusers about the stolen tax receipts of Andalusia as Scipio had done in the same situation eighteen centuries before him: as his brother was about to produce the accounts which would clear them, Scipio wrested them from his hands and in a magnificent—nay, *quixotic*—gesture, he tore them to pieces and scattered them on the floor of the Senate. Yet Scipio was no impractical dreamer; Cervantes recalled with admiration his aplomb when he stumbled and fell upon landing in Africa—to turn this omen to advantage,

---

[6] Plutarch's dialogue is an extrapolation of Ulysses' adventure with the sorceress Circe in the *Odyssey*. Gryllus is a talking pig, i.e., a man turned into an animal by the enchantress. Plutarch shows that Gryllus actually prefers this state to that of leading the life of a human being.

[7] Cf. Freud's slip from Spanish into Italian—"Scipione"—in his letter of 1928 (above, p. 302), which demonstrates his knowledge of this derivation. Moreover, one of his letters to Silberstein is signed "Cipion, *non imperador romano*," indicating that the connection to Scipio was of personal significance to him.

[8] One of the indications that this was a conscious and deliberate choice occurs in Quixote's paean to Dulcinea, whose merits are asserted in the face of her handicap of not being descended from illustrious ancestors like the Scipios. It should also be noted that both Scipio Africanus and his father before him had conquered Spain during the Punic Wars; it was at this time that Seville's Roman predecessor, the city of Italica, was founded by Scipio.

[9] Freud's choice of the secret pseudonym "Cipion" for himself betrays that his openly declared identification with Hannibal was ambivalent at best and more probably stood as a thin screen hiding his partisanship for Rome. This may account for his curious slip about Hannibal's Italian campaign, previously discussed by Gedo (1968).

he promptly grasped the soil with both hands, exclaiming that he would not permit Africa to escape him![10]

The story of Cipion, that of the life Cervantes would have wished to lead, is never told in the *Colloquy*. He had had to settle for the life of the sycophant Berganza; the last episode of the *novela* concerns four artists in the hospital who have been unable to find an "intelligent, generous, and magnanimous" patron. The dogs comment wryly, "most persons of this sort come to die in hospitals." The very name "Berganza" may be a reference to sycophancy; it is perhaps a corruption of "Braganza," title of the Portuguese duke who had a claim to the vacant throne equal to that of Philip II but allowed himself to be bought off with extravagant bribes. Compare this to the rewards for Cervantes' extraordinary efforts in Philip's service, for his intrepid insistence on fighting in the forefront at Lepanto in spite of a debilitating fever. Listen to Cervantes' self-disgust about what he had been driven to do by necessity, put into the mouth of Berganza:

> It is of [humility] I avail myself when I would enter any household, having first taken a good look to make sure that it is the kind of a house that can afford to keep and maintain a large dog. I then station myself at the door, and when I see some stranger coming in, I bark at him, but when the master comes I lower my head and run up to him, wagging my tail and licking his boots. If they beat me, I put up with it and, with the same meekness as before, fawn upon the one who has given me the blows . . .

We may infer that Cipion and Berganza represent complementary halves of an internal dialogue in the mind of Cervantes. Although on the surface the adventures of Berganza form just another picaresque tale, albeit the most refined example of that peculiar Hispanic genre (see Putnam, 1952), the responses of Cipion add to the *novela* a deeper layer which transforms it into something unique and without precedent, the record of a journey of introspection: "for it will be better to spend the time this way than in seeking to learn about the lives of others." It would seem that the youthful Freud read his Spanish primer with full understanding and retained its precepts permanently.[11]

Berganza's earliest memories concern the Slaughter House of Seville, where he served the "bullies and ruffians . . . without soul or conscience" who lived by killing, stealing the meat, and quarreling over the spoils. At

---

[10] Cf. *Don Quixote*, Part II, chap. 58. References to this book will henceforth be made in the following manner: (II/58). Because of the numerous editions of the works of Cervantes available at present, page numbers for quotations from this author will not be given. The Chapters within *Don Q* are invariably brief and make pagination references superfluous.

[11] An interlocutor in the *Colloquia* of Erasmus had already put forward the ideal of refraining from irreversible actions until one acquires self-knowledge (see Huizinga, 1924). The analytic principle of abstinence had thus been prefigured in the 1520s.

that time, the dog's name had been "Gavilan," meaning a member of a gang of rogues, and he recalls himself as having had a "dirty butcher's mouth." Fearing his master's disfavor, he escaped to the countryside, where he found similar conditions among the shepherds. He comments bitterly on the difference between these realities and the picture of pastoral life in romances such as Cervantes' *Galatea*. Cipion concurs with anguish: "it is impossible for people in this world to get along together unless there is mutual trust and confidence"; yet in actuality "the defenders are the offenders . . . the watchman robs, and the guardians kill." So much for childhood.

In the next episode, Berganza becomes a student at the Jesuit school of Seville as an attendant of the pampered sons of the mercantile bourgeoisie. This fleeting exposure to people of good will and honor is soon terminated by "a calamitous fate," as he is reduced to a menial job and put at the mercy of the household slaves. His indignation at human depravity boils over when he is required to act as silent witness to their amours, and he ragefully attacks the black wench who is in control of his food supply. Once more he runs away, but now his next master is a corrupt policeman in league with a gang of racketeers, an adventure that also ends with his turning on the unworthy person upon whom he is dependent. He then joins a company of soldiers on their way to foreign wars and receives training in the performance of tricks which permit him to earn his living on the stage. As the story proceeds, he becomes more and more self-assured and competent to deal with the world as it is; the incidents of his adventures parallel the life of Cervantes, with a period of relatively tranquil residence among the Moors and eventual entry into artistic circles. He finally joins Cipion in the service of someone connected with the Hospital at Valladolid, where the colloquy is actually taking place.

The turning point of Berganza's life, the encounter that changes him from a childlike innocent, ever hoping for impossible ideal conditions and filled with narcissistic rage (see Kohut, 1972) about the actualities of society, into what Freud was to call a "practical philosopher," is the discovery of his own origins and the acknowledgement of his true nature. An elderly sorceress recognizes him as the enchanted son of a fellow witch, i.e., a human being. This is why "wrongdoing and the speaking of evil are something we inherit from our forebears and drink in with our mother's milk"—dogs are not afflicted with these characteristics. When Berganza recounts the fact that he has learned about the mysterious delivery of a pair of puppy dogs by a witch, we are suddenly shown that Cipion is his twin by the latter's excited abandonment of the posture of the detached philosopher in order to speculate on "the remedy for our plight." Cipion quickly concludes that the story must be a hoax; the witch "was at once foolish, cunning, and malicious—if I may be pardoned for speaking that way of our mother, or rather of your mother, for I will not have her for mine."

At any rate, the sorceress gave Berganza the precepts by which he was to live: "always be as good as you can, but if you have to be bad, do your best not to appear so." In view of the fact that the old sorceress ended her days as a hospital matron, we are left with an uncanny doubt about the purport of the dogs' residence at the hospital. Throughout the dialogue, Cipion and Berganza are concerned about their tendency to be malicious but never succeed in curbing their backbiting, even when they decide to punish it by biting their own tongues. When Berganza commits the next offense, he reneges on this pledge with "today a law is made and tomorrow it is broken, and perhaps that is the way it should be . . . Leave tongue-biting to the devil; I don't intend to bite mine . . . what I want to do now [is] to refrain from biting my tongue."[12]

The Colloquy of the Dogs thus deals with the problem of evil: man's innate aggressiveness, his identifications with parental malice and corruption, and his narcissistic rage about the manifold disillusionments of life, especially those provoked by the deficiencies of caretaking persons. This existential dilemma can only be transcended by a few bewitched individuals who will be regarded as children of the devil by society at large—they are the creative personalities. The fate of those untouched by this magic wand of fortune is shown in the *novela* closest in theme to the *Colloquy, Rinconete, and Cortadillo.*[13]

These ordinary adolescents have escaped from backgrounds of poverty and shoddiness to make their way in the world by petty thievery and fraud. They are typical picaroons—lovable rogues who provide for their own needs with the innocent rapacity of animals. When they attempt to get by through these means in the Andalusian metropolis, they are promptly sucked into the center of a sophisticated mafia which regulates their activities, confiscates their spoils, and grants them a meager wage. Monipodio is the head of this efficient bureaucracy, the tentacles of which infiltrate every aspect of society. Everyone is corrupt, cowardly, cruel, and faithless. Rinconete and Cortadillo are incorporated by this Leviathan in spite of their desperate awareness of the fact that it will consume them in a short time. Such, then, is Man's Fate: the fate that awaited Miguel and Rodrigo de Cervantes in Seville, Sigmund Freud and Eduard Silberstein in Vienna—

[12] Cervantes is gently reproaching Erasmus through this device for having allowed himself to ridicule his intellectual opponents in the *Colloquia* (Huizinga, 1924, pp. 157–158).

[13] We have thus far been unable to ascertain whether Freud was familiar with any of the *novelas* beyond the *Colloquy*. However, a man who presents his fiancée with the works of Calderón (Jones, 1953, p. 174) is not likely to have missed these "settings for the jewel of truth" (Bell, 1947). Moreover, the Academia Castellana departs from the *Colloquy* in one major detail: in Freud's version, the hospital in which the dogs live is relocated from Valladolid to Seville. We cannot exclude the possibility that this may have been an unmotivated error based on truncation of the story in Freud's primer (the early episodes of Berganza's adventures take place in Seville, and therefore it may be natural to assume that he also ends up there); we prefer to believe that it represents a condensation of the biography of Berganza with those of Cortadillo and Rinconete, who make their way to Seville on the *camino real* through La Mancha and enroll in the Academy of Monipodio.

unless they could utilize some inner resource to create a novel solution for themselves.

The solution of Cervantes is presented in *Don Quixote.* The First Part of this greatest of cautionary tales does more than satirize childish literary genres; on a deeper level, it is an ironic signpost to the desires of childhood "to reform the world by force of arms" (Brenan, in Nelson, 1969), a memento to a discarded part of the youthful Cervantes, i.e., to his grandiose self. As Bell (1947) has concluded, "the main theme of *Don Quixote* was clearly the presumption of Don Quixote, the presumption of Sancho, the presumption of Cervantes, of Spain, of modern man" (p. 221). Freud, with his penetrating psychological vision, saw it (1905) as a comedy at the expense of childish reactions to the actualities of life. We can best illustrate this point by comparing Don Quixote's reaction to the primal scene with that of Berganza. In contrast to the dog's rageful response when he had been made to witness the blatant sexual peccadilloes of his masters, Quixote (I/46) reacts with total refusal to perceive reality. When Sancho reports that he has seen the supposed·Queen Micomicona "rubbing noses with one that is here every instant and behind every door," his master indignantly accuses him of slander. The girl has to rescue Sancho from Quixote's narcissistic wrath by suggesting that the "good squire" may not have borne false witness: he had really seen what he had reported, but this vision had been brought about by "diabolical enchanters." Every threat to the perfection of the infantile self or to that of the idealized parental imago is warded off through similar magical thinking. In this regard, the very name of the beloved Dulcinea is "rare and significant" (I/1); this magical private meaning is betrayed by its etymology—in old French, *doulcinée* signified a precious and ridiculously unnatural girl, *une précieuse ridicule,* but for Quixote Dulcinea is precious in all earnestness.

The personal development of the mature Cervantes may be inferred from his treatment of the theme of his daughter's promiscuity in one of his late plays and in the Exemplary Novel, *The Jealous Estramaduran.* In this work, a rich man of seventy marries a naïve fifteen-year-old whom he keeps in complete seclusion lest she be seduced by someone who can offer her a sexual life. An adventure in the spirit of the *Decameron* culminates with the old man observing the girl in bed with a young rake. He states his reaction in these words:

> My vengeance shall fall upon myself, as the person most culpable of all, for I ought to have considered how ill this girl's fifteen years could assort with my threescore and ten. . . . I do not reproach you, misguided girl . . . but that all the world may see how strong and how true was the love I bore you, I shall give proof on my death-bed . . . [in my will I shall recommend that] she marry that young man. Thus she will see that . . . I wish her to be happy when I am no more, and to be united to him whom she must love . . .

Cervantes then shows the consequences of this renunciation: instead of pursuing a life of sexual freedom, the girl became a nun "in one of the most austere and rigid convents in all Seville." The internalization of morality is shown to depend on the transformation of parental narcissism into empathy (see Kohut, 1966).

In the Second Part of *Don Quixote*, Cervantes summed up the experiences of a heroic life. The Knight of the Rueful Countenance ultimately learns to tolerate actuality and thus comes home at the end "victorious over himself, which is the highest kind of victory" (II/72). We know that he now stood for the author in the most explicit way, for he speaks in his own voice on the last page: "For me alone was Don Quixote born, and I for him; it was his to act, mine to write; we together make but one." As Bell (1947) has pointed out, in his *Journey to Parnassus* Cervantes addresses himself in words almost identical with those he puts into the mouth of Quixote: "Every one builds his own fortune and I have built mine, but not with the necessary prudence, so that my presumption has come to nought." Quixote only regrets that the destruction of his illusions has come about so late that it leaves him no time to devote his life to some better purpose (II/74).

Cervantes was fully aware of his own genius, however, as repeated references within his writings indicate, and he certainly did not look upon ambition as undesirable or a pathological trait: "men of low rank . . . raise themselves by their ambition or by their virtues . . . only those are seen to be great and illustrious that show themselves so by their virtue, wealth, and generosity. . . . There are two roads . . . by which men may reach wealth and honours; one is that of letters, the other that of arms" (II/6). He amplifies this list beyond the spheres of his own capacities through the mouth of Sancho Panza (II/8), who is able to prove that no secular accomplishment can equal saintliness with regard to the degree of the ambition motivating it.[14]

Victory over oneself therefore did not mean the abandonment of ambitions or the surrender of high ideals; Freud was correct in discerning that Cervantes had remained an idealist. It was his capacity to see his own ideals through a screen of wisdom and humor, i.e., his triumph over his archaic narcissism, that constituted his victory and his greatness. Quixote ceases being a ridiculous, childish figure when (II/17) he makes a distinction be-

---

[14] The successful attainment of seemingly unrealistic ambitions recurs as a theme in a number of Cervantes' works (e.g., the *novelas The Little Gypsy* and *The Illustrious Kitchen Maid*, as well as the play *Pedro, the Artful Dodger*). In each case, it is expressed through the revelation that the family-romance fantasies of a beautiful young girl have been based on reality after all. Cervantes' assessment is most clearly stated in the play. The voice of "rationality" is "all amazed at the imperious claim this humble girl is making, for though she is of low state her claims are all ambitious, and I marvel to see with what mad gusto she aspires to soar aloft and even touch the sky." However, the voice of wisdom, that of Pedro, the author's alter ego, replies, "She is right and you should not ridicule her. It pleases me to see with what fierce pride she brings her tools and drills her upward way. I, too, who am dull-witted have my fancies, and dream of being Emperor and King; why there are times when I rave and believe that I am master of the entire world." (Cf. Kohut, 1971.)

tween human behavior viewed from the vantage point of an external observer and its meaning within the intrapsychic world:

> No doubt . . . you set me down in your mind as a fool and a mad-man,
> and it would be no wonder if you did, for my deeds do not argue anything
> else. But for all that, I would have you take notice that I am neither so mad
> nor so foolish as I must have seemed to you. . . . All knights have their own
> special parts to play; let the courtier devote himself to the ladies, let him add
> lustre to his sovereign's court . . . but let the knight-errant explore the corners
> of the earth and penetrate the most intricate labyrinths, at each step let him
> attempt impossibilities . . . for to seek these, to attack those, and to vanquish
> all, are in truth his main duties. I, then, as it has fallen to my lot to be a
> member of knight-errantry, cannot avoid attempting all that seems to me to
> come within the sphere of my duties.

In this key passage, Cervantes conveys his knowledge of the road to victory
over oneself: the choice of an activity suited to one's talents and endowed
with the perfection formerly reserved for the self and its pursuit without
reserve or regard for external criticism. In achieving literary success close
to the age of sixty with the First Part of *Don Quixote*, Cervantes had
proven that the quixotic pursuit of seeming impossibilites may sometimes
bear fruit: for him alone was Don Quixote born—it was Quixote's nature
to act, Cervantes' to write.

The Second Part of the novel therefore celebrates the triumph of intrepid
perseverance in imposing an artist's vision on the public, as well as the
internal victory over his own archaic grandiosity. Everywhere Don Quixote
and Sancho are now received as famous and worthy personages; everyone
they encounter is delighted to accept their eccentric vision of reality, i.e.,
the *aesthetic* illusion, as an improvement over the naturalistic viewpoint
of ordinary people. The spokesman for this cultivated audience is the gentle-
man of Barcelona, who reproves those attempting to interrupt Quixote's
activities (II/65):

> "O señor . . . may God forgive you the wrong you have done the whole
> world in trying to bring the most amusing madman in it back to his senses.
> Do you not see, señor, that the gain by Don Quixote's sanity can never equal
> the enjoyment his crazes give? . . . may Don Quixote never be cured, for by
> his recovery we lose not only his own drolleries, but his squire Sancho Panza's
> too, and any one of which is enough to turn melancholy itself into merriment.[15]

The sustaining ideal of a vision of perfection is essential to the artist
if he is to have the strength to withstand the lengthy mortification of being
undervalued as a person before he has imposed himself on the audience

---

[15] This theme was more fully developed in *The Man of Glass*, another of the
Novelas Ejemplares, which deals with the vulnerability of the artist who has not
as yet created what his genius promises to make possible. The belief that the self
contains within it treasures that should be exhibited to the public, as in a glass case
or *vitriera*, is concretized as a delusion. Cervantes implies that his decision to seek
more immediate glory on the battlefield had been necessitated by his incapacity to
tolerate the tension between the estimate of his own worth and the response of
the public which—perceptively—failed to appreciate his juvenilia.

as a hero. As Quixote puts it (II/32), "to deprive a knight-errant of his lady is to deprive him of the eyes he sees with, of the sun that gives him light, of the food whereby he lives . . . a knight-errant without a lady is like a tree without leaves, a building without foundation, or a shadow without the body that causes it." There can be no question that Cervantes is referring to a part of his own mental structure. Furnished with such internal structure, he could even withstand the unbearable verdict pronounced on one of his characters by the latter's wife: *"Come me ve pobre no me estima"*—she despises me because I am poor. And where do these sustaining ideals originate? Once more, let us listen to the wisdom of Quixote:

God knows whether there be any Dulcinea or not in the world, or whether she is imaginary or not imaginary; these are things the proof of which must not be pushed to extreme lengths. I have not begotten nor given birth to my lady though I behold her as she needs must be, a lady who holds within her all the qualities to make her famous throughout the world . . . (II/32).

Sustaining ideals are thus self-created, albeit never by parthenogenesis.

Perhaps we have said enough about Miguel de Cervantes to provide some tentative answers to our problem, that of the meaning of the Academia Castellana for Freud; in any case, we must curb our own presumption before we embark on enterprises beyond our means. It may be fitting to close our survey of the universe of Cervantes by echoing the lines he wrote about himself in a prefatory sonnet to the *Novelas Ejemplares:*

> *Bien, Cervantes insigne, conociste*
> *La humana inclinación*[16]

IV

Sigmund Freud spent the summer of 1872 in Příbor; some of the earliest surviving records of the Academia Castellana were dispatched to Berganza from there. This was the summer of the disappointing affair with Gisela Fluss described a quarter-century later in *Screen Memories* (1899):

It was my first calf-love and sufficiently intense, but I kept it completely secret. After a few days the girl went off to her school . . . and it was this separation after such a short acquaintance that brought my longings to a really high pitch. I passed many hours in solitary walks through the lovely woods - . . . and spent my time building castles in the air [p. 313].

In the light of Freud's intense preoccupation with *Don Quixote* earlier in his adolescence, one is forcibly reminded of that chapter of the great novel (I/26) "in which are continued the refinements wherewith Don

---

[16] Noted Cervantes, you knew Man's inclinations well (our translation).

Quixote played the part of a lover in the Sierra Morena."[17] It may be inferred that Martha Bernays was not the first girl whom Freud had cast in the role of Dulcinea. Jones (1953) may therefore have reached a false conclusion in asserting that Freud had failed to speak to Gisela out of shyness: a knight-errant does not wish to converse with his lady; he needs her to embody his ideals. Freud's contemporary claim in a letter to Gisela's brother, Emil Fluss (see Freud, 1969), that "there was more irony, yes, mockery than seriousness in this whole flirtation" cannot be dismissed as mere sour grapes or concealment (cf. Gedo and Wolf, 1970).

Let us recollect Freud's own interpretation of the screen memory from Příbor (1899): the core of the conflict which gave rise to it concerned the temptation "to give up your unpractical ideals and take on a 'bread-and-butter' occupation." Implicit in this conflict is the tension between the platonic and a coarsely sensual love for women. In some manner not known to us, Gisela Fluss did not meet Freud's ideal standards; perhaps this disillusionment is echoed in Sigmund's depreciating reproach to her brother, "Oh, Emil, why are you a prosaic Jew?" On the occasion of Gisela's marriage in 1875, Cipion sent Berganza a scathing parody of Latin poetry celebrating nuptials in a corrupt Homeric style in which the bride is mocked for her "dull spirit," her "small brain," and her striving for petit-bourgeois goals (cf. Stanescu, 1967, Rogawski, 1970). At any rate, by the time he returned to Vienna in the late summer of 1872, Freud invariably referred to Gisela Fluss as "Ichthyosaura" (i.e., an extinct fish-lizard): the knight-errant had lost his lady through the machinations of wicked enchanters.

Although we have disagreed with Jones's conclusion that the outcome of this affair led to the repression of Freud's erotic impulses (Gedo and Wolf, 1970), we must concur with his view that it prepared the way for a decade of strict celibacy filled with scholarly pursuits. It was not until April, 1882, that Freud found his Dulcinea in Martha Bernays; after meeting her while she was visiting his sisters, he observed her from a distance for several weeks before approaching her with the verdict that she was like "the fairy princess from whose lips fell roses and pearls" (Jones, 1953, p. 103). We assume, therefore, that the traumatic disillusionment with Gisela Fluss had reawakened Freud's extraordinary sensitivity to the imperfections of his archaic objects. As Kohut has shown (1968, 1971), before the secure internalization of a workable set of guiding ideals, such failures on the part of idealized objects generally lead to regressions to relatively more primitive states of the grandiose self—the mental states satirized in the First Part of *Don Quixote*.

It is not possible to specify at this time the historical factors in Freud's early life which may have predisposed him to this narcissistic vulnerability in adolescence. Jones (1953, pp. 7, 22) has noted that his father's business

---

[17] Similarly, Deutsch (1937) in her discerning exposition of Quixote's adolescence remarks on the love episode with the peasant girl from Toboso as "the typical behavior of a boy in adolescence."

reverses caused the boy to be "disillusioned in a specially painful manner." He implies that Jakob Freud temporarily lost his son's esteem when Sigmund was twelve, when the father told the son about his humble submissiveness in the face of a crude anti-Semitic attack.[18] The severity of the problem was even more impressive in relation to women, if we may judge from Freud's readiness to form intense friendships with men in contrast to his hesitancy with girls. In his letters to Fliess (Freud, 1887–1902), Freud stressed the life-saving significance of the availability of a nannie after the birth and death of his brother Julius during his infancy. In his self-analysis he recovered memories of this woman encouraging him to steal from his parents in her behalf and of her dismissal from the Freuds' employ for her thefts (Letter 70, pp. 218–221). We need not belabor the disillusion-ment caused by the disappearance of such a figure; what perhaps deserves more emphasis is that the attachment to a surrogate mother at such an early age also betokens some disturbance in the primary mother-child relationship.

Whatever the genetic precursors may have been, it would seem that Sigmund Freud entered adolescence still searching for idealized parental imagoes and that he found what he needed in the writings of Cervantes. Identification with the great novelist's humor and wisdom concerning his own grandiosity as well as with the unworkable idealizations of his char-acters apparently permitted Freud to avoid the consequences of acting out in a quixotic manner—the episode with Gisela Fluss having been the single known exception. He followed the example of the *Colloquy* in borrowing strength from twinship with someone who was presumably struggling with the same problems.[19] Most important of all, in Cervantes himself he found a great man who had successfully overcome the consequences of a back-ground of poverty and degradation, paternal weakness, and female corrup-tion. The solution lay in the internalization of an austere morality adhered to through self-knowledge and self-control. Berganza ceased being a picaroon after learning about his real nature from the sorceress.

Freud was to make "learning about his real nature" into his life's work; the Academia Castellana thus prefigured the whole psychoanalytic enter-

[18] Jakob Freud was apparently in agreement with Berganza about the proper method for getting along in a hostile environment. Jones contends that Freud's admiration for Hannibal stemmed from the Semitic general's refusal to submit to the Romans. It should be recalled, however, that Scipio Africanus defeated Hannibal in the end, thus avenging his own father's disastrous humiliation by the Carthaginian at the battles of the Ticinus and the Trebia. It is all very well to admire good losers, but adolescents need to identify with the bigger battalions!

[19] Another permanent acquisition from the *Colloquy* became a regular feature of Freud's writing style: this was the employment of a fictive dialogue to express varying perspectives about some matter. We have described in a previous paper (Gedo and Wolf, 1970) how, at about this same time, Freud was incorporating certain stylistic attributes of the Latin poet Horace. Doubtless he made similar identifications with selected aspects of other great men; Goethe and Shakespeare (whom he started to read at age eight and probably soon confronted in English) may have been as crucial to him at other times as was Cervantes in adolescence.

prise. The role of Cipion, that of listening to a life's story and making occasional comments to facilitate the flow of the material, has left its stamp on the professional activity of the psychoanalyst. Even more crucial in its impact was the explicit purpose of the *Novelas Ejemplares:* that of the moral improvement of Man. If the Academia Castellana was but an unpublishable, juvenile Exemplary Novel, *The Complete Psychological Works of Sigmund Freud* constitute the greatest accomplishment in the genre in the history of the modern era (cf. Gedo, 1972a), and Philip Rieff's designation of Freud as the saving moralist of our civilization is clearly justified (1959).[20]

When Freud visited the Athenian Acropolis in 1904, he experienced an episode of derealization which he later interpreted (1936) as the result of his disavowal of the feelings of triumph and superiority he had then developed in relation to his father. Jakob Freud had declared, when the seven-year-old Sigmund had invaded the parental bedroom in order to urinate, that his son "would never amount to anything" (Jones, 1953). Cervantes would have known better: the small boy who boldly reverses the situation of the primal scene, a Scipio avenging the ravages of Hannibal in Italy, would have pleased him for the "mad gusto . . . to soar aloft and even touch the sky" (see above, n. 14).

And that is why the *camino real* from Pŕibor to the Acropolis of Athens traverses La Mancha on its way to Seville.

BIBLIOGRAPHY

Bell, A. (1947), *Cervantes.* Norman: University of Oklahoma Press.
Brenan, G. (1969), Cervantes. In: Nelson, L. (ed.), *Cervantes—A Collection of Critical Essays.* Englewood Cliffs: Prentice-Hall.
Deutsch, H. (1937), Don Quixote and Don Quixotism. *Psychoanal. Quart.,* 6:215.
Eissler, K. (1971a), *Discourse on Hamlet and "Hamlet."* New York: International Universities Press.
———— (1971b), *Talent and Genius.* New York: Quadrangle Books.
Ellenberger, H. (1970), *The Discovery of the Unconscious.* New York: Basic Books.
Erasmus of Rotterdam (1487–1535), Selected Letters. In: Huizinga, J. *Erasmus and the Age of the Reformation.* New York: Harper and Row, 1957.
Freud, E. (ed.) (1960), *Letters of Sigmund Freud.* New York: Basic Books.
———— (ed.) (1968), *Sigmund Freud Briefe 1873–1939.* 2 Aufl. Frankfurt: Fischer Verlag.
Freud, S. (1887–1902), *The Origins of Psychoanalysis,* ed. M. Bonaparte, A. Freud, and E. Kris. New York: Basic Books, 1954.
———— (1899), Screen Memories. *Standard Edition,* 3:303-322. London: Hogarth, 1962.
———— (1901), The Psychopathology of Everyday Life. *Standard Edition,* 6. London: Hogarth, 1960.

[20] Of course, Freud, like Cervantes and Shakespeare before him, was the inheritor of a great moral tradition of introspective humanism going back to Socrates. This tradition reached its acme prior to Cervantes in the *Essays* of Montaigne. The history of this tradition and its bearing on psychoanalysis will be discussed in future studies.

—— (1905), Jokes and Their Relation to the Unconscious. *Standard Edition*, 8. London: Hogarth, 1960.

—— (1912–13), Totem and Taboo. *Standard Edition*, 13:1–161. London: Hogarth, 1955.

—— (1923), Letter to Señor Luis Lopez-Ballesteros y de Torres. *Standard Edition*, 19:289. London: Hogarth, 1961.

—— (1936), A Disturbance· of Memory on the Acropolis. *Standard Edition*, 22:239–248. London: Hogarth, 1964.

—— (1969), Some Early Unpublished Letters of Freud. *Internat. J. Psycho-Anal.*, 50:419–427.

Gedo, J. (1968), Freud's Self-Analysis and His Scientific Ideas. *Amer. Imago*, 25:99–118.

—— (1972a), The Dream of Reason Produces Monsters. *J. Amer. Psychoanal. Assn.*, 20:199–223.

—— (1972b), Caviare to the General. *Amer. Imago*, (in press).

—— (1972c), Panel report: The Methodology of Psychoanalytic Biography. *J. Amer. Psychoanal. Assn.*, 20:638–649.

Gedo, J. and Wolf, E. (1970), Die Ichthyosaurusbriefe. *Psyche*, 24:785–797.

Huizinga, J. (1924), *Erasmus and the Age of the Reformation.* New York: Harper and Row, 1957.

Jones, E. (1953), *The Life and Work of Sigmund Freud.* Volume I. New York: Basic Books.

Kohut, H. (1966), Forms and Transformations of Narcissism. *J. Amer. Psychoanal. Assn.*, 14:243–272.

—— (1968), The Psychoanalytic Treatment of Narcissistic Personality Disorders: Outline of a Systematic Approach. *Psychoanalytic Study of the Child*, 23:86–113.

—— (1971), *The Analysis of the Self.* New York: International Universities Press.

—— (1972), Thoughts on Narcissism and Narcissistic Rage. *Psychoanalytic Study of the Child*, 27:360–400.

Lowenfeld, M. (1956), Sigmund Freud. *J. Amer. Psychoanal. Assn.*, 4:682–691.

Miller, J., Sabshin, M., Gedo, J., Pollock, G., Sadow, L., and Schlessinger, N. (1969), Some Aspects of Charcot's Influence on Freud. *J. Amer. Psychoanal. Assn.*, 17:608–623.

Putnam, S. (1952), Introduction. In: Cervantes, M. de (1613), *Three Exemplary Novels*, trans. and introd. by S. Putnam. London: Cassel & Co., 1952.

Rieff, P. (1959), *Freud: The Mind of the Moralist.* New York: Viking Press.

Rogawski, A. (1970), Young Freud as a Poet. In *Celebration of Laughter*. Los Angeles: Mara Books.

Schlessinger, N., Gedo, J., Miller, J., Pollock, G., Sabshin, M., and Sadow, L. (1967), The Scientific Styles of Breuer and Freud in the Origins of Psychoanalysis. *J. Amer. Psychoanal. Assn.*, 15:404–422.

Schoenau, W. (1968), *Sigmund Freuds Prosa.* Stuttgart: J. B. Metzlersche Verlagsbuchhandlung.

Spitzer, L. (1969), On the Significance of Don Quijote. In: Nelson, L. (ed.), *Cervantes—A Collection of Critical Essays.* Englewood Cliffs: Prentice-Hall.

Stanescu, H. (1965), Unbekannte Briefe des Jungen Sigmund Freud an Einen Rumanischen Freund. *Neue Literatur*, 16:3, 123–129.

—— (1967), Ein Gelegenheitsgedicht des Jungen Sigmund Freud. *Deutsch für Ausländer*, Jan. [1967]:13–18.

Starkie, W. (1964), Introduction. In: Cervantes, *Don Quixote de la Mancha.* New York: Signet Classic (New American Library of World Literature.)

Wolf, E. (1971), Sigmund Freud: Some Adolescent Transformations of a Future Genius. In: *Adolescent Psychiatry*, 1:51–60. New York: Basic Books.

Freud's Cultural Background

HARRY TROSMAN, M.D. (*Chicago*)

In order to do full justice to the scientific and cultural tradition to which Freud's thought is related, it would be necessary to cover a wide variety of topics. In this essay, however, I confine myself to those sources which are usually regarded as literary, political, or broadly cultural rather than scientific; thus I do not aim at comprehensiveness. In addition, the influences discussed in this investigation are presumed to have affected Freud at a young age, before he immersed himself during his early twenties in the scientific work of von Brücke's physiological laboratory. In the following sections I shall deal with Freud's link with romanticism, particularly as reflected in his view of nature, the political and cultural milieu of Vienna in the latter half of the nineteenth century, the influence on Freud of the Jewish tradition, and Freud's secondary school education, with its classical emphasis on Greek and Latin texts.

Nature and Politics

Men of thought who find a universe emptied of God fill the conceptual void. The mind requires a manner of accounting for order and energy, a regulatory agency, preferably impersonalized and inoffensive to empiricism. With the decline of the theological point of view and the coming of romanticism at the beginning of the nineteenth century, Nature was credited with the power previously attributed to a deity.

Although the adolescent Freud showed an early interest in the study of nature, this interest vied with involvement in another derivative of the romantic movement—the arena of revolutionary politics. The revolutions of 1848, the subsequent concessions to bourgeois demands, the tottering monarchies, and stirring nationalist movements made a political career a promising choice for able young men in the early 1870s. Thus nature and politics—the first a field for learning something of the world, the second the means for changing it—were twin enthusiasms of the young Freud.

Before discussing the view of nature in Freud's thought, I shall briefly consider the broad cultural movement we have come to designate as "romanticism" or the "romantic movement." Beres (1965) has depicted the relationship between the romantic tradition and psychoanalysis and has described the elements they have in common: "In Freud's writings on art, religion, and civilization there are thoughts which have led recent writers to designate him as a neo-romanticist. . . . I think the writers are correct . . . though I see no need for the 'neo'" (p. 409). "Psychoanalysis is one of the culminations of the Romanticist literature of the nineteenth century," wrote Trilling (1950, p. 44).

Romanticism is a current of thought which has a high regard for spontaneity and emotional expressiveness. It can be viewed as a revolt against the neoclassical style in literature and art that characterized the end of the eighteenth century. A shift toward increasing concern with ordinary people and everyday speech occurred in the arts. Forms became more experimental, themes that previously had been taboo were taken up. Nature and the individual were glorified, and a heightened emphasis was given to passion and sensibility, as exemplified by Goethe's *The Sorrows of Young Werther*. A positive value was attached to the irrational; psychological processes of an unconscious nature were regarded as routes to higher truths. Man was seen as complex, his nature as conflicted and ambivalent. An appreciation for the value of early childhood experience and the conception of an unconscious, hidden human nature were accompanied by a high regard for imaginative over logical mental processes.

Historically, the movement is associated with the political upheavals of the end of the eighteenth century, the American War of Independence and the French Revolution; both produced Declarations of the Rights of Man. Literary figures took up the interest in nationalism and liberation. The exploration of private mental states ("feeling is all," stated Goethe) encouraged an interest in introspection, the dream, the uncanny, and the supernatural. In its more extreme forms romanticism led to a suspicion and depreciation of reason, knowledge, and rationality.

The romantic movement was given a great impetus by German writers of the early nineteenth century, many of whom Freud knew well and quoted. The lyric poetry of Goethe and Heine, the writings of Jean Paul Richter and E. T. A. Hoffmann, of Herder and other folklorists, spread their influence throughout Europe and reflected a view of Nature not unlike a theme from Wordsworth:

> One impulse from a vernal wood
> May teach you more of man,
> Of moral evil and of good,
> Than all the sages can.
>
> [1950, p. 377]

Although it is not the intent to highlight here the romantic influence at the expense of the positivist and rationalist side of Freud's heritage, it can hardly be minimized. Freud was fully aware of the literary and philosophic tradition not only in writings of German origin but in the half-dozen languages he read. Goethe had translated into German Diderot's novel *The Nephew of Rameau*, which contains an explicit and unambiguous statement of the Oedipus complex, and Freud quoted the passage several times:

If the little savage were left to himself, preserving all his foolishness and adding to the small sense of a child in the cradle the violent passions of a man of thirty, he would strangle his father and lie with his mother [Freud, 1916–17, p. 338].

The conception of a hidden element in human nature and the dangers of blunting the emotional life were prominent in the writings of Byron— with whom Freud was also familiar (Jones, 1953, I, pp. 172–173; Reik, 1968, p. 648).

The romantic influence had even permeated into the psychiatric writings of the nineteenth century (Ellenberger, 1970, pp. 210–15). Indeed, it was in part as a counterromantic reaction against an excessive reliance upon poorly conceptualized, and vaguely understood, subjective states that psychiatry moved into a more organic and objectively descriptive phase in the second half of the century (Zilboorg and Henry, 1941).

In its excesses, romanticism tended toward one-sided attitudes: a repudiation of rationality and reason, a rejection of all artistic norms, a glorification of force, and a revival of pantheism. The latter became identified with *Naturphilosophie* and the German philosopher Schelling. But most significantly, the romantic movement produced an essential shift in the mentality of the nineteenth century through its emphasis on nature.

What is Nature? Nature may be characterized as anything which exists, anything which is apprehended by the senses but not created by man. In its simplest sense (and omitting capitalization) nature refers to landscape—mountains and valleys, the world of growing things, trees, grass, flowers, animals—flora and fauna. Nature (now occasionally capitalized, as in The Standard Edition of *The Complete Psychological Works of Sigmund Freud*) also denotes the creative and controlling force of the universe. Nature is distinct from culture and society, if not, indeed, opposed to both. Nature may be not only benign or indifferent to man, but also cruel and attacking. Occasionally, man-made artifacts which have some initial charm or beauty (such as castles and cathedrals), and which show the ravages of time and the effects of natural forces, are considered a part of nature. The ruins of Tintern Abbey as experienced by Wordsworth became transformed into a natural object.

To the romantics, the state of nature, though primordial, was the fullest expression of man's being; as man grew, his increasing involvements with a world unrelated to nature were anticlimactic, if not corruptive. Civilized man could only strive for the reattainment of his original unity with natural forces. The Philosophy of Nature promulgated by Schelling supported a belief in the indissoluble unity of natural and spiritual forces. Nature, it was suggested, could not be understood in terms of mechanical or physical concepts. The organic and visible world arose from a common spiritual principle, a world soul, which produced matter, living nature, and the mind of man.

At the risk of casting too wide a net, it is possible to note links between the romantic philosophers and the more abstract theorizing of psychoanalysis. The Philosophy of Nature put forth a law of polarities, a dynamic interplay between those antagonistic forces which govern the existence of natural phenomena. This dualistic principle later found its echo in the bipartite instinct theory of psychoanalysis.[1]

The notion of a primordial state followed by a series of metamorphoses also evokes recollections of genetic and developmental approaches. To the romantic philosopher, the unconscious was considered a true bond linking man with nature and permitting an understanding of the universe through mystical ecstasy or dreams.

Evidences of the romantic interest in nature can be seen early in Freud's development. His choice of a career as a natural scientist was made at seventeen, after he had heard Goethe's essay on Nature read at a public lecture.[2] Goethe had exclaimed:

Nature! We are surrounded by her, embraced by her—impossible to release ourselves from her and impossible to enter more deeply into her. Without our asking and without warning she drags us into the circle of her dance and carries us along until exhausted we drop from her arm. . . .
She has a purpose and broods continuously. . . . She reserves to herself an all-embracing intention, which no one discovers. . . .
She has set me within. She will also lead me without, I commit myself to her. She may command me. She will not hate her work. I have not spoken of her. No, what is true and what is false, it is she who has spoken it. Hers is all the blame; hers is all the praise.

The essay is a challenge to uncover the hidden secrets of nature, to find knowledge through a pantheistic mysticism. Man is powerless and submissive. Nature is pictured as an omnipotent mother, who is unfathomable, creating and destroying, changing and eternal. Although no one can comprehend her fully, love is the only means of understanding her (Goethe, 1893, pp. 207–213).

---

[1] Bernfeld and Jones regard "the solemn oath" sworn by Dubois-Reymond and von Brücke when they embarked on their scientific careers as prototypical of the pledge exacted by the mechanistic school in which the young Freud learned the rudiments of science. Even this program, however, requires scientists to investigate "matter, reducible to the force of attraction and repulsion," thus recalling the duality of the Philosophers of Nature (Bernfeld, 1944; Jones, 1953, pp. 40–41). Cranefield has called attention to the romantic underpinnings of von Brücke's teachings (1966).

[2] Or at least it was assumed by many that Goethe had written the essay. In actuality the ideas were Goethe's but were recorded by a Swiss theologian, Tobler, following a conversation with Goethe. Years later, Goethe incorporated Tobler's essay into his collected works, believing it was his, since the ideas were so consistent with his own line of thought (Freud, 1925–35, pp. 8–9 n).

Although Freud's first enthusiam for science soon suffered because of his inability to find an arena in which he felt he could make use of his natural gifts (1925–35, p. 9), he did not lose his enthusiasm for the Goethe essay. More than twenty-five years later he referred to it as *unvergleichlich schön* [incomparably beautiful] (1900a, p. 443).[3] However, by this time, he was also prepared to acknowledge that the "Nature" of the essay had other meanings. He cited a patient whose mental illness was attributed to the reading of Goethe's essay. The young man, who cried "Nature! Nature!" was referring, stated Freud, to the sexual sense of the word.

Freud's references to nature are extensive. Echoing Goethe, he wrote of the secrecy of nature. Discovering the sexual etiology of neuroses, he told Fleiss, "I have the distinct feeling that I have touched one of the great secrets of nature" (Freud, 1887–1902, p. 83). Elsewhere he stated that one of the "constraints of Nature to which mankind is subject" is the fact that procreation is entangled with the satisfaction of the sexual need (Freud, 1898, p. 277). Writing of Leonardo da Vinci, he viewed his interest in nature as a sublimation for the kindly mother who nourished him (Freud, 1910, pp. 122–123). In another context, nature was credited with keeping love fresh and guarding it against hate (Freud, 1915, p. 299).

But nature in Freud is also cruel and terrorizing. The task of civilization is to defend us against nature, which brings earthquakes, floods, storms, diseases, and death. Man first responds to the inexorable power of nature by humanizing this force over which he has little control. When he finds, however, that natural forces conform to independent and autonomous law, they seem to lose their human traits. They are the Moira (Fates), superior even to the gods (Freud, 1927, pp. 15–19). Finally, Freud combined nature with the power of Eros, the power to create and multiply life. Our bodily organism thus becomes a minute part of the superior power of nature. "Oh, inch of nature" he quoted, without recalling the source, in reference to the state of the helpless infant at birth (Freud, 1927, pp. 15–19; 1930, pp. 86, 91, 121; Reik, 1968, p. 648).

Perhaps one of Freud's most revealing references to nature occurs in a repeated misquotation. Commenting on the advisability of not deceiving patients about their terminal illnesses and counseling submission to the inevitable, he stated, "Shakespeare says: 'Thou owest Nature a death'" (Freud, 1887–1902, p. 276). The quotation, a remark of Prince Hal's to Falstaff from 1 *Henry IV* actually reads, "Thou owest God a death." Freud made the same error on two subsequent occasions, once in association to a dream, later in referring to the belief that death is the necessary outcome of life (1900b, p. 205; 1915, p. 289). He thus partially impersonalized and deanimated those forces to which man must submit, deprived the powers of their masculine identity, and removed the conception from a religious framework.

[3] Poorly translated as "striking" in The Standard Edition (1900b, 5:440).

Thoughts concerning nature accounted for the immutable in the human condition. Nature might be a source of endless fascination, a storehouse of wisdom and creativity; however, man could do little but submit to its inexorable laws or merely fend off its destructive effects. Politics, on the other hand, insofar as it dealt with the man-made, held out the promise, at least during Freud's adolescence, of bringing about incisive changes. He recalled that as a boy of six when his mother rubbed her hands together to show him we are made of earth and he saw the blackish scales of epidermis, he acquiesced in the belief of our inevitable return to Nature (1900b, p. 205). But as a boy of eleven or twelve he could share in the hope of social reform promised by the *"Bürger"* Ministry formed after the ratification of the new Austrian Constitution in 1867. Indeed, until a few months prior to entering the university in 1873 he could still aspire to a political career, and even subsequent to matriculation he still maintained a political interest.

In the latter half of the nineteenth century Vienna was the capital of a quasi-feudal state administered by a ruling family whose control was insecure. The Austro-Hungarian Empire was made up of a polyglot collection of Czechs, Magyars, Germans, Croatians, and Slovaks; few of the inhabitants thought of themselves as distinctively Austrian. The "German spirit" of high culture and social humanism was admired by the German-speaking intelligentsia, and the monarchy felt threatened by political movements which promoted closer ties with Germany.

It is interesting to consider Freud's choice of career as a reaction to the bankruptcy of the liberal political culture of nineteenth-century Vienna. For a time, the liberal middle class, devoted to the values of advanced German thought but not the ideal of German nationalism, was dominant. Several of the liberal Cabinet ministers in the government of 1867 were Jews who, by and large, adhered to the values of the progressive German-speaking bourgeoisie (Freud, 1900a, p. 193). J. N. Berger, one of the ministers admired by Jakob Freud and the eleven-year-old Sigmund, stated, "the Germans in Austria should strive not for political hegemony, but for cultural hegemony among the peoples of Austria." They should "carry culture to the East, transmit the propaganda of German intellection, German science, German humanism" (Schorske, 1967, p. 343).

Although the Bourgeois Ministry urged a program of liberal reform and attempted to mitigate the power of the upper classes, its net result was failure. It did not succeed in unifying the divergent national elements within the Austro-Hungarian empire, nor could it control the explosive lower classes. Instead, states Schorske, "the liberals unwittingly summoned from the social depths the forces of a general disintegration" (1967, p. 344). New antiliberal and antimonarchial mass movements consisting of Czech nationalism, Pan-Germanism, Christian Socialism, Social Democracy, and later, Zionism, were ready to replace an ineffectual and short-lived spirit of moderate liberalism. Although morally committed to supporting the rights of minority groups within the empire, the German-speaking middle class realized that any concessions to Bohemia and Moravia would weaken their own power and create disorganization. By the early and middle 1870s, the academic intellectuals—both students and faculty—were prepared to give up imperial stability and middle-class oligarchy for the promise of a unifying German nationalism. But under the influence and eventual leadership of Georg von Schönerer, the Germanic nationalist movement became progressively illiberal and totalitarian. In 1878, Schönerer declared in the Austrian Reichsrath, "If only we already belonged to the German Empire!" The next year he began to show his anti-Semitic leanings and railed against "the semitic rulers of money and the world." In 1882 Schönerer raged at the "sucking vampire . . . that knocks . . . at the house of the German farmer and craftsman"—the Jew (Schorske, 1967, pp. 351–352).

Schönerer's anti-Semitic appeals had a strong attraction for the Austrian lower classes who were inclined to blame their economic ills on the Jewish capitalists, and their more proximate representatives, the Jewish peddlers. The artisan who had previously made and sold the product of his trade in his own home was now replaced by the itinerant peddler who went from house to house developing his own clientele. Schönerer's anti-Semitism was largely motivated by his own internal needs, and it became apparent that it was one manifestation of an intrapsychic disturbance which finally culminated in social ostracism and a jail sentence when he physically attacked a political opponent. But the obvious advantages of using prejudice to organize latent social discontent were not lost.

A few years later, Karl Lueger made use of the anti-Semitic feelings of the lower classes for opportunistic political purposes. Unlike Schönerer, he was a man of some culture and charm, and furthermore he was less driven by intense psychopathology. Five years after Schönerer's initiation of anti-Semitic sentiment into the German nationalistic movement, Lueger began to use it as a focus for the organization of the Christian Socialist party. Pan-Germanism became of less interest to Lueger after he had collected a sufficient majority of Viennese artisans to lead him to a political victory as mayor of Vienna in 1895. Schorske states that the last gasp of Austrian liberalism may well have been the emperor's refusal to ratify Lueger as mayor on two occasions before he was finally forced to do so in 1897. The Fliess correspondence informs us that Freud broke a temporary smoking fast in order to celebrate this autocratic action of the emperor against Lueger on the first occasion in 1895 (Freud, 1887–1902, p. 133). Lueger's anti-Semitism lacked the rancor of Schönerer's, and he apparently modulated it by treating some Jews with favor. "Der schöne Karl," as Lueger was known, became famous for his statement of flexible anti-Semitism. "I will decide who is a Jew," he stated.

But let us return to an earlier phase of Freud's life. From 1873 to 1877, during his early university days, he belonged to a German nationalist group, the *Leseverein der deutschen Studenten,* which, after several years, was disbanded through governmental pressure because of its anti-Austrian leanings. The association attracted young Viennese such as Freud who were interested in political changes and were Germanic in sympathy. Germany was regarded not only as the seat of an advanced nationalism but also as a haven from an oppressive and outdated oligarchy (McGrath, 1967).

Freud, while still at the gymnasium, seriously considered a political career, and until the spring of 1873 he planned to study law as a preparatory step. Much later, he stated that Heinrich Braun, his inseparable friend at the time, had awakened in him a "host of revolutionary feelings" (E. L. Freud, 1961, p. 379), and during his early adolescence these competed with his budding scientific interests.[4]

It is ironic that the political movement of German nationalism which was originally associated with freedom from the Austrian yoke and which attracted enthusiastic young intellectuals, shortly became repressive and baldly anti-Semitic. In the 1870s it had represented the highest aspirations of students like Freud who saw in the movement toward Pan-Germanism closer links with the culture of Goethe as well as a more genuine expression of their political identity. Indeed the adherents, many of whom were young Jews, saw alliance with Germany as a socialist goal. The students of Freud's generation, in contrast to their fathers, for whom German nationalism was no positive objective, were radicalized through their pride in German culture. In the *Leseverein* (reading society), student discussion frequently revolved around the manner in which the "stable bourgeois world of their liberal fathers could best be overturned" (McGrath, 1967, p. 185).

Bismarck's creation of a united German empire in 1870 had given a sense of reality to the aspirations of the German-speaking students at the University of Vienna. Freud's *Leseverein* took Schopenhauer, Wagner, and Nietzsche as ideational leaders. It was believed that a new and artistically vital culture, opposed to the excessive rationalism of the past, had to be created. Political activity was to appeal to the integrated man and not regard his rational aspect as more important than his emotional side. Freud's friend Heinrich Braun was elected to office in the *Leseverein* and participated actively over several years. In 1877 Braun was one of the joint signers of a letter to Nietzsche declaring devotion to his outlook and offering to follow in the wake of his criticism of liberal society. But it is doubtful whether Freud's active interest continued much beyond his first years at the university. Even in an early debate with Victor Adler, the subsequent

[4] Freud eventually lost touch with Braun, though Braun is referred to in the associations to the "Count Thun" dream as one of his school fellows who "seemed to have taken Henry VIII of England as his model." Braun married four times and later had a distinguished political career. It is noteworthy that the dream association concerns a revolt against an unpopular schoolmaster. Although Braun was the moving spirit in planning the revolt, the leadership in the assault was left to Freud (Freud, 1900b, pp. 211–212.

leader of the Austrian Socialist party—which probably occurred at a meeting of the *Leseverein*—he was already "full of materialistic theories" (Freud, 1900b, p. 212). Soon he was to become totally immersed in scientific activity.[5]

Thus, from his early adolescent years Freud was swayed by both the romantic regard for nature and the world of practical politics. He retained a love for the Moravian woods of his childhood and the beautiful ruins close to the town of his birth (Freud, 1969, p. 426). His response to Goethe's essay, a latter-day expression of this interest, already heralded his transition toward a scientific orientation. Under the influence of Heinrich Braun, he developed an interest in revolutionary politics. But by the 1880s when anti-Semitism had become an ingredient of German nationalism, Freud had dissociated himself from political goals. His membership in the *Leseverein* terminated in 1877, a few years before it was prohibited by governmental edict. But it is likely that his interest had already waned by the previous year, when he entered von Brüche's laboratory and for the first time felt that he had found his niche (Freud, 1925–35, p. 9).

Interestingly enough, we hear of an appeal to the remnants of Freud's nationalistic interests several years later. In 1885, Freud had come to Paris to study with Charcot at the Salpêtrière. One evening at a gathering at the home of Charcot, the French neurologist Gilles de la Tourette baited Freud by predicting a ferocious war between France and Germany. Freud promptly countered that he was a Jew, and aligned himself neither with Germany nor Austria. That evening he wrote his fianceé, Martha Bernays, that he found such conversations very embarrassing, for he felt something German quickening within him. However, he immediately added, he had long ago decided to crush such stirrings (E. L. Freud, 1961, p. 216).

In spite of the political ferment, several observers are united in the belief that the vitality of Vienna in the last half of the nineteenth century fostered a spirit of creativity (Zweig, 1943; Barea, 1966; Schick, 1968–69; Sachs, 1944). Intellectual values were highly prized, learning was treasured, art and science were idealized. "There is hardly a city in Europe where the drive toward cultural ideals was as passionate as it was in Vienna," stated Stefan Zweig (1943, p. 12). A country which for centuries had been politically expansionist now found itself unsuccessful as a military power and looked for supremacy on artistic levels.

However, a striving for excellence was not characteristic of the totality of the educated classes. The Austrian ruling class, the old aristocracy of the emperor's court, settled for the status quo. They were content to prac-

---

[5] Of interest, however, is the fact that Freud's subsequent teacher, Theodor Meynert, whom he initially followed with "deep veneration," was an active participant in the *Leseverein* and frequently lectured to the membership on psychiatry. (Freud, 1900b, p. 437; McGrath, 1967).

tice their casual refinements and enjoy their intellectual sluggishness. In this regard, they resembled the French courtiers who had preceded them by a century.

The drive toward scientific and artistic supremacy was characteristic of the flourishing middle class and was encouraged by the wide receptivity of the city for the assimilation of divergent people and cultures. Viennese Jews who had lived peacefully in the city for two hundred years—although without full civil rights until 1867—took on the sponsorship of art supported by the nobility in earlier generations. "Nine-tenths of what the world celebrated as Viennese culture in the nineteenth century was promoted, nourished or even created by Viennese Jewry," stated Zweig (1943, p. 22). Nor were the Viennese Jews artistically productive in any specifically Jewish way; Mahler and Schönberg in music, Hofmannsthal, Schnitzler, and Beer-Hofmann in literature, Max Reinhardt in the theater—all saw themselves as European or Viennese rather than Jewish.

"What spirit engendered such a concentration of creative powers in Vienna?" asked Schick (1968–69, p. 531). He inventoried the surrounding idyllic landscape, the well-planned educational system, the profundity of wit, the peculiar Viennese vacillation in prizing both reality and fantasy, and the simultaneous enjoyment and cynical disparagement of the creature comforts. But to catalogue such factors and attempt to apply them to Freud leaves one with a sense of dissatisfaction, particularly when we consider how lacking in Freud's basic outlook is any suggestion of fin-de-siècle fashionable world-weariness. Antithetical to Freud's sense of the tragedy of the human condition is the well-known Viennese epigram, "the situation is hopeless but not serious."

Perhaps we do best if we consider creative activity such as Freud's as operating in opposition to ongoing ideational currents. Freud had something like this in mind when he discussed the influence of his native city on his thought. Ridiculing the belief that psychoanalysis owed its character to the alleged sexual looseness of Vienna, he proposed that discoveries such as his were more likely to occur in the presence of exceptional restrictions on sexual satisfaction. Freud suggested that the crucial significance of a particular locality in the development of intellectual ideas might well be the degree of openness with which free observations are permitted. Here Freud was able to point with favor to his milieu. The Viennese, he believed, were less embarrassed and less prudish regarding sexual relationships than Northern or Western European city dwellers (Freud, 1914a, p. 40). Cultural life was not characterized by hypocrisy or a need to practice dissembling either for its own sake or in the interest of so-called higher idealistic aims. Indeed, Hanns Sachs, in fact no greater lover of Vienna, made a similar observation, although he remained firm in the conviction that "the allegation that Vienna has put her stamp of origin on Freud's work is a hollow pretense" (1944, p. 19). However critical Vienna felt to Freud, at least its character did not blur his vision.

The Jewish Tradition

A more vital matter concerns Freud's link with the Jewish tradition and Jewish life and thought. Although he discarded any adherence to religious belief or ritual, he never repudiated his Jewish identity. Out of his earliest tendency to find Semitic military heroes for idealization, he freely and incorrectly attributed a Jewish identity to Napoleon's general, Masséna, and sympathized with the Carthaginian Hannibal as a fellow member of an alien race (Freud, 1900b, pp. 196–198). He believed it unworthy and senseless to deny one's Jewish identity at a time when baptism to Christianity was by no means uncommon (Bakan, 1965, p. 46). Being a Jew, he believed, prepared him to take a position of solitary opposition against a compact majority (Freud, 1925–35, pp. 8–9), enabled him to be free of prejudices, repudiate arbitrary authority (Freud, 1926, p. 274), and respect intellectual values (Bakan, 1965, pp. 48–49; Freud, 1934–38, p. 115). In later life he realized that his early familiarity with the Bible had had "an enduring effect" upon him (Freud, 1900b, pp. 97, 334; 1925–35, p. 8).

The experiences of Freud's family of origin were typical of the lot of the central European Jew. Toward the middle of the nineteenth century, permitted new freedom in traveling and in seeking economic opportunity, the Jews began to infiltrate the central European cities from the eastern countryside. The first-known traces of the Freud family were in Lithuania; the family then moved to Galicia. Freud's father and mother were both born in Galicia and had moved to Příbor in Moravia by the time Sigmund was born. When he was three they moved to Leipzig for a year, before settling in Vienna.

In the towns of central Europe the ancient laboring guilds were inadequate to cope with the needs of expanding populations. Hence Jews with commercial experience drifted from region to region as needs arose for the transmission of goods and services. "Many remained petty tradesmen looking for opportunity, always hopefully expecting something to turn up but rarely finding security," states Handlin (1967, p. 165). Freud in later life described his father in similar terms.

In view of the uncertainty of the political and economic situation, and in response to emancipation, a secular education became an enthusiastically sought prize. Handlin points out that Jews who emigrated to America prior to 1900 showed no such eagerness for schooling. "In Austria and Germany, by contrast, the university became the object of young people's ambition. . . . In this society *Bildung*—the possession of defined cultural symbols—carried with it a status that could partially compensate for the disadvantages of affiliation with a minority discriminated against for centuries" (Handlin, 1967, p. 165). Suddenly, the generation of Jews of which Freud was a member was precipitated into Western society and modern life. The attempt to wrestle with the problems of their new secular lives led at times to great feats of creativity and innovation.

Commenting on the mode of thought transmitted through the Jewish tradition, Handlin states:

The insistent confidence that an orderly arrangement of the universe made all phenomena susceptible to rational comprehension was characteristic of a people whose culture, for centuries, had stressed the need for interpreting every particular action and event in the light of the Divine purpose of creation. The sense of divinity was no longer immediate for those whose outlook was increasingly secular; but the sense of purpose and meaningfulness remained even for those who had moved away from traditional modes of thought [1967, p. 168].

In assessing the significance of his Jewish background Freud tended to give credit to the broad cultural attitude that was part of his religious legacy rather than systematic Judaic knowledge or specific content. Although Abraham pointed out to him the "Talmudic" nature of his thought, nowhere do we see any real familiarity with the Talmud nor any citations from it (E. L. Freud, 1961, p. 153; Abraham and Freud, 1965, p. 36). He was of course deeply interested in Moses. He particularly identified with the Jewish military leader. "I have often felt," he wrote Martha, "as though I had inherited all the defiance and all the passions with which our ancestors defended their Temple and could gladly sacrifice my life for one great moment in history" (E. L. Freud, 1961, p. 215). But specific Jewish sources for his thought are not striking.

Although Freud was provided with some religious instruction in his boyhood, his liberal teachers attached no great value to knowing the Hebrew language and literature. What he acquired in childhood, he soon lost, describing himself in his Preface to the Hebrew translation of *Totem and Taboo* as "ignorant of the language of holy writ" (1912–13, p. xv).

Bakan bases his supposition that Freud was influenced by the Jewish mystical tradition on similarities between psychoanalysis and the Kabbala, citing particularly the similarity in techniques of interpretation and the importance that both attach to sexuality. He also points out Freud's interest in numerological discussions and concern for discovering hidden meanings in trivialities. He suggests that Freud was interested in dissembling the mystical influence and took steps to cover his tracks so that this would not be discovered. He proposes that Freud's interest in law was related to his interest in becoming a rabbi and quotes from a Jewish scholar who claimed that he had discovered the Zohar and other books on Kabbala in Freud's library in Vienna.

Bakan's evidence is not impressive. He cannot discuss the Jewish mystical tradition in terms of its unique attributes, and he acknowledges that there are many similarities between Jewish mysticism and other cultural movements of the time, for example, romanticism. His interpretations are poorly supported, as, for example, when he suggests that the pseudonym "Dora" for one of Freud's patients is a cover for the word "Torah." We have evidence that Freud was far more interested in the law as preparation for a political career than the rabbinate. The argument that Freud wanted to hide such mystical influence because he feared rejection by the scientific community is contradicted by Freud's openness about his Jewish identity throughout his writings and the pride he took in establishing links with his past. In my perusal of the Freud libraries in London and New York, I found no literature dealing with the Kabbala or any significant collection of Judaica.

Nevertheless, in attempting to evaluate factors in Freud's cultural background, it is best not to dismiss readily a possible source of influence. Freud himself came to believe that his interest in the significance of numbers was related to an unconscious incorporation of Jewish mysticism.

In a letter to Jung of 1909, he stated:

Some years ago, I discovered that I had the conviction I would die between the ages of 61 and 62. . . . It all began in the year 1899, when two events occurred simultaneously; first I wrote *The Interpretation of Dreams*, and second, I was assigned a new telephone number—14362. A connection between the two could easily be established; in the year 1899, when I wrote *The Interpretation of Dreams*, I was 43 years old. What more natural, then, that the other numbers should refer to the end of my life, namely, 61 or 62. Suddenly, there was method in the madness. The superstition that I would die between 61 and 62 showed itself to be the equivalent of a conviction that I had fulfilled my life's work with *The Interpretation of Dreams*, didn't have to produce anything further, and could die in peace. You will admit that with this knowledge the thing no longer sounds absurd. . . . You will find confirmation here, once again, of the specifically Jewish nature of my mysticism [Jung, 1961, pp. 361–363].

Reference has already been made to the affinity which existed between the Jews and the Germans in the nineteenth century. German culture in its universalist form, as exemplified by Goethe and Schiller, provided emancipated Jews with a ready source for involvement in the Western ideal. A Jewish writer of the 1880s wrote:

To no other people have the Jews grown so close as they have to the Germans. They are Germanized not only on German soil, but far beyond the German boundaries. . . . There must be correspondence in the basic disposition [of the two people] which made Germany and all things German particularly attractive for the Jews, and the Jews an especially useful complement to the German character [Kahler, 1967, p. 24].

The special attraction of the Jews "for all things German," the love for the language, the literature, and the land is illustrated by an anecdote that belongs to a later period. In the 1930s, after the German writer Erich Maria Remarque had emigrated, a Nazi official tried to woo him with the promise of much honor if he would return to Germany. When he refused, the Nazi said "Are you not a bit homesick?" "Homesick?," Remarque said. "No. I am not Jewish" (Kahler, 1967, p. 33).

Freud responded to German culture and, as I have previously mentioned, while in Paris felt the Teutonic tug. However, he was not submerged by the attractions of national identity. He used his identity as a Jew to maintain a freedom from chauvinistic restrictions when nationalistic ideals were no longer useful to him. He experienced the attractions of nationalism, as well as the repudiation of such narrow allegiances. As we have seen, by his mid-twenties, anti-Semitism had clearly cast its shadows over nationalist aspirations and Freud was fully taken up with his scientific life.

Freud's Classical Education

By "classicism" we denote certain values characteristically revealed in the literature and art of Greece and Rome. The essential elements have been filtered through the neoclassical revival of the eighteenth century, and subsequently the emphasis was placed on restraint, order, serenity, and repose. Classicism has come to emphasize the ideal over the real, the abstract over the concrete, reason and intellect over the emotions. But, in actuality, the affective part of life was not neglected among the ancients.

Sterba has pointed out the intense humanistic bent in the classicism of antiquity (1969). Although order and integration were valued, there was no slighting of the instinctual life and the pleasure-seeking components to the personality. Freud wrote of the glorification of instinct among the ancients in contrast to the modern idealization of the object (1905, p. 149). He acknowledged the importance with which the Greeks treated the dream and stated that he was following in the footsteps of the dream interpreters of antiquity (1916–17, pp. 86–87). Generally, Freud, whose knowledge of classical writings and art was extensive, turned to classical antiquity to illustrate the power of irrational instinctual forces more often than qualities of order, control, and integration.

Freud's secondary school education took place in the classical gymnasium with its heavy emphasis on Greek and Latin. Under the influence of educators and humanists such as Alexander and Wilhelm von Humboldt, German-speaking and European education had rediscovered classical antiquity at the beginning of the nineteenth century (Sterba, 1969). The humanistic tradition, developed during the Renaissance in Italy in the fifteenth century as a reaction against the authoritarian restrictions of the Middle Ages, found its visible form in the university preparatory schools of the nineteenth century. Universalism, order, and harmony were to be arrived at through exposure to the highest levels of Western thought as exemplified by the classical ideal. The formal discipline acquired by the mind in the mastery of the rudiments of the literature and language of Greece and Rome would carry into other modes of thinking and provide a basis for an educated outlook.

Along with the reverence for the classical ideal, several side effects resulted from the gymnasium experience. The teachers were usually ambitious men of learning and ability who saw themselves entering careers of scholarship and advancement. It was not unusual for universities to recruit their faculty from the classical gymnasium, and many scholarly papers, the product of teacher and pupil collaboration in the secondary school, were produced. The classical gymnasium was the prestige school, and it became identified with the attainments of the "educated man." The author who wrote for readers educated in the classical gymnasium could leave his Latin and Greek quotations untranslated. Robert Waelder described the culture shock that followed his arrival in the United States when he discovered that educated men could not be relied upon to understand Greek and Latin quotations (Sterba, 1969, p. 437).

The curriculum of the classical gymnasium called for hard work and a skill with languages. After a two-year preparatory period in Latin, which Freud began at nine, he was assigned Livy's *History of Rome*. Freud read much of Ovid's *Metamorphoses* with its poetic rendering of many of the Greek myths. Sallust, the Roman historian, Cicero's *Orations*, Virgil's *Eclogues* and *The Aeneid*, Horace's poems, and Tacitus' *History* rounded out a rather full exposure to Latin. In Greek, Xenophon's *Anabasis* and *Cyropaedia* familiarized Freud with the Greek struggle with the Persians of the fourth century and the character and education of Cyrus. In Herodotus he read of the death of Darius, Xerxes' invasion of Greece and the Battle of Thermopylae. Demosthenes' orations, Sophocles' *Ajax* and *Antigone*, Homer's *Iliad* and *Odyssey*, and Plato's *Apology* and *Crito* were read in the original Greek over a period of almost six years.

Did the readings leave an impression? Freud refers on several occasions to *The Aeneid*. Not only does he use a quotation from it as the motto for *The Interpretation of Dreams*, but he also recalled with ease Dido's curse on Aeneas when it was forgotten by a young man Freud described in the *Psychopathology of Everyday Life* (Freud, 1901, pp. 8–11). In contrasting the classical reverence for instinct with the modern repudiation of instinctual life he doubtless falls back on Plato, Ovid, and perhaps Catullus. Freud first read of the favorite hero of his youth, Hannibal, in the pages of Livy. The assigned portion of the *History of Rome* covers the Second Punic War, the character of Hannibal, and the campaign against Rome. A line from a Horatian Ode read in 1873 was quoted as a memorial to Karl Abraham in 1926. The use of Greek names for crucial psychological concepts (Oedipus, Eros and Thanatos, Narcissus), the frequent references to classical myth, the shared values regarding morality and aesthetics, the fascination with Greek and Roman sculpture and archaeology—all attest to the indelible impression of the classical gymnasium.

How did Freud react to his secondary school curriculum? Darwin, similarly educated, stated that the classical curriculum had stultified his mind. The general negative reaction to the classical influence is highlighted in Butler's book *The Tyranny of Greece over Germany* (1935). In Freud's case we hear of only one episode of rebellion directed toward his teachers. Once when he was fifteen, he states, "We had hatched a conspiracy against an unpopular and ignorant master. . . . The leadership in the chief assault was allotted to me" (Freud, 1900b, pp. 211–212). We hear of no reprisal for this rebellious confrontation, nor did his conduct interfere with his making the honor roll that year, as in every other year of his gymnasium career. He wrote of his teachers with affection when his secondary school asked its distinguished graduates to comment in a festschrift celebrating the fiftieth anniversary of the foundation of his school. It was his classical education which provided him with his "first glimpse of an extinct civilization which in my case" he stated, "was to bring me as much consolation as anything else in the struggles of life" (Freud, 1914b, p. 241).

Freud's library, now in London, documents his fascination with the culture of Greece and Rome. He continued a lifelong interest in the history, archaeology, art, and literature of classical antiquity. He had an extensive collection of art and archaeological objects, subscribed to archaeological journals, and had more than an amateur's knowledge of the field. It is not surprising that the founder of psychoanalysis should be interested in glimpses of extinct civilizations. Archaeology and psychoanalysis have obvious links with one another. Both value the understanding of the past through present-day remnants (Bernfeld, 1951). It is likely that an additional factor in Freud's love for the literature of antiquity was the opportunity it provided for authenticating the universal nature of psychoanalytic findings. He was sustained by the awareness that discoveries made in a specific clinical situation had a general applicability and had already been hinted at in cultures centuries old. Classical antiquity could provide a surety for findings clinical experience first revealed.

In summary then, Freud had already been exposed to a wide cultural and humanist tradition in his pre-scientific days. Through an interest in German literature and particularly the writings of Goethe, he became conversant with the tradition of romanticism and its regard for the irrational and unconscious. Although intrigued by the romantic concern with the powers of nature, he responded, not philosophically, but with an interest in observation. His native city provided an environment which encouraged an openness and acceptance of learning and innovation. His early political aspirations fostered an attitude of independence and an unwillingness to bow to authority, and the Jewish tradition provided the strength to tolerate prejudice and opposition. His classical education provided a complex substratum upon which universals concerning the human mind could be tested.

Although I began this survey with a discussion of romanticism, it is fitting to end by highlighting Freud's classicism. In the sense in which psychoanalysis attempts to find order in chaos, synthesis among conflicting irrational forces, integration and self-knowledge in place of warded-off unconscious impulses, Freud blended two broad movements in the history of Western thought. Both romanticism and classicism provided an impetus toward an empirical investigation of psychic reality.

BIBLIOGRAPHY

Abraham, H. C. and Freud, E. L. (1965), *A Psychoanalytic Dialogue: The Letters of Sigmund Freud and Karl Abraham, 1907-1926.* New York: Basic Books.

Bakan, D. (1965), *Sigmund Freud and the Jewish Mystical Tradition.* New York: Schocken Books.

Barea, I. (1966), *Vienna.* New York: Alfred A. Knopf.

Beres, D. (1965), Psychoanalysis, Science and Romanticism. In: *Drives, Affects, Behavior,* M. Schur (ed.) Vol. 2. New York: International Universities Press.

Bernfeld, S. (1944), Freud's Earliest Theories and the School of Helmholtz. *Psychoanal. Quart.,* 13:341-362.

Bernfeld, S. C. (1951), Freud and Archeology. *Amer. Imago,* 8:107-128.

Butler, E. M. (1935), The Tyranny of Greece over Germany. New York: The Macmillan Co.

Cranefield, P. G. (1966), Freud and the "School of Helmholtz." *Gesnerus,* 23:35-39.

Ellenberger, H. (1970), *The Discovery of the Unconscious.* New York: Basic Books.

Freud, E. L. (ed.) (1961), *The Letters of Sigmund Freud* 1873-1939. London: Hogarth.

Freud, S. (1887-1902), *The Origins of Psychoanalysis: Letters to Wilhelm Fliess, Drafts and Notes 1887-1902.* Bonaparte, M. Freud, A. and Kris, E., Eds. New York: Basic Books, 1954.

—— (1898), Sexuality in the Aetiology of the Neuroses. *Standard Edition,* 3:261-277, London: Hogarth, 1962.

—— (1900a), *Die Traumdeutung.* Gesammelte Werke 2/3, London: Imago Publishing Co., 1942.

—— (1900b), The Interpretation of Dreams, *Standard Edition* 4 & 5, London: Hogarth, 1954-1955.

—— (1901), The Psychopathology of Everyday Life. *Standard Edition* 6, London, Hogarth, 1962.

—— (1905), Three Essays on the Theory of Sexuality. *Standard Edition* 7, London, Hogarth, 1953.

—— (1910), Leonardo da Vinci and a Memory of His Childhood. *Standard Edition* 11, London: Hogarth, 1957.

—— (1912-13), Totem and Taboo. *Standard Edition* 13, London, Hogarth, 1955.

—— (1914a), History of the Psychoanalytic Movement. *Standard Edition* 14, London, Hogarth, 1957.

—— (1914b), Some Reflections on Schoolboy Psychology. *Standard Edition* 13:241-244, London, Hogarth, 1955.

—— (1915), Our Attitude Toward Death. *Standard Edition* 14, London: Hogarth, 1959.

—— (1916-17), Introductory Lectures in Psychoanalysis. *Standard Edition* 16, London, Hogarth, 1963.

—— (1925), Letter to the Editor of the Jewish Press Centre in Zurich. *Standard Edition* 19:338, London: Hogarth, 1961.

—— (1925-35), An Autobiographical Study. *Standard Edition* 20, London: Hogarth, 1961.

—— (1926), Address to the Society of B'nai B'rith. *Standard Edition* 20:273-274, 1959.

—— (1927), The Future of an Illusion. *Standard Edition* 21, London: Hogarth, 1961.

—— (1930), Civilization and Its Discontents. *Standard Edition* 21, London: Hogarth, 1961.

―――― (1934–38), Moses and Monotheism. *Standard Edition* 23, London, Hogarth, 1964.

―――― (1969), Some Early Unpublished Letters of Freud. *Internat. J. Psycho-Analysis*, 50:419–427.

Goethe, J. W. (1893), Essay on Nature, translated by T. Bailey. *Maxims and Reflections of Goethe*, New York: Saunders.

Handlin, O. (1967), Jews in the Culture of Middle Europe. *Studies of the Leo Baeck Institute*, M. Kreutzberger (ed.), New York: Frederick Unger Publishing Co.

Jones, E. (1953), *The Life and Work of Sigmund Freud*. Vol. 1, New York: Basic Books.

Jung, C. G. (1961), *Memories, Dreams, Reflections*. New York: Pantheon Books.

Kahler, E. (1967), The Jews and the Germans. *Studies of the Leo Baeck Institute*, M. Kreutzberger (ed.), New York: Frederick Unger Publishing Co.

McGrath, W. J. (1967), Student Radicalism in Vienna. *J. Contemp. Hist.*, 6:183–201.

Reik, T. (1968), *The Search Within*. New York: Funk & Wagnalls.

Sachs, H. (1944), *Freud, Master and Friend*. Cambridge, Mass.: Harvard University Press.

Schick, A. (1968), The Vienna of Sigmund Freud. *Psychoanalytic Rev.*, 55:529–551.

Schorske, C. E. (1967), Politics in a New Key: An Austrian Triptych. *J. of Mod. Hist.*, 39:343–386.

Sterba, R. F. (1969), The Psychoanalyst in a World of Change. *Psychoanal. Quart.*, 38:432–454.

Trilling, L. (1950), *The Liberal Imagination*. New York: Viking Press.

Wordsworth, W. (1950), *The Poems of Wordsworth*. London: Oxford Standard Authors.

Zilboorg, G. and Henry, G. W. (1941), *A History of Medical Psychology*. New York: Norton.

Zweig, S. (1943), *The World of Yesterday*. New York: Viking Press.

Minister to a Mind Diseased: *Freud at the* Allgemeine Krankenhaus

ERNEST S. WOLF, M.D. (*Chicago*)

Forty-seven years ago Freud (1925) wrote about his psychiatric training: "I followed his [Brücke's] advice, left the physiological laboratory and entered the General Hospital as an Aspirant . . . and worked in various departments of the hospital, among others for more than six months under Meynert . . ." Though Freud was unenthusiastic about medicine, Meynert's lectures had been the only medical ones that had aroused his interest as a student. Working in Meynert's psychiatric clinic constituted Freud's chief purely psychiatric experience (Jones, 1953). Freud was assigned to Meynert's clinic from May 1 to the end of September, 1883; he spent two months in the male wards and three months in the female. The familiarity with psychiatric patients and their illnesses gained during these five months[1] must have been of inestimable value for the future psychoanalyst. This brief communication is an attempt to reconstruct Freud's psychiatric experience, as far as is possible, on the basis of obtainable hospital records.[2]

The material upon which this report is based consists of forty-eight case records from the Allgemeine Krankenhaus in Vienna. These patient charts generally comprise an admission note, a brief history of the illness, a past history with special emphasis on family history, the findings of a physical examination, as well as an assessment of the patient's mental state.[3] Sometimes additional information was obtained from the patients' families or other outside sources. Progress notes were recorded at irregular intervals. Abstracts of the decisions about diagnosis and the disposition made by the "Kommission" were included, as were face sheets summarizing the patients' vital

[1] Freud was in error when he recalled "more than six months" in 1925.
[2] We wish to thank Mr. Irving Stone for his gracious generosity in making available to us these records upon which he based one chapter of his biographical novel of Freud, *The Passions of the Mind*.
[3] There did not yet exist formal "Mental Status" examinations in the modern sense of this term.

336

statistics, such as age, religion, marital status, occupation, address, place and country of birth, legal information about guardianship, and, in addition, condensed medical information about diagnosis, symptomatology, etiology, organic disease, and disposition.

The forty-eight cases have admission dates which are irregularly scattered from April, 1880, to April, 1885. Sixteen of the patients were in residence when Freud arrived on Meynert's service, and nine more were admitted while he was there. The rest were discharged before he came or did not gain admission until after he left. It is not known how these cases were selected, but there is nothing to indicate that the selection was other than a random sample.[4] It seems justified to conclude that these records in their aggregate give an authentic and comprehensive picture of psychiatric practice on Meynert's service during the early 1880s.

The patients described in this sampling ranged in age from thirteen years to seventy; the average age was forty-two. Twenty-five of the patients were males, twenty-three were females. Sixteen were single, twenty-three were married, three were widowed, and the marital status of three is not known. Thirty-eight had been born in Austria, mainly in Vienna. The ten foreign-born patients had come from Hungary, Bavaria, Bohemia, Galicia, Moravia, Silesia, and Würtemberg. The occupations of the adult patients, or in the case of some of the women that of their spouses, were distributed as follows: twelve skilled workers, eight unskilled laborers, four landowners, four office workers, three farmers, three civil servants, two musicians, two manufacturers, one each of businessman, student, army officer, and clergy; the occupations of five patients were unknown. One thirteen-year-old son of a jailer probably was still in school. The population was Roman Catholic with the exception of four Jewish patients, all of whom, it is interesting to note, had been born in Hungary. The average length of hospital stay was twenty-one months, with the shortest recorded time having been fifteen days; the longest hospitalization was seven years, six months, and twenty-seven days.

A wide gamut of diagnoses had been made, and most patients received more than one diagnostic label. The most frequently made diagnosis was *madness*, followed by *idiocy, mania,* and *progressive paralysis*. Other diagnoses in order of decreasing frequency were *chronic alcoholism, delirium tremens, insanity, confusion, epilepsy, feeblemindedness, persecution mania,* and *melancholy*.

The most frequently observed symptoms were *persecution-maniacal ideas, excitements, confusion, mental deficiency,* and *hallucinations*. Other symptoms recorded were, in decreasing frequency, *feeblemindedness, tremor, facial paresis, anxieties, epileptic fits, apathy, disturbance of speech, staggering gait, soiling, urge to move, amnesia, fear, stupidity, change of mood, religious-maniacal ideas, restlessness,* and *depression*.

---

[4] The sequence of the case numbers indicates a random distribution.

Hundreds of patients were hospitalized during the five-year period. Of the forty-eight patients discussed here, seven were discharged as cured, eight left the hospital on probation, and twelve were transferred to another institution, apparently a regional asylum. Twenty patients died; the fate of one is not recorded.

The records do not mention any treatment procedures addressed to the mental disturbances except occasional sedation with chloral hydrate, the rare use of tincture of opium, or the application of electric stimulation. Other medications were given for coughs and for diarrhea, both apparently rather frequent organic symptoms.

Autopsies were performed when permission had been granted by the deceased's family; this was obtained in the majority of cases. Most of the reports of the postmortem examinations were, like the clinical records, written in German; yet it is interesting to note that a few are in Latin.

It is evident that the patients were not too dissimilar from those whom one might find in a usual psychiatric ward of a modern General Hospital. One perceives a preponderance of functional psychoses, most of which probably would be diagnosed as schizophrenic or paranoid in current nosology, while a somewhat smaller group might be designated now as suffering from chronic alcoholism, epilepsy, or chronic organic brain disease. The most outstanding difference evident from a comparable sampling of contemporary hospitalizations seems to be the relative infrequency of severely depressed patients; and, of course, today the diagnosis, prevention, and treatment of lues has greatly reduced the incidence of general paralysis.

Case 351 is presented here as an illustrative example of the clinical material. J. D., a thirty-nine-year-old single bank clerk, was admitted in June, 1882.[5] Mr. D. had been living in Vienna with his mother when it was noticed that within a period of several weeks his behavior began to change, with increasing absentmindedness, forgetfulness, and disregard for what is appropriate, both at home and in public. Professor Schlager was consulted, and he found the patient to be in a state of mental disturbance as a result of a progressive ailment of the brain. He commented on Mr. D.'s restlessness, his purposeless buying, and his stealing, which included the compass from an optician's shop. Professor Schlager noted that Mr. D. was not aware of being ill and that he resisted when anyone tried to restrain him from senseless behavior: he then became excited and showed disturbed mental functioning. Professor Schlager advised that the patient could not be left to himself and recommended admission to an insane asylum for reasons of safety and treatment. A day later the patient was admitted.[6] At that time he appeared confused and restless, and on one occasion he knocked the glass panes out of several hospital windows with the comment that

---

[5] This patient was being treated during the time of Freud's attendance there.

[6] Not many patients arrived with such a detailed referral note from their own doctors.

he was trying to create some business for his brother, a glazier. Upon examination it was found that Mr. D. was apathetic, gave false answers, and mixed correct dates with incorrect ones. His speech was incoherent. He claimed to be married, to have five children, and to be the owner of a store that sold silk. He thought it took a man with a good stomach to deal with the "high and mighty." He reported that his father, a glazier, had died at age seventy-one of edema of the lungs, while his mother still felt well enough to be active and running eighteen hours a day. The patient himself felt perfectly well, and, as the reason for being in the hospital he mentioned his desire to see the pictures, presumably meaning those hanging on the walls and fancying himself to be a connoisseur. He thought the building to be a private mansion, and he did not notice any mental patients—only nice people. The food and service he found to be excellent; he planned to write an article for a newspaper about that. He asserted that he could speak five languages and that he was immensely rich. It was observed that the patient made these statements in an indifferent manner, not caring about contradictions. At times he would lie on the floor and throw his clothes around. There was increasing weakness of all functions, but especially those of judgment and orientation, in addition to the changing delusions of grandeur that were presented without affect. Sleep was not disturbed, nor were appetite or bowel function. Dr. Tilkowsky made a diagnosis of progressive paralysis, and the "Kommission" declared Mr. D. to be *idiotic*. He was given daily electric treatments with induction current and sulfur baths for pain. In August the treatment was changed to potassium sulfate baths; however, no relief of pain was noted until September. Mr. D. was friendly with the physicians, but wrote letters complaining about the hospital and threatened to hang himself on the first best nail if he could not get out soon. He also gave instructions for large stock purchases on the exchange. In November he was given morphine daily to help his insomnia, and in December this was changed to chloral hydrate and long warm baths. One month later he was noted to be improved, friendlier, busy at work with a fret saw. From his letters it was evident that he was improving markedly, though there was still some confusion. In November, 1883, he was discharged on probation.

One can discern that the patients were attentively examined and the observed psychopathological phenomena meticulously recorded. In those pre-Kräpelinian days symptomatology and nosology were not yet systematized, and the present-day psychiatrist may therefore easily get the misleading impression of haphazard investigations. Little etiological speculation can be recognized except some cryptic comments pointing to heredity and alcohol. Interest apparently focused on careful clinical description and the collection of anatomical and histological data through postmortem examinations. In the absence of specific treatment methods the therapeutic regimen seemed designed toward support, maintenance, and restoration of general physical well-being. The tone of these physician's reports reflects a detached and scientifically interested concern without a trace of impatience or unkindness in the face of a difficult task. Similarly, it seems reasonable to assume that Freud purchased his psychiatric experience by the labor of meticulous observations. Three of the admission notes are signed "Dr. Freud" and will now be reported in somewhat more detail.

Case 45/83 was a forty-five-year-old wood-seller from Vienna who was admitted to the hospital in May, 1883. Freud noted on admission a high-grade maniacal excitement with an urge to move, dance, and jump all the time. The patient would attempt to beat anyone coming near him, and during the preceding night he had run around without clothes, carrying a candle, and had to be forcibly brought back into his apartment. Freud's impression: "potator," "idiot." The subsequent record shows the patient to have fluctuated between states of *excitement* and *apathy*, with many *persecution-maniacal ideas, confusion,* and *disorientation.* He became progressively more ill and died in June, 1884, of pneumonia.

Case 480 was a sixty-two-year old maid who had been born in Bavaria and who was admitted in August, 1883. Freud noted on admission that the patient had been unable to work and *excited* at night, but that she had not been dangerous to her surroundings. He observed that she answered questions in a *feebleminded* way and had no sense of time or place. She had hallucinatory visions of her father. This woman was transferred unchanged to another hospital two years later with the diagnosis of *idiocy.*

Case 503 was a sixty-nine-year-old beneficiary from Vienna admitted in August, 1883. Freud's note reports that she had been ill for more than a quarter year and had been treated by Dr. Visaric for five to six weeks. The patient, he notes, said she has been suffering from gout for years. Her father and her brother had died of ailments of the brain. She now looked neglected, she believed, because her family had *persecuted* her for suffering from syphilis. She also complained of *sleeplessness* and *excitements.* Freud observed that she was quiet and had *hallucinations* in which she was accused of the most terrible things. This patient gradually worsened and died of tuberculosis in October, 1886. Diagnosis was *Madness,* and the face sheet indicated *heredity* as the etiology.

One cannot be sure, of course, whether these admission notes, though signed "Dr. Freud,"[7] were actually written by him. They are in no way remarkable and cannot be distinguished from the notes written by other physicians.

In summary these patient records provide evidence that in Meynert's psychiatric clinic Freud met with a broad and intensive exposure to a wide range of the usual severe psychiatric illnesses admitted to a psychiatric ward of a General Hospital. Perhaps this experience contributed to his growing sensitivity to the inner conflicts which bedevil Man. And, perhaps,

---

[7] The available records are typescripts, and authenticity of the signatures therefore cannot be verified.

it was during his assignment at Meynert's clinic that he learned that "nothing in life is so expensive as illness—and stupidity" (Freud, 1913, p. 133).

BIBLIOGRAPHY

Freud, S. (1913), On Beginning the Treatment. *Standard Edition*, 12:133–150, London: Hogarth, 1961.
—— (1925), An Autobiographical Study. *Standard Edition*, 20:10–137, London: Hogarth, 1957.
Jones, E. (1953), *The Life and Work of Sigmund Freud*. Vol. 1. New York: Basic Books.

VII

APPLIED
PSYCHOANALYSIS

On Oscar Wilde

ALEXANDER GRINSTEIN, M.D. (*Detroit*)

This paper is a small fragment from my forthcoming book, which is a psychoanalytic study of Oscar Wilde. At the very outset I would like to indicate some of the problems in doing such a psychoanalytic study. It is always difficult to deal with a historical figure because of the limited availability of personal material. This is especially true in the case of Wilde. There are no journals, no diaries, and only two (very brief) dreams have been recorded. In addition, Wilde was so vain and so affected, such a *poseur*, and his writings and speeches were so filled with deliberate deception, that his real self was often obscured by a "mist of words."

Despite these difficulties, however, there are important primary sources: Wilde's extant letters have now been published in unexpurgated form; his statements in court during his trials are a matter of public record; and all his writings are available. In addition to these sources, there are a number of excellent biographies. By studying this material I have endeavored to piece together something of a dynamic formulation of Oscar Wilde's personality, a psychoanalytic picture of Oscar Wilde if you will. This picture, however, is at best a sketch—incomplete and imperfect.

I am mindful, of course, of the fact that using literary productions as a basis for understanding an author's personality presents certain dangers and possibilities of error. We cannot have the author confirm or disprove our hypotheses. Hence, we can never be entirely certain what dynamic determinants in the author's personality were responsible for his choice of material. Thus, even though we may recognize that certain themes are parallel or even identical with what is known about the life of an author, there is always an element of conjecture as to whether these themes actually provided the determining factors for a particular work. When one sees that these themes appear repeatedly in the author's work, however, and when one knows certain biographical facts about him, then the supposition that these biographical events served as important determinants is greatly strengthened. Moreover, if the author utilizes these autobiographical events

Originally presented to the Michigan Association for Psychoanalysis, Detroit, April 20, 1968. Presented also to the Chicago Institute for Psychoanalysis, September 23, 1969.

and then provides material which furnishes us with a genetic explanation for them, as Wilde does, then, even though we are dealing with fictional material, we may suspect that the author himself was trying to provide a psychological explanation for these autobiographical events.

Wilde died on November 30, 1900, at the age of forty-six, at the Hotel d'Alsace in Paris. His death was caused by an intracranial complication of a suppurative otitis media and an abscess in his ear, on which he had had an operation a short time before. According to Brasol (one of Wilde's biographers), Dr. Maurice Tucker, the physician who examined him prior to his death, stated that Wilde had "all the signs of syphilis" (Wiegler, 1929, as cited by Brasol, 1938, p. 384), but thus far I have been unable to find out exactly what these signs were, let alone any definite confirmation that he ever actually had the disease.

During the last year of his life Wilde became quite deaf and developed extensive red blotches over his body—"like a leopard," he wrote. He believed that these blotches came from a kind of "blood poisoning" and blamed it on eating mussels. He was treated with arsenic and strychnine but without much success (Hart-Davis, 1962, pp. 817–818). Besides the deafness and the skin disease, there was evidence of a general deterioration of Wilde's personality. He drank excessively, including great quantities of absinthe. He became inordinately dependent on his friends for his support, repeatedly asking them for money which he then immediately squandered. He suffered horribly from depression, social ostracism, isolation, and loneliness. As far as his homosexual practices were concerned, he was "hand in glove with all the little boys" on the Paris boulevards. Stories that Wilde became a drunken, unshaven, shabbily dressed bum wandering around Paris in a confused state, are quite untrue, however. He remained clever and witty and, as far as I can gather, was entirely in possession of his faculties until just before his death.

There is no doubt that Wilde was left a broken man by the experiences of the three trials which plunged him from the height of fame in early 1895, when *The Importance of Being Earnest* and *An Ideal Husband* were both playing in London to packed houses, to the abyss of social stigma and ostracism in May of the same year, when he was reviled and spit upon. The horrors of total degradation and dehumanization during the two years of hard prison labor completely crushed him. Whatever glimmer of hope Wilde may have had for his rehabilitation after his release from prison ultimately had to be abandoned. To avoid further painful publicity, he left England and was barred by court order from ever seeing his family. Probably the most bitter experience of all during these years was the disintegration of his intimate relationship with Lord Alfred Douglas.

From the time that he was released from prison on May 19, 1897, until his death three years later, Wilde wrote two articles on prison life, which were published in the *Daily Chronicle* (May 28, 1897, and March 24, 1898), and completed his "Ballad of Reading Gaol" (August, 1897). Apart from these he was unable to write anything new. His letters, however, remained clear, lucid, and reasonably rational.

It is not my intention in this paper to give the complicated and rather sordid details of Wilde's trials. It should suffice to provide the following brief information for purposes of orientation.

Oscar Wilde began his fatal friendship with twenty-one-year-old Lord Alfred Douglas, the third son of the Marquess of Queensbury, in 1891, a relationship which became a passionate, homosexual love affair. Evidently, the character of their association was so obvious that the marquess, a very cruel, sadistic man, divorced from Lord Alfred's mother because of his flagrant extramarital affairs, sought to break off the relationship between his son and Wilde. After many unsuccessful attempts to do this, he left his card at Wilde's club, the Albemarle Club, in London on February 18, 1895, four days after the opening of *The Importance of Being Earnest*. On the card he wrote: "To Oscar Wilde, posing as a sodomite" (which he misspelled "Somdomite"). The club porter put the card in an envelope and did not show it to anyone. Wilde received the card some ten days later. Lord Alfred, determined to have his father prosecuted for his own personal reasons, persuaded Wilde to press libel charges against Queensbury. Despite repeated advice to the contrary, Wilde pressed such charges, lying to his legal counsel that there was absolutely no truth to the allegations. Queensbury in turn found a number of people of very questionable reputation who were willing to testify on his behalf concerning Wilde's abnormal practices. The marquess was acquitted of the charge of libel on April 5. Realizing the danger, Wilde's friends, his wife, and his legal counsel all encouraged him to flee the country. For various reasons, however, Wilde could not bring himself to go. He was arrested later the same day and charged with a violation of the Criminal Law Amendment, Section ii, enacted in 1885, which made homosexuality, whether practiced in public or private, a punishable offense. After two trials, Wilde was convicted and sentenced on May 25, 1895, to the maximum penalty: imprisonment for two years at hard labor. All evidence points to the fact that, although Wilde was guilty and admitted this in his writings, the sentence imposed by the seventy-seven-year-old presiding justice, Alfred Wills, was unduly harsh and sadistic.

Wilde's action in bringing a libel suit against the Marquess of Queensbury and the whole manner in which it was done—his woefully driven disregard of everyone's advice that he not go through with it, his lying to his counsel, etc.—clearly were not based on reality demands but undoubtedly were brought about by internal forces. It is interesting to note that, while in his last year at Oxford, Wilde had said: "I'll be a poet, a writer, a dramatist. Somehow or other, I'll be famous, and if not famous, I'll be notorious . . . " (Holland, 1960, p. 27). It would thus appear that Wilde attempted to fulfill all aspects of this prediction. He became a poet, a writer, a dramatist. He became famous, but the unconscious need to be notorious as well served to spur him to provoke a legal action that resulted in his punishment and ruin.

Strange as it may seem to us today, during the first trial, some of Wilde's literary productions were used by the defense as evidence against him to prove his homosexuality, i.e., that he was "posing as a sodomite." The most notable of these was his only novel *The Picture of Dorian Gray*, portions of· which· were read in open court. It is obvious to us today, just as it was to many of Wilde's contemporaries, that one cannot very well use a literary invention or creation of a writer as either an indictment against him or as a *proof* of anything about his personality. Nonetheless, there are some striking parallels between the life of Oscar Wilde and those of Lord Henry Wotten and Dorian Gray. We are, of course, not interested in using Wilde's writings as an indictment against him as was attempted during the trials. We are interested, however, in trying to understand something about his personality dynamics and his psychopathology, as revealed from his publications and his other writings.

The Picture of Dorian Gray first came out in America on June 20, 1890, as a story in the July issue of *Lippincott's Monthly Magazine*. In other words, it was written before Wilde met Lord Alfred Douglas. The novel, the form in which *Dorian Gray* is best known, was published in April, 1891. In addition to making many changes from the original version, Wilde added six new chapters and a preface in order to answer the storm of violent criticism and indignation as to its "immorality" that the story had aroused in England.

Let me now briefly review *The Picture of Dorian Gray*, with emphasis on the details that are pertinent in connection with this paper.

While visiting his friend, the artist Basil Hallward, Lord Henry Wotten talked with him about his almost completed full-length portrait of Dorian Gray, a young man of "extraordinary personal beauty." The painter confided that Dorian "now and then [was] horribly thoughtless, and seem[ed] to take a real delight in giving [him] pain" (p. 25).

While the men were talking, Dorian, a somewhat naïve, petulant, narcissistic youth of twenty, arrived to pose for the finishing touches on his portrait. Lord Henry attempted to seduce him into gratifying his forbidden impulses. He said: "Every impulse that we strive to strangle broods in the mind, and poisons us. . . . The only way to get rid of a temptation is to yield to it. Resist it, and your soul grows sick, with longing . . . " (p. 29). "Nothing can cure the soul but the senses, just as nothing can cure the senses but the soul" (p. 31). Dorian immediately became attracted to Lord Henry. The older man proceeded to extol the virtues of youth and the damaging ravages of age: ugliness, wrinkles, sallowness, and dull eyes. He declared: "Our limbs fail, our senses rot. We degenerate into hideous puppets, haunted by the memory of the passions of which we were too much afraid, and the exquisite temptations that we had not the courage to yield to" (p. 32).

When Hallward finished his painting, Dorian looked at it with joy. But, as Lord Henry's comments on the evanescence of youth stirred him greatly, he expressed the wish: "If it were I who was to be always young, and the picture that was to grow old! For that—for that—I would give everything! . . . I would give my soul for that!" (p. 34).

The next day Lord Henry called on his uncle to learn from him some of the details of Dorian's background. These facts, omitted in the original story, are important in our understanding of the dynamics of Dorian's personality. Dorian Gray was the grandson of the last Lord Kelso. His mother was Lady Margaret Devereux, an extraordinarily beautiful and romantic girl who had run away with a penniless young infantry officer. A few months after the marriage the young man was killed in a duel at Spa. Evidently Lord Kelso had paid some "Belgian rascally adventurer" to insult his son-in-law in public. The Belgian had then "spitted this man as if he had been a pigeon." Lady Margaret never spoke to her father after that and died within a year, soon after Dorian's birth. Although he was independently wealthy from another inheritance, Dorian would also inherit Kelso's money and property when he came of age. Kelso evidently was a mean, tyrannical, quarrelsome and "loveless" man.

Later, in a conversation with his aunt, Lord Henry indicated that he could "sympathize with everything, except suffering. . . . The less said about life's sores the better" (p. 44). What is so significant about this remark, coming as it does after the discussion of Dorian's traumatic background, is that it indicates the author's view about the importance of suppression (and ultimately repression) from consciousness of unpleasant and painful events.

A month after the completion of his portrait, Dorian fell in love with a beautiful seventeen-year-old Shakespearean actress named Sibyl Vane. In the relationship that developed between them, the girl did not learn Dorian's name but referred to him as her "Prince Charming."

In the only digression in the story, Wilde informs the reader that Sibyl had a brother, James, a year her junior, who was on his way to becoming a sailor and had orders to leave for Australia. James had cautioned Sibyl to beware of her Prince Charming and vowed that if this man ever did her any wrong, he would kill him.

Within a month after he met Sibyl, Dorian announced to Lord Henry and Hallward that he was engaged to her. He invited his friends to the theater with him to watch her perform in *Romeo and Juliet*. That evening, however, her acting was so poor that many of the audience hissed and left.

Dorian felt that Sibyl had entirely altered. The previous evening she had been a great artist; this evening she was commonplace and mediocre. Following this performance, Sibyl told Dorian that she would never act again. Since she had fallen in love with him, she had realized what reality was and therefore could no longer *act* being in love, for that would be profanation. Furious that she had thrown away her talent, Dorian told her contemptuously that she had killed his love. Sibyl begged him not to leave her. She admitted that what she had done was foolish and promised Dorian that she would try to act. Dorian regarded her as being absurdly melodramatic, however, and disdainfully left.

Later, when he arrived home, Dorian saw that a change had taken place in his portrait. There was a touch of "cruelty around the mouth as clearly as if he had been looking into a mirror after he had done some dreadful thing" (p. 77). Although at first he could not believe what had happened, he realized that the picture would change with every sin he committed. "The picture, changed or unchanged, would be to him the visible emblem of conscience" (p. 79). He determined to resist temptation, decided that he would return to Sibyl, beg her forgiveness, marry her, and try to love her as he had before.

He went to the table and wrote a passionate letter to Sibyl, imploring her forgiveness. Just then Lord Henry came into the room and informed him that Sibyl had committed suicide by taking cyanide, soon after Dorian had left her. Although the young man's initial reaction was that it was terrible, Lord Henry persuaded him not to let a thing like that upset him but to dine with him and go the opera where they would meet his sister, Lady Gwendolyn.

Dorian could hardly believe what had happened, feeling that he had murdered Sibyl. He said: "Strange, that my first passionate love-letter should have been addressed to a dead girl. Can they feel, I wonder, those white silent people we call the dead? . . . Oh, Harry, how I loved her once! It seems years ago to me now" (p. 83).

At this point in the story Oscar Wilde writes that "once, in boyish mockery of Narcissus, Dorian had kissed, or feigned to kiss, those painted lips that now smiled so cruelly at him. Morning after morning he had sat before the portrait, wondering at its beauty, almost enamoured of it . . ." (p. 88).

The next morning, when Hallward visited Dorian to express his sympathies for Sibyl's death, Dorian remarked: "Don't talk about horrid subjects. If one doesn't talk about a thing, it has never happened" (p. 89). During the course of the visit Dorian goaded the painter into admitting his homosexual attraction to him.

After Hallward left, Dorian covered the painting and had it carried to his old schoolroom at the top of his house, a room which was used for storage. It had not been opened since the death of his grandfather when Dorian was sixteen. After the picture was installed there, Dorian locked the door and kept the key with him. Dorian realized that his picture "had a corruption of its own, worse than the corruption of death itself—something that would breed horrors and yet would never die. What the worm was to the corpse, his sins would be to the painted image on the canvas. They would mar its beauty, and eat away its grace" (pp. 96–97).

In the years that followed, Dorian participated in all manner of pleasures and sins. In spite of his debaucheries, his youthful physical appearance did not change. Only his picture changed. He lived in luxury, entertained lavishly, dressed extremely well, and was the model of fashion. He studied perfumes and music. He collected jewels, embroideries, tapestries, textiles, and ecclesiastical vestments. For periods of time he would not go to the lonely locked room of his boyhood, but then he would find himself compelled to view the changes in the picture, at times with loathing and at times with pride.

On occasion he would become so obsessed that he would be overcome by intense anxiety that some one might have broken into the attic room and looked at the picture. At these times he would suddenly leave his guests, even if he were at his country house, and rush back to town to examine the door of the room where his picture was kept, to see if it had been tampered with. He was dreadfully afraid that somebody might steal the portrait and that then his secret would be revealed. He felt that if anyone saw the picture it could be regarded as evidence against him.

Around eleven o'clock in the evening on the ninth of November, the eve of Dorian's thirty-eighth birthday (his thirty-second in the original story), while walking home from visiting Lord Henry, Dorian met Basil, whom he had not seen for a long time. The painter told him that he had wanted to see him before he left for a six months' visit to Paris. Dorian invited Basil into his house. The painter told him that he had heard evil gossip about him. He mentioned the sullied reputation that many women, including Lord Henry's sister, Lady Gwendolyn, had acquired since their association with Dorian and named a number of young men whose friendship with Dorian had been fatal. Basil wanted to hear from Dorian himself whether these rumors were true or false.

Dorian contemptuously told Basil that he would show him his soul. He then led him to the locked attic room and revealed the portrait to the horrified artist, reminding him of the wish he had uttered at the time the painting was completed. The figure in the painting was so dreadful that "the rotting of a corpse in a watery grave was not so fearful" (p. 122). Suddenly Dorian was seized with a feeling of uncontrollable hatred for Hallward. Picking up a knife, he plunged it "into the great vein that is behind the ear, crushing the man's head down on the table and stabbing him again and again" (p. 123).

The next day Dorian summoned Alan Campbell, a young man with whom he had at one time presumably been involved in a homosexual affair, and blackmailed him into destroying the painter's body.

Later that evening, Dorian went to an opium den, but the presence of an erstwhile homosexual acquaintance convinced him to go elsewhere. As he left, a prostitute addressed him as "Prince Charming." A sailor drowsing in the den, heard this, and then rushed after Dorian. When he caught up with him in the dark, he told him he would kill him, saying: "You wrecked the life of Sibyl Vane, and Sibyl Vane was my sister. She killed herself. I know it. Her death is at your door. I swore I would kill you in return. For years I have sought you. . . . I knew nothing of you but the pet name she used to call you. I heard it tonight by chance . . ." (pp. 144–145).

Frightened at the prospect of being killed, Dorian asked Vane how long ago his sister had died. When the man replied that this had happened eighteen years before, Dorian had him look at his face in the light. Seeing before him a lad of twenty, Vane realized that he had made a mistake. He pleaded with Dorian to forgive him. Dorian left. The prostitute followed Vane, however, and told him that Dorian was much older than he looked, that it was almost eighteen years since he had made her what she was.

A week later Vane traced Dorian to his house. Dorian was terrified that Vane would kill him, as he himself had murdered the painter. But a short time later Vane was accidently shot by a hunter on Dorian's country estate, thus putting an end to Dorian's anxiety.

A change now took place in Dorian's personality; he wanted to become good. He had met a peasant girl and was quite sure that he loved her, so he determined not to have sexual relations with her. When he told this to Lord Henry, the latter laughed at him and told him that the girl would be disappointed.

By this time Lord Henry was divorced and Campbell had committed suicide. One evening Dorian asked Lord Henry what he would say if he told him that he had murdered Basil, to which the latter replied: "It is not in you, Dorian, to commit a murder" (p. 160). That night Dorian began to think about the three men (Vane, Campbell, Hallward) who had died because of him. He resolved to be more kindly in the future, and, as he had not seduced the peasant girl, he thought there might now be some change for the better in the portrait.

When he went to view it, he found, however, that it was even more hypocritical and more loathsome than ever. There seemed to be blood on the hands and feet of the painting. He determined that he would destroy the picture which he regarded as evidence against him. Seizing the knife with which he had stabbed Basil, he decided that, if it had killed the painter, it would kill the painter's work and all that it meant. He would kill the past and then he would be free. With this he stabbed the picture with the knife. A cry was heard, followed by a crash.

Finding the door locked, the servants, who had been alarmed by the sounds, had to climb in through the balcony and found "hanging upon the wall, a splendid portrait of their master as they had last seen him in all the wonder of his exquisite youth and beauty. Lying on the floor was a dead man, in evening dress, with a knife in his heart. He was withered, wrinkled, and loathsome of visage. It was not till they had examined the rings that they recognized who it was" (p. 167).

Tempted as I am to discuss from a psychoanalytic standpoint the dynamics of this fascinating story, some of which are evident from the above synopsis, including such themes as the *doppelgänger*, "the uncanny effect," the role of the mother, the significance of the picture as the superego, Dorian's aggression against his grandfather, etc., I must refrain. These subjects and others will be taken up in great detail in my forthcoming book. I will limit my remarks to a few topics.

Some of the hero's problems can be understood as a clinical case study drawn from Oscar Wilde's presentation of the "facts" about Dorian's unfortunate background, "facts" that he added in the book version. I will briefly summarize some of the psychodynamics operative in Dorian's personality. The hero's fears about aging, deterioration, and death, set in motion by Lord Henry's remarks, were founded upon the tragic circumstances of his parents' death and his having to live at the home of his hated and feared grandfather. To cope with these anxieties Dorian elaborated many characterological defenses, among which were narcissism and an identification with his grandfather as the aggressor. This identification probably became intensified after his grandfather's death. Dorian felt that by his cruelty, he was responsible for Sibyl's death, just as his grandfather had been responsible for the death of Dorian's young mother. By his action, Dorian also probably attempted to undo what had happened to him in his infancy. Now it was he who abandoned a love object, rather than being the one who was left abandoned by his mother's death. Dorian's identification with his grandfather became progressively more complete after he himself came of age and presumably became the heir of his grandfather's fortune. Further identification with his grandfather was manifested in the changes that took place in Dorian's picture where he became old and even had blue veins like his grandfather. With his act of murdering Basil Hallward, the man who "fathered" his picture, Dorian's identification with his grandfather became complete. He stabbed the painter just as the Belgian employed by his grandfather had spitted Dorian's father "as if he had been a pigeon." On one level, the picture in its final stage represents Dorian in the very image of his hated grandfather. Since he could no longer tolerate the person that he had become, he finally endeavored to kill this person within himself and perished in the attempt.

I would now like to discuss Sibyl Vane's death. Although, as we have seen, there were early determinants of Dorian's personality difficulties, and although the stage for the story was set in the painter's studio at the time of Dorian's fatal wish, the actual changes in his picture, and hence in his personality, occurred only *after* his first act of cruelty: his repudiation of his love for Sibyl. Dorian's initial reaction to her death was one of horror and dismay. He felt responsible for it; was visibly affected by it; and reacted in a way that by any standard would be considered quite normal. As Lord Henry talked with him, however, he gradually assumed the defense of completely suppressing any feelings about Sibyl's death. As I indicated above, he went out to dine, to the Opera, and was introduced to Lady Gwendolyn, Lord Henry's sister. Later, Dorian justified his incomprehensible behavior to Basil by his verbalization that "if one doesn't talk about a thing, it never happened." It is unlikely that this suppression and the ultimate repression of his grief and guilt could have developed following Sibyl's death unless such defense mechanisms had been established earlier in Dorian's life.

Following Sibyl's death Dorian developed a number of complicated reactions. In part these served to ward off his feelings of guilt for the responsibility of her death; in part they served to ward off his deeply felt longing for her. In an attempt to find a substitute for the lost, real love object, he developed an almost frantic search for some satisfying material possessions.

I have already related Wilde's description of how once "in a boyish mockery of Narcissus," Dorian "kissed or feigned to kiss those painted lips that now smiled so cruelly at him." This narcissistic action following Sibyl's death may be understood as an expression of Dorian's desire to be reunited with the lost love object. Quite frequently in our clinical practice we hear of a child who kisses or hugs himself in reaction to having lost a love object, expressing in this way his wish to be reunited with it. Dorian's flurry of heterosexual behavior, particularly his affair with Lady Gwendolyn, Lord Henry's sister, immediately following Sibyl's death may also be regarded as an attempt to revive a lost relationship. Of particularly major significance, moreover, is the fact that Dorian's overt homosexual activity began after Sibyl's death. In addition to these reactions the personality of Dorian underwent continued deterioration. He went from one "sin" to another, and ultimately committed murder.

Let us now return to Oscar Wilde himself. It has been conceded by most writers that *The Picture of Dorian Gray* reveals much about its author, so much so that, as I have already told you, it was used in court as evidence against him. Some have commented on the fact that the character of Lord Henry Wotten is very much like that of Oscar Wilde. There is little doubt that Lord Wotten's cynicism, sarcasm, and wit, his marital difficulties, and his propensities to tempt young men were attributes of Wilde's personality. In addition to this, moreover, Dorian Gray himself represents certain aspects of Wilde. Introduced to homosexual practices in 1886 by his friend Robert Ross, who was seventeen years old at that time, Wilde seemed to be already undergoing a personality deterioration in 1890 when *Dorian Gray* was written. He became more estranged from his wife, and at the time of his arrest in 1895 Constance Wilde indicated that he had been "mad for the last three years." Many of the people who knew him commented on the change in his physical appearance during these years. He was described during this period as "unpleasant" and "bloated" (see Sherard, 1915, as cited by Brasol, 1938, p. 212). His gaze was half-veiled, his eyes expressionless under lids that seemed heavy with inexpressible weariness. Brasol believed it only natural that a life of unbridled lust that came from a surfeit of success or of money (Sherard) should have "left upon Wilde a hideous impress like that which Dorian perceived in the beautiful features of his own portrait" (Brasol, 1938, p. 213).

In his letters from Reading Gaol, Wilde himself indicated that he had been "suffering from the most horrible form of erotomania, which made him forget his wife and children, his high social position in London and Paris . . . and left him the helpless prey of the most revolting passions" (July 2, 1896). He described himself as being for the two years preceding his ruin the "prey of absolute madness—the insanity of perverted sensual instincts" (November 10, 1896). On April 1, 1897, he wrote that his "record of perversities of passion and distorted romances would fill many scarlet volumes. . . . Tired of being at the heights I deliberately went to the depths in the search for new sensations. What the paradox was to me in the sphere of thought, perversity became to me in the sphere of passion."

Earlier in this paper I indicated that some of Wilde's biographers (Sherard, Harris) believed that there was an organic basis for Wilde's deterioration. According to Sherard (Brasol, p. 221), Wilde contracted syphilis while at Oxford and received mercury injections. Sherard believed that some of Wilde's teeth may have turned black and become decayed because of this treatment. He relates that, prior to proposing to Constance Lloyd (they were married May 29, 1884), Wilde went to see a physician who assured him that he was completely cured. Sherard goes on to say, however, that shortly after the birth of Vyvyan, Wilde's second son, on November 3, 1886, he discovered that his syphilis, which had been dormant, had returned. Just what his symptoms were is not stated. According to Sherard, Wilde believed that if he were to continue sex relations with his wife, he would infect her or have a syphilitic child. It was around this time that he turned to homosexual practices. While it is possible that Wilde may have been concerned about injuring his wife, it is questionable that this was actually the determinant of his turning toward homosexuality at this time.[1]

It seems to me that Wilde's characterization of the changes that took place in the picture of Dorian Gray may have represented his perception of the changes that were taking place within himself at this time (1890). The question arises as to whether these changes were the result of some process of organic deterioration, such as syphilis, or had solely a psychogenic basis. It is extremely doubtful that these changes were organic. There was no change in Wilde's handwriting such as would be associated with neuro-

---

[1] It is of incidental interest that in the novel of Dorian Gray Oscar Wilde gave the date of Basil's murder as November 9, the eve of the hero's thirty-eighth birthday, while in the original story he gave his age as thirty-two. If we apply this to Oscar Wilde, adding thirty-two to 1854, the year of his birth, we come up with 1886, the year Vyvyan was born and the year Wilde began his homosexual relations with Ross. The date of the murder itself, then, would be shortly after Vyvyan was born! Vyvyan Wilde was born on November 5, 1886.

syphilis, and no loss of his artistic creativity. He wrote some of his best plays after this date including *An Ideal Husband, Salomé, Lady Windemere's Fan,* and *The Importance of Being Earnest.* The unconscious significance of the perception of the deterioration was that it was probably equated with castration. We may even suspect that the gruesomeness of the painting which Wilde describes before the final scene may have had this meaning, among others, for him. The adjectives that Wilde used to describe the picture—bloody, boggy, wrinkled, twisted, deformed, etc.—may all be applied to his view of, or his perception of, the female genital.

Let us now consider some of the psychological determinants of Wilde's personality difficulties insofar as these can be determined. In order to do this I must now digress and provide the following important background information about Oscar Wilde. He was born in Dublin on October 15, 1854. His father, a rude, crude, dirty man, was a famous ear surgeon and author of many books on a variety of subjects, including archaeology, and an important treatise on otology. Early in 1864 he was knighted at Dublin Castle for his services to statistical science, especially his work with the Irish census.

Sir William Wilde's extramarital affairs were well known, and he fathered a number of illegitimate children. One of his natural sons later became associated with him in his medical practice. Sir William's sexual behavior achieved particular prominence, however, as a result of his association with Mary Travers, who first came to see him in 1854, when she was nineteen. They had an affair, and she subsequently accused him of having chloroformed her and of then having had sexual relations with her while she was unconscious. Through a complicated set of circumstances, the matter culminated in a trial in December, 1864, when Oscar was ten years old. The outcome of the trial was that the jury assessed the damages to Miss Travers at one farthing, thus, in effect, finding Sir William not guilty of her claim that he had seduced her. The whole matter received a great deal of publicity, and Sir William, formerly a famous man, dropped out of active medical practice and public life. Although he continued to do some writing, he gradually deteriorated.

There can be little doubt that Oscar Wilde heard a good deal about these events. At the time of the trial he was away at Portora Royal School, and the boys there must have talked about it a good deal since it was a highly salacious and scandalous affair involving a famous figure. The story is related that one day during his school days young Oscar exclaimed that "nothing would please him more than to be the leading figure in a great trial and to achieve fame as the defendant in a case of Regina v. Wilde" (Pearson, 1946, p. 18). I venture to suggest that out of his unconscious need to repeat his father's experience Oscar Wilde provoked the trial of Alfred Douglas' father (a man also involved in flaunting his extramarital affairs), thus creating a situation in which his own personal and sexual life was brought before the public eye. Like his father, Oscar Wilde himself became the object of scandal and fulfilled the prediction of notoriety that he had made years before. The results of the trial also brought about a deterioration of his personality similar to that suffered by his father.

Oscar Wilde's mother, née Jane Francesca Elgee, an authoress in her own right under the pen name of "Speranza," had also been involved in legal action, but this was before Oscar's birth and was related to the cause of Irish nationalism. A discussion of these matters is beyond the scope of this paper.

After the birth of their first son, Willie, in 1852, Lady Wilde badly wanted a daughter. When Oscar was born, she dressed him in girl's clothes. Although this was not so unusual in those days, the intent behind it, the degree to which this was carried out, and the length of time it persisted seemed to have contributed to her son's feminine identification.

When Oscar was around three, his sister, Isola Francesca, was born. She died around ten years later on February 23, 1867. Oscar was twelve years and four months old at the time and away at school, but her death affected him deeply. The doctor recorded that "Oscar's lonely and inconsolable grief found its outward expression in long and frequent visits to his sister's grave in the village cemetery" (Pearson, 1946, p. 18). A number of years later (1881) Wilde published the poem "Requiescat" [in Pace: May she rest in peace] in his sister's memory. He refers to her: "Lily-white, white as snow, / She hardly knew / She was a woman, so / Sweetly she grew." The last two lines of this poem indicate how attached he was to her, for he wrote: "All my life's buried here, / Heap earth upon it." In another poem "Ballade de Marguerite" (1879) he wrote: "O mother, you know I loved her true; / O mother, hath one grave room for two?"

Isola's death must have been very significant for him. After his death an envelope was found in his possession on which was written "My Isola's Hair, Obit. February 23, 1867. She is. not. dead. but. sleepeth." Mark 5:39. Other expressions written on the envelope were "Thy will be done," "Resurgam." [I shall rise again], "She rests in peace." "God is love." Of even greater interest is the fact that on either side of what appears to be a box or coffin on which is written "My Isola's Hair," Wilde drew a crucifix with the initials O and I, and I and O. Both crucifixes are on mounds of earth as though over graves: his own as well as Isola's. There are two wreath-like figures connected by a bond near the top of the envelope. One of these has an O on it; the other an I. This bond between the O and the I wreaths suggests the strength of the relationship and identification between Oscar Wilde and his sister. The fact that this envelope was taken with him to Europe and thus preserved when so many of his personal effects were lost after his death is a further testimonial to its importance.

It is interesting to note that for many years Oscar Wilde lied about his age, saying that he was born in 1856, an error that is even perpetuated in the *Encyclopaedia Britannica*. Curiously, his mother also lied about her age, making herself two years younger (Wilson, 1942, p. 180). The truth that he was born in 1854 was actually disclosed at the time of his first trial, when Queensbury's defense counsel, Edward Carson, produced a copy of Wilde's birth certificate. Various writers have claimed that Wilde lied about his age in order to appear younger or perhaps to repress the early period when he was dressed as a girl. We may suggest as an alternative possibility that Wilde lied about his age because he thereby expressed his wish to be born at an age when his mother was pregnant with his sister. In later years, Wilde said that he would have named his second child Isola if it had been a daughter. It may be of significance that his homosexual behavior began at this time.

I have already indicated the striking parallels between Oscar Wilde and Dorian Gray insofar as their personality deterioration is concerned. Now I would like to go a step further, because I feel that Wilde, by giving the genetic determinants of Dorian's personality deterioration, provides us with a clue to his own personality difficulties.

What I want to discuss now deals further with Sibyl Vane and her pertinence to Oscar Wilde. Sibyl, it will be remembered, was three years Dorian's junior. The name "Sibyl" is very similar to "Isola," who was, as we have already seen, three years *his* junior. Although the name "Isola" derives from a different source than "Sibyl," the two names are close enough in sound to be readily interchangeable. Examples of such transpositions of names are frequent in Wilde's writings.

Dorian's immediate reaction to Sibyl's death was that his cruelty was responsible for it. It was partly because of Lord Henry's influence and partly because he realized that the picture would bear the burden of his guilt that Dorian was able to repress his guilt and to embark upon a career of debauchery and crime. It is striking that Dorian's first love letter was to a dead person. He says: "Strange that my first passionate love-letter should have been addressed to a dead girl. Can they feel, I wonder, those white silent people we call the dead?" There are, moreover, many allusions to death in connection with the picture in the story. Wilde writes: "What the worm was to the corpse, his [Dorian's] sins would be to the painted image on the canvas." The figure in the painting was so dreadful that "the rotting of a corpse in a watery grave was not so fearful . . ." The picture thus served, in part, to represent those people for whose death Dorian felt responsible, including Sibyl.

Let us now consider the possibility that Oscar Wilde unconsciously equated Sibyl Vane with his sister Isola, and apply the sequence of events in the story to the historical events in the life of its author. We may then surmise that Wilde was saying that the etiology of *his* personality disturbances, his homosexuality, his debauchery, and ultimately his deterioration, began with Isola's death. Like the hero in his story, Wilde, too, may have felt responsible for the death of a girl three years his junior and attempted to deal with it by many complicated defenses: narcissism, a suppression and repression of his grief, an exaggerated consideration for material things rather than genuine personal relationships, homosexuality, etc. Like Dorian, Wilde may also have wondered whether "they feel . . . those white silent people we call the dead." In his poem "Requiescat" he gave the ability of sensation to his dead sister, for he wrote: "Tread lightly, she is near / Under the snow, / Speak gently, she can hear / The daisies grow."

We may assume that apart from his relationship to his mother (a theme that I am purposely omitting in this presentation) the first heterosexual object that had a great emotional significance for Wilde was his sister. Dorian's wonder that his "first passionate love-letter should have been addressed to a dead girl" probably refers to Oscar Wilde's feeling about Isola and to the envelope mentioned above.

There is a further interesting parallel between the story and reality that may be pertinent in this connection. You will recall that in the story, after Dorian learns of Sibyl's death, he goes to the opera with Lord Henry and his sister, Lady Gwendolyn. We may suspect that Wilde's introduction of Lord Henry's *sister* into the story just at this point, almost as a replacement for the dead Sibyl, indicates that Wilde was attributing a sister significance to Sibyl and was alluding directly to his own feelings about *his* sister, Isola. This is especially convincing if we bear in mind that Lord Henry clearly stands for Oscar Wilde.

Lady Gwendolyn's name comes up again in the story only once more. That is when Basil Hallward, just before he is murdered, mentioned the sullied reputation Lady Gwendolyn had acquired as a result of her association with Dorian. At the end of the story, Dorian decides not to have sexual relations with the peasant girl, thus assuring himself of goodness and a change for the better. If we look at all this material together—Dorian's sexual relations with Lady Gwendolyn, who represents a dead sister, and his later decision not to have sexual relations with the peasant girl—and apply this genetically to Wilde's dynamics, it would seem to indicate his guilt over forbidden incestuous feelings toward Isola.

In the book Wilde introduces James Vane, Sibyl's brother, who represents the avenger for his sister. He is determined to kill the man responsible for her death. James represents a foil for, or another aspect of, Dorian's personality. The theme of the avenging brother would seem to be applicable to Wilde. Though he probably felt guilt and responsibility for Isola's death, he may also have tried to blame her death on someone else and may have wanted to avenge her.

In the story Wilde characterized Dorian's grandfather (or *uncle* in the original version) as the one fundamentally responsible for all the hero's difficulties. Dorian's aggression against him is apparent by his murder of Basil, the painter who "fathered" the picture. What is especially interesting is the detail that Dorian plunged a knife "into the great vein that is behind the ear."

It will be remembered that Oscar Wilde's father was a famous otologist.

In his book *Aural Surgery* Sir William, writing of the treatment of mastoid infections with engorgement and floculation, recommended that "we should not hesitate to make a free incision at least an inch in length. The head should be firmly secured against some unyielding substance, and the blade of a stout scalpel inserted steadily until the point reaches the bone . . . sometimes . . . to the depth of nearly an inch. . . ." This operation has been called "Wilde's incision" and is sometimes still performed (Wilson, 1942, p. 214). Thus, the two elements which Oscar Wilde selected for use in his novel—*knife* and *ear*—are both connected with his father's profession. These elements may express, among other things, his own murderous rage against his father, which was the result of many complex factors, among which may have been that he held him responsible for Isola's death.

Earlier in this paper I indicated that when one sees certain themes appear repeatedly in an author's work and when one knows certain biographical facts about the author, then the supposition that these biographical events served as important determinants of the author's literary material is greatly increased. This is indeed the case with Oscar Wilde.

The theme of being in love with a young girl who dies before experiencing sexual gratification or achieving maturity appears in a number of his publications. His poem "Requiescat" expresses this clearly. In 1881 Wilde wrote "Charmides," a lengthy poem in which the dead hero is made love to by a dryad who is then killed, and the two are permitted to have a moment of passion in Hades. This fascinating poem, full of autobiographical significance and with much primal-scene material, contains a reversal of elements, for here there is a dead boy who is made love to by a dryad instead of a young boy who makes love to a dead girl.

In the story *The Fisherman and His Soul* (1891) there is an interesting variant of this theme. To live under the sea with a young mermaid with whom he had fallen in love, a young fisherman cut away his soul, and his soul went about committing all sorts of crimes. You will readily see that the dissociation between the hero and his soul in this story is similar to that between Dorian Gray and his picture. After three years, and at the instigation of his soul, the fisherman left the mermaid to seek other female companionship (human). At the end of the story, the mermaid died of grief, and the guilt-ridden, heartbroken fisherman embraced her form, kissing her passionately until he was washed into the sea to his death.

In her book on Wilde, Frances Winwar observes that Wilde seldom described feminine loveliness and that when he did, the attributes that he used "were of white lilies, cool ivory, the shadow of a white rose in a mirror of silver [Salomé]—everything that was removed from the warmth of life" (p. 31). I think that her observation is a valid one. It is interesting to note that Constance Wilde was born in 1857, around the same time as Isola. In describing Constance to Lily Langtry, Wilde wrote that she had "great coils of heavy brown hair which make her flower-like head droop like a blossom and wonderful ivory hands . . ." (1962, p. 154).

One of the most impressive examples of the importance of the theme of a dead young girl may be found in the expanded version of Wilde's *Portrait of Mr. W. H.* (1891). The original version of this story was also brought up at the time of Wilde's first trial, where it was referred to, although not read (Hyde, 1948, p. 130). In the story Wilde attempted to understand Shakespeare's passions by carefully studying his sonnets. Using the content of the sonnets as evidence, Wilde identified the bard's homosexual friend as Willie Hughes and traced the course of the relationship between them.

After a lengthy discourse about homosexual love which was not published at the time of the original version of the story, Wilde, without any apparent connection, wrote the following, which is clearly about himself:

> How curiously it had all been revealed to me! A book of Sonnets, published nearly three hundred years ago, written by a dead hand and in honour of a dead youth, had suddenly explained to me the whole story of my soul's romance. I remembered how once in Egypt I had been present at the opening of a frescoed coffin that had been found in one of the basalt tombs at Thebes. Inside there was the body of a young girl swathed in tight bands of linen, and with a gilt mask over her face. As I stooped down to look at it, I had seen that one of the little withered hands held a scroll of yellow papyrus covered with strange characters. How I wished now that I had had it read to me! It might have told me something more about the soul that hid within me, and had its mysteries of passion of which I was kept in ignorance. Strange, that we knew so little about ourselves, and that our most intimate personality was concealed from us! Were we to look in tombs for our real life, and in art for the legend of our days? (1966, pp. 1195–1196).

Thus we see that even with the framework of explaining Shakespeare's homosexuality Wilde brought in material that clearly had to do with a dead young girl who could only have represented to him his sister Isola.

I would like to conclude my presentation by quoting the following lines from "The Ballad of Reading Gaol," which, as I said earlier, was Wilde's last literary production, apart from his two letters to the *Daily Chronicle*.

> *Yet each man kills the thing he loves,*
> *By each let this be heard,*
> *Some do it with a bitter look,*
> *Some with a flattering word.*
> *The coward does it with a kiss,*
> *The brave man with a sword!*
>
> *Some kill their love when they are young,*
> *And some when they are old;*
> . . . .
> *The kindest use a knife, because*
> *The dead so soon grow cold.*

I feel that these lines, written in another context, express a psychological truth about their author and confirm our formulation about his feeling responsible for the death of a love object (particularly his sister, Isola). It may well be that Wilde's imprisonment and his emotional participation in the hanging of the trooper, Charles Thomas Wooldridge, on July 7, 1896, confirmed in his mind that he was indeed guilty and beyond salvation. Like the doomed trooper, Wilde felt that he, too, "had killed the thing he loved," and so he too "had to die."

BIBLIOGRAPHY

Brasol, Boris (1938), *Oscar Wilde—The Man—The Artist—The Martyr*. New York: Charles Scribner's Sons.

Hart-Davis, Rupert, ed. (1962), *The Letters of Oscar Wilde*. New York: Harcourt, Brace & World.

Holland, Vyvyan (1960), *Oscar Wilde, A Pictorial Biography*. London: Thames and Hudson; New York: Viking Press.

Hyde, H. Montgomery, ed. (1948), *The Trials of Oscar Wilde*. London: W. Hodge.

Pearson, Hesketh (1946), *Oscar Wilde, His Life and Wit*. New York/London: Harper & Bros.

Sherard, Robert H. (1915), *The Real Oscar Wilde*. London: Hodder.

White, Terence de Vere (1967), *The Parents of Oscar Wilde, Sir William & Lady Wilde*. London: Hodder and Stoughton.

Wiegler, Paul (1929), *Genius in Love and Death*. New York: A.M.C. Boni.

Wilde, Oscar, (1966), *The Complete Works of Oscar Wilde*. London/Glasgow: Collins.

—— "The Fisherman and His Soul." In *The Complete Works of Oscar Wilde*, pp. 248–272.

—— "The Picture of Dorian Gray." *Lippincott's Monthly Magazine*, 1890, July:3–100.

—— *The Picture of Dorian Gray*. In *The Complete Works of Oscar Wilde*, pp. 17–167.

—— (1962), *The Letters of Oscar Wilde*. Ed. Rupert Hart-Davis. New York: Harcourt, Brace & World.

—— "The Portrait of Mr. W. H." In *The Complete Works of Oscar Wilde*, pp. 1150–1201.

Wilson, T. G. (1942), *Victorian Doctor. Being the Life of Sir William Wilde*. London: Methuen; New York: L. B. Fischer, 1946.

Winwar, Frances (1940), *Oscar Wilde and the Yellow Nineties*. New York: Harper & Bros, 1941, 1958.

Psychoanalytic Object-Relations Theory, Group Processes, and Administration: Toward an Integrative Theory of Hospital Treatment

OTTO F. KERNBERG, M.D. (*Topeka*)

The purpose of this paper is to formulate an integrative set of theoretical propositions providing a common frame of reference for the different treatment modalities in the psychoanalytic hospital. Such a theoretical structure should also permit the establishment of clearer boundaries among the various therapeutic modalities utilized in the hospital so that they can be optimally geared to an individual patient's needs. Finally, this frame of reference also may contribute to decreasing the traditional tensions between administrators and clinicians by providing a conceptualization of their actual professional and functional interdependence.

I. The Concept of Structural Change in the Light of Object-Relations Theory

In psychoanalytic theory, the term "structural intrapsychic change" (in the direction of clinical improvement) refers to changes in the relationship between the ego, the id, the superego, and external reality. In clinical terms, this means changes in impulse-defense configurations, that is, changes in the defensive structures which determine the boundaries between ego, superego, and id. Changes in impulse-defense configurations require, according

Director, C. F. Menninger Memorial Hospital, Topeka, Kansas.

to psychoanalytic theory, modification of these defenses so that unconscious conflicts may become conscious and may be resolved in consciousness. Such conflict resolution, in turn, modifies the impulse-defense equilibrium in the direction of more effective ego functioning, brings about a broadening of the sphere of the mature ego, greater ego autonomy, and better gratification of instinctual needs as well as of reality demands.

From this theoretical viewpoint, structural intrapsychic change requires psychoanalysis or psychoanalytic psychotherapy. Such changes as do occur in patients within a hospital setting would be predominantly behavioral changes rather than structural intrapsychic changes. Nonanalytic psychotherapy and other hospital treatment devices would hardly be able to modify unconscious intrapsychic conflict. Indeed, one finds many patients whose behavior changes in response to the social pressures within the hospital, but who then revert to previous behavior patterns once they leave the hospital system.

A modified formulation of intrapsychic structure and of structural intrapsychic change, which incorporates recent findings regarding the intrapsychic structures of severely regressed (particularly borderline and psychotic) patients, opens the possibility of obtaining change in these intrapsychic structures by means of particular therapeutic functions of the hospital as a social system. This modified conception of intrapsychic structure and of structural intrapsychic change is an application of psychoanalytic object-relations theory (Guntrip, 1961; Sutherland, 1963; Jacobson, 1964; Kernberg, 1971a). This theory proposes, in essence, that the basic units of the intrapsychic structures are constellations of self-images, object-images, and affect-dispositions which reflect particular internalized object-relationships represented by such self-object-affect units. These units of internalization of object-relationships coalesce into more complex psychic structures (such as the ideal self and ideal objects), and these structures, in turn, finally determine the ego, the superego, and the id in their definite forms.

The earliest intrapsychic units of this kind are undifferentiated self-object images linked with primitive, overwhelming affect dispositions of either a pleasurable or a painful, frightening nature (Jacobson, 1964). All pleasurable internalized experiences condense into a primitive self-object image determining the ego core; all unpleasurable ones are also condensed and are then first "expelled" (as a primitive "non-me") and later projected. These are the earliest libidinally-invested and aggressively-invested internalized object-relations. At a later stage of development, self- and object-images are sorted out from each other in both pleasurable and painful constellations. This separation of self- from object-images, and the maturation and development of perceptive and cognitive functions, influence each other and contribute to the delimitation of boundaries between self and outside world (ego boundary).

The next stage of development consists of an integration of libidinally and aggressively invested self-images culminating in an integrated self-concept, and an integration of object-images (originally of a multiple, primitive, fantastic kind) into constellations of object-representations resembling ever more closely—and permitting the realistic perception of—real, external objects (parental figures, siblings, etc.). The integration of self-images brings about a contrast between an evermore realistic perception of the self (real self) and idealized fantasy formations of the self (which, in turn, integrate into the ideal self). Realistic integration of object-images contrasts real object-images with idealized ones representing parental figures of a magical, all-need-gratifying kind (ideal objects).

A condensation of the ideal self and of ideal objects determines the ego ideal, which will form part of the superego. A remnant of primitive, condensed self-object images invested with aggression and projected outside determine persecutory parental images, because they distort the perception of early frustrating experiences in terms of persecutory fantasies. Internalization of such persecuting, primitively conceived objects (particularly of the parental forbidding and punishing functions) determines sadistic forerunners of the superego. The ego ideal and these sadistic forerunners become integrated as the early superego, and later expand with more realistic internalization of parental demands and prohibitions (Jacobson, 1964).

The integrated self-concept, plus the related, increasingly realistic, libidinally invested object-images constitute ego identity, a basic organizer of the ego. Thus, the self (or integrated self-concept) becomes the center of the world of internalized object-relations, a world constituted by the self plus the totality of object-images. The self is part of the ego; that part of the ego not related to the world of internalized object-relations is represented by the totality of nonpersonified ego functions and structures. Ego integration establishes a firm repressive barrier against internalized self- and object-images linked with intolerable or forbidden sexual and aggressive needs, so that the id acts as the consolidating reservoir of repressed units of self- and object-images linked with unacceptable affective dispositions. Thus, psychic development culminates in the establishment of the definite structures of the mind as described by Freud (ego, superego, and id).

This theory of intrapsychic structure has important consequences for the conceptualization of structural intrapsychic change, and of the role of hospital treatment in achieving such structural change.

First, the substructures which jointly determine the overall psychic structures are no longer to be viewed simply as impulse-defense configurations, but as dynamic structures, each involving an impulse-defense configuration in the context of an internalized object-relationship.

Second, structural change occurring after consolidation of an integrated superego, ego, and id, is radically different from structural change occurring in patients who have not achieved such integration. In the case of neurotic patients and patients with neurotic character pathology, where ego, id, and superego are integrated (although involved in pathogenic conflicts and defensive operations), the activation of any particular object-relationship within the treatment situation simultaneously reflects conflicts between these overall intrapsychic structures. The defensive mechanisms in these conflicts center around repression and related mechanisms (the classical mechanisms of defense of the ego, superego, and id). Under these circumstances, much preliminary interpretive work needs to be done if the patient is to reach the point of structural change, because defensive operations (such as pathological character traits) are secondarily integrated into and protected by the overall psychic structure involved. In addition, because of the abstraction and depersonification of internalized object-relations within the ego and superego, reactivation of these relations in the therapeutic situation takes time.

In contrast, in patients with borderline character pathology and in the psychoses, there exists a lack of integration of the ego, lack of integration of the superego (with projection of personified superego nuclei), and an "infiltration" of ego functions with primitive instinctual derivatives. This infiltration derives from the predominance of a different set of defense mechanisms from those centering around repression in better integrated patients. At the level of borderline personality organization and in the psychoses, there is a predominance of splitting and other related, primitive defensive operations (such as projection, projective identification, primitive idealization, denial, omnipotence, and devaluation), all of which have in common their defense of the psychic apparatus against conflict by mutual dissociation of contradictory, primitive ego states. Each of these mutually dissociated, primitive ego states reflects a primitive, internalized object-relationship, a basic unit of self- and object-image, and a corresponding primitive affect-disposition, relatively unintegrated and hence easily activated in the interpersonal field (Kernberg, 1967). There thus exists, in the patient's interactions in the hospital, a potential for rapid development of new relationships representing primitive object-relations. This affords the opportunity for a diagnosis of the pathogenic conflicts involved, because the patient's interpersonal relationships in the hospital reflect quite directly these primitive intrapsychic dispositions.

Third, from this viewpoint, one might consider two levels of internalized object-relationships: (1) a basic primitive level, characterized by multiple self- and multiple object-representations corresponding to primitive fantasy formations linked with primitive impulse derivatives; and (2) a higher level of internalized object-relationships, characterized by sophisticated, integrated self-images and by sophisticated, integrated object-images linked with higher levels of affect-dispositions; all of these higher-level object-relationships reflect more accurately the early childhood experiences and conflicts between the individual and his real parental figures and siblings.

These two levels of object-relationships differentiate transference neurosis from transference psychosis. Transference psychosis, in contrast to transference neurosis, is characterized by loss of reality testing in the transference situation. Clinically, this loss of reality testing is reflected in delusional thoughts involving the analyst, possible appearance of hallucinations in the analytic hours, activation of primitive, overwhelming affective reactions in the transference, and the patient's loss of a sense of separate identity from the analyst. The dynamic mechanisms of this loss of reality testing in borderline patients are different from those in psychotic patients; but there is one general characteristic of transference psychosis (in both borderline and psychotic patients) which differentiates it from transference neurosis: in the transference neurosis a more realistic, dyadic, Oedipal-triangular, or sibling relationship is mobilized, while in transference psychosis primitive object-relationships are activated, with multiple self-images and multiple object-images representing the deepest layers of the mind (Kernberg, 1971b). These primitive, multiple object-relationships are of a fantastic nature, and do not reflect actual, past interactions with the parents (as do the higher-level transference reactions of transference neurosis); rather, they reflect early fantasy structures (fantastic relationships with inner objects) which are normally submerged within the structure of more "realistic" transference dispositions in the context of an integrated ego and superego.

As stated before, this conceptualization has important theoretical and clinical implications for hospital treatment. In the psychoanalytic treatment of neurotic patients and of patients with higher-level character pathology, transference neurosis develops gradually, and primitive object-relationships only emerge in the transference after the working through of higher-level psychic structures and defenses. In contrast, in the hospital, patients are seen who suffer from severe character pathology, borderline personality organization, or psychotic reactions. In all of these cases, primitive levels of structural development predominate, and primitive object-relationships are immediately activated intrapsychically and in the interpersonal field. Thus, it is possible to observe directly, and also to gradually influence intrapsychic conflict by means of an understanding, confronting, and (technically) neutral hospital team which can clarify and consistently modify the primitive object-relationships activated in the interpersonal field. The concept of a "neutral" hospital atmosphere derives from Anna Freud's (1946) concept of the technical neutrality of the psychoanalyst, and his equidistant attitude from id, superego, external reality, and acting ego; neutrality in this regard implies a potential alliance with the observing ego of the patient.

II. Psychoanalytic Theory of Small Groups and the Activation of Primitive Object-Relations in the Social Field

Insofar as the hospital represents a social structure organized around group processes with varying degrees of structuralization, the patient is faced with participation in a setting which reinforces in varying degrees the activation of primitive object-relationships. Impressive clinical evidence exists which indicates that, regardless of the degree of maturity and psychological integration of the individual, small, closed, unstructured groups—as well as large groups with minimal structure and no clearly defined task relating that group to its environment—tend to bring about an immediate regression of the individuals involved, toward the activation of defensive operations and interpersonal processes that reflect primitive object-relationships.

In other words, a potential exists in all of us for activation of primitive levels of psychological functioning when the ordinary social structure is lost, when suspension of ordinary social roles occurs, and when multiple objects are present simultaneously in an unstructured relationship (thus reproducing in the interpersonal field a multiplicity of primitive, intrapsychic object-relationships). Our theoretical understanding of why this surprising development takes place in groups is still insufficient, but the fact that it does occur—and particularly in individuals with severe character pathology, borderline, or psychotic syndromes—makes the hospital an impressive diagnostic (and potentially therapeutic) tool in understanding primitive levels of internalized object-relations, and in modifying them in a controlled social system. However, this activation requires a sufficient degree of flexibility, or lack of structuralization within the hospital milieu, if such a regression is to occur. An excessively regimented hospital routine may block this regression and obscure its full observation. An excessively regimented hospital may also foster pathological dependency and apathy in patients (as well as in staff), thus artificially increasing regression in certain patients.

Such immediate activation of primitive levels of functioning does not occur in a dyadic relationship such as a standard psychoanalysis or individual, psychoanalytically oriented psychotherapy. Although severely regressed patients may develop a transference psychosis rather soon, even in individual psychotherapy and psychoanalysis, this is not true for less regressed patients, who usually take quite a long time before reaching a similar level of primitive object-relationships in individual treatment. Yet, such nonregressed patients may immediately present an activation of primitive levels of functioning in group situations.

The implication is that there exists a potential in all of us for both an activation of higher-level object-relationships which leads to transference neurosis in individual treatment, and for an activation of primitive levels of object-relationships leading to "psychotic" situations in groups. However, the more severely regressed the patient, the more the activation of primitive object-relationships spills over into the individual treatment setting as well, and the more his intrapsychic problems also contaminate immediately the social field of the group situation. It may well be that the primitive transference dispositions that can be observed in the early hours of psychoanalysis in many patients, and that then go underground for varying periods of time, reflect the predisposition to activate primitive object-relationships under conditions of uncertainty and role diffusion similar to those which are maximal in group situations.

An additional implication of these two levels of activation of internalized object-relationships is that the higher, "dyadic-triangular" level may become particularly activated in individual therapeutic relationships, and the lower or "groupish" level may become particularly activated in unstructured group situations. This conceptualization permits the development of a theory of treatment combining individual and group treatment modalities to deal simultaneously with different levels of intrapsychic conflicts, and the combination of these two types of modalities in different proportions, or at different points in time, according to the nature of the individual patient's psychopathology. However, the psychological processes activated in individual and group therapeutic processes overlap, and (as will be mentioned later) the use of a combination of individual and group therapy in many cases is still controversial.

Another hypothesis implicit in all that has been said is that the potential for activation of primitive object-relationships may be much stronger in neurotic and normal persons than psychoanalytic exploration within a dyadic situation (the standard psychoanalytic situation) may indicate. It may well be that because the relationships within the family setting represent social structures which reinforce dyadic and triangular object-relationships, they protect the psychic apparatus from its regressive potential for activation of multiple, fantastic, primitive object-relationships.

Following Erikson (1956), introjection, identification, and ego identity have been defined as a progressive sequence in the process of internalization of object-relations (Kernberg, 1966). Introjection represents the most primitive type of internalization of the self-, object-, and affect-components of the basic intrapsychic units mentioned before. Identification represents a higher-level type of introjection, within which both self- and object-representations are more elaborate, delimited, precise; the affect-disposition linking the self- and object-representations is more "toned down," differentiated, less diffuse and intense than in the case of introjection. Identification presupposes a higher level of development of the perceptive and cognitive abilities of the child, to the point of recognizing the role aspects of interpersonal interaction. "Role" implies the presence of a socially recognized function that is being carried out by the object or by both participants in the interaction.

Introjections coalesce with similar, later ones, and gradually develop and are integrated into identifications. In turn, identifications are reshaped by later ones, then combine and are integrated into an overall ego identity. Introjections form the core of similar, related identifications. It may well be that the potential for regression from a certain identification to the underlying, more primitive introjection is quite prevalent, and that the role enactments of ordinary interpersonal relationships protect the higher-level identifications from such a regression. Also, there may be a normal potential for reestablishment of a certain identification after some temporary regression to a component introjection. This might explain part of the rapid regression that occurs in certain group situations, and the rapid recuperation from such regression: groups may induce such regression by elimination of the usual role reinforcement of normal interpersonal interactions.

The role aspects of the relationships between baby and mother, and between the child, its parents, and siblings may obscure the "groupishness" in all of us. The individual relationship between psychoanalyst or psychotherapist and patient may contribute to activation of such dyadic and triangular infantile and childhood relationships, and determine a situation in which the primitive level of internalized object-relationships only becomes available after the working through of higher-level psychic structures and defenses. Again, a general implication is that treatment might take place simultaneously on a dyadic (individual therapy) and on a group level, and simultaneously tap intrapsychic life at different levels of development and structuralization.

Even highly trained, relatively healthy, and mature professionals in the behavioral sciences present activation of primitive emotional processes in unstructured group situations. Developments within group-dynamics experiences, within psychoanalytic institutes, and within professional organizations related to the behavioral sciences provide sufficient illustration that, in certain group situations without precise role definitions and without a clear-cut external task, primitive types of defenses, primitive object-relationships, and, even more interestingly, deep personal conflicts may come to the surface rapidly. This is a further illustration of the regressive potential in all of us, which is different (in the speed of production and recovery) from the regressive moves within a standard psychoanalytic situation. Within a dyadic psychotherapeutic relationship, regression occurs to object-relationships of the childhood Oedipal level, or to pregenital levels of development within the dyadic, triangular, and sibling family setting; regression may occur to primitive object-relationships and early defensive structures of the ego, but this latter type of regression usually takes a long time. In contrast, the regression in group situations is very rapid, leads immediately to defensive operations and types of object-relationships of the primitive, early level, and is transitory in the sense that recovery rapidly occurs again outside the group setting.

Bion's analysis of the regressive phenomena that occur in small groups when their task structure ("work group") fails is relevant here (Bion, 1959; Rioch, 1970). He described the development of certain basic emotional reactions within the group ("basic-assumptions group"), reactions which exist potentially at all times but become activated particularly at times of breakdown of the task group. He described the "fight-flight" assumption, the "dependent" assumption, and the "pairing" assumption as the predominant constellations of the basic-assumptions group. What is particularly striking is that the defensive mechanisms activated within the basic-assumptions group correspond to the defensive operations characteristic of primitive, internalized object-relationships. Indeed, impulses, defenses, and object-relationships of that primitive level of intrapsychic development become evident in the basic-assumptions group.

Main (1957), in analyzing the group reaction of nursing staff involved in the treatment of predominantly borderline, and some psychotic patients ("special" cases) within the hospital, found that these patients managed to activate group phenomena in this nurses' group similar to those of Bion's basic-assumptions group. The implication is that regressed (particularly borderline) patients may, under certain conditions, activate their intrapsychic object-relationships in the interpersonal relations of the staff of the hospital: the patient induces in his social field a reenactment of the conflicts within his intrapsychic world. The combination of massive projection, omnipotent control, denial, primitive idealization, and, above all, splitting of staff reflects both the intrapsychic mechanisms involved and the behavioral means by which staff relationships are distorted in terms of the patient's intrapsychic world. Stanton and Schwartz (1954), in turn, have demonstrated how splits and covert conflict in the interpersonal and social field of the hospital may intensify intrapsychic conflict and disorganization in the kind of "special" (borderline, and in some cases psychotic) patients mentioned above. In short, a reciprocal reinforcement develops between the patients' intrapsychic conflicts and the potential cleavages and stresses within the social system of the hospital.

All of this provides evidence about the rapid activation of primitive levels of defensive operations in the context of primitive, internalized object-relationships in certain groups, and in social and administrative situations within the hospital. The question may now be raised, granted that such an activation of early intrapsychic, object-relations–determined structures occurs in the interpersonal field, what is the therapeutic (in contrast to the merely diagnostic and educational) potential of such an activation?

Psychoanalytic exploration of the patient's interpersonal field within the hospital may greatly contribute to the diagnosis of his intrapsychic conflicts, and may be utilized therapeutically in two ways: (1) within psychoanalytic group therapy which directly interprets to the patients as a group the activation of primitive conflicts within the group as a whole; and (2) within the hospital therapy, that is, within the individual-psychotherapeutic approach of the hospital therapist who interprets to the patient as an individual the total interpersonal situation which the patient has created around himself, and how this interpersonal situation reflects his conflictual, intrapsychic object-relationships. The working-through process in these two therapeutic situations is different. In psychoanalytic group therapy (following, as has been implied, the orientation of Bion [1959], Ezriel [1950], and Sutherland [1952]), the working through occurs not from the viewpoint of the individual patient's genetic development but from the viewpoint of the genetic development of the group as a whole. The working through of the deeper layer of object-relationships on the part of each individual patient occurs in repetitive cycles, in a "disorderly" fashion from the individual's point of view but not from the point of view of the total group history. The intensity and the clarity of the controlled social situation of the small group are the strength of this psychoanalytic group approach.

The examination of the individual patient's evolving deployment of primitive object-relationships in the social field of the hospital may be better accomplished by the hospital therapist's systematic examination with the patient of his interpersonal experiences in the hospital. These interpersonal experiences include all of the patient's interactions with hospital staff and with other patients. The hospital therapist integrates the many observations of staff in their interactions with the patient. As team leader of the staff involved with the patient's treatment, he facilitates the development of an integrating understanding of the patient's impact on the total social system of the floor or section, and communicates this understanding to the patient.

This examination of the patient's total impact on the social system requires a "neutral" hospital milieu, that is, an attitude of staff basically equidistant from the different intrapsychic and external agencies involved in the patient's conflicts, and reflected in an overall friendly and generally tolerant, an interested and intellectually alert hospital atmosphere. This atmosphere is in contrast to two extremes: (1) the hospital run with a "barracks" atmosphere which interferes with the full development of the patient's pathological object-relationships, and (2) the hospital with such a lack of unified structure that a complete examination of the patient's interpersonal field becomes impossible. This atmosphere also fosters free and open communication and interactions between all staff members and the patient, and encourages staff to use their specific technical skills, their psychological understanding, and their personality in maximizing the patient's opportunities for meaningful human relations in the hospital.

In addition, the possibility exists for combining such group- and hospital-therapy approaches with a more standard psychoanalytic or psychoanalytically oriented, individual psychotherapeutic procedure, within which a systematic development of transference analysis leading to the crystallization of higher-level object-relationships and conflict resolution would become the main task, in the context of the dyadic, patient-therapist relationship. I have described in earlier papers (Kernberg, 1968, 1971b) a modified psychoanalytic procedure for patients with borderline personality organization, characterized by: (1) systematic elaboration of the (particularly negative) transference in the "here and now" only, without attempting to achieve full genetic reconstructions; (2) interpretation of the defensive constellations of these patients as they enter the transference; (3) limit-setting in order to block acting out of the transference, with as much structuring of the patients' life outside the hours as necessary (for example, by means of hospital structure) to protect the neutrality of the therapist; and (4) systematic clarification of the patients' perceptions in the hours (Frosch, 1970).

Psychoanalytic exploration of the patient's interactions in the total social field of the hospital (hospital therapy), within a small, closed, unstructured group (psychoanalytic group therapy), and in individual psychotherapy or psychoanalysis cannot be, in clinical practice, as sharply delimited from each other as implied above. Primitive levels of object-relationships will develop, even rapidly, within the individual treatment setting of borderline and psychotic patients; transference analysis, the examination of the patient's interaction within the small group, and within the hospital at large will necessarily overlap. However, an additional frame of reference may contribute further to the delimitation of the functions of all these different treatment modalities. I am referring here to A. K. Rice's systems theory of organization which treats the individual, the group, and the social organization as a continuum of open systems (Miller and Rice, 1967; Rice, 1963, 1965, 1969).

III. A Systems-Theory Approach Integrating Psychoanalytic Object-Relations and Small-Group Theories with a Theory of Hospital Administration

Open systems are characterized by exchanges with the environment which are defined by input, conversion, and output phases. Rice proposes that the individual, the group, and the social institution may be seen as such open systems, and that properties common to the functions and structure of open systems may be applied to all three. The practical implication is that a common set of laws may be established regulating individual, group, and institutional functioning, and, particularly, that the boundaries between individual, group, and institution, and between the institution and its environment can be examined in an integrative frame. What follows is a brief summary of the pertinent aspects of Rice's theories.

All open systems carry out tasks in their exchanges with the environment. The essential task which an open system must carry out to survive is called the primary task. In a given system, there may be several primary tasks which may constitute constraints for each other. In general, all task performance is limited by constraints, and, in order to carry out a task successfully, a system must have a definition of the task, an understanding of the processes necessary to carry it out, and a view of the constraints limiting task performance. Each system must include a control function which will permit the analysis of the environment, the internal reality of the system, and the executive organization of task performance within such a reality. This control function must be at the boundary between the system and its environment (because by definition, open systems must exchange material with the environment to survive; the primary task of any open system, therefore, involves exchange with the environment). The control function must also include the function of determining and preserving the boundary of the system. Breakdown of system boundaries implies breakdown of control of the open system, and this, in turn, brings about breakdown in carrying out the primary task, thus threatening the survival of the system. This theory may be applied to patients, groups, and to the hospital as a social system.

In the case of the psychic life of an individual, the ego may be conceptualized as the control function, ego boundaries as the boundaries defined and protected by ego functions, and the person's intrapsychic world of object-relationships as the inner space or inner world of the system. Rice (1969) proposes that in the mature individual the ego function mediates the relationship between the external and the internal world, and thus takes a "leadership" role in relation to the individual and exercises a "management" control function. The primary task of the individual is to satisfy the instinctual and object-oriented needs of his internal world by means of interactions with his social environment, adapting to and creatively modifying his interpersonal world in terms of his intrapsychic needs, and elaborating intrapsychic needs in terms of external reality. Psychopathology may be seen as varying degrees of breakdown of the control function (ego), with consequent breakdown of both adaptation to the environment and gratification of basic intrapsychic needs.

In the case of the group, the group leader may be seen as the control function; the primary task of the group is that which determined the existence of this group in the first place; and the activation of primitive object-relationships within the group structure (Bion's "basic assumptions group") represents the internal world of object relations of the group (Rice, 1969). From the viewpoint of hospital treatment, groups may be classified into three general types: (a) task groups, which are organized to carry out a task involving interchange with the environment (work projects, study groups, etc.); (b) group-dynamics groups in which the task consists of learning experimentally about the psychodynamics of group behavior; and (c) psychotherapeutic groups in which the task is the examination of psychological developments within the group for the purpose of treating the psychopathology of the group members.

The following considerations regarding the leadership of these three types of groups always refer to functional leadership, which is derived from a series of activities or achievements related to the tasks that need to be carried out by the group. This concept is in contrast to the concept of leadership as a personality attribute, and of the leader as a charismatic figure. In other words, functional leadership is contrasted to leadership linked to personality structure. Functional leadership may be carried out by an individual or by a group of individuals, and it may shift within the task group in response to shifting requirements.

The leader of the task group has to be able to define the task, carry out or delegate responsibility for the different phases and subdivisions of the task, and evaluate performance in examining the relationship between the internal and external world of the group (measuring task performance or conversion by the differences between input and output). He also must be able to detect and utilize the emotional constellations (basic assumptions) of the group, which will remain more and more in the background as task performance improves. Reduction of task performance (because of excessive constraints or poor leadership) activates basic group assumptions and basic group leadership and challenges the task group leader.

In the group-dynamics group, the "consultant" leads the group in the task of observing its own behavior and learning from it. The nature of this task greatly intensifies the development of the basic-assumptions group, the need for the consultant to interpret the assumptions as far as they become resistance to learning, and the need to maintain an optimal balance between experiencing and observing on the part of the entire group membership.

The therapist of a psychotherapeutic group is the leader for the task of psychological exploration, with techniques similar to those of group dynamics, but with the additional goal of linking learning about primitive object-relationships and the related defensive mechanisms which are activated in the group with the respective intrapsychic conflicts of the group members.

For the hospital as an organization, hospital administration represents the leadership or management carrying out the control functions of the system. In the case of the psychoanalytic teaching hospital, the primary tasks of the system are patient care, education, and research. The creation and protection of an optimal social atmosphere within the hospital to permit the development and examination of intrapsychic, interpersonal, intragroup, and intergroup processes for therapeutic purposes are specific tasks of the psychoanalytic hospital which maximally emphasizes the need for functional task-oriented leadership. The therapeutic community is a special organization within the hospital or within sections of the hospital; it is geared to an open examination of all the social processes occurring within the hospital or section, for the purpose of maximizing the therapeutic opportunities for (1) individual treatment (individual psychotherapy or psychoanalysis, and hospital therapy); (2) group treatment (group therapy and task groups); and (3) group-dynamics experiences (for educational purposes and for the development of leadership among the hospital staff). The therapeutic community will be examined further later on.

In summary, the primary task of the individual is to negotiate with the environment so as to fulfill the needs that stem from his own internal world; his control function, including boundary control, is the ego. In the case of the group, the primary task is that for which the group has become organized, and its control function is the group leader or group leadership.

The equilibrium between the group focusing around the task (task group) and the group focusing around the activation of primitive object-relations in its social field (basic-assumptions group) depends on the extent to which the task is clear and defined, the adequacy of task leadership, and the examination of the basic assumptions that are either included in the task or taken into consideration as task constraints. In the case of the hospital, the primary task is to carry out the purposes for which the hospital has been established and continues in existence, and the control function is represented by hospital administration. Consideration of the emotional needs of hospital staff is a basic constraint on task performance, just as basic group assumptions are a basic constraint on the task or work group. In the case of the psychoanalytic hospital, focusing on the emotional life within the social field of the hospital becomes a primary therapeutic function, and the therapeutic community is one task system for carrying out this function. This is the great advantage of a therapeutic community: a basic constraint (the emotional needs of groups within the hospital) becomes a major task objective (the study of emotional conflicts as a learning experience in conflict management and emotional growth).

Within this model, psychopathology may be conceptualized as breakdown of the control function, failure in carrying out the primary task, and threat to the survival of the system: in the case of the individual, we see breakdown of the ego and emotional catastrophe; in the case of the group, breakdown of group leadership and paralysis in basic assumptions; in the case of the hospital, breakdown of administration, failure to carry out the task, and loss of morale. Breakdown of boundary control is the main manifestation of breakdown in the control function; loss of ego boundaries is a primary cause of loss of differentiation between self and nonself, and a basic characteristic of the psychoses.

IV. An Integrative Conceptualization of Treatment Modalities within the Hospital

Treatment, within this conceptualization, may be defined as the introduction of a "consultant" (therapist) to the system. The consultant's primary task is to diagnose the nature and causes of the breakdown in the control function; to facilitate reestablishment of boundary control, an adequate redefinition of the primary task and its constraints, and the redefinition, reorganization, and carrying out directly or by means of delegation of the overall primary task. The consultant needs to be an expert in the field in which the breakdown occurs (individual, group, or organization). He must be sufficiently outside the system to be able to examine its internal and external environment objectively. The consultant needs to negotiate with the system the nature and limits of his task, renegotiating it as he himself redefines the nature and limits of his task. The consultant, in interacting with the system in conflict, establishes a task system of its own; this system needs, in turn, a definition of its primary task and of its boundaries; the main boundary of the consultant is the time boundary: a consultant without a clearly defined time boundary tends to become confounded and confused with the control function of the system (individual, group, or organization).

Applying this conceptualization to ("formal") individual psychotherapy, we might say that the psychotherapist acts as a consultant to the patient, diagnosing his control function (ego), the nature, causes, and extent of its breakdown, diagnosing also the nature of the internal world (internalized object-relationships) and the environment, and the nature of the transactions which would be necessary to satisfy the patient's internal needs within his given environment. In short, the psychotherapist focuses on both the control function and the internal world of the patient. Insofar as individual psychotherapy tends particularly to activate the higher level of internalized object-relationships, individual psychotherapy and psychoanalysis activate the patient's potential for dyadic, Oedipal-triangular, and sibling relationships (transference neurosis). However, as we have seen, in borderline patients and in psychotic patients, individual psychotherapy also directly activates primitive object-relationships together with remnants of the control function (ego), directly negotiating such primitive object-relationships in a fragmented, disorganized way. From this viewpoint, ("formal") individual psychotherapy of borderline and psychotic patients may be conceived as a clarification, within each of the fragmented ego states that are activated in the transference, of the patient's relationship with reality, and of the particular object-relationship activated at that point. Clarification becomes interpretation of the patient's perceptions and the realistic aspects of the treatment hours, simultaneously with interpretation of his primitive, internalized object-relationships in the transference. In the case of severely regressed psychotic patients, the disintegration of the ego may interfere with the minimal work needed to separate internal needs from reality perception; in these cases, a shift in the psychotherapeutic task to a predominant focus upon the control function (ego) may be the first stage of treatment, until sufficient observing ego is present to participate in the therapeutic task of sorting out reality from intrapsychic needs.

In group psychotherapy, the focus is predominantly on primitive object-relationships and related defensive operations as they become activated in the basic-assumptions group. In psychoanalytic group psychotherapy, the focus is primarily on the internal world of object-relationships, with less emphasis on the nature of the individual patient's control function (ego). The implication is that in contrast to individual psychotherapy, which may be indicated for all patients along the continuum of psychosis-borderline-neurosis, analytic group psychotherapy is most indicated where the patient's control function is stable enough to be able to participate in the examination of the basic group assumptions, that is, in the case of neuroses and borderline conditions. Group dynamics is not a therapeutic modality as such and would be reserved for staff trained as experts in the treatment of individual, group, and therapeutic community modalities (and as experts in organizational leadership).

Focus on boundary control between groups focuses sharply upon the qualities and deficiencies of group leadership (Rice, 1965). The therapeutic communty examines patient, staff, and combined patient-staff leadership, including that of hospital administration. Sociological research in the hospital in recent years has stressed the therapeutic value of such an open examination of leadership, authority, and power struggles within the hospital (Rubenstein and Lasswell, 1966).

The therapeutic community and individual hospital therapy operate at a similar level of simultaneous examination of internal object-relationships and the control function (ego). Insofar as the therapeutic community utilizes group methods and thus activates the basic-assumptions group, it contributes to the activation of primitive object-relationships and may examine them and the related defenses as developments in the social field; insofar as the therapeutic community is geared to task performance (that is, to the negotiation of the needs of task performance of different groups within the hospital), and to the related intergroup relationships (particularly staff-patient relationships), the focus of the therapeutic community is on the control function as well.

However, the therapeutic community requires that sufficient individual control function (ego) be present for participation in the stressful community examination of breakdown and correction of intergroup boundaries, and thus excluding the more severely regressed psychotic patients. In contrast, the therapeutic community might be an ideal model for somewhat less regressed psychotic patients and for those with borderline conditions in which deficit of the control function (ego), and yet some preservation of it, is predominant.

Individual hospital therapy may be compared to the therapeutic community in that it also focuses predominantly on the individual's control function (ego), that is, on the extent to which the patient is able to negotiate his intrapsychic needs within the interpersonal environment of the hospital. Insofar as the hospital therapist communicates to the patient the effects of the patient's behavior on the interpersonal field in the hospital, and the intrapsychic implications of the distortions created by the patient in the interpersonal field, the hospital therapist also focuses upon the patient's internal world of object-relations. However, insofar as the hospital therapist focuses upon the "here and now" of the patient's interactions in the hospital (in contrast to transference analysis within "formal" individual psychotherapy), issues of control, of multiple boundary relationships with other patients, staff, and task systems, predominate in the hospital therapist's work. The hospital therapist represents the entire hospital to the patient, in the same way that the therapeutic community reflects the hospital or section social system and permits its examination by the entire group of patients. The hospital therapist may not be able to carry out such a complex task with severely regressed psychotic patients who are seriously withdrawn or isolated from the social life of the hospital. In contrast, in this function the hospital therapist is of maximal use to the borderline patient who needs a "consultant" to clarify his interactions within the hospital social system.

The hospital therapist carries out a particular boundary function between the hospital as a social system and the individual patient as an open system. Insofar as the hospital therapist makes decisions concerning the patient's life, he really shifts from a "consultant's" role to an auxiliary ego role, that is, he becomes the "management" of the patient. This implies abandonment of neutrality in a technical sense, at the risk of losing the monitoring capacity to evaluate the patient's ego resources for carrying out management functions himself. However, this radical change in the hospital therapist's role is necessary, particularly for patients with little motivation for change. Groups or social organizations without the will to survive would die; it is an aspect of medical, indeed humanitarian, ethic that we "take over" for a patient whose control function has broken down and who would, psychologically (and sometimes physically), die if we would not "move in." The hospital therapist, therefore, really becomes a "hospital administrator" in the case of severely regressed psychotic patients; this may also be true, to a lesser extent, for some borderline patients.

By definition, task groups within the hospital minimize the activation of primitive object-relationships (basic assumptions) in them, and maximally activate the potential for task leadership, cooperation, task orientation, and reality orientation in patients. Therefore, they directly reinforce the individual's control function (ego). Task groups seem ideally indicated for psychotic patients and borderline patients, but are not so necessary in the treatment of neurotic patients. Roughly speaking, one might classify task groups in the hospital by professions (Brocher, 1970): the nursing profession would specialize in the establishment of family-living task groups, the activities department in the establishment of work and recreational task groups, the social worker in the establishment of social reintegration and rehabilitation task groups. At this time, we are in the early stages of a reexamination and redefinition of professional roles and functions in our hospital[1] in the light of the theoretical model presented in this paper.

In summary, hospital treatment could be formulated as the simultaneous diagnosis and treatment of the patient's control function and his internal world of object-relationships. Analytic group psychotherapy would examine deeply the intrapsychic world of object-relationships; it is ideally indicated for patients with a strong control function (particularly patients functioning on a neurotic level), and only to a lesser extent for patients on a borderline level. Task groups which examine the control function maximally and the

[1] C. F. Menninger Memorial Hospital.

internal world of object-relationships minimally would be most clearly indicated for patients with serious deficits in their control functions, such as psychotic patients and borderline patients, rather than for neurotic patients. Individual psychoanalytic psychotherapy or psychoanalysis would be indicated for the entire range of psychiatric patients (with the exception of specific or individual contraindications), in that it deals with different levels of object-relationships, and with the corresponding problems in the control function (ego). The therapeutic community, with a predominance of emphasis on the control function over the internal world of object-relationships, but with a sharp focus on the reality of interpersonal interactions in the hospital, appears ideally indicated for the less regressed psychotic patients and particularly for borderline conditions. Hospital therapy is similar in its approach and indications to the therapeutic community, and would naturally combine with it. The hospital therapist as a hospital administrator would reflect the particular need for "taking over" in the case of severely regressed psychotic patients (and some borderline patients, too), functioning in this case (and in contrast to all other "consultant" functions of individual therapist, group therapist, therapeutic community leader, and hospital administrator) as an auxiliary ego.

The implication of this examination of different treatment modalities in terms of Rice's open-system theory, psychoanalytic object-relations theory, and psychoanalytic theory of small groups is that group therapy, individual therapy, therapeutic community, hospital therapy (and management), and task groups may be integrated in a common theoretical frame and, in varying proportions, are part of the treatment of psychotic, borderline, and neurotic individuals. In general terms, severely regressed psychotic patients require hospital management (including medication), individual psychoanalytic therapy, and task groups as the main modalities of treatment; borderline patients require individual psychoanalytic therapy, therapeutic community and/or hospital therapy, and task groups; neurotic patients (including "higher-level" character pathology), require psychoanalysis, or, if that is contraindicated or unavailable, individual psychotherapy and/or group psychotherapy. However, in practice the differentiation of treatment modalities cannot be made as sharply as within such an ideal model. Classifying patients into neurotic, borderline, and psychotic conditions is certainly not sufficient for the purpose of treatment indication: the indication of treatment modalities for any particular patient has to depend upon highly individualized judgments, and could not be arrived at on the basis of this schematic outline alone.

The combination of individual and group psychotherapy for neurotic patients is controversial: there exists a danger of transference splitting and transference acting out; the opinions about this are divided, and the advantages and disadvantages of sole or combined modalities seems to need much further research. Individual psychoanalytic psychotherapy and psychoanalysis seem ideally geared to focusing on dyadic relationships in depth over the entire range of psychopathology. Group psychoanalytic psycho-therapy and group dynamics tend to activate rapidly primitive levels of object-relationships and pathological character defenses of the individual which may need a long time to become fully exposed in the individual treatment situation. Individuals who have undergone psychoanalysis first and group experiences later have been able to reconfirm findings from their own psychoanalysis within the group situation. Yet it is an open question whether any group experience may permit the full range of integration of emotional learning available in psychoanalysis.

To this point, the intrapsychic world of object-relationships has been separated sharply from the patient's ego. Although for clinical purposes they may be separated, the internal world of object-relations and the control function (ego) do, however, have common roots. It may well be that satis-factory development of the earliest dyadic relationship between baby and mother is a prerequisite for the establishing of a basic ego core, of basic trust, and the related capacity for a therapeutic alliance (Winnicott, 1954; Zetzel, 1966). The relationship between internalization of object-relation-ships and the development of the ego and psychic structures in general has already been examined briefly. Psychoanalytic object-relations theory constitutes a basic theoretical tool in this analysis, as I have outlined else-where in a more detailed synthesis of this theory (Kernberg, 1971a).

The implication of everything that has been said so far is that the hospital as a social system may provide various therapeutic structures which activate to varying proportions the patient's control function and the patient's in-ternal world of object-relationships.

It is important to stress the human, personal element in the therapeutic process. The therapist ("consultant") cannot help the patient grow as a human being without authentic respect and concern for him. And one crucial aspect of the patient's learning process in treatment ("managerial skill") is the development of concern for himself, as well as the capacity of establishing an authentic relationship with the therapist (Ticho, 1971). Thus the patient is influenced both by what the therapist does and what the therapist is. The therapist's availability as a real person, as somebody willing to understand and to help—a good, real object in contrast to the patient's transference distortions—is crucially important in the treatment. In this connection, the patient-therapist unit might be described as a higher-order "unit" of object-relationship: a higher-order self, a higher-order affect of hope and anticipation of help, a higher-order helpful object (Myerson, 1971). Only within this conceptualization may treatment be formulated as the learning of "managerial skills" in order to understand oneself, one's boundaries, one's internal needs, one's environment, and one's life tasks; only in this way can structural intrapsychic change be formulated as im-provement in the control function (ego), and as improvement in the capac-ity of the patient to carry out his primary task (the expression of his intra-psychic needs in ways that are adaptive to his environment).

With these reservations, psychological treatment may be conceptualized as a particular form of (conscious and unconscious) learning for leadership of one's own self. This brings us to another assumption regarding the therapeutic functions of the psychoanalytic hospital: namely, that the administration of the hospital itself may be utilized for purposes of learning about managerial and leadership functions and preconditions.

V. Functional Hospital Administration as a Model and Precondition for the Therapeutic Community

The staff may learn about management at the individual, group, and organizational level by open examination of the administrative system of the hospital, and hospital management may understand the therapeutic needs of the psychoanalytic hospital from the viewpoint of Rice's theory of administration. In this conceptualization, psychoanalysis and psychoanalytic psychotherapy become a particular theory and technique of "management consultation," and psychoanalytic object-relations theory (including the psychoanalytic theory of small groups) links the understanding of the internal world of the individual, the group, and the organization in one common frame of reference. Administrative theory, insofar as it concerns itself with the analysis of the control function, and with leadership of organizations, of groups, and of individuals, may be integrated conceptually with the psychotherapeutic approaches of the hospital. Hospital administration, within this conceptualization, has to provide functional (task-oriented) leadership to create an open social atmosphere conducive to examining the administrative process itself. The norms, expectations, and values which the administrator communicates in his relationships with staff are likely to be recommunicated by staff to patients; lack of authenticity in staff-staff relationships will foster and legitimatize similar behavior in patient-patient and patient-staff relationships, especially in those involving the exercise of authority (Dolgoff, 1971).

Failure of hospital management implies a breakdown in the boundary functions of the hospital, a breakdown in its capacity for carrying out the primary task, and, therefore, also a breakdown, to varying extents, of all task systems within the hospital (including staff, patient, and staff-patient task groups). The deterioration of task groups activates basic-assumptions conditions within groups and in intergroup relationships to such an extent that primitive conflicts, primitive defensive operations, and the loss of task leadership all make open, rational examination of the hospital as a social system impossible. Therefore, the therapeutic potentials of individual and group activities deteriorate. In contrast, with efficient hospital administration and maintenance of functional task leadership, all task systems throughout the hospital may function adequately, and partial breakdowns in intraorganizational task systems can be localized, diagnosed, and treated. The preservation of task boundaries and of task leadership maximizes open examination of the hospital as a social system and mobilization of the therapeutic potentialities of such an examination.

Effective hospital management requires adequate definition by the hospital management of the primary task (or tasks) of the hospital, definition of the constraints, and establishment of priorities and of compromises among priorities and constraints on a functional basis. Hospital management needs to have adequate control over hospital boundaries, which implies stable, fully delegated authority regarding all hospital functions from the hospital board to the director or managing team. Such stable, clearly defined, non-ambiguous authority needs to be delegated in turn by the hospital administration to hospital staff in a stable, clearly defined and delimited, unambiguous way along functional, task-determined lines. Hospital administration, in order to carry out the boundary-control functions of the hospital, must provide adequate representation of the external environment to the hospital staff, and must communicate the internal needs of the hospital to the external environment with which the hospital relates in carrying out its task. In the case of the psychoanalytic hospital, strict administrative boundaries should be matched with wide-open professional doors (open examination of all professional issues), so that changing needs, demands, and constraints from the environment can be explored, analyzed, and incorporated in the decision-making process. Such an administrative structure should involve opportunities for learning about administration by means of open examination of its functioning for all hospital staff (although in varying degrees, and in accordance with the specific professional functions of hospital staff).

The therapeutic community is an organized social structure within the hospital, centering around the community meeting of patients and staff; it also requires meaningful, stable, and delimited delegation of authority from hospital administration to staff and from staff to patients; as an organization, it should afford open interchange between staff and patients in the process of carrying out their respective functions within their respective delegated authority.

The therapeutic community is the comprehensive organization of the social system for psychotherapeutic purposes within the hospital or a hospital section (Jones, 1968; Caine and Smail, 1969; Edelson, 1967; Falck, 1969). The community meeting is only one of its aspects, although a very crucial one. The community meeting includes all staff and all patients who form part of the social system included in the therapeutic community. The total authority invested in the therapeutic community must be less than that invested in the administrative head of the hospital or section; the community meeting permits public recognition of what the extent and limits of this authority are, and what further delegation of this authority will be invested in particular component systems of the community.

Delegation of authority in professional matters should not be done on an ideological, pseudo-democratic basis, but on a functional one (Zaleznik, 1970). For example, delegation of authority regarding medical matters has to go to the physicians of the community. If authority is delegated regardless of the professional expertise, skills, experience, and motivation of staff and patients, role diffusion, ambiguities, and breakdown of task systems will occur. This may have very regressive, demoralizing, and, ultimately, anti-therapeutic effects.

The primary task of the therapeutic community is the treatment of patients and not the expression of an equalitarian ideology (Falck, 1969; Zaleznik, 1970). All explorations of group conflicts, of task requirements and constraints, of interpersonal difficulties and characterological problems of individual patients, should have a therapeutic function. The design, organization, and actual carrying out of tasks by individuals and groups, by staff, patients, and staff-patient task forces should also have an ultimate therapeutic purpose. The functions of the therapeutic community may thus be grouped into: (1) analysis and strengthening of the control function of individual patients, groups, and of the total community; and (2) analysis and modification of the internal world, the intrapsychic and interpersonal object-relations of patients as individuals and within groups.

These functions may be carried out within the community meeting or delegated to groups, task forces, or individuals within the community. For example, "group-living meetings" may be designated to examine and resolve conflicts between individual patients, groups of patients, or between patients and staff: as long as these meetings deal with the "here and now" only (and do not attempt to explore transference implications in terms of their genetic origins), they represent therapeutic community functions delegated to a particular subsystem of the community. "Floor meetings" may deal with concrete tasks of the daily life in the hospital, again representing one delegated function of the therapeutic community.

Group-living meetings, floor meetings, and other meetings may, of course, be organized regardless of the existence of a therapeutic-community model at the hospital or section. The advantage of the therapeutic-community model is that it incorporates, by definition, the total social field of the patients' interactions in the hospital or sections. It includes in its realm formal and "spontaneous" groups, overt and covert stress and conflict in the social system; above all, it permits a functional definition of roles and tasks for staff and patients alike, and in this way maximizes the functional organization (in contrast to a hierarchical one) of the hospital or section (Falck, 1969). Functional organization, in turn, permits an optimal openness of exploration of the social field for the therapeutic purposes mentioned above.

Patient government meetings, staff meetings, and joint patient-staff meetings should be geared to exploring tasks and task constraints within the hospital, particularly task constraints created by the development of basic-assumptions groups within hospital group processes. The traditional philosophy of the therapeutic community implies that open communication, democratization, full information sharing, and open confrontation of conflicts have therapeutic values: we can now examine these assumptions in the light of the hypotheses formulated earlier regarding hospital administration.

Patient organization may indeed be a helpful therapeutic agent, in that patients as a group may function as a "normal," effective social system (Falck, 1969) and, by means of such effective functions, improve the control function (ego) of individual patients and their capacity for interpersonal relationships. However, effective functioning of patient groups requires adequate patient leadership, clear task definition, and stable and nonambiguous authority vested upon such patient leadership. If the tasks carried out by patients are not meaningful but trivial, if delegation of authority from staff to them is ambiguous, and if patient leadership is ineffective, regression of the patient group to a basic-assumptions group, as well as ineffectiveness and failure, will develop; thus, patient groups may actually become antitherapeutic agents promoting hopelessness, passivity, cynicism, and despair. The democratization of social functions within the hospital may be therapeutic insofar as it is opposed to an authoritarian power structure (Rubenstein and Lasswell, 1966), which usually goes hand in hand with nonfunctional hospital administration. However, democratic decision-making may or may not coincide with, or bring about, functional, task-centered leadership. Staff and patients have different functions, authority, and expertise: efforts to deny this reality by means of "democratic" political procedures may lead to role diffusion, breakdown in task performance, abandonment of task-determined leadership and of individual responsibility.

Patients do have the capacity for helping each other as individuals and as groups; however, for groups to be helpful they must be task-centered, and so must be their relationships with other groups within the hospital. In the last analysis, effective leadership within all therapeutic group structures, including the therapeutic community, depends upon authority delegated from hospital administration. Dissociation of leadership of the therapeutic community from hospital leadership can only lead to failure of the therapeutic community. Not everything that goes on in therapeutic community meetings is therapeutic; not everything that is democratic means effective decision-sharing; and not everything that is open communication means improvement in intrapsychic and interpersonal relationships. One must acknowledge actual differences between staff and patients with regard to skill and expertise; an optimal balance has to be achieved between open communication and the right of privacy (within an open-communication system in which confidentiality cannot be guaranteed).

If the therapeutic community is geared to active problem-solving within the social system of the hospital, it has to be directed by active, task-oriented leadership. If the therapeutic community is seen only as a large "group-dynamics" exercise, in which basic assumptions can be explored at the expense of realistic tasks to be carried out, aimlessness, unproductivity, hopelessness, and cynicism may soon ensue. Contradictions in the administrative structure of the hospital or section, between formal and informal aspects of the hospital social system, between a "pseudo-psychoanalytic" hospital philosophy (Novotny, 1971), and a manipulative system of control over patients on the part of staff will soon come out in the open if the therapeutic community, and particularly the community meeting, functions effectively. If open ventilation of these problems is not then coupled with adequate means for bringing about change, the community meeting will become simply a "griping session" (not only for patients, but for staff as well). Open examination of conflicts needs to be matched with tools to solve these conflicts: it is the experience of successful task performance which gives meaning to the open examination of task constraints. For such experiences to occur, the therapeutic community needs to be clearly differentiated from group-dynamics experiences. (As earlier mentioned, group-dynamics experience is essentially not a therapeutic but an educational tool.) The actual leader of the therapeutic community must be willing and able to assume administrative authority, and to assure himself of such delegated authority from hospital administration.

VI. Summary

A conceptual model for a philosophy of treatment within the psychoanalytic hospital has been outlined. This model includes and attempts to integrate several theories: (1) a theory of intrapsychic structure and of structural change derived from psychoanalytic object-relations theory; (2) a theory of activation of primitive object-relationships and related primitive defensive operations within small, unstructured groups, and of reciprocal reinforcement in such groups of the intrapsychic and the interpersonal field; (3) a theory of two general levels of activation of intrapsychic object-relationships, a "higher" (dyadic-triangular) one predominantly activated in individual psychotherapeutic relationships, and a "lower" (primitive) one particularly activated in nonstructured groups; (4) a theory of organizations as open systems, focusing around the issue of control function (leadership or management) and internal needs (an internal world) at the level of the individual, the group, and the hospital; (5) a theory ranging therapeutic modalities (including individual, group, and community methods) according to selective activation of problems in the control functions and/or problems in the expression of internal needs, and an application of this range to the prescription of treatment modalities for psychotic, borderline, and neurotic patients; (6) a theory of hospital administration (including therapeutic community models) derived from the theory of the organization as an open system mentioned above.

BIBLIOGRAPHY

Bion, W. R. (1959), *Experiences in Groups*. New York: Basic Books.

Brocher, T. (1970), Personal Communication.

Caine, R. M. and Small, D. J. (1969), *The Treatment of Mental Illness*. New York: International Universities Press.

Dolgoff, T. (1971), Personal Communication.

Edelson, M. (1967), The Sociotherapeutic Function in a Psychiatric Hospital. *J. Fort Logan Ment. Health Center*, 4:1–45.

Erikson, E. H. (1956), The Problem of Ego Identity. *J. Amer. Psychoanal. Assn.*, 4:56–121.

Ezriel, H. (1950), A Psychoanalytic Approach to the Treatment of Patients in Groups. *J. Ment. Sci.*, 96:774–779.

Falck, H. (1969), Personal Communication.

Freud, A. (1946), The Ego and the Mechanism of Defense. New York: International Universities Press, pp. 30–32.

Frosch, J. K. (1970), Psychoanalytic Considerations of the Psychotic Character. *J. Amer. Psychoanal. Assn.*, 18:24–50.

Guntrip, H. (1961), *Personality Structure and Human Interaction*. New York: International Universities Press.

Jacobson, E. (1964), *The Self and the Object World*. New York: International Universities Press.

Jones, M. (1968), *Social Psychiatry in Practice*. Baltimore, Maryland: Penguin Books.

Kernberg, O. (1966), Structural Derivatives of Object Relationships. *Internat. J. Psycho-Anal.*, 47:236–253.

—— (1967), Borderline Personality Organization. *J. Amer. Psychoanal. Assn.*, 15:641–685.

—— (1968), The Treatment of Patients with Borderline Personality Organization. *Internat. J. Psycho-Anal.*, 49:600–619.

—— (1971a), New Developments in Psychoanalytic Object-Relations Theory. Presented at the Annual Meeting of the American Psychoanalytic Association, Washington, D.C. (Unpublished).

—— (1971b), Diagnostic and Therapeutic Implications of Ego Weakness. Panel Presentation at the Mid-Winter Meeting of the American Psychoanalytic Association, December, 1970. (Unpublished)

Main, T. F. (1957), The Ailment. *Brit. J. Med. Psychol.*, 30:129–145.

Miller, E. J. and Rice, A. K. (1967), *Systems of Organization*. London: Tavistock Publications.

Myerson, P. G. (1971), Personal Communication.

Novotny, P. (1971), The Pseudo-Psychoanalytic Hospital (Notes on the Institutionalization of Countertransference Acting Out Patterns). Unpublished.

Rice, A. K. (1963), *The Enterprise and Its Environment*. London: Tavistock Publications.

—— (1965), *Learning for Leadership*. London: Tavistock Publications.

—— (1969). Individual, Group and Intergroup Processes. *Human Relations*, 22:565–584.

Rioch, M. J. (1970), The Work of Wilfred Bion on Groups. *Psychiatry*, 33:56–66.

Rubenstein, R., and Lasswell, H. D. (1966), *The Sharing of Power in a Psychiatric Hospital*. New Haven & London: Yale University Press.

Stanton, A. A. and Schwartz, M. S. (1954), *The Mental Hospital*. New York: Basic Books.

Sutherland, J. D. (1952), Notes on Psychoanalytic Group Therapy. I. Therapy and Training. *Psychiatry*, 15:111–117.

—— (1963), Object Relations Theory and the Conceptual Model of Psychoanalysis. *Brit. J. Med. Psychol.*, 36:109–124.

Ticho, E. (1971), Personal Communication.

Winnicott, D. W. (1954), Metapsychological and Clinical Aspects of Regression Within the Psycho-Analytical Set-Up. In: *Collected Papers*, Chapter XXII, pp. 278–294. 1958.

Zaleznik, A. (1970), Personal Communication.

Zetzel, E. R. (1966), The Analytic Situation. In: *Psychoanalysis in the Americas*, ed. Robert E. Litman. New York: International Universities Press.

Index

Abreaction, 275
Abstractions, 44, 47, 49
Academia Castellana, 302
"Acting out," 208, 210, 233, 236
Action, 160, 233
Activity–passivity conflict, 160f.
Adaptation, 168
Adler, A., 31
Adolescence, 107, 115
Advances in psychoanalysis, 29
Affective discharge, 284
Affects, 233, 272
Aggression, 9, 21, 53, 365
Aging, 353
Alarm clocks, 12
Alienation, 28
Allgemeine Krankenhaus of Vienna,
    336–341
Ambivalence, 252
Ambivalent symbiosis, 248, 251
American Psychoanalytic Association,
    application for membership, 266
Anality, 109
Analysis, well conducted, 25, 111
"Analyst as mother," 260
"Analytic," 218
Analytic encounter, 44
Analytic parlor games, 6
Analytic situation, 9, 11, 19, 25, 115, 117,
    212, 231–246, 258, 268, 274
Analytic success, 19
Anna "O," 14
Annihilation, 236
Anthropomorphism, 160
Anticipation, 55
Anti-Semitism, 324
Anxiety, 69
"Aphanisis," 121
Archaeology, 83
Archaism, 217, 219
Archimedes, 33
Architecture, 77
Aristophanes, 225
Art, 24, 86, 140, 155, 157, 226
Artists, 77, 312f.
Assessment of candidate progress, 289,
    290
Atomism, 78

Attention, 130, 199–215
    cathexis, 188
Attentiveness, devoted, 11
Attitudes
    complementary, 119
    hidden, 217
Auden, W. H., 5, 35
Austro-Hungarian Empire, 323
Authors, 345
Autism, 247, 257, 259, 260
Autobiographical events, 345
Autobiography, 303
Automatisms, 85, 209, 221

Bakan, D., 67
Beauty, 219
Behavior, "symbolic," 52
Behavioral change, 364
Beres, D., 78
Bernfeld, S., 97
Bertalanffy, L., 47
Beyond the Pleasure Principle, 163, 222
Biochemistry, 62
Biography, general theory of, 245–362
Biography and criticism
    Cervantes, 299–317
    S. Freud, 216–228, 299–341
        Project for Scientific Psychology,
        88–103
    D. Rapaport, 200–207
    P. Ricoeur, 216–228
    Oscar Wilde, 345–362
Biology, 58
Bisexuality, 112
Blame, 162
Borderline patients, 122, 209, 364, 366,
    367, 371, 377
Boundary control, 376, 378, 383
Brahe, Tycho, 32
Brain, 50
Braun, Heinrich, 325

Candidates as patients, 285–294
Capacity for experience, 206, 207, 209
Case presentations, 277
Catharsis, 275
Cervantes Saavedra, Miguel de, 299, 303,
    304, 311, 312, 313

Chance and Necessity, 59
Change, 227–228
Child analysis, 242
Choice, 161
Choice of treatment, 379, 380, 381
"Classicism," 331
Classificatory theories, 42–44
Clinical conferences, 266, 276, 277
Clinical literature, 84
Colloquy of the Dogs, The, 302, 303,
    305, 307, 308, 309
Communal organization, 4
Communication, 33, 118, 125, 137, 154,
    224, 242, 243, 254
  unconscious, 119
Competitiveness, 256, 257
Conceptual categories, 128
Conceptual codes, 209–210
Conceptualization, 265, 266, 274
Conflicts, 27, 181, 184, 208, 271, 273, 283,
    364
  passivity, 109
Consciousness, 51, 207, 130, 272, 273
  altered states of, 131
  conditioning of, 92
Consultant, psychiatric, 376, 381
Contemplation, 22
Copernicus, 7, 31
Coping, 272
Core psychic structures, 271
Cornford, F. M., 29
Counseling, psychotherapeutic, 11, 258
Countertransference, 119, 252, 266, 282,
    283, 291, 292
Creativity, 25, 75, 76, 141, 257, 327
"Criteria of Reality," 94
Crystalline structure, 61
Cybernetics, 64, 126–127, 204
Culture, 318–335
Cure, 231, 235

Darwin, C., 8, 24, 54, 66
Data processing, 128
Death, 69, 106, 358, 359, 360, 361, 362
Death instinct, 53, 70, 84, 91, 223
Deduction, 39
Defense mechanisms, 186, 210, 271, 353,
    354, 364, 366, 370
  unconscious, 185
Delusional reality, 236, 244
Dependency, 247
Depth psychology, 4, 5, 10
Descartes, R., 118, 223
"Descriptive explanatory theory," 47
Desexualization, 108
Desires, 221, 224
  "semantics of," 222
Determinism, 161
Detractors of psychoanalysis, 3–4, 29
Deutsch, H., 119

Diabetes, 67
Diagnosis, 337, 338, 339, 366
"Dialectic," 218
Differentiation, 249
"Disclaimed action," 162
"Discomfort," 21*n.*
DNA, 66
Don Quixote, 299, 300, 310, 311, 312,
    313
Douglas, Lord Alfred, 347
Drawings (of patients), 242, 243
Dream interpretation, 150
Dreams, 93, 144, 221, 226
  blanket, 146
  cathedral, 235
  economy of, 145–146
  phallic, 150
Drives, 28, 272
  organization, 271
  suppression, 21
Drugs, 22
Dyadic relationships, 219, 225, 369, 370

Eastern philosophy, 22
Ego
  adaptive, 168
  autonomy, 160
  boundaries, 251, 254, 364
  core, 364, 381
  "defect," 250
  development, 247
  distortions, 244
  fragmentation of, 255
  functions, 94, 126, 164
  "infiltration" of, 240, 249, 272, 274,
      366
  ideal, 15, 365
  identity, 365
  incompleteness of, 249
  integration, 265
  psychology, 104
  states, primitive, 366
Einstein, A., 49
Empathy, 14, 119
Energy, psychic, 24, 71, 91, 108, 201, 206
Entropy, 59, 201
Epigenetic processes, 64
Epistemology, 118, 216, 217
Erasmus, 305, 306
Erikson, E., 169
Espace Humaine, 238
Euclid, 29, 33
"Existential facts," 238
Existentialism, 167*n.*
Exoskeleton, 259
Explanation, causal, 42

Failure, 287
Family relationships, 249

Fantasies, 109, 271
  homosexual, 104
Fechner, G., 56
Federn, P., 34
Feelings, 252, 253
Fenichel, O., 174
"First 'Freudian' Book," 97
Fixation, 249
Fluss, E., 29
Fluss, Gisela, 313, 314
Formalism of psychoanalysis, 73, 74
Free association, 11, 44, 122, 144, 231
Freud, A., 106, 122
Freud, S., 29
  adolescence, 313–316, 318
  education, 331, 332, 333
  Jewishness, 328
  library, 333
  and literature, 301, 319, 320
  and nature, 322
  and numerology, 330
  obsolescence, 26
  pessimism, 217
  and politics, 323, 325, 326
  psychiatric training, 336–341
  screen memory from Pribor, 314
  self-analysis, 232
  Silberstein correspondence, 301–302
  tolerance, 34
  Totem and Taboo, 232
  and Vienna, 327
Freudian discoveries, 6
Fusion, 71

Genetic viewpoint, 47, 48
German nationalism, 324, 325
Gestures, 221
Gitelson, Maxwell, 114
Goals of the psychoanalytic process, 271
Goethe, J. W., 321
Gospels, 7
Greeks, 33, 73, 75
Group(s)
  dynamics, 9, 15, 18, 363–388 *passim*
  survival of, 123
  therapy, 371, 377
Guilt in schizophrenia, 250
Guttman, S. A., 26
Gymnasium, 331, 332, 333

Hallucinations, 254, 256
Hannibal, 306, 315
Hartmann, H., 164
Hayek, F. A., 46
Healthy adults, 250
Hebephrenia, 256
Helmholtz, 90
Helplessness, 252
"Hermeneutical" methods, 217, 219

History, 10
Homeostasis, 55
Homosexuality, 347, 348, 354, 361
Honesty, 29
Hospital
  administration, 382–386
  therapist, 379
  treatment, 364, 367, 371, 372, 379
Human nature, 319, 320
Human relationships, 249
Humour, 300

"I," 162, 167–168
Id, 365
  psychology, 104
Ideal objects, 364, 365
Ideal self, 364, 365
Idealism, 311, 313
Identification, 119, 259, 300, 369
  with the aggressor, 353
  projective, 120
Identity, 160, 169, 255
Illusions, 231–246 *passim*
"Impossible professions," 281
Impulse–defense configurations, 182, 363
Impulses, 184
  of cruelty, 53*n.*
  instinctual, 49
Incest, 232, 233
Incorporation, 109
Individuation, 247, 249, 250
Induction, 40
Infantile sexuality, 101–102
Infants, 239, 240, 241
Information theory, 66, 129, 202
Insight, 7, 10, 12, 121, 235, 283
Instinctual drives, 104, 272
Instincts, 53–72, 104–116, 163, 222
  primary, 55
Intentionality, 164
Internalization, 364, 365
International Journal of Psycho-Analysis, 168
International relations, 3–25
Interpretation, 150, 160, 174, 179, 192–213, 217, 220, 228, 231, 238, 273
Interpretation of Dreams, 48, 150
Interrupted activities, 183
Intrapsychic needs, 374
Intrapsychic structure, 364
Introductory Lectures, 48
Introjection, 110, 183, 251, 254, 255, 256, 369
Introspection, 14
Intuition, 68, 119
Invariant reproduction, 65
Irma dream, 100
Isolation, 123
Israel Institute for Psychoanalysis, 125*n.*

James, W., 28, 55
Jealous Estremaduran, The, 310
Jealousy, 255, 256, 257
Jews, 327, 328, 329

Kant, I., 54, 216, 218
Kantian principles, 218-219
Kekulé, 80
Kepler, H., 31
Kitchener, E., 28
Kleist, E. C. von, 16
Knowledge, 39, 41
  "empty," 41
Kohut, H., 121-122, 170, 171
Korzybski, L., 46
Kraus, Karl, 21
Kuhn, I., 74, 83

Langer, S., 47
Language and linguistics, 123, 136, 232,
  233, 237-238, 243-244, 245, 301
Laws, scientific, 76
Leaders, messianic, 17
Leadership, 374
Learning, 199-215, 265-279
  in psychotherapy, 207-213
Leseverein der Deutschen Studenten, 325
Listening, 238
Little Hans, 53*n.*
Logic, 40
Los Angeles Institute for Psychoanalysis,
  26*n.*
Love, 249
Lueger, Karl, 324

Macrostructures, 273
Magical control, 241
Man, inner life of, 22
Maculinity and femininity, 112
Masochism, 110*n.*
Maternal shield, 259, 260
Mathematics, 41
Maturation, 249
Meaning, 165
Melville, H., 16
Memory, short term, 202
Mental
  apparatus, 48, 89, 103, 127, 153, 166
  health, 22-23
  hospitals, 363-388
  representation, 125-158
Mentation, 45, 48, 243, 244
Metapsychology, 39, 45, 47, 159, 160
Methodology, 275
Microstructures, 273
Milner, Marion, 242, 243
Mind, 180, 189
Models of mental apparatus, 48
Monod, J., 59
Morphogenesis, 65

Mother-child relationship, 240, 241, 248,
  249, 257
Motivation, unconscious, 10, 15, 27, 49
Mourning, 106
Multiple function, 163
Music, 22, 24

Narcissism, 15-18, 110*n.*, 170, 257
  character, 122
  resistance, 286
  self, 170
Nationalism, 323
Nature, 318, 320
Negation, 236
"Negative entropy," 60
"Neuronic inertia," 91
Neuroses, 24, 193
  genesis of, 28
Neurosis, compulsion, 69
Neurotic patients, 365
Neutral therapist responses, 259
Neutralization, 108
New York Psychoanalytic Society, 77
Newton, T., 31
"Normalcy," 69
Normality, 22, 115
Northrop, R., 44
Novelas Ejemplares, 299-301
Nunberg, H., 75
Nursing staff, 371

Object cathexis, 108
Object-images, 364
Object loss, 354
Object love, 121
Object relations, 111, 122, 242, 363-388
  internalized, 111, 365, 366
  primitive, 367, 368, 369
  theory, 364
Object-representations, 265
Observation, 40-42, 84
Oedipus complex, 106, 113
Omnipotence, 236, 241
  archaic, 17
On Aphasia, 97
Oppenheimer, O., 73
Orality, 109

Pain, psychic, 235
Pantheism, 321
Paradigm, 74
Paranoia, 15
Paranoid symbiosis, 248
Parapraxis, 176
Parent-child relations, 289
Parricide, 232, 233
Passivity, 174, 187
  conflict, 109
"Patient as mother," 260
Patient organization, 385

Patient as therapist, 248, 260
Patient–analyst relationship, 247, 249, 255, 256
Patient–physician relationship, 247–262
Peace, 24
Penis envy, 113
Perceptions, 121, 153, 241, 242
    preconscious, 119
"Period of hesitation," 239
Persecutory fantasies, 365
"Perturbations," 67
Perversions, 113
Peterfreund, E., 45n.
Philosophy, 118, 216–228
    scientific, 39
Physics, 75
Physiology, 55
Piaget, J., 219
Picture of Dorian Gray, The, 348–359
Pittsburgh Conference on Training
        Analysis (1965), 280, 289
Play, 240
Poems, 140
Plutarch, 306
Politics, 3–25
Predictions, 47
Primary process, 91, 125, 132
"Principle of constancy," 56, 91
"Problematic," 218
"Processes," 133n.
Project for a Scientific Psychology, 50
Projection, 251, 364
Psychiatry, history, 336–341
Psychic conflict, models of, 48
Psychic development, 240
Psychic structure, 104
Psychoanalysis
    as a cultural factor, 7, 14
    ethics of, 226
    history, 299–341
    is dialectical, 225
    and literature, 345–362
    methodology, 39–52, 53–72
    progressive, 31–33
    and psychology, 14
    and romanticism, 319
    and science, 73–87
    as a science, 25
    and society, 3–35
    therapeutic, 5, 11
    therapeutic process, 231–246, 247–262, 265–279
Psychoanalysts, 234, 250, 259, 260, 268, 274, 275, 276
    as scientists, 85
Psychoanalytic
    candidates, 79, 265, 274, 278, 294
    curriculum, 265
    data, 117
    process, 111, 122, 231, 250, 259, 265,

Psychoanalytic process (continued)
    267, 273, 277, 278
    seminars, 265
    societies, 305
    technique, 258, 259
    training, 265–279
      analysis, 280–295
      goals of, 77, 265, 267, 270, 271, 279–294
Psychobiology, 161
Psychological equilibrium, 21, 25
Psychoneuroses, 22
Psychopathy, 235
Psychotherapeutic relationship, 11, 370
Psychotherapists, 377, 381
Psychotherapy
    brief, 12
    individual, 377, 378
Psychotic relationships, 15, 364, 366, 367, 371, 377

Quantum mechanics, 74

Rapoport, A., 42
Rapaport, D., 200, 237
Reaction formation, 210
Real self, 365
Reality, 46, 282, 283, 284, 291
Reality-oriented functions, 133
Reality testing, 272, 273, 289, 366
Re-analysis, 234
Reason
    ascendancy of, 18
    inferential, 41
Referral, 234, 236
Regression, 240, 248, 251, 272, 364, 368, 370
Rejection, 252
Relating, 242
Relevance of psychoanalysis, 4, 13
Reliability, 257
Religion, 35
Remembering, 233
Reparation, 243
Repetition compulsion, 57, 65, 68, 223
"Representation," 104
Repression, 27, 349
Research, 8, 10, 91, 200
Resistance, 156, 174, 179, 240, 256, 286, 290
Responsibility, 177n.
Results of analysis, 10
Ricoeur, P., 118, 216–228
Rimbaud, A., 244
Rinconete and Cortadillo, 309
"Role," 369
Romanticism, 318, 319
Russell, B., 40, 44

Sadism, 53n.
Sancho Panza, 300

Schizoid patients, 256, 257
Schizophrenia, 247, 250
   chronic, 258
Schönerer, Georg von, 324
Schopenhauer, F., 27
Schreber case, 15
Schrodinger, 59
Science, 25, 39, 75, 117
   empirical, 41
   history of, 31, 82
Scipio Africanus the Elder, 306, 315f.
Secondary process, 49, 133, 272, 273
Secret of life, 64
Secret societies, 303
Selection of candidates, 287
Self, 160, 171–172, 249, 256, 365
   archaic, 17
   sustaining, 219
Self-analysis, 281, 282, 293
Self-annihilation, 18
Self-centered functions, 133
Self-concept, 364, 365
Self-esteem, 16
"Self-evident," 41
Self-images, 364
Self-object-affect units, 364
Self-observation, 208
Self-preservation, 56
Separation anxiety, 253, 254
Sexuality, 28
Shakespeare, W., 361
Shame, 287
Sign, 134–137
Skilled behavior, 211
Sleep, 131
Slips of the tongue, 176
Social psychology, 3–25
Sociology, psychoanalytic, 24
Solipsism, 217, 219, 223
Space, 231–246
Speech, 221
Stengel, E., 98
Stereotyped comments (by patients), 254
Structural change, 272, 273
Structural concept, 73–87
Structural intrapsychic change, 363, 364
Structural theory, 48, 78, 85
Structure, concept of, 75, 76
Studies on Hysteria, 89
Suggestion, 275
Suicide, 236
Suitability of cases, 233, 257
Superego, 271, 365
   formation, 104, 105–116
Supervision, 266, 267, 281, 287
Survival-negative mechanisms, 56
Symbiosis, 247–262
   pre-ambivalent, 248, 252
Symbiotic relatedness, 250, 251, 252, 253
"Symbiotic therapist," 249

Symbolic discourse, 231
Symbols and symbolism, 40, 125, 137–138, 220
Synthetic Function, 75
Systems theory, 47, 373–376
Systems UCS., 49
Szasz, T., 58

Taboos, 233
Tape recordings, 117
Task performance and task groups, 373–376, 379, 383
Teaching–learning situation, 275
Teleonomy, 65
Termination phase, 19, 25, 104, 105, 269, 293
Thanatos, 223
Theory formation, 39
Therapeutic
   alliance, 122, 233, 268, 269
   community, 375, 378, 383, 384, 385
   distance, 321
   space, 231, 235, 237, 242, 243
   symbiosis, 247
Thermodynamics, second law of, 59, 226
Thought, 50
   secondary process, 49
   and thinking, 125
   unconscious, 49
Toucher pour voir, 241
Touching, 241, 243
Toulmin, H., 46
Training analysis, 265, 280–294
"Transcendental analysis," 218
Transference, 45, 122, 174, 227, 231, 249, 273, 282, 283
   interpretations, 247
   neurosis, 107, 110, 268–270, 366, 367
   psychosis, 366, 367
Transitional objects, 239, 241
"Treat versus teach" issue, 281
Treatment modalities, combined, 369, 380
Triadic relationships, 369, 370
Typical analytic hour, 144

"Unbehagen," 21*n.*
Unconscious, 10, 118, 143, 154, 300
"Unconscious communication," 154–155, 187
Unconscious mental processes, 92
Unintegrated states, 240, 245
Utopia, 23

Validation of psychoanalytic inference, 277
Values, 4
Variations in the psychoanalytic process, 270, 271

Vertical circles, 147–153
Victorian age, 28
Vienna, 323, 326
Viennese psychiatry, nineteenth century, 336–341
Violence, in the analytic situation, 236, 237
Voir, 243
Vorstellung, 104

Waelder, R., 49, 83, 163
"Wholistic" approach, 86
Whyte, L., 78
"Wild ego analysis," 169

Wilde, Oscar, 345–362
  homosexuality, 354, 355
  sister's death, 357, 358
  trials, 347, 348
Wilde, Isola Francesca, 357
Wilde, William, 356, 360
Winnicott, D. W., 239–245
Wisdom, 79
Wish-fulfillment, 93
Wish-systems, 232, 233
Withdrawal, affective, 122
Words, 117, 209, 231, 232, 244
Working alliance, 286
Working through, 272, 274, 371